Seignelay Colbert de Castlehill (1735–1811)

Alain Alcouffe
Editor

Seignelay Colbert de Castlehill (1735–1811)

A Bishop Between Scottish Enlightenment and Counter-Revolution

palgrave
macmillan

Editor
Alain Alcouffe
Toulouse Capitole University
Toulouse, France

ISBN 978-3-031-75272-8 ISBN 978-3-031-75273-5 (eBook)
https://doi.org/10.1007/978-3-031-75273-5

Translation from the French language edition: "Seignelay Colbert de Castlehill (1735–1811)" by Alain Alcouffe, © Presses de l'Université Toulouse 1 Capitole 2022. Published by Presses de l'Université Toulouse 1 Capitole. All Rights Reserved.

This Palgrave Macmillan imprint is published by the registered company Springer Nature Switzerland AG
The registered company address is: Gewerbestrasse 11, 6330 Cham, Switzerland

Acknowledgements

This book is the result of the colloquium of 8-9-10 December 2020[1] held remotely thanks to the platform of the Institut catholique de Toulouse. The idea for the colloquium arose from a meeting in November 2019 between Alain Alcouffe, Bernard Callebat and Andrew Moore, whose 1989 dissertation had been made available by the Inter-Library Loans Service [Sally Williams] and whose contact details had been found by David Collard, Development and Alumni Relations Office at the University of Bristol. Andrew Moore brought to the project a stock of documents copied from the Archives Départementales de l'Aveyron and over three years hundreds of exchanges and further research have resulted in a bilingual web site, with the help of Chloe Seddon, making available all our knowledge of Seignelay Colbert of Castlehill https://colbertdecastlehill.com/.

The character of Seignelay Colbert de Castlehill had emerged from research on Adam Smith's stay in Toulouse and the contrast between the multiple facets of this character and the paucity of records about him. So many people have contributed information about his life, family, career or encouraged the development of the project that we will no doubt

[1] We would like to thank the historians who kindly joined the scientific committee of the conference, Nigel Aston, Bernard Callebat, Gerard Carruthers, Francis Hutcheson, Philippe Delvit, William Doyle, Christine Fauré, Stéphane Gomis, Gilbert Larguier, Clotilde Prunier, Valérie Sottocasa.

forget some, but we would like to thank James Brennan and Robert Preece, historians of Inverness, who have enlightened us about Seignelay's parents, starting with his baptismal certificate, and about education in Inverness in the eighteenth century. Colin Powell, Archivist, Buccleuch Living Heritage Trust gave us access to Colbert's correspondence with the Duke of Buccleuch after his return to Britain during the French Revolution. Edward Corp has given us information on the protections Colbert enjoyed from the Pretender's Court. Carole Jacquet and Anne Roels, Irish Cultural Centre, have recovered prize books obtained by Colbert during his studies at the College of Scotland.

We would not forget Julie du Boberil, Jeanne de Gérin-Ricard, André Algrin, Régis de la Roche, the descendants of Lancelot/Lachlan Colbert de Castlehill, Seignelay's uncle, who have kept the memory of their cousin alive, and have provided access to a very enlightening family monograph on these Franco-Scottish relations.[2]

In these Covid-19 years, no research would have been possible without the help of archivists and librarians who have identified and found for us multiple traces of Colbert. I would like to thank Ralph Mclean and Robert L. Betteridge at the National Library of Scotland, Emily Teyssèdre-Jullian and Pierre Lançon at the Société des gens de lettres de l'Aveyron, Ellen Cordes, Head of Technical Services at the Lewis Walpole Library at Yale, René Andrieu at the Archives de l'évêché de Rodez, Françoise Launay and Nicolas Rieucau at the Condorcet Archives, and Alison Mason at the Highland Archive Centre Ronan Tallec carried out research at the Archives Nationales and Wolfgang Mager kindly translated the Latin of the eighteenth century. Édouard Bouyé, former director of the Cantal archives, sent us his book on the Enfarinés of Cassaniouze. Alain Drulhe Carrère has digitised Colbert's book, les *Élémens*, kept at the Rodez Media Library.

We thank Hélène Cussac (French Society for the Study of the eighteenth century), Penelope J. Corfield, President International Society for Eighteenth-Century Studies (ISECS), Andrea Kaszewski, Society of Antiquaries of Scotland, Dr. Annie Tindley, the Scottish History Society, Gerard Carruthers and the Scottish Catholic Historical Association, Craig

[2] François de la Roche-Saint André, *Famille Cuthbert Colbert De Castlehill*, Château-Gontier: Éditions de l'hôtel de Sancé.

Smith, Eighteenth-Century Scottish Studies Society. Dr. Allan Kennedy, History Scotland.

We do not forget the many colleagues with whom we were able to exchange views, Caroline Barrera, Gérald Bray, Kirsty Carpenter, Monique Cuilleron, Florent Garnier, Chandra Mukerji, Daniel Szechi, Felix Waldmann, David Worthington.

We would like to thank the DRAC Occitanie, which has authorised us to reproduce the portrait of Seignelay, and the National Library of Scotland for the map of Inverness.

We would like to thank Christiane Alcouffe for her advice, her patience and her many proofreadings. We thank the Presses universitaires de l'Université Toulouse 1 Capitole for their support and Mrs Anne Blandin for her tenacity.

Contents

Notes on Contributors

Alain Alcouffe is Emeritus Professor of Economics at University of Toulouse. He served as Director of Toulouse University Network (2001–2005) and President of the International Walras Association (2013–2015). His research interests lie in corporate governance, business intelligence, ecological economics, economic history and history of economic thought. He edited the *Mathematical Manuscripts of Marx* (Economica, 1985), coedited *Business Cycles in Economic Thought: a history* (2017, Routledge) and *Macroeconomic theory and the eurozone crisis*, (Routledge, 2018) he coauthored *Adam Smith in Toulouse and Occitania*, (Toulouse, 2018) (English edition, 2020, Palgrave).

Guy Astoul was an associate professor at the IUFM in the Midi-Pyrénées region, and has researched teaching and rural life in the Midi. In particular, he has studied disputes over tithes and seigneurial rights between Limousin and the Pyrenees, on the eve of the French Revolution. An associate member of STUDIUM-FRAMESPA at the Université Toulouse Jean-Jaurès, and a member of the Académie de Montauban, he is president of the Société montalbanaise d'étude et de recherche sur le protestantisme.

Gilles Bancarel, Doctor of Letters, author of numerous works on the History of the Two Indies and Abbé Raynal (1713–1796) https://www.crlv.org/users/bancarel . He is a member of the Société des Lettres Sciences et Arts de l'Aveyron, the Société Archéologique, Scientifique et

Littéraire de Béziers, a corresponding member of the Académie de Montpellier, and a corresponding member of the Académie de Marseille. He is president of the Société d'Étude Guillaume-Thomas Raynal www.abbe-raynal.org which organized events devoted to Raynal for his bicentenary in 1996 and his tercentenary in 2013, under the patronage of UNESO. He is preparing an edition of Abbé Raynal's correspondence.

Julien Béchard has researched the articles devoted to the episcopacy of Mgr Colbert de Castlhill by *Les Nouvelles Ecclésiastiques*, the Jansenist weekly published from 1728 to 1803. The Jansenists had many grievances against the French episcopate in the 18th century. They accused the first order of exercising despotic power over the second-order clergy and the lay faithful as a whole. The bishops were neglecting their role as defenders of the faith, allowing incredulity to grow throughout the kingdom, and making pacts with the Church's enemies, the Philosophers. Although Gallican, the episcopate was in continual conflict with the Jansenists and parliamentarians in order to defend the Church's interests, notably the independence of its jurisdiction. The first opposition newspaper, *Nouvelles Ecclésiastiques*, relayed this pejorative view of the episcopate to a wide audience, showing the evils of the Unigenitus bull for the Church and exposing the persecution Jansenists suffered at the hands of ecclesiastical authority.

He is doctor in Canon Law, he has worked on Jansenist parish law and the Jansenist curé in the Nouvelles Ecclésiastiques. He is currently a teacher-researcher at the Institut Catholique de Vendée. He is also archivist and cultural heritage officer at the Institut des Frères Maristes. He is continuing his research into the history of Congregational teaching in France and the authority of the superiors of religious congregations.

Dominic Aidan Bellenger is an Associate Member of the Faculty of History, University of Cambridge, where he is a Senior Research Associate at the Von Hugel Institute and a Senior Member of St Edmund's College. He is a Fellow of the Society of Antiquaries and the Royal Historical Society. He is the author of two books on the French Exiled Clergy, the subject of his doctoral dissertation.

Marie-Paule Biron defended her history thesis, *Les messes clandestines* en France *pendant la Révolution*, in 1987, under the supervision of Jean Tulard. She is a member of the Société des Lettres Sciences et Arts de l'Aveyron. She has published numerous articles on the history of the Church during the Revolution and Restoration.

Maïté Bouyssy defended her thesis *Thirty years later, Bertrand Barère or the rhetoric of the Ténare* in 1992, and produced some thirty articles on Bertrand Barère, the usual rapporteur of the Committee of Public Safety in the second year. A specialist in the cultural history of politics in the XIXe century, she has edited a *Vincenzo Cuoco, Des origines politiques du XIXe siècle* at the Publications de la Sorbonne and published in 2012 *L'urgence, l'horreur, la démocratie, essai sur le moment frénétique français, 1824–1834*, and in 2016 *Une histoire culturelle de la Révolution, le Salon imaginaire de Bertand Barère.*

Timothy R. Day holds a Ph.D. in transnational and comparative history from Central Michigan University, with specializations in modern France and Britain . He studied at the University of Angers and at Erasmus University Rotterdam as part of his MA in European History. He received his BA from Purdue University in the United States, where he later taught history and academic composition as a visiting professor in 2020–2021. He is currently an English teacher at the International Language Training Center in Chişinău, Moldova.

Christine Fauré Director of research emerita at the CNRS, scientific editor of *Les Déclarations des droits de l'homme de 1789*, Payot, 1992; *Les Manuscrits de l'abbé Sieyès*, Champion, 1999 and 2007; *Nouvelle Encyclopédie Politique et Historique des Femmes*, Belles-Lettres 2010, English edition Routledge and Spanish edition Akal; *Autobiographie d'Alexandra Kollontaï*, Fayard, 2024. She is the author of : *La démocratie sans les femmes*, PUF, 1985, in English Indiana University Press; *Ce que déclarer des droits veut dire : histoires*, PUF et Belles Lettres, 1997–2011, Prix de l'Académie des Sciences morales et politiques; *Mai 68 jour et nuit*, Gallimard, 2018; *Les néo-conservateurs à la française*, Milan, Mimesis, 2015; *Ces idées qui ont fait le Mouvement de Libération des Femmes*, XVIIIe–XXIe siècles, Chryséis éditions, 2022.

Patrick Ferté is an emeritus lecturer at the University of Toulouse-Jean Jaurès and a member of the Framespa laboratory (UMR 5136—UT2J-CNRS). A specialist in the history of ancient universities, his first book was devoted to the University of Cahors in the Age of Enlightenment (1974), followed by a pioneering thesis on the student populations of the University of Toulouse (1679–1793). Since then, he has written around a hundred books and articles on the subject, including a 7-volume Répertoire prosopographique des Étudiants du Midi de la France (2002–2015). Co-director and co-author of the 3-volume Histoire de l'université de Toulouse (2020) and an international collection on Les Étudiants de l'exil (PUM, "Tempus", 2009).

Bernard Fixes is a priest of the diocese of Rodez, with a master's degree in history and a master's degree in theology.

Jennifer Morag Henderson is a writer, based in the Scottish Highlands. Her first book, the biography "Josephine Tey: A Life", was listed as a Book of the Year by the Observer, the Independent, and the Telegraph, and acclaimed by reviewers in the Wall Street Journal, TLS, Literary Review, and elsewhere. Her second biography, "Daughters of the North: Jean Gordon and Mary, Queen of Scots", was longlisted for the prestigious Highland Book Prize. Jennifer has degrees from the University of Glasgow and Dalhousie University (Canada), and studied French at the French Institute in Edinburgh, and at the Université de Caen. www.jennifermoraghenderson.com

Gilbert Larguier Honorary Professor at the University of Perpignan Via Domitia, Gilbert Larguier has been interested in the history of the South from the end of the medieval period to the beginning of the XIXe century, using a variety of approaches economy, society, institutions... with his thesis, Le drap et le grain en Languedoc, Narbonne et Narbonnais (1300–1789), the study of the origin and evolution of Languedoc taxation in its implications at the level of the communities, the Estates of Languedoc and the kingdom and, in a comparative perspective, the analysis of the specificities of Languedoc, Roussillon and the Catalan countries, which are close, but so different in many respects.

Jean-Baptiste Masméjan is a lecturer in legal history at Nantes University. A specialist in the history of social law, he is interested in revolutionary committees, and more specifically in the Comité de mendicité. He defended his thesis in 2021 (L'assistance par le travail à l'aune du traitement de l'indigence au XVIIIe siècle : idées et institutions l'exemple lyonnais).

Andrew Moore born in 1950 in Neuilly-sur-Seine, France, spent his entire school career in France before passing his baccalaureate in 1968. He worked in various roles including oenologist, entrepreneur, and consultant in France and England. He studied history at the University of Bristol from 1985 to 1989, focusing on the French Revolution under Professor William Doyle. There, he wrote a dissertation titled "Seignelay Colbert of Castlehill during the pre-revolutionary years: a bishop of the ancien régime." Alain Alcouffe invited Moore to help prepare a conference on the bishop and manage the website colbertdecastlehill.com. Moore preserved his research documents for 35 years, now being transferred to the Highland Archives in Inverness. Retired as a French teacher, he splits his time between Somerset and Cotentin.

Clotilde Prunier is Professor of British History at Université Paris Nanterre. She is the author of *Anti-Catholic Strategies in Eighteenth-Century Scotland* (Peter Lang, 2004) and of articles on various aspects of the Scottish Mission in the eighteenth century. She has co-edited *Debating the Faith: Religion and Letter Writing in Britain 1550–1800* (Springer, 2013) with Anne Dunan-Page and is currently working on a monograph on the European networks of the Scottish Mission in the eighteenth century.

Hiroki Ueno Ph.D., Senior Researcher and Lecturer at SFC Research Institute and the Faculty of Economics, Keio University, Japan. Teaching the history of social thought at several universities including the University of Tokyo, he is also a vice-president of Ueno Medical Corporation, Japan. He is a founder of the East Asian Intellectual History Network (EAIHN). His recent articles include: "Educating a Young Aristocrat during Grand Tour: Moral and Political Economy in Adam Smith", Journal of Scottish Philosophy 21.1 (2023): 75–96; and "The Scottish Enlightenment" in DIGIT.EN.S: The Digital Encyclopedia of British Sociability in the Long Eighteenth Century (online open access, co-authored with Iain McDaniel.

CHAPTER 1

Introduction

Alain Alcouffe and Andrew Moore

Abstract This introductory chapter sets the stage for an in-depth exploration of Abbé Colbert de Castlehill, a complex and influential figure in 18th-century France. Drawing on newly discovered archival materials, it outlines Colbert's journey from his Presbyterian roots in Inverness to his prominence within the French Catholic Church. The chapter highlights Colbert's interactions with significant contemporaries, including Adam Smith, and his role in pivotal historical events such as the French Revolution. It delves into Colbert's intellectual contributions, particularly his social thinking and his involvement with the Comité de mendicité. Additionally, the chapter examines his later years, marked by his exile in London and his pastoral correspondence during the turbulent revolutionary period but also his part in the edition of Mme du Deffand-Walpole correspondence. This introduction aims to frame the multifaceted narrative of Colbert's influence and legacy, preparing readers for the detailed analyses presented in the book, which cover various

A. Alcouffe (✉)
Université of Toulouse Capitole, Toulouse, France
e-mail: alain.alcouffe@ut-capitole.fr

A. Moore
Independent Researcher, L'Etang Bertrand, France

A. Alcouffe (ed.), *Seignelay Colbert de Castlehill (1735-1811)*,
https://doi.org/10.1007/978-3-031-75273-5_1

aspects of his life and impact, from his early years in Scotland to his significant role in the Gallican Church and his enduring legacy in both France and Scotland.

Keyword Colbert de Castlehill · Adam Smith · Duke of Buccleuch · French Revolution · Gallican Church · Comité de mendicité · Calas affair · Scots college · Exile in London · Inverness

The Circumstances of the Research

For economists, concerned with the history of their discipline, the months spent in Toulouse by Adam Smith after the publication of his first work in 1759 and before the publication of The *Wealth of Nations* remained an enigma. Thus, the chapter devoted to Toulouse in the first major biography[1] of Adam Smith was based on letters sent to Hume by a mysterious *Grand vicaire écossois*, who Philippe Massot-Bordenave discovered was Seignelay Colbert. The Scottish archives shed light on the links forged in Toulouse between Smith, his pupil, the Duke of Buccleuch and their guide, the Abbé Colbert de Castlehill. But there was very little information on this *cicerone* and some data that might have seemed well established would turn out to be wrong. Starting with his date of birth, for which 'official' documents from Seignelay's lifetime, such as the portraits of the representatives to the Estates-General, give as 1736, whereas the Inverness baptismal register, kept in the Scottish Archives, clearly states that he was baptised (by a Presbyterian minister) in 1735. Further Colbert was celebrated at the beginning of a key moment in the Revolution, on 25 June 1789, five days after the oath of the *Jeu de Paume*, marking the end of the Ancien Régime, when the Bishop of Rodez, one of the few prelates to have accepted the idea of joint deliberations of the representatives of the three orders, was carried in triumph through the streets of Versailles by the people.[2] This same prelate, who had presided over the short-lived Provincial Assembly of Haute-Guyenne

[1] John Rae, *Life of Adam Smith*, London: MacMillan. 1895.

[2] Claude-François Beaulieu, *Essais historiques sur les causes et les effets de la Révolution de France*, Paris, Maradan, tome 1, p. 277, An IX (1801), Louis BLANC, *Histoire de la révolution française*, Paris, Langlois & Leclercq, 1847, Tome 2, p. 297.

set up on an experimental basis as part o f a reformist programme by Necker, emigrated to London after refusing to take the constitutional oath in 1791, unlike Loménie de Brienne, whose vicar-general he had been for eighteen years in Toulouse. Ten years later, he opposed the concordat of 8 April 1802 between Napoleon and Pius VII and led the resistance to the numerous 'concordataire' clergy well established in his Rouergat diocese, until his death in 1811.

The State of Previous Research

This break with the French Revolution, as well as the refusal of the Concordat, contributed to his oblivion, since the judgements of Catholic historians were hardly tender towards him, while on the other side, this atypical and unclassifiable prelate did not attract attention. A few biographical notes from the nineteenth century recalled his career in a more or less incomplete way, while local historians, according to their discoveries, published some of his letters in the publications of the *Société des lettres de l'Aveyron*. In 1865, Victor Advielle, a civil servant, librarian and collector, devoted some pages to him.[3] In Scotland, the *Celtic Magazine*, which retraced the fate of the Cuthbert family, published some of the dates of his life.[4] He also appears in the book by J. G. B. Bullock, MD, *The Cuthberts, Barons of Castlehill and Their Descendants in South Carolina and Georgia*, Washington: 1908.

After the Second World War, Jacques Bousquet, the curator of the Aveyron archives, studied the measures taken by Seignelay in relation to a family dispute within a Protestant family in Millau: 'Un precedent of l'affaire Finally en Rouergue (1786). Mgr Colbert de Castlehill, le pensionnat-couvent de l'Arpajonie et les protestants de Millau" in *Revue du Rouergue*, 1953. Finally, a handwritten note by Henri Guilhamon, professor of history at Cahors and editor of the Voyage de Richeprey,[5] summarised a communication to the *Société des Lettres de l'Aveyron* in

[3] Victor Advielle. *The Scots In Rouergue* By Mr. Victor Advielle ... (15 June 1865). Paris: Edinburgh.

[4] James D. Mackenzie. "The Cuthberts of Castlehill. *The Celtic Magazine*", No. XLII. April, 1879. Vol. IV, pp. 227–30.

[5] Jean-François Henry de Richeprey, Henri Guilhamon. *Journal des Voyages En Haute-Guienne de J.-F. Henry De Richeprey*. Rodez: Commission des archives historiques du Rouergue 1952. Then Société des lettres, sciences et arts de l'Aveyron 1967.

which he listed sources on the life of Seignelay found in the Archives of Haute-Garonne.

A few decades later, Andrew Moore used the departmental, diocesan and Society of Letters archives of Aveyron to write his degree dissertation on the bishop. Unfortunately, this work, which he had taken care to translate into French, was lost by the Departmental Archives of Aveyron, while the English version lay dormant in the Bristol University Library.[6] Bernard Fixes studied the pastoral activities of Seignelay in 1989.[7] A new stage was reached with Philippe Massot-Bordenave's journey to Scotland, which enabled him in his thesis to underline the links he had established with the Duke of Buccleuch, Smith's pupil, and to open up other avenues thanks to the archives of the Buccleuch family.[8] More recently, Gautier Louyriac devoted a thick master's thesis to his administration of the diocese of Rodez.[9]

Finally, the search for traces of Seignelay has benefited from multiple contributions in Inverness, Rodez, but also in Paris, Toulouse, Caen, Reims and Harvard, because if unfortunately, Seignelay Colbert's papers disappeared when his possessions were dispersed at auction, many letters were preserved by their addressees in collections, not all of which

[6] Andrew Moore, *A Bishop of the Ancien Régime: Segnelai Colbert de Castlehill in the Pre-Revolutionary Years*, University of Bristol, 1988.

[7] Bernard Fixes, "Le clergé séculier dans le diocèse de Rodez à la fin de l'Ancien Régime". *Bulletin de littérature ecclésiastique*, tome XC. pp. 47–68, January-March 1989.

[8] Alain ALCOUFFE, Philippe Massot Bordenave, *Adam Smith à Toulouse et en Occitanie*, Toulouse : Privat, 2018. (The book used documents produced in Massot-Bordenave 2013 PhD thesis).

[9] Gautier Louyriac, *Le Diocèse de Rodez à la fin du XVIIIe siècle. Part 1: state of the diocese of Rodez under the episcopate of Mgr Seignelay-Colbert (1781–1789)*. Université Jean Jaurès, 2016.

have been explored,[10] while details emerged from some correspondence between third parties.[11]

Researching Sources

The first document, preserved in the National Archives of Scotland, is of course the baptismal certificate of 13 August 1735 for Seignelai Cuthbert of Castlehill, a first surprise since the biographical records put his birth date at 1736. The baptismal officiant was Alexander Mc Bean, nicknamed the *John Knox of the North*, the Presbyterian minister of Inverness.[12] If we add that his grandfather was an Episcopalian bishop and that his two uncles who had emigrated to France publicly abjured Presbyterianism in order to convert to Catholicism,[13] we can see that Seignelay's 'Catholic' origins are less obvious than what will be put forward by two bishops at the time of the enquiry prior to his consecration as bishop of Rodez. But the baptismal certificate introduces another singularity: the first name of the future bishop is rather incongruous: Seignelai. This was the spelling of the village of Seignelay until a letter from Colbert designated it as Seignelay. No saint seems to be attached to this name, which François

[10] We are thinking here of the Vatican Archives, to which the pandemic prevented access, but also, in Toulouse itself, of the correspondence of the Présidente du Bourg, which contains letters from Colbert; but the family archives are dispersed between the municipal archives of Toulouse, the Departmental Archives of Haute-Garonne and the Municipal Library of Toulouse. Colbert frequently travelled to Paris and kept the Présidente du Bourg informed of her son's studies and the political situation. On the Présidente du Bourg, see Christine Dousset, "La présidente Du Bourg: diffuser et mettre en pratique ses lectures. Réflexion à partir d'un exemple toulousain", in Isabelle Brouard-Arends, Marie-Emmanuelle Plagnol-Diéval. *Femmes éducatrices au siècle des Lumières*, Rennes: P.U.R., 2007, pp. 75–92.

[11] For example, the *Correspondence of Mme du Deffand and Horace Walpole*. Andrew Moore and I have been able to collect 350 documents or texts by Colbert or concerning Colbert's chronology. See https://colbertdecastlehill.com/timeline/.

[12] The copy of the birth certificate was provided by James Brennan of Inverness. MacBean's nickname is reported in Fraser Mackintosh, Charles. 1898 *An Account of the Confederation of the Clan Chattan; Its Kith and Kin*. Glasgow: John Mackay.

[13] The manuscript of Charles Rabache de Fréville, parish priest of the abbey of Saint Germain des Prés, reports the abjurations of Lachlan Cuthbert/Colbert (who would later francize his first name to Lancelot) and Alexandre on 8 March and 12 April 1734, respectively, pp. 175–6 in Pierre Gasnault. *Histoire De La Paroisse De L'abbaye De Saint-Germain-Des-Prés À Paris*. Paris, Paris Musées, 2004.

Falc'hun attributes to a Celtic origin.[14] On the other hand, it is impossible not to link it to the family of the Great Jean-Baptiste Colbert. The destiny of the young Highlander is indeed a consequence of Jean-Baptiste Colbert's claim to have the nobility of his origins recognised, in defiance of all plausibility. The fable of the noble origin of the Colberts hardly deceived contemporaries and probably not the Great Colbert himself, but genealogists have claimed to have established it and in the church of the Cordeliers in Reims a tombstone bears the inscription: 'Ci-gît li preux chevalier Richard Colbert, dit li Escossois ki [three words deleted] 1300. Priez pour l'âme de il'. The inscription was followed by a shield with the knight's arms bearing a serpent twisted in pale. Below this shield were two verses in Gothic letters: "En Écosse, je us le berceau / Et Rheims m'a donné le tombeau.[15]" The origin of this tombstone is highly suspect and there is nothing to link the Colbert family to this famous knight, but very opportunely the grandfather of Bishop Seignelay undertook to claim it and the Scottish Parliament registered this request.[16] This made it easier for J.B. Colbert's children to enter the circles of the nobility, even if few people were fooled. It especially facilitated the emigration of two of Seignelai's uncles (Lachlan, who made a career in the army and whose descendants still remember him, and Alexander, who was known as the Abbé Colbert). So when Seignelai's father died accidentally, his grandmother, Jeanne Hay, the daughter of the former Episcopal bishop of Moray, undertook to send him to France to join his uncles.

On arriving in France in 1747, Seignelay did not immerse himself in the French intellectual world: in addition to his contacts with his two uncles, he was studying at the Collège des Écossais, which he did not have to attend at all.

[14] François-Marie Falc'hun, *Celtic Place Names. First series, Valleys and plains* / by; with the collaboration of Bernard Tanguy, 1909–1991.

[15] "In Scotland was my cradle Rheims gave me a grave", Mathieu STOLL, Thierry Sarmant, *Le Grand Colbert,* Paris: Tallandier, 2021, p. 28.

[16] Warrant for a bore brieve to Charles Colbert, marquis of Seignelay, *The Records of the Parliaments of Scotland to 1707*, K.M. Brown et al. eds (St Andrews, 2007–2022), https://www.rps.ac.uk/search.php?action=print&id=47702&filename=jamesvii_trans&type=trans date accessed: 10 October 2022.

He did not 'leave' until late in 1761.[17] The role of Scottish culture in his education should not be underestimated. It is not known whether he had a private tutor or went to school in Scotland, but his subsequent years at the Scots College provided him with a solid grounding in culture of antiquity. Indeed, when he transferred to the Collège d'Harcourt, where he took part in the *Concours général* organised among the rhetoric students, he won the 'prix d'honneur' in Latin speech in 1754.[18] During his early years in France, this brilliant student was recommended to the exiled King of Scotland, James III, at Saint Germain en Laye.[19]

Seignelay's activities in the following years are not well known. He studied law at the faculty of Reims, a choice which can be explained either by the links between the family of Jean-Baptiste Colbert and the city of Reims, or more prosaically by the reputation of the faculty of Reims for granting degrees easily. In any case, there is also a link to the Douglas affair, which agitated the Scottish high nobility but which also aroused public opinion.

Seignelay's role was modest but he seems to have served as an interpreter and guide (already) to the Douglas family investigators seeking to prove Lady Jane's pregnancy and her deposition taken by Adam Smith, who like Hume, rather on the side of the Hamiltons, was careful not to make any assertions that might be detrimental to the Douglas family.[20]

The question then arises as to how David Hume and Abbé Colbert could have become so close so quickly, as Colbert's letters to his 'cousin' show, to the extent that Hume recommended him to Smith and the latter made Toulouse, where Colbert had arrived at the beginning of January 1764, his home port for most of the Duke of Buccleuch's *Grand Tour*.

[17] Brian Michael Halloran, *The Scots College, Paris, 1653–1792*. PhD thesis, University of Saint Andrews, p. 319.

[18] He was the second student of the College, after La Harpe, to win a prize in the general competition. Henri Louis A. Bouquet 1891. *The former Collège d'Harcourt and the Lycée Saint Louis*. Paris, Delalain. A certificate of the prize can be found in the Aveyron archives.

[19] Edward Corp has kindly pointed out letters between the treasurer and private secretary of James III showing interest in the young Seignelay, who was also recommended to Arthur Richard Dillon (7 October 1753).

[20] Colbert's deposition was taken on 5 October 1765 by Adam Smith, a few days before he left Toulouse. See note 1 p. 260 in William R. SCOTT. *Adam Smith As Student and Professor*. New York: Augustus M. Kelley, 1937.

There is no doubt that a great friendship and even familiarity had developed between the three Scots during Smith's and the Duke's stay in Toulouse (March 1764 - October 1765) and during his exile in England after 1792 Seignelay still refers, in his correspondence with the Duke, to Smith, their common friend, and benefits from the Duke's assistance.[21] The correspondence of Smith, Colonel Barré and Colbert himself with Hume, as well as Colbert's letters to the Duke, shows a cheerful character, never losing an opportunity to make a witty remark, very hostile to superstition, horrified by the fate of Calas, but doing justice to David de Baudrigue, the capitoul who first accused Jean Calas in the death of his son, when the English embassy wrongly accused him of prevarication and extortion against foreign Protestants who had died in Toulouse.

In 1767, Colbert became the commendatory abbot of Val Richer, a Cistercian abbey which was the offshot of Clairvaux, and he remained so until he became Bishop of Rodez. The archives of the Calvados department contain a great deal of correspondence showing the difficulties in which the abbey's finances found themselves and the hesitant beginnings of Colbert's management as he had to call on his uncle Alexander to restore a difficult situation.

For Colbert, the year 1770 was also marked by the publication in Basel under the pseudonym of Baron de C** of a work, *Les Elémens du Droit de la nature et de la Morale Naturelle. Adressé aux nations civiliséeset policées de l'Europe*.[22] There seem to be only two surviving copies: one is kept in the library of the Assemblée nationale[23] and the other in the Médiathèque de Rodez.

Seignelay's accession to the episcopal see of Rodez in 1781 at the age of 46 was a remarkable success for a Scot with no powerful patrons. Episcopal careers in the Gallican church of the eighteenth century have been studied in detail by Michel Péronnet.[24] Family relations sometimes

[21] Crispin Powell, archivist to the Duke of Buccleuch, has kindly provided us with Colbert's letters to the Duke during the French Revolution.

[22] *The elements of natural law and natural morality. Addressed to the civilised and policed nations of Europe.*

[23] The history of this library goes back to works collected by the Committee of Public Instruction, created on 14 October 1791. See Catalogue des livres de jurisprudence, d'économie politique et d'administration, composant la bibliothèque de la Chambre des députés, Paris, Didot, 1833.

[24] Michel C. Peronnet, *Les évêques de l'ancienne France*, Paris: Champion, 1977.

played a decisive role, but in the eighteenth century the lengthening of the life span of prelates slowed down the rotation of seats, so that the wait forced episcopal candidates to make themselves familiar to the assembly of bishops in order to hope for consecration. Colbert thus had the opportunity to present a report on the difficulties of collecting tithes to the small assembly of the clergy in 1780.[25] But it was still necessary to pass the examination of the file collected by the nuncio and transmitted to the pope (the Roman information). Two bishops were found to guarantee that Seignelay came from a Catholic family, Jean-Baptiste-Joseph de Lubersac, bishop of Chartres and Marie-Charles-Isidore de Mercy, bishop of Luçon.[26] The *Scots Magazine* quickly greeted the new bishop in its June 1781 issue mentioning that he was also Count of Rodez and President of the Provincial Assembly of Rouergue (a confusion with Upper Guyenne). In the latter capacity, he was to continue the reforms initiated by his predecessor, Jérôme Champion de Cicé, 'a friend and disciple of Turgot'.[27] In this capacity, he administered the use of funds for charity workshops. As the cadastre (land register) was the big issue in Rouergue, he supported Richeprey's efforts, as his correspondence with Condorcet shows.[28]

But in the same month of May 1782, Colbert published under the same pseudonym B^{on} de C de C a *Projet d'un traité de paix générale et perpétuelle entre les différentes puissances chrétiennes de l'Europe précédé d'explications préliminaires* (sl; s d.). The book is in the Bibliothèque Nationale together with a long letter of about ten handwritten pages addressed directly to King Louis XVI. It is difficult to determine the origin and fate of this book: was it managed by Loménie de Brienne or was the new bishop trying to play a personal card?

[25] Pierre-Louis de La Rochefoucauld, *Procès-verbal de l'assemblée-générale extraordinaire du clergé de France tenue à Paris au couvent des Grands-Augustins en l'année mil sept cent quatre-vingt*. Paris: Desprez.

[26] The notice is dated 3 February 1781, Arch. Nationales, MC/ET/LXXXII/581. We would like to thank Ronan Tallec who made a copy for us and Wolfgang Mager (University of Bielefeld) who kindly summarised and commented on it.

[27] Léonce de Lavergne, *Les assemblées provinciales sous Louis XVI*, Paris: Calmann Lévy, 1879 [1863].

[28] Letter of 11 May 1782, kept in the Archives of the Académie des Sciences, of the Acad. des Sciences. Session pocket of 15 May 1782. Document IDC 601.

Before the elections for the Estates-General, Colbert wrote to his Jacobite (and Freemason) friends Barneval: "We are here in all the turmoil which must naturally precede this great event... It is a great revolution which is going to take place, I have no doubt that it will turn out for the good, and I desire it more than I can express to you".[29] Colbert was at the heart of the movement, as Arthur Young points out[30] and in his role in rallying the clergy to the Revolution, which led to his being carried in triumph to Versailles on 25 June 1789.[31] The obstacles to Colbert's support for the Revolution soon multiplied: firstly, on 2 November 1789, the Assembly voted the decree placing the clergy's property at the disposal of the Nation. Of course, these effects were largely virtual, such as the counterpart according to which the State would assume the costs of worship and provide for the maintenance of hospitals and the relief of the poor. The confrontation with the Catholic Church continued with the Civil Constitution of the Clergy adopted on 12 July 1790 and, above all, on 27 November 1790, the Assembly demanded that all bishops and parish priests swear an oath of loyalty to the Constitution. We must admit that we do not know what his perception of events and reactions was from July 1790 to May 1792. Louis Servières reported decades later the testimony of Abbé Malrieu who boasted that he had convinced him to refuse the revolutionary prescriptions and emigrate in the spring of 1791[32] but in reality Colbert discreetly remained in Paris under scabrous conditions until the spring of 1792 if we are to believe the gossip that followed him to England.[33] In reality, we only know from a letter sent to the Duke of Buccleuch that he ended up in England in May 1792. Eventually, Abbé Grégoire, a French Catholic priest, constitutional bishop of Blois and a revolutionary leader who visited London after 1792, wrote that

[29] Gaston Martin, "Les Élections aux États généraux dans le Sud-Ouest. Some unpublished documents", in *La Révolution française*, t. 81, January-December 1928, pp. 231–236.

[30] On 22 June 1789, Young reports that he dined with "the Duke of Liancourt at the Palace: there were many noblemen and deputies of the communes, among others, the Duke of Orleans, the Bishop of Rhodez, the Abbé Sieyès and M. Rabaud-Saint-Étienne. Young, Arthur. 1792. *Travels during the Years 1787, 1788, and 1789*. Bury St. Edmonds: W. Richardson, p. 117.

[31] See supra note 40.

[32] Louis SERVIERES, *Histoire de l'Église du Rouergue*, Rodez, Carrère, 1874.

[33] See Marion Lochhead, John Gibson Lockhart. London: John Murray. 1954, pp. 176–7 and infra the contribution of Jennifer Henderson.

Bishop Colbert "was welcomed especially by the Duke of Gordon",[34] grand master of the Grand Lodge of Scotland (1792–4). Abbé Grégoire reports also that Lord Launderdale told him that "this prelate, by his virtues, honored humanity".

The aim of the colloquium was to draw the portrait that a career as extraordinary as Colbert's deserves. Many aspects remain unknown to us, but the various papers allow us to follow an itinerary stretching between the Highlands, Paris, Toulouse, Rodez and finally London, and finally to bring us closer to a man of the eighteenth century, born a protestant in Scotland, arriving in France as a teenager, reaching the highest functions of the Gallican Church, forced to return to Great Britain where he is moved to find the harbour of his childhood during a trip to Scotland.

Much remains to be discovered as to Bishop Colbert' activities once back in Britain. He was an active member of the Cuthbert family, frequented his brother Lewis, now returned from Jamaica and settled in Bristol, travelling to Scotland on family business and to visit the Duke of Buccleugh. He officiated at ceremonies for Catholic families and corresponded with clergy in Rodez who did not subscribe to the new elected Bishop Debertier who had replaced him. He visited Walpole and worked with Miss Mary Berry on the publication of Walpole's correspondence with Mme du Deffand.

Principally perhaps, following the 1801 Concordat between Napoleon and the Pope, he was one of the main animators and supports of the schismatic 'Petite Eglise', which counted nigh on 100.000 members by the time of his death. Seignelay Colbert/Cuthbert died on 15 July 1811 (of a bladder inflammation) at the Twickenham house of his relative Lord Gray, a previous Postmaster General of Scotland. He was buried at Saint Pancras cemetery.

This book is divided into four parts which follow, loosely speaking, the great steps of his life (Parts One to Three), while Part Four compares his destiny with some of his contemporaries.

Part One is devoted to the singular curriculum vitae which carries Colbert from Inverness to the see of Rodez. In Chapter 2, writer Jennifer Morag Henderson places the Colbert family in the context of its geographical environment, Inverness, the capital of the Highlands. Knowledge of the Colbert/Cuthbert family, their standing in Scotland

[34] H.L. Carnot, *Mémoires de M. Grégoire, [...] précédé d'une Notice historique sur l'auteur*, Paris, J. Yonet, 1840, t. II, p. 257.

and their religious background help to make sense of Colbert of Castle-hill's later decisions. Henderson recalls the Jacobite rebellion of 1745. It is in its aftermath that Seignelay's family sent him to France while his younger brother, Lewis, followed a very different path, holding the patent office of Provost Marshal of Jamaica and becoming an advocate of slavery.

In Ueno Hiroki's Chapter 3, the author remarks that Colbert not only connects the Enlightenment and the Revolution in France, but also the French and Scottish Enlightenment worldwide. He turns his attention to the long-lasting relationship between Colbert, Smith and his pupil, the Duke of Buccleuch. Colbert attended the Parisian salons very young and was befriended by David Hume. Colbert's sociability was not only practically useful to Smith and Buccleuch, but also essential to the moral education of the young duke himself.

In Chapter 4, Gilbert Larguier looks at the role assigned by Loménie de Brienne to his vicar-general: to deputise for him at the Toulouse diocesan *assiette*, one of the key cogs in the provincial administration. For almost twenty years, Colbert's main task was to monitor and even direct the work of the *assiette*. This chapter documents the role played by the vicars-general of the prelates of Languedoc, which often remained in the shadows. Colbert's years in Toulouse were a long preparation for the future Bishop of Rodez, who was to preside over the provincial assembly of Haute-Guyenne.

Despite his many duties, Loménie's vicar-general found the time to write a treatise on morality in the aftermath of Smith's visit in Toulouse, which is reviewed by Timothy Day in Chapter 5. Such a treatise, produced by a Catholic clergyman, shows that the influence of the philosophers reached its peak in the second half of the eighteenth century. Colbert's treatise focuses on the role of man in the natural order of things, presenting the objects of his study to those who have the natural right to maintain peace and concord between nations. Colbert's treatise is valuable as an historical document because its content brings a certain clarity and emotion to an increasingly complex discourse on the Enlightenment.

Part Two of the book examines Colbert's role and actions prior to and during the initial stages of the French Revolution. The representatives of the clergy to the Estates-General of 1789 were elected using voting procedures allowing all members of the clergy (including female congregation members) to take part, directly or indirectly. Local tradition reports that Colbert was elected with some difficulty, proposing reforms in the training and the compensation of the lower orders of clergy.[35] The Cahier de Doléances of the Rouergat clergy provides evidence that it was aspiring to a more democratic management, both for its own concerns and for the nation.

In Chapter 6, Julien Béchard scrutinises the treatments of Loménie de Brienne, Champion de Cicé and Colbert in the *Nouvelles Ecclésiastiques*. This French Jansenist weekly was founded in 1728 to fight against the implementation of the Unigenitus Bull (1713) and to support Jansenists who were being harassed by the royal or ecclesiastical authorities. The episcopacy of Mgr Colbert de Castlehill did not escape the harsh analysis of the Jansenists. For *Les Nouvelles*, the episcopacy of the Bishop of Rodez was merely a continuation of that of Mgr Loménie de Brienne, Archbishop of Toulouse from 1763 to 1788, one of the bishops most criticised by the newspaper.

In Chapter 7, Guy Astoul examines the attitude of the clergy in May–June 1789. Since the first meeting of the Estates-General on 5 May 1789, the clergy had been deeply divided on the question of voting by order. 19 ecclesiastical figures, including some bishops, were the first to join the Third Estate, on June 16, and the very next day they associated themselves with the proclamation of a National Assembly. Among these prelates who recognised the need for reform, there were the Archbishop of Bordeaux, Champion de Cicé, of Vienne, Lefranc de Pompignan, of Chartres, de Lubersac, de Chalmazel, bishop of Coutances and Seignelay Colbert de Castlehill, Bishop of Rodez. Astoul analyses the extent to which this rallying was decisive in the evolution of events at a decisive time, in line with the recent historiography which stresses the religious origins of the Revolution.[36] Many of them later regretted their commitment to the Revolution and were forced to emigrate, as explained in Part Three.

The honeymoon period between the National Assembly, Colbert and the other progressive prelates did not dissipate immediately after the first months of the Revolution. Jean-Baptiste Masmejan recalls in Chapter 8 that, as Bishop of Rodez and President of the provincial assembly of

[35] See, Barrau, Eugène de. 1873. *1789 en Rouergue: Étude historique et critique des institutions électorales de l'ancien et du nouveau régime: 1er Volume. sénéchaussée de Rodez*. Rodez: Vve Carrère.

[36] Van Kley, Dale K., *The Religious Origins of the French Revolution*. New Haven and London: Yale University Press, 1996.

Haute-Guyenne, Colbert de Castlehill set out to provide local poor relief by establishing charitable workshops and supporting charitable foundations. It was only natural that during the Constituent Assembly he should find himself a member of the Begging Committee, which he joined as vice-President. Despite the Bishop of Rodez remaining committed to the protection of Church property and the role of the clergy in providing aid, his involvement with the Committee was consistent. Most of his work focused on hospital issues and the treatment of incurable patients.

The gulf between the Church and the Revolution began to widen on 2 November 1789, when the Constituent Assembly decided that the property of the Catholic Church's clergy should be made available to the Nation to pay off the State's debts. The next step after expropriation was the reorganisation of the Catholic Church through the Civil Constitution of the Clergy (CCC), adopted on 12 July 1790. In the next months, the king delayed signing the legislation, while the Constituent Assembly, on 27 November 1790, voted to require the clergy to sign an oath of loyalty to the Constitution. Eventually on 26 December 1790, Louis XVI finally gave his public assent to the Civil Constitution, allowing the process of administering the oaths to proceed in January and February 1791. Colbert not only refused to take the oath but encouraged the priests of his diocese to follow his example.[37] Consequently, the new law deemed him to have resigned, his see was declared vacant, and Claude Debertier was elected Bishop on 20 March 1791.[38] Colbert was soon to adopt a hard line, as can be seen from his letters to the priests of his diocese. Bernard Fixes' Chapter 9 explains the Rouergat context and establishes the position of the priests who were faced with an agonising choice. It is very likely that the position of their bishop influenced their decisions. The massive refusal of the priests to sign, which had far-reaching consequences, illustrates the rupture between the Church and the Revolution.

Part Three is devoted to the two last decades that Colbert spent in Britain, where he arrived in 1792. During his last three years in France, Colbert had entered the Scots College in Paris in 1747 and had kept in touch with his family. His uncle, Abbé Alexander Colbert, had strong

[37] See Lettre écrite par M. l'Evêque de Rodez., a M***. Curé & Vicaire forain de son Diocese. A Paris, le 8 Janvier 1791.

[38] Sabatié, Amans-Claude. 1912. *Debertier, évêque constitutionnel et le clergé de Rodez*. Paris : Beauchesne.

links with influential members of the Scottish Catholic community, but Colbert seems to have had very little contact, if any, with the Scottish Mission until 1790. By then, John Farquharson, the Rector of the Scots College in Douai, had established a connection with Colbert who, alongside another member of parliament, Merlin of Douai, actively supported the Rector's endeavours to preserve the Scots College from the worst effects of the French Revolution. Two years later, the now refractory Bishop of Rodez was again called on to help the Scottish Mission in its attempt to resolve its dispute with Alexander Gordon, Principal of the Scots College, Paris, at a time when events in France threatened its very existence. In Chapter 10, Clotilde Prunier seeks to explore the role the Bishop of Rodez really played in those two major crises for the Scottish Mission, which ultimately failed to secure its Scots Colleges in France, and she then examines the nature of Colbert's relationship with the Scottish Mission during his years of exile in Britain.

Colbert's correspondence and the testimony of his contacts with the Scots Mission prove he was still in Paris in May 1792 while he wrote to the Duke on 22 October 1792 that he was all ready to spend some time in England[39] Having been ousted from the bishopric in March 1791, Colbert continued to work in Paris, both for his diocese and for the Scots College. Perhaps he was counting on a return to grace, or thought that his Scottish origins would protect him from the persecution that befell Mgr de la Marche, the bishop of Saint Pol de Léon, at the end of March 1791 and which led de la Marche to move to England, the first prelate of the Gallican church to find refuge there.[40] This "precursor" of Colbert whose see was located on the coast had prepared for an exile by transferring some funds via a ship smuggling contraband to England. Very little is known about Colbert's own exile. It is true that from May 1792 onwards, measures against refractory priests multiplied: proscription (26 May 1792) and banishment (26 August 1792)[41], not to mention the September massacres, encouraged the Gallican Prelates to escape from the "cannibals" Colbert denounced in his letter to the Duke. One third

[39] See Colbert's timeline.

[40] See Chapter 1 of Plasse, François-Xavier. 1886. *Le clergé français réfugié en Angleterre* 1. Paris: Soc. Générale de Libr. Cathol. u.a.

[41] "Clergy who have not taken an oath of allegiance to the new government are to leave France within two weeks or be deported to Guiana" Carpenter, Kirsty, *Refugees of the French Revolution: émigrés in London, 1789–1802*. London: Palgrave, p. 186.

of the clergy emigrated with the largest wave during the summer of 1792 while almost three quarters of the prelates eventually emigrated, most of them before mid-1792.[42]

In Chapter 11, Patrick Ferté has attempted to reconstruct the network of relationships that underpin the period of Colbert's exile across the Channel, whether in Scotland or London. This network was forged well before the Revolution in four converging centres of friendship, (1) with his first mentors, the bishop of Chartres, Lubersac, his character witness and his patron in Toulouse, Loménie de Brienne and above all in his diocese of Rodez since 1781; (2) with the liberal La Rochefoucauld family, particularly the Duchesse d'Enville and her nephew the Duc de Liancourt, followers of Turgot and Adam Smith; (3) at the Sorbonne, through some of his fellow students but above all through his professors, some of whom were from Rouergue and whom he later met again in London; and (4) his British connections also played a major role, due to his Scottish origin, but Ireland was just as decisive in this instance. These four focal points, split into segments to clarify the presentation, are most often intertwined: some of the Irish refugees he met or ordained in Toulouse or Rodez became professors at the Sorbonne before fleeing to England or Dublin (to the Catholic College of Maynooth); others were from his Rouergat flock, who themselves obtained a chair at the Sorbonne and/or a position as chaplain or confessor to the royal family. The fact remains that these four foci, which formed a solid network, shared the same ideology and converged into exile, usually in London.

At the dawn of the Revolution, there were 139 bishops of the Gallican Church. Only four of them (including Loménie de Brienne and Talleyrand) took the oath and most of the refractory prelates emigrated to neighbouring countries. Eventually seventeen reached Great Britain and settled in London, hoping that the situation in France would improve. Instead, the situation worsened over the following two years. If Year II (September 1793-September 1794) marked the apogee of de-Christianisation, the persecution which encompassed not only the refractory clergy but also the constitutional one persisted right through the period of the *Directoire* and the first year of the Consulate, until the Concordat of 1801 between the First French Republic and the Holy See, signed by First Consul Napoleon Bonaparte and Pope Pius VII on

[42] See p. 411, Les défis de la modernité (1750–1840) sous la responsabilité de Bernard Plongeron, tome X, *Histoire du christianisme*, Paris: Desclée, 1997.

15 July 1801 in Paris after one year of negotiations.[43] It was carrying out a complete reorganisation of the church, since all the bishops were to resign their sees, which would be filled again by the First Consul according to the procedures in force before 1789. The negotiations between Napoleon and the Pope did not involve the former bishops who were scattered around various countries. Almost all the bishops exiled in London, including Colbert, rejected the Concordat; but a few of them, such as Boisgelin de Cucé who lead the rallying of the clergy in 1789 alongside Colbert, resigned on 7 November 1801, returned to France in January 1802 and was appointed archbishop of Tours on 9 April 1802, then Cardinal on 17 January 1803.

In Chapter 12, Dominic A. Bellenger provides an overview of the life and thought of the French Bishops resident in London following their emigration relating to the Civil Constitution of the Clergy, published in 1790. Their life, in great contrast to their former existence, was dependent on the charity of the British state and limited self-help. It was centred on French chapels which provided spiritual and material comfort. They had an uneasy relationship with their English fellow Catholics and their leaders, and the Vicars Apostolic of the London District were aware that their identity as Catholics and Frenchmen made them doubly suspect. Leadership among the bishops themselves was provided by the Bishop of St Pol de Léon in Brittany, a devout and business-like prelate, who acted as an intermediary with the British authorities. Others, like Dillon of Narbonne and Colbert himself, had personal links with their land of exile. Colbert cultivated his British contacts, who included Horace Walpole, and busied himself alongside his episcopal colleagues in presenting a united front in opposition to Napoleon's Concordat. Their 'memoir', signed by 14 bishops on 23 December 1801—including Colbert—was a spirited defence of the pre-Revolutionary Gallican Church of which they regarded themselves as the 'faithful remnant'.

The positions taken by Colbert during the Revolution appear consistent with his conception of the separation between Church and State as well as his conception of the Papacy, both rooted in Gallicanism and Jansenism. In a letter to the Duke of Buccleuch (5 November 1793),

[43] Xavier Maréchaux records the various reactions of exiled bishops to changes in religious policy during the decade 1791–1801 in his article: Réorganiser l'Église après la Révolution: les évêques d'Ancien Régime et le Concordat de 1801. *Napoleonica*. 2019/1 (N° 33), pp. 67–98.

he seems to be disillusioned about the future of the church and about his own future, avowing that "if French affairs do not recover, I would be a farmer in Scotland if I were not a bishop in France. There are many ways to pass at least gently through life and I am no longer [so] difficult as that".[44] Despite his temptations to emigrate to America, he remained a guide for the refractory clergy of the diocese of Rodez as well of Toulouse, replacing an ageing and tired Dillon. In Chapter 13, Marie-Paule Biron examines Colbert's correspondence with his priests in Rouergue, revealing his reactions to the Revolution. Initially enthusiastic about the early reforms, his optimism turned to doubt when they disrupted the balance between society and the Church. As a Gallican, Colbert had navigated the balance of power between royalty and the Pope but realised a separation of powers was needed to oppose the Civil Constitution of the Clergy.

With the Concordat, Mgr Colbert found himself faced with two protagonists who undermined his principle of the separation of powers. While he sought to fight openly against Bonaparte, who wanted to tame the Church through the Concordat, Colbert wanted, through dialogue and with the support of his Gallican *confrères* in exile in London, to make the Pope recognise that, under pressure from temporal authorities, he had exercised a power to dismiss the bishops not granted to him by the Church. Faced with his failure, in the face of Bonaparte and the Pope's refusal to listen to him, Mgr Seignelay fell back on the "Little Church", whose ideals he did not necessarily share.

Part Four displays three figures who belonged to a greater or lesser extent to his network of social contacts from the 1770s onwards. These include the Abbé Raynal, born in Lapanouse in Aveyron in 1713 and deceased in Chaillot in 1796, Abbé Sièyès, born in1748 in Fréjus and deceased in 1836 in Paris, and Bertrand Barère, born in 1755 in Tarbes and deceased in the same town in 1841. One can be surprised to find these figures linked to freemasonry among these essays devoted to a Gallican Bishop, as in the eyes of most people, there is a deep gulf between the two institutions.[45] Nevertheless, as Michel Taillefer, historian

[44] We are indebted to Crispin Powell, archivist, who transmitted us this Letter from the Buccleuch archives.

[45] Gilles Bancarel sustains that there is no evidence that Abbé Raynal was a freemason. Christine Fauré holds the same for Abbé Sieyès.

of Toulousan freemasonry, put it: "From the introduction of Freemasonry in France around 1725 until the end of the Ancien Régime, Catholics and Freemasons lived in harmony, or rather there was no problem of conscience in being both a Catholic and a Freemason".[46] Nineteenth-century Catholic historians, often obsessed by the part played by freemasonry, never suspected Colbert to be an initiate, but nevertheless, his links with masonry are manifold. Colbert's father belonged to the Inverness lodge, as his uncle, Lachlan, belonged to the lodge of the Royal Ecossois.[47] According to Pierre Chevallier,[48] there is no evidence till now that Loménie de Brienne himself was a freemason as his network of contacts (beginning with his own sister-in-law) included many freemasons. Soon after his arrival in Toulouse, Colbert formed a lifelong friendship with the Barnaval family, founders of the first lodge in Toulouse. It is noticeable also that Francis Scott, the 2nd Duke of Buccleuch, the grandfather of Henry, the pupil of Smith, held the office of Grand Master of Freemasons from 24 June 1723 to 24 June 1724. Henry himself is frequently quoted in the freemasonry events.[49]

Gilles Bancarel, in Chapter 14, examines the relationship between Colbert and Abbé Raynal. Bishop Colbert de Castlehill came to Rouergue following his appointment to Rodez on 28 January 1781, for a period characterised by great instability due to revolutionary events. He played an active role in the development of his diocese, presiding over the work of the Provincial Assembly of Upper Guyenne initiated by his predecessor Champion de Cicé. This innovative institution of the Ancien Régime, initiated by Louis XVI and his ministers, which put into practice the ideas of decentralisation on the eve of 1789, disappeared with its instigators with the arrival of the new regime. The chapter examines the evolution and future of this institution in the light of the initiatives taken in its favour by Mgr Colbert and Abbé Raynal.

[46] Michel Taillefer, 2014. *Études sur la sociabilité à Toulouse et dans le Midi toulousain de l'Ancien Régime à la Révolution*. Toulouse: Presses de l'université du Mirail (2020: Openedition).

[47] Among the witnesses of Lachlan's abjuration was the Chevalier Ramsay who introduced freemasonry into France in about 1725 (See https://chevalierramsay.be/).

[48] See his *Histoire de la franc-maçonnerie française*, Paris: Fayard, 1974, p. 306.

[49] Róbert Péter, Ed., *British Freemasonry*, 1717–1813 Volume 5 Rsepresentations, London: Routledge, 2016, pp. 120, 124, 395.

In Colbert's network of contacts, the Duke Larochefoucauld Liancourt is a major figure as shown in Chapters 8 and 11. He was close to famous freemasons, despite (in his biography written by his son) the latter insisting that "it had once been impossible to lead him astray in the society of d'Alembert, Baron d'Holbach and Condorcet".[50] Anyway, according to Arthur Young, Colbert and Sieyès frequented the salon of the Duke in the heady days of June 1789. From the Revolution to the dawn of the twenty-first century, the historiography from the counter-revolutionaries as well from the freemasons themselves agreed that Abbé Sieyès was already a freemason in Fréjus and later a member of the Nine Sisters lodge. Nowadays the lack of evidence forces historians to be more cautious but there is no doubt of his close connections with freemasons, beginning with Chamfort.[51]Christine Fauré, in Chapter 15, discusses how two ecclesiastical figures became involved in the French Revolution of 1789: Seignelay Colbert de Castlehill, former Grand Vicar of Toulouse, and Abbé Sieyès, author of "Qu'est-ce que le Tiers État?". Both were involved in provincial politics and later met in Versailles shortly before the General Estates transformed into the National Assembly. Despite their differences, both defended the tithe and shared a rational, abstract view of administrative reform. Colbert eventually chose religion, while Sieyès, driven by events, focused on governance.

Colbert was a man of the Enlightenment, like Sieyès, whose actions constitute a link between the ideas of emancipation and their revolutionary application.

The last figure, examined in Chapter 16, is that of Bertrand Barère. His relationship with Colbert as with freemasonry is tenuous but beyond doubt. He lived in Toulouse from October 1772 to March 1788, i.e. from 17 to almost 33 years, first as a law student and then as a lawyer in the parliament, while Colbert was vicar-general till 1781 and then President of the Provincial Assembly of Haute-Guyenne, which must have provided plenty of opportunities to assess each other's strengths and weaknesses. If some doubt is allowed for Loménie, LaRochefoucauld

[50] *Vie du duc de La Rochefoucauld-Liancourt*. Frédéric-Gaëtan La Rochefoucauld, son fils, 1831, p. 86.

[51] One can compare the very assertive Louis Amiable, 1897. Une loge maçonnique d'avant 1789, la loge les Neuf Soeurs Paris: Alcan and the very cautious Éric Saunier 2014. De la Franc-maçonnerie révolutionnaire à la Franc-maçonnerie en Révolution, *La chaîne d'union*, (N° 67), pp. 30–35.

or even Sièyès, Michel Taillefer provides evidence of the early affiliation of Barère to freemasonry in Tarbes in 1781 and then to Loge Encyclopédique (Toulouse, 1788) but Taillefer concludes that Barère's "involvement in the fraternity was very limited and cannot be used as an argument in favour of the thesis that the French Revolution was the result of a Masonic plot".

Maïté Bouyssy's work explores how Bertrand Barère used academic eulogies in Toulouse to gain prominence, leveraging connections with influential figures like Loménie de Brienne and Castlehill. Through these eulogies, Barère subtly acknowledged his debts to his benefactors by praising "great men" and patrie. This reflects the emerging ideas of nationalism and law. Bouyssy also highlights how the Philanthropy Committee of the Encyclopaedic Lodge in Toulouse united young leaders to establish local administration and promote justice, including defending the innocent. These efforts, influenced by Turgotine and Catholic Enlightenment thought, were pivotal during the Constituante, where Barère played a key role.

Finally Andrew Moore, in a valedictory tribute to Bishop Colbert, 'discovered' in curious circumstances while researching for a dissertation in the Rouergue, tries to understand the influence on his life of a number of dualities which echo some of his own. For example Protestant and Catholic, Scottish and French, commoner and noble, conformist and rebel. In this, he maintains, Colbert/Cuthbert was unique. The only bishop not born in France or one of its colonies, he was also the only not to go into exile, but to return home. He was completely self-made. He had to create his own networks, shine as a scholar and find sources of finance and employment. He had to be articulate, sociable, diligent and reliable. He rose to a position of some eminence and influence within his adopted context, while remaining throughout a Cuthbert and maintaining his family ties in Britain, a useful and sustaining fallback, as events developed.

Moore makes use of his assumed familiarity with the bishop, a ghostly companion for some forty years, to try to understand some of the factors that underpin his extraordinary life, and hopes this collection will lead to further research, and more revelations on the life of a very remarkable man.

This collection of articles, first published in France in 2023, can only be a welcome addition to the history of the French Revolution by casting light on one of its most intriguing, and central, participants. Bishop Colbert/Cuthbert's career is completely unique, and it is hoped these texts will stimulate further research from scholars far and wide.

PART I

From Inverness to Rodez: The Singular Making of a Gallican Bishop

CHAPTER 2

Cuthbert of Castlehill: A View from Inverness

Jennifer Morag Henderson

Abstract Writer Jennifer Morag Henderson places the Colbert family in its geographical environment, Inverness, the capital of the Highlands. Colbert of Castlehill is little known there, but there are various sources available in Scotland that can help shed some light on his life and family. Using her local knowledge and expertise in Scottish and especially Highland records, she presents what these records can reveal about the environment in which Seignelay grew up. Knowledge of the Colbert / Cuthbert family, their standing in Scotland, and their religious background, can help to make sense of Colbert of Castlehill's later decisions. Matching research on Colbert in France with contemporary Scottish and Highland research on the same historical period gives new insights. Placing Colbert's life in the context of the Jacobite rebellion of 1745 and its aftermath gives a different perspective, while viewing his choices in the French Revolution alongside his brother's pro-Slavery stance similarly opens up new areas for discussion.

J. M. Henderson (✉)
Inverness, Scotland
URL: https://www.jennifermoraghenderson.com

A. Alcouffe (ed.), *Seignelay Colbert de Castlehill (1735-1811)*,
https://doi.org/10.1007/978-3-031-75273-5_2

Keywords Castlehill · Cuthbert · Scotland · Inverness · Jacobite · Culloden · Slavery · Jamaica · Gaelic · Highlands

The organisers of the 2020 conference on Seignelay Cuthbert of Castlehill have said that "it would certainly be no exaggeration to assert that no other Scot exercised as much influence on events in France in the second half of the eighteenth century"—but Seignelay is actually very little known in his home city of Inverness, or in the wider arena of Scottish history. However, sources available in Scotland can help to shed light on Seignelay's life and family. This paper aims to highlight the existing information in Highland and Scottish archives and to share local knowledge which may be of help to other researchers. This includes the history of the Cuthbert family, their standing in Scotland and their religious background; their involvement in the Jacobite rising of 1745 and the Battle of Culloden; and Seignelay's brother Lewis' involvement in the slave trade and financial problems in Jamaica. Full details of sources are in the footnotes.

Seignelay grew up in Castlehill House, just outside Inverness, on the road to Culloden, a location that still exists. However, researching 'Castlehill' immediately presents some problems, as there is more than one area locally associated with that name, and in fact confusion over names is the first barrier to researching Seignelay.[1] There are many variations of Seignelay's name, something which is unsurprising given that he was trilingual, speaking English, Gaelic and French, and the name was recorded differently by speakers of different languages. Meanwhile, there is more than one 'Castlehill' in Inverness: there is the hill where Inverness Castle stands—and there is Auld Castlehill. An area near the centre of Inverness, Auld, or Old, Castlehill was Cuthbert family land. The name Castlehill then in turn became associated with the area just outside the modern city of Inverness, on the road to Culloden, where Castlehill House was situated, even when the Cuthberts no longer owned that land. However, most of the local debate around the name (Auld)

[1] 'Castlehill' is very difficult for French speakers to pronounce the way it is said in Scotland, and I have seen French sources with variations like 'Gast-Le-Hill' which effectively mask who they are talking about. I will refer to 'Seignelay Cuthbert of Castlehill' in this paper, as being the name he was generally known by in Scotland.

Castlehill centres around the idea that it may or may not refer to the original site of Macbeth's castle.[2] While Shakespeare's play Macbeth is obviously the main place where most people encounter this name, the real Macbeth in fact ruled Scotland for a considerable time longer than his fictional counterpart. The local debate around Castlehill is full of layers of discussion of literature, culture and politics. None of this is strictly relevant to Colbert of Castlehill, but without that knowledge then searches through Scottish or Highland writings on 'Castlehill' make little sense.

Maps of the area from Seignelay's time show the Castlehill House and lands clearly marked.[3] Castlehill House sits at the centre of the Cuthberts' estate, which stretched from the eastern edge of the burgh of Inverness up to the high ground of Drummossie Moor, and east towards the village of Croy. There was good farmland around Castlehill House, Muckovie and Stoneyfield, but Inshes is marshy, boggy ground. There were 49 named families listed on a nineteenth-century rent roll,[4] but the real number of people on the Castlehill land would have been much higher, as this list would not include sublets. Although it could seem a large tract of land to modern eyes, it was relatively small for a Scottish landowner: it would have given the Cuthberts high status and power in the Inverness area, but far less on a national or international scale.

Castlehill House itself, Seignelay's childhood home, is a large dwelling place. It has been greatly altered and is now substantially Georgian, but part of the original building still remains.[5] The building is still a family home, though the current occupants have no link to the Cuthbert family. Recently, Castlehill House and its owners were in the local

[2] See, for example, *On the Site of Macbeth's Castle at Inverness*, John Anderson, 1828.

[3] The National Library of Scotland hold old maps: this military map from 1725 clearly shows "Cuthbert of Castlehill" https://maps.nls.uk/military/186.html (*A Generall Survey of Inverness and the Country Adjacent to the Foot of Loch Ness*, ca 1725. MS.1647Z.02/76b). Their other online maps offer opportunities to compare over time.

[4] In papers relating to Lewis Cuthbert's debts, bound in the Fraser Mackintosh collection in Inverness Reference Library, item 3313, p. 41

[5] Canmore, National Record of the Historic Environment (Historic Environment Scotland) here: https://canmore.org.uk/site/13514/inverness-castlehill-castlehill-house. See also SUAT Ltd "Archaeological Evaluation of Castlehill, Caulfield Road, Inshes", 11th Dec 2000, Inverness Library reference MR/CAM/JN04). Norman NEWTON 'The Georgian Mansions and Public Buildings of Inverness', Ness Book Fest, 5th October 2019 (unpublished).

Inverness news, during a debate over the naming of a nearby carehome—the carehome had first tried to call itself 'Culloden House' and then 'Castlehill House', both names of local well-known buildings, but there were several objections: this is important not just for the passing local interest, but to show the emotive interest raised by historical houses in the Culloden area and what this means for filtering search results.[6] In particular anything connected with the Jacobite defeat at the battle of Culloden attracts notice, both locally and further afield. The Jacobites (from the Latin for James 'Jacobus') had hoped to return the descendants of King James VII to the British throne; the battle of Culloden saw the end of their hopes. The defeat of Bonnie Prince Charlie (Charles Edward Stuart, or The Young Pretender) at Culloden by the Government troops in 1746 was a massive turning point for the Highlands in particular, as the area suffered brutal reprisals. Attention remains focused on Culloden Battlefield, particularly in the light of current political events around Scottish independence, and the massive impact of cultural and literary associations such as the 'Outlander effect' (tourism brought in by the Outlander books and television series). The 'Outlander effect' not only has a significant measurable economic effect on the major Scottish industry of tourism, but also influences some current thinking around the battle of Culloden.

Symposium organisers Andrew Moore and Professor Alain Alcouffe thought that Bonnie Prince Charlie had stayed at Castlehill House the night before the battle of Culloden, i.e. 15th/16th April 1746. Research found evidence that the Prince actually arrived at Castlehill slightly earlier, on 18 February 1746, staying for one or two nights. From the 18th February to 3rd March, Bonnie Prince Charlie was in the area of Inverness, either at Castlehill or Culloden. On 3rd March he took lodgings in Inverness. The night before the battle, the Prince led a failed night march to nearby Nairn, which had aimed to surprise the Government troops. On retreat, the Prince returned to Culloden House.[7] Bonnie Prince Charlie's brief stay at Castlehill is normally ignored in favour of his longer stay at

[6] https://www.pressandjournal.co.uk/fp/news/inverness/1868696/new-cradlehall-care-home-finally-resolves-name-problems/.

[7] Jacqueline Riding, *The Jacobites* (London: Bloomsbury, 2017), p. 383. Royal Archives, Cumberland Papers Box 13/306: Letter from Mrs Isabella Stewart to Anne Haldane her sister, Inverness 29 March 1746 (with thanks to Richard Knight).

Culloden House—particularly as Culloden House is closer to the battlefield, strategically important as being the home of Duncan Forbes (who was on the Government side), and currently operates as a hotel, drawing strongly on its links with the history of Culloden.[8]

Seignelay's uncle Lachlan fought at Culloden, and there are several sources which shed more light on his life. Lachlan fought with the Royal Eccossois (Royal Scots), a regiment of French exiles on the Jacobite side: he was already living in France before 1746, and returned there afterwards, where he was a contact for Seignelay in Paris. Lachlan is specifically mentioned in a letter from Lewis Gordon to the Laird of MacLeod in the Culloden Papers. Lewis Gordon was the fourth son of the 2nd Duke of Gordon, and, in company with other families who made sure to have a foot in each camp, may have been a Jacobite as proxy for his brother (who remained officially on the Government side). Lewis Gordon was making plans to move wounded men and prisoners; writing from Aberdeen to the Laird of MacLeod, who was based at Culloden, he added a short postscript: "Colonel Colbert desires his compliments to be made to his Brother Castlehill".[9] It seems characteristic of the Cuthbert family that the reference is to Lachlan's family ties. We don't know whether Lachlan ever did manage to see his family, but he was captured at Culloden and "On 7th January 1747/8 [Lachlan][10] wrote from the Marshalsea Prison[11] to Andrew Stone that John Gray, an officer, had been lying in irons in the New Prison, Southwark, ever since he came from Scotland…"[12] In company with other French nationals, Lachlan was sent back to France.[13]

[8] In addition to his brief stay at Castlehill, Bonnie Prince Charlie also stayed at Kilravock Castle, the home of the Rose family. Seignelay's family were related by marriage to the Roses of Kilravock, and of course family ties were very important to Seignelay.

[9] *Culloden papers: correspondence from 1625 to 1748* ed H.R. Duff (1815), No. DXXII. (digital version available online).

[10] "Colonel Colbert of the King of France's Service".

[11] Marshalsea was a notorious prison in London. It became well known later through the work of Charles Dickens: Dickens' father spent time there

[12] *The Prisoners of the '45*, Volume 1, Publications of the Scottish History Society, Third Series, Vol 13 (ed Sir Bruce Gordon Seton and Jean Gordon Arnot, Edinburgh: University Press, 1928); available as a pdf through the NLS: https://deriv.nls.uk/dcn23/1266/1380/126613805.23.pdf.

[13] Database of Jacobite officers, Centre for Robert Burns Studies, University of Glasgow: "Colbert, Lancelot Cuthbert. Major, Royal Scots. T, Culloden. Banished."

Meanwhile, Seignelay and his family remained in Culloden, where they began to experience significant problems. Following in the family tradition, Seignelay's father George Cuthbert was a prominent official in Inverness.[14] Previous Cuthberts had been Town Provosts (head of the local Government), and the family name recurs frequently in Burgh Council records and church records.[15] Inverness Town House[16] has one painting labelled 'Cuthbert', dating from 1730, when George was Sheriff-Substitute.[17] George was second-in-command to Simon Lord Lovat, who is better known as the notorious 'Old Fox' of Jacobite legend. Lord Lovat was eventually beheaded in London.[18] After Culloden, the Government army behaved particularly harshly in Inverness, and any official who thought to have helped the Jacobites would have been suspect. Government troops were stationed at Castlehill House, where, it is alleged, they caused considerable damage: "great numbers of… corn of all sorts

https://www.gla.ac.uk/schools/critical/research/researchcentresandnetworks/robertburnsstudies/ourresearch/jacobiteofficersdatabase/thedatabase/c/.

[14] A. Gerald Pollitt, *Historic Inverness* (Perth: The Melven Press, 1981), pp. 139–142.

[15] The Highland Archive Centre in Inverness holds the Burgh Council records (which start in the eighteenth century), and church records (from 1640). A search on Inverness Museum's digital filing system brought up several results for charters that mentioned various Cuthberts, dating from the 1400 s to 1600 s. Most of these charters have been transcribed and could be accessed, but from the dates and names they don't seem particularly relevant to Seignelay Cuthbert's life, and would only provide background information about his family.

[16] An impressive Victorian Gothic building which has recently been refurbished https://www.highlifehighland.com/inverness-museum-and-art-gallery/inverness-town-house-2/.

[17] The painting is dated 1730 and is the subject of some debate as it is hung with paintings of Provosts, but there was no Provost Cuthbert at this date, so it's not known who is in the picture (*A Guide to Inverness Town House*, Highland Council, 2008). This picture is also available to view online at www.ambaile.org.uk. (reference: TITLE Provost Cuthbert EXTERNAL ID: AB_INVTOWNHOUSE07_51. ASSET ID 426. "This portrait of Provost Cuthbert hangs in Inverness Town House, in the Council Chamber. The date on the frame is 1730. The artist is unknown. There was no Provost Cuthbert serving in 1730 but ex-Provosts are given the courtesy title of Provost. The family of Cuthbert was one of the most powerful families in Inverness in its day and several Cuthberts served as Provost, often more than once, between 1556 and 1646. The painting could be any one of them." Alternatively, I suggest that the possibility that it could be a picture of Seignelay's father.

[18] In the *Culloden Papers: Correspondence from 1625 to 1748* ed H.R. Duff (1815) CCCLXX, George Cuthbert is linked with the Old Fox; see also article *On the Site of Macbeth's Castle at Inverness*, John Anderson, 1828, p. 240.

destroyed, the tenants impoverished, so that they could not pay their rent, several thousand trees cut down for firing to the army, the manor house of Castlehill rifled, and [the Cuthberts'] house in the town of Inverness made an hospital of... the loss sustained thereby exceeds two thousand pounds at the lowest computation."[19] This is a considerable sum of money—although the Cuthberts may already have been experiencing debt problems.[20] In 1739, fellow local landowner Duncan Forbes had written "The greatest part of my neighbours are in a very tottering condition. I am sorry that ther is no great appearance that Castlehill, Clava and several others can keep their estates."[21] However, things came to a head for the Cuthbert family when George died suddenly in a fall from his horse in 1748. He left a family of eight young children and considerable debts. Local hearsay talked darkly of a curse that had fallen on the Cuthberts to punish them for their behaviour, recalling with long memories the way the family had seized property in a "high-handed" manner after the Reformation, and a more recent occasion when the Cuthberts had been involved in the brutal and unnecessary burning of two local women suspected as witches.[22]

However, Old Lady Castlehill, Seignelay's formidable grandmother Jean Hay, stepped in to help her grandchildren, as reported by historian Charles Fraser Mackintosh. Jean Hay lived with her son, daughter-in-law and grandchildren at Castlehill House, and previously her own father, the Right Reverend William Hay (Seignelay's great-grandfather), had also lived with the Cuthbert family.[23] The Rev Hay was the former Bishop of Moray, but had lost his position after refusing to take an oath of fealty

[19] Petition of "Jean Cuthbert of Castlehill" to "Their Excellencies the Lords Justices of the Regency", quoted in the *Northern Chronicle* Wednesday 30 March 1904, accessed through the British Newspaper Archive https://www.britishnewspaperarchive.co.uk/ (digital portal of the British Library).

[20] The Cuthberts' money situation is sometimes rather vague. There certainly were debts, but also a large amount of money coming in. See also Charles Fraser Mackintosh *Letters of Two Centuries, Chiefly Connected with Inverness and the Highlands, from 1616 to 1815* (Inverness: A & W Mackenzie, 1890), p. 171.

[21] *Culloden papers: correspondence from 1625 to 1748* ed H.R. Duff (1815), p. 151.

[22] *Reminiscences of a Clachnacuddin Nonagenarian* (Inverness: Donald Macdonald, 1886), pp. 93–101; Charles Fraser Mackintosh, *The Cuthberts of Castlehill.*

[23] Charles Fraser Mackintosh *Letters of Two Centuries, Chiefly Connected with Inverness and the Highlands, from 1616 to 1815* (Inverness: A & W Mackenzie, 1890), p. 122; Charles Fraser Mackintosh *The Cuthberts of Castlehill.*

to William and Mary in 1689. William and Mary had come to the throne after King James VII & II had been deposed. One important reason for King James losing his throne was his Catholic religion, but the situation was complex and James was supported by people of other faiths, including Episcopalians. This strong Episcopal background in the Cuthbert family might suggest why Seignelay and his family had some Jacobite sympathies—and why Seignelay (and earlier his uncles Alexander and Lachlan) later felt little qualm at converting to Catholicism, despite the fact that Seignelay was baptised in the Presbyterian Church and his father was a prominent Freemason.[24]

Jean Hay decided to appeal to her own family to help the Cuthberts of Castlehill. In about 1750 she carried Seignelay and his brother Lewis off down to London, where her own brother Dr Hay lived, to seek assistance.[25] In London, Jean Hay also set in motion an official complaint to the British Government, asking for redress for the damage that Government soldiers had caused to Castlehill House and Estate.[26] The Cuthberts were welcomed down south: an anonymous letter written from London in 1754 and full of gossip about "Inverness youths in London" particularly praised Seignelay's brother: "Lewie Cuthbert is one of the sweetest-tempered, sensible, promising young boys I ever knew. I love him very much, and Dr. Hay continues to use him with the strongest affection, and is exerting himself to get him into the East India Service. Lewie cannot fail of doing well wherever he goes, and if he lives will do honour to all of his concerns." The letter continued "and God grant that the rest of

[24] The baptism record for Seignelay shows that the minister was Presbyterian Alexander MacBean. There is a lengthy description of a mason's meeting attended by George, Seignelay's father, and a subsequent argument in 1740 in several local newspapers: *Aberdeen Evening Express*, Thursday 10 April 1879 and *Press and Journal* Saturday nineteenth April 1879. The Episcopal Church in Scotland had retained many of the rituals of the Catholic Church. The appointing of bishops was a particular sticking point in religious debates in Britain and especially Scotland.

[25] Charles Fraser Mackintosh, *The Cuthberts of Castlehill*; Charles Fraser Mackintosh *Letters of Two Centuries, chiefly connected with Inverness and the Highlands, from 1616 to 1815* (Inverness: A & W Mackenzie, 1890). I have had some correspondence with local researcher Jim Brennan, who has tried to find out more about Dr Hay: his research was inconclusive, but he suggests that Dr Hay might in fact be Jean Hay's nephew, rather than brother, and that he could be the same Dr Hay (1715–78) who was an MP.

[26] From internal evidence in the quoted petition, it would seem that it was written about 1751, and that Jean Hay had been in London for ten months. *Northern Chronicle* Wednesday 30 March 1904.

Lady Castlehill's children when they grow up, may promise as well, and be as lustry as those that are already abroad in the world."[27] Dr Hay had told his sister Jean that he couldn't help all her grandchildren, but had suggested applying to the well-known French branch of the Cuthbert family to see if they could do anything. Two of Jean's sons, Lachlan and Alexander, were already in France, and now she sent Seignelay to join them.[28]

Although Seignelay was given other baptismal names which he apparently sometimes used, his French name suggests how important his family rated the connection with the French Colberts.[29] The 'Bore Brieve' or Birth Brief[30] of the Scottish Parliament of 1685, applied for by Colbert, Minister to Louis XIV, details the supposed history of the Cuthbert family, their links to other noble families, including the Scottish royal family, and then to the French Colbert branch.[31] Though to some extent an "imaginary genealogy",[32] it traces the family tree of the Cuthberts, going back to the Gaelic Mic Sheorsa of 1371. It was exactly what Jean-Baptiste Colbert in France had hoped for: his family were merchants, but he had become the Minister of Finances to Louis XIV, the Sun King. Colbert became one of the Sun King's most trusted advisers, carrying out a programme of economic reform that helped to make France the dominant power in Europe but, despite his power and influence, he still felt the need to try and explain away his background as the son of a merchant. Even acquiring the barony of Seignelay did not make him a nobleman,

[27] Charles Fraser Mackintosh, *Letters of Two Centuries, Chiefly Connected with Inverness and the Highlands, from 1616 to 1815* (Inverness: A & W Mackenzie, 1890), p. 240.

[28] I have seen different dates for when Seignelay arrived in Paris: on the Colbert de Castlehill website timeline, 1746 is given, with a reference to Halloran's book on the Scots College, with an alternative of 1750. If Jean Hay's petition was c1751, and she had been in London for almost a year when that was written, the second date of 1750 seems far more likely, particularly as it would place it after Seignelay's father's death.

[29] The record of Seignelay's birth records his name as "Seignalai Cuthbert"; records at the Scots College record "Antonius Johannes C de C-H", according to the timeline on the Colbert de Castlehill website.

[30] The 'Bore Brieve' or 'Birth Brief' was a type of birth certificate in old Scots, detailing the genealogy of the family.

[31] *Reminiscences of a Clachnacuddin Nonagenarian* (Inverness: Donald Macdonald, 1886), pp. 93–101; A. Gerald Pollitt *Historic Inverness* (Perth: The Melven Press, 1981); and First Statistical Account of Scotland (p. 633) (ed. John Sinclair).

[32] Charles Fraser Mackintosh, *The Cuthberts of Castlehill.*

he had to somehow prove that he had been born with noble blood in his veins. His link with the Scottish Cuthbert family gave him this. The Bore Brieve proved the importance of the Cuthberts to the lasting satisfaction of both the French and Scottish branches of the family.

Two of Jean Hay's sons, Lachlan and the Abbé Alexander, were already in France. Lachlan was to climb through the ranks in the Royal Scots regiment, marry, and has to this day descendants in France. The Abbé had bought back Castlehill House for the family in the 1770s, following their problems after Seignelay's father's death, (though he himself was barred from holding property in Scotland because he was living abroad, and a Catholic),[33] but he also did his best to help his nephew.

Seignelay went to the Scots College in Paris,[34] where he excelled in languages—unsurprisingly, since he already spoke English, Gaelic and French. His letters are fascinating for their use of the three languages—for example, a letter to the Duke of Buccleuch, where he writes in French, despite English being their native tongue, but throws in Gaelic words when he wants to talk obliquely.[35] A later letter, written when he was exiled in England, talks of the sensation he caused when he spoke Gaelic to Highland cattle drovers: "they were not a little surprised to hear a man they did not know speak Erse [Gaelic], but when they heard that it was by a French bishop, they could not temper their astonishment".[36]

Seignelay would not have been the only Highlander in France, as many Jacobites (including his uncles Alexander and Lachlan) were exiled there, and Seignelay always made an effort to meet with Scots arriving

[33] Charles Fraser Mackintosh, *The Cuthberts of Castlehill*. The Abbé supposedly bought Castlehill Estate in 1779, so this was a long-term project. Documents in the Highland Archive Centre relating to Lewis Cuthbert's will (Lewis Cuthbert Executory Papers 1793–1824 D75/1–4) mention an Alexander Cuthbert who may be the Abbé.

[34] There are some Scottish archives relating to this which may bear further examination: Aberdeen University's Special Collections include documents relating to the collection (undigitized): https://www.abdn.ac.uk/special-collections/documents/SLA_PDF/ca001.pdf. A book *The Scots College Paris, 1603–1792* by Brian Halloran was published by Scottish publisher John Donald in 2001; this is based on Halloran's 1996 PhD (available online). It contains several brief mentions of Colbert.

[35] Letter of 18 September 1766. See Alain Alcouffe and Andrew Moore, La correspondence de Mgr Seignelay Colbert de Castlehill, évêque de Rodez et du duc de Buccleuch, in *Études Aveyronnaises, Rodez: Société des lettres, sciences et arts de l'Aveyron*, 2020, pp. 342–363.

[36] Letter of 21st October 1792, *ibidem*. It would be a particular sensation given the suppression of Highland culture after Culloden.

in France, such as David Hume and Adam Smith, seeing their nationality as a common bond which transcended both religion and politics. It is possible that, through his contact with other Scots there are other individual letters or references in other Scottish archives, which I have not uncovered. It was unusual, however, for a Scot to be promoted within the French Church as Seignelay was, and his appointment to the post of Bishop of Rodez did attract attention in Seignelay's home and the English-speaking press: "On Sunday April 22. John Seignelay Colbert, or Cuthbert, was consecrated Bishop Rodez Rovergue, by Stephen Charles Lomenie de Brienne, Archbishop of Toulouse, assisted by John de la Croix de Castries, Bishop of Vabres, and John Augustus de Chastenet de Puysequi, Bishop of Carcassone, in the presence of a numerous assembly of persons of the first distinction in France, friends of the Bishop-elect, and of the principal nobility and gentry, British subjects, who were then in this city. This gentleman is the eldest son of the late Mr. Colbert of Castlehill, in Invernessshire, in Scotland. He came to France at the age of fourteen years, and was placed by his uncle, a Roman Catholic clergyman, in the Scotch College at Paris, where he remained some years. He was afterwards in the college of Harcourt, and in both these colleges always distinguished himself by his good behaviour, and diligent application to his studies. He returned to the Scotch College, received priestly orders, was made Vicar-General in the diocese of Toulouse, and on account of his extraordinary parts and great merit, has been raised to the episcopal dignity, which very seldom happens to a foreigner in France. He is not only Bishop, but also Count of Rodez, and President of the States of Rovergue. He is, at present, about 46 years of age, of a very becoming appearance, and is endowed with a solid judgement, and a remarkable good heart."[37]

Seignelay's work as a published author is also now recorded in Scotland, with copies of his writings (in the original French) available in the National Library of Scotland. However, most Scottish description of Seignelay's time in France invokes his historical connection with the Colbert family through the Bore Brieve, and his achievement in becoming Bishop of Rodez, with no mention of his actions in Versailles. As the

[37] This same report appears almost word-for-word in several papers: *Belfast Newsletter*, 18–22 May 1781, p. 2; *Scots Magazine*, Friday 1 June 1781; *Caledonian Mercury*, Monday 14 March 1781.

Revolution turned to the Terror, Seignelay may have wished to disassociate himself from voting with the Third Estate, so this may reflect how Seignelay presented himself after 1792. Charles Fraser Mackintosh's comprehensive article about the Cuthberts says only that the Bishop of Rodez "on the breaking out of the French Revolution, had to fly from France", with no indication that Seignelay had any agency or influence on events. Alternatively, it may reflect the interests of the time and place: Inverness commentary on the Cuthberts focuses on what became of the whole family, particularly the fortunes of Seignelay's brother Lewis, who became mired in debt: "sons of [the Cuthberts] rank high in the church and armies of France, and … the Bishop of Rodez is brother to Lewis Cuthbert Esq., Provost Marshall of Jamaica."[38]

Since the brothers Lewis and Seignelay had left Castlehill together for London, they had remained close. There is a record of Lewis visiting Seignelay in Paris in 1792[39] and shortly afterwards Seignelay went into exile in London, where he moved in with his brother.

Seignelay's letter of 1793 movingly recounts his return to Scotland and his roots: "I was enchanted to see Scotland again, especially the place of my birth. I found, it is true, things very small in comparison with the images that I had in my head: but my heart had lost nothing there and all my affections were rediscovered, on seeing what I had left, 45 years ago".[40] He seems to have returned to Inverness several times[41]: "The Bishop of Rodez, said to be the last foreign representative of the Cuthbert family, visited Inverness about the year 1803, and was obliged to prolong his residence in the country, owing to the hostilities then carrying on between Great Britain and France," recalled one elderly Invernessian in his memoir. He continued, "[The Bishop of Rodez] took great interest in the success of the Inverness Academy and contributed towards its funds,

[38] A. Gerald Pollitt, *Historic Inverness* (Perth: The Melven Press, 1981), pp. 139–142.

[39] Charles Fraser Mackintosh, *Letters of Two Centuries, chiefly connected with Inverness and the Highlands, from 1616 to 1815* (Inverness: A & W Mackenzie, 1890), p. 171.

[40] Letter of 5 November 1793: See Alain Alcouffe and Andrew Moore, La correspondence de Mgr Seignelay Colbert de Castlehill, évêque de Rodez et du duc de Buccleuch, in Études Aveyronnaises, Rodez: Société des lettres, sciences et arts de l'Aveyron, 2020, pp. 342–363.

[41] The letter just quoted is from 1793. *Nonagenarian* mentions a visit of 1803. The *Inverness Courier* Tuesday 28 October 1884 mentions an 1806 visit. Files on Lewis Cuthbert's debts (bound in the Fraser Mackintosh collection in Inverness Reference Library, item 3313) state Seignelay was in Scotland (Edinburgh) on 1st August 1806 (p. 112).

he also procured the valuable services of M. Villimer, a Frenchman, as teacher of the French language at the Institution."[42]

The Inverness Royal Academy was (and is) a well-known school in Inverness, which had been set up only a few years before—prior to that, boys like Seignelay would have been educated at home, or in a small private establishment with only a handful of pupils.[43] The Academy, under that name, came into being after 1787, but the kernel of the school existed, and it's possible that the Cuthberts were already linked to the institution that became the Academy because they had been educated there. However, because the Cuthbert family were one of the leading families in Inverness, they may well have just wished to subscribe to the project as the idea for a good school grew. Seignelay and Lewis were typical of Invernessians of their generation and standing in that they contributed funds to it.[44] The history of the school has been traced in detail.[45] Pierre Villemer, the teacher recommended by Colbert of Castlehill, took up his position in 1810 or 1811. Described as a "French exile" and "a man of culture", he taught French, Spanish and Italian at the school, earning an annual salary of £30, plus extra fees from private pupils. He published a long poem, in French, sometime before 1824, entitled *Astronomie*, the cost of printing of which was covered by subscription from friends and former pupils. Pierre Villemer petitioned the school for an increase in his salary, claiming that he was having to take on private pupils and teach till late at night and this was affecting his health. The school did not increase his salary, and he fell into debt. He died on the

[42] *Reminiscences of a Clachnacuddin Nonagenarian* (Inverness: Donald Macdonald, 1886), pp. 93–101.

[43] Robert Preece, *Song School, Town School, Comprehensive: A History of Inverness Royal Academy* (Inverness: For the Right Reasons, 2011).

[44] Although actually Lewis Cuthbert did not contribute all the money that he had promised to the Academy, and the school was listed as a creditor in the court case and dispute over Lewis' will, asking for £10 16 4d (papers relating to Lewis Cuthbert's debts, bound in the Fraser Mackintosh collection in Inverness Reference Library, item 3313, p35).

[45] Robert Preece, *Song School, Town School, Comprehensive: A History of Inverness Royal Academy* (Inverness: For the Right Reasons, 2011); Charles Bannerman, *Further Up Stephen's Brae: the Midmills Era at Inverness Royal Academy*, 2010.

1st December 1825, and his wife and daughter were given £15 to cover the expense of their return to their home of London.[46]

However, the majority of recent study into the families donating to the Inverness Royal Academy, including the Cuthberts, has been into how their money was made through the slave trade.[47] Lewis Cuthbert was a slave owner and slave factor in Jamaica.[48] Around the time that Seignelay returned to London in 1792, Lewis gave evidence to a Westminster enquiry into slavery, where he stated that he believed that slave owners did a good job of looking after their slaves for good commercial reasons, and that the system of slavery should be maintained.[49] The affirmation of the Revolution in France that 'all men are created equal' had been taken up by the slaves in the Carribean, and the Haitian Revolution had surely contributed to the British Government's examination of the system of slavery in the neighbouring island of Jamaica. Lewis Cuthbert's attitude to the slaves, although it was entirely typical of the times, can be compared and contrasted with Seignelay's somewhat unusual support of and vote along with the Third Estate in Versailles.[50]

[46] Robert Preece, *Song School, Town School, Comprehensive: A History of Inverness Royal Academy* (Inverness: For the Right Reasons, 2011), p. 108, p. 131.

[47] Major recent Highland studies of northern Scottish links to the slave trade include the work of David Alston, which focuses on Scots in Dutch Guiana: personal webpage: http://www.spanglefish.com/slavesandhighlanders/index.asp?pageid=446643.

Online article on Grenada mentions Lewis Cuthbert as raising money for charities in Scotland: https://grenadanationalarchives.wordpress.com/2016/03/01/grenada-heritage-from-the-caribbean-back-to-scotland/ as does this similar article https://www.cambridge.org/core/journals/rural-history/article/from-the-caribbean-to-the-scottish-highlands-charitable-enterprise-in-the-age-of-improvement-c1750-to-c1820/CABF4A077D56E23D217A13F73F573990 (partial access only) and the work of Professor David Worthington of the University of the Highlands and Islands, which looks at very early involvement of the Highlands in slavery, eg *Sugar, Slave-Owning, Suriname and the Dutch Imperial Entanglement of the Scottish Highlands before 1707* https://www.tandfonline.com/doi/full/10.1080/03096564.2019.1616141.

[48] *Legacies of British Slave Ownership* project, through University College London: Lewis Cuthbert page: https://www.ucl.ac.uk/lbs/person/view/2146650219. See also https://www.jjhc.info/cuthbertlewis1802.

[49] https://www.jjhc.info/CuthbertLewis1802. *Minutes of the Evidence taken at the Bar of the House of Lords*, 1792, available online.

[50] One of Seignelay and Lewis' other brothers, James, moved to Georgia, where he also kept slaves. There is a record of him offering a reward for a runaway slave. See https://sites.rootsweb.com/~rykbrown/cuthbert-castlehill.htm#George%20Cuthbert,%2010th%20of%20Castlehill.

Lewis' fortunes fluctuated. There were huge fortunes to be made and lost in Jamaica. Lewis Cuthbert stated that he fully bought back the estate of Castlehill in 1780, for £14,000, and between 1792 and 1795 he maintained a house in the north at Cradlehall.[51] Cradle Hall was a big house on the Castlehill lands—there is no record of why Lewis chose to stay there rather than Castlehill House itself, but perhaps it was more modern or more suited to his family. However, by 1796 Lewis was in considerable debt, due to "severe dry weather" which would "greatly affect the Crop",[52] and also to unrest in Jamaica (the Second Maroon War, part of the ongoing bloody conflict over slavery and British rule): in a letter of 17th April 1796 Lewis wrote "Martial law [has now] ceased... and business is resumed once more; and I trust that matters will come round again in the course of the present year. Not one individual in this island has experienced greater inconvenience and real loss than I have done; the latter exceeds upwards of L.7000 Sterling."[53] In particular, Lewis Cuthbert owed a large sum of money to his London banker Abram Robarts. Lewis made over Castlehill to Abram Robarts, with the provision that Robarts did not do anything with the estate for two years—Lewis seemed to believe that his fortunes would rise again, and he might have been able to buy back Castlehill, ending the letter quoted above by saying "If I live some years longer, and remain capable of attending to business, I have no doubt of bringing up my lee-way." Unfortunately for Lewis, however, when he died in 1802 a large balance was still due to Robarts. Robarts began to portion up and sell off not only the Castlehill lands, but also the contents of Lewis' former family home, including personal items from Cradlehall: local Inverness lawyer and historian Charles Fraser Mackintosh records, in his article on the Cuthberts of Castlehill, that he bought Lewis Cuthbert's tea service. A good portion of the Castlehill lands were sold to neighbouring landowner Duncan Forbes, but Lewis

[51] The information on Lewis' purchase of Castlehill comes from the papers relating to his debts, bound in the Fraser Mackintosh collection in Inverness Reference Library, item 3313. The Abbé Alexander had been involved in the purchase, so it was more complicated than Lewis makes it appear. Charles Fraser Mackintosh's article *The Cuthberts of Castlehill* mentions that he lived at Cradle Hall. The area of Cradlehall is very close to Castlehill, on the road from Culloden to Inverness.

[52] Highland Archive Centre, D75, letter from Lewis Cuthbert.

[53] Papers relating to Lewis Cuthbert's debts, bound in the Fraser Mackintosh collection in Inverness Reference Library, item 3313, p. 8 of appendix.

Cuthbert's other creditors objected to Robarts selling off his assets before their debts were paid, and further sales were halted. A lengthy court case over Lewis Cuthbert's debts dragged on for thirty years until 1832.[54] Seignelay was involved in this court case both as a creditor—as Lewis had left him in his will provision for £150 per annum—and also as a mediator: he met several times with Abram Robarts in London, and then on the 1st August 1806 Seignelay arranged a meeting of Lewis Cuthbert's creditors at the Royal Exchange Coffeehouse, Edinburgh. The meeting, held in a place where the prominent members of the Scottish Enlightenment had often gathered, was successful, with the creditors able to agree a way forward—though this did not shorten the court proceedings, as more creditors appeared, and the death of Robarts caused further delays and involved further people.[55]

Debts did not mean that the Cuthberts were penniless, however—Lewis' position in Jamaica had brought considerable money, and they

[54] There are details of Lewis Cuthbert's debts, and the original attempts by both Abbé Colbert and Lewis Cuthbert to buy back Castlehill House in Charles Fraser Mackintosh's article, including the text of a letter from the Abbé to his sister.

Original papers from the 1832 court case, occasioned by Lewis' death, are bound in the Fraser Mackintosh collection in Inverness Reference Library, item 3313.

The Highland Archive Centre contains the Lewis Cuthbert Executory Papers 1793–1824: refs: D75/1 Papers re process of Claim by William Brooke, Lt. Colonel 5th Dragoon Guards vs the Estate of Lewis Cuthbert of Castlehill [1 bundle] 1793–1809.

D75/2 Papers re process of claim by the estate of Thomas Hankey against the estate of Lewis Cuthbert [1 bundle] 1804–1809.

D75/3 Papers re process of claim of estate of Peter Franklin, late collector of customs in Jamaica Against the estate of Lewis Cuthbert of Castlehill [1 bundle] 1800–1824.

D75/4 Papers re process of claim by Rev. Charles Wallington of Ealing (Later Worthing) on the estate of Lewis Cuthbert [1 bundle].

These papers show the claims made on Lewis Cuthbert's estate after he died, with increasingly belligerent letters from creditors. There were huge amounts of money to be made in Jamaica, but also huge amounts to be lost—investors were used to large fluctuations, and Lewis seems to have died at a point where his fortunes were going down, even though he and his family had every expectation of them rising again. A letter from his son George then describes how he has "sustained the misfortune of losing my father who died… [letter ripped]…severe illness". George's following letter dissembles somewhat, but faced with persistent creditors, the debts were eventually paid after "considerable parts of the Scotch Estate [were] sold to an amount exceeding £20,000".

The Archive Centre also holds a Cuthbert family tree, drawn up by the Centre's professional genealogist, and based on the information in the Bulloch book.

[55] Original papers from the court case are bound in the Fraser Mackintosh collection in Inverness Reference Library, item 3313. For creditors' meeting see page 112, and minutes of the meeting in appendix p. 20.

had substantial properties in both Edinburgh and London.[56] Although Castlehill had been bought originally for £14,000, the sale of the estate brought in £52,321.[57] Seignelay continued to live with family and to embark on various visits to others of his social class, as well as his work within the schismatic church. There are snippets of information from various sources which show glimpses of his life: he was involved in discussion over the possibility of emigrating to Canada with Catholic Highlanders from the island of Uist[58]; a memoir written by one of Seignelay's nephews records that Seignelay gave him the gift of a cheque for £50 when he embarked on his career as a solicitor—a substantial amount of money for the time, which brings up some questions over how Seignelay was funding his life; while in contrast a rather couthy sketch of him visiting John Gibson Lockhart (the son-in-law of famous Scottish writer Walter Scott), presents Seignelay as a harmless and rather incongruous figure of some fun: "the Abbé de Colbert, who was by birth a Scotsman... he so endeared himself to his flock that during the Revolution he was, for a long time, safely hidden. When, at length, obliged to leave his see, he was aided by a lady of frail virtue in Paris, who from the liking she had to the good Bishop, hid him in her lodging and then procured his escape... he made his way to Britain carrying nothing with him but a huge wig-block without which he never afterwards travelled...". The story continues with the wig-block being misplaced and Seignelay coming down to dinner in his own "venerable grey hair, which being much admired by the ladies, the Bishop never again resumed the wig."[59]

[56] On the *Legacies of British Slave Ownership* website run by UCL, two addresses are given for Lewis Cuthbert: Castlehill in Inverness, and 63 George Street, Edinburgh. https://www.ucl.ac.uk/lbs/person/view/2146650219.

[57] Papers relating to Lewis Cuthbert's debts, bound in the Fraser Mackintosh collection in Inverness Reference Library, item 3313, p. 189.

[58] See *Emigration from the Scottish Catholic Bounds, 1770–1810 and the Role of the Clergy*, PhD by Kathleen Toomey, University of Edinburgh, 1991, p. 217;'Some Refugee French Clerics and Laymen in Scotland, 1789–1814' by James Mcgloin in the Innes Review, (1965.16.1.27); http://www.jamaicanfamilysearch.com/Members/MemoirGeorgePinnock.htm; *Legacies of British Slave Ownership* webpage Home Page: https://www.ucl.ac.uk/lbs/; original papers from the court case are bound in the Fraser Mackintosh collection in Inverness Reference Library, item 3313.

[59] Marion Lochhead, *John Gibson Lockhart* (London: John Murray, 1954), pp. 176–177.

Seigneley's niece married Scots peer and politician Lord Gray, and it was at Lord Grey's house that Seignelay died.[60] Family connections were always important to Seignelay, and through various genealogies, popular both in the nineteenth century and today, we can find out more about his life.[61]

Meanwhile in Inverness, the Cuthberts became viewed as a tragic family and the story of the witches' curse that brought down their fortunes was often invoked. The sale of the Castlehill estate by the Cuthbert family would have affected hundreds of people in the local area.[62] The very public nature of the sale by Abram Robarts, which included the sale of household items from Cradlehall, and the ensuing court case, would have done much to damage the Cuthberts' reputation and would have given the impression locally that the family was now penniless. The *Highland News* of Saturday 9 April 1904 described one of the last remaining members of the Cuthbert family in Inverness: Peggy 'Cubbart' was in the Fish Market, "anxious to make a bargain for a fresh haddock for dinner for herself and her brother… As you look into Peggy's time-worn face you see at once that she is the scion of a noble family. Would you be surprised to know that the old woman is among the last of the Cuthberts of Castlehill, a family that for centuries was held in high esteem in Inverness and the surrounding district: but, alas! It is little heard of now." The life of Seignelay Cuthbert of Castlehill has been half-remembered and forgotten in the Highlands—until now (Fig. 2.1).

[60] An obituary of the Dowager Lady Gray in the *Perth and Cupar Advertiser* of Friday 7 January 1859 specifically mentions the Cuthbert / Colbert family link, suggesting that the Grays were proud of the connection.

[61] See J.G.B. Bulloch, *The Cuthberts, Barons of Castle Hill & Their Descendants in South Carolina & Georgia* Washington D.C.: 1908. Online genealogies brought up several references to Seignelay Cuthbert of Castlehill, with the most informative being https://sites.rootsweb.com/~rykbrown/cuthbert-castlehill, the personal site of a Canadian called Ryk Brown who was related to the Cuthberts of Castlehill, and https://www.jjhc.info/cuthbertlewis1802.

[62] Based on the fact that there were 49 named families on the rent roll given in the papers relating to Lewis Cuthbert's debts (bound in the Fraser Mackintosh collection in Inverness Reference Library, item 3313). The estate also paid contributions to local ministers and schoolteachers, so their influence was wide.

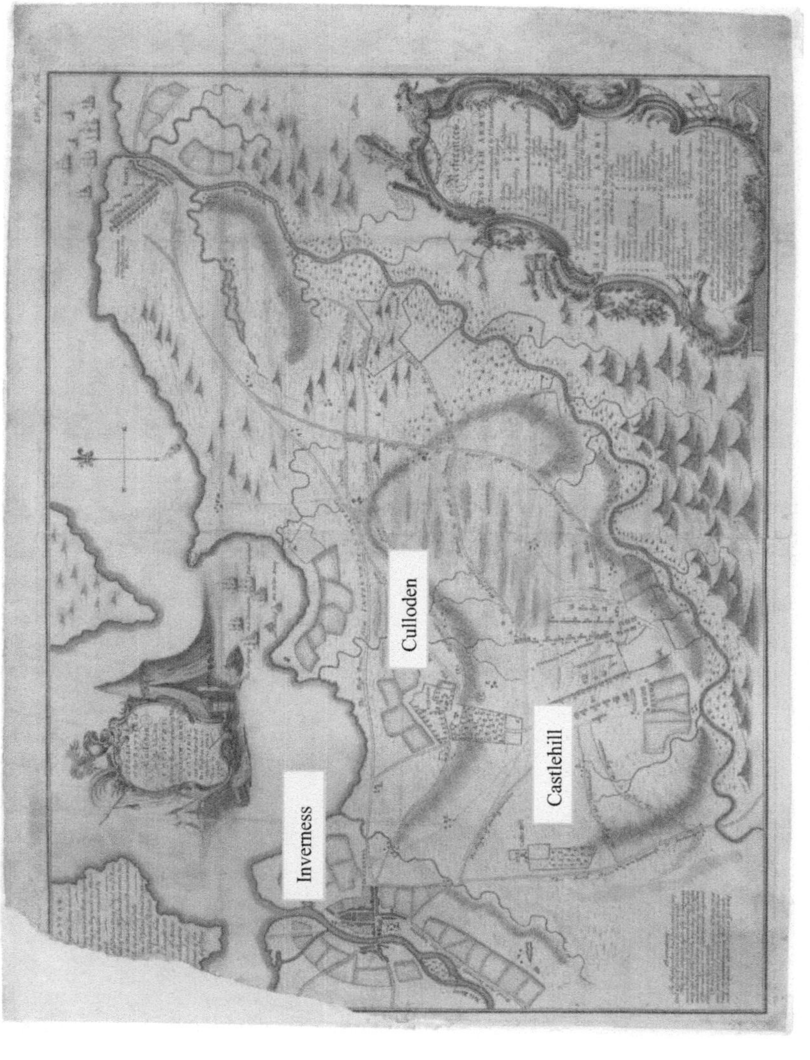

Fig. 2.1 Map of Inverness and Culloden (*Source* National Library of Scotland—NLS)

CHAPTER 3

Adam Smith, the Duke of Buccleuch and Colbert de Castlehill as 'Strangers' in Toulouse

Hiroki Ueno

Abstract Recent scholarship on the French Enlightenment has discovered an intriguing figure, Colbert de Castlehill, who played a significant role in the early stage of the French Revolution. He not only bridges the Enlightenment and the Revolution in France, but also the French and Scottish Enlightenments worldwide. In the context of the study of Adam Smith, Colbert has been known merely by his name, but the situation has gradually been changing. Compared to the highlighted scene of Smith's encounter with François Quesnay and other Physiocrats in Paris, the days Smith and his pupil the Duke of Buccleuch spent in Toulouse and Southern France during the first half of their Grand Tour was considerably ignored. In Southern France, it is David Hume's friend Colbert de

English version largely revised and focused on Colbert.

H. Ueno (✉)
Keio University, Tokyo, Japan
e-mail: h.ueno83@keio.jp

A. Alcouffe (ed.), *Seignelay Colbert de Castlehill (1735-1811)*,
https://doi.org/10.1007/978-3-031-75273-5_3

Castlehill who was possibly of the greatest importance to Smith's landing on local societies. Colbert had a kind of Humean talent cultivated in Parisian sociable settings before arriving in Toulouse, whose sociability would have not merely been practically useful to Smith and Buccleuch, but also essential to moral education for the young duke. The chapter particularly illustrates his "Voltairian" spirit characterised by his public interventions with the polemical issues of the age that were accompanied by the morally impartial perspective.

Keyword Colbert of Castlehill · French Revolution · Grand tour · Adam Smith · Scottish enlightenment · Toulouse · Sociability · David Hume · Duke of Buccleuch · Intellectual development

Colbert de Castlehill has long been known merely by his name among Adam Smith scholars. As is widely discussed in this collection of papers, having played a significant role in the early stage of the French Revolution, he bridges the Enlightenment and Revolution in France. But Colbert can also be an intriguing figure who bridges the French and Scottish Enlightenments worldwide when seen from another perspective, on which this chapter focuses. Here I shall particularly deal with Colbert as a key person for the Duke of Bacculeuch's Grand Tour based in Toulouse, during which time Smith, after having resigned a professor in moral philosophy at Glasgow, accompanied the young duke as a private teacher. This tour is well-known thanks chiefly to Smith's encounter with François Quesnay and other Physiocrats in Paris, which was a marked episode for the history of economic thought; however, the days Smith and his pupil Buccleuch spent in Toulouse and South France are, as will be shown below, no less important to the intellectual development of Smith's moral argument (and probably his political economy as well) owing considerably to the existence of this Scottish-originated clergyman.

For the two Scottish travellers who arrived in France in February 1764, Abbé Colbert appears to have played a pivotal role in their choice of Toulouse and their long stay in *Occitania* (South France). This seemingly a little strange choice should be explained, despite the fact that classical biographers of Smith tend to regard this choice as natural. The presence of Charles Townshend as the exclusive financial supporter of this Grand

Tour cannot be neglected.[1] Sympathised with by Smith, Duke's tutor, Townshend's critical opinion about the *grandes villes* such as Paris and London in terms of moral education for young noblemen would have surely prevented the two Scottish travellers from planning to spend all the time in Paris. Assured by Townshend's letter,[2] Smith and Townshend's chief end appears to educate the Duke to be a noble gentleman and statesman proper for leading the country, by teaching him the art of government or 'science of a legislator' including political economy, as well as by cultivating the suitable moral and political virtues for his expected position.[3] For this purpose, Toulouse may have been better than the too attractive Paris, in order for the two Scots to sufficiently keep tranquil time for being dedicated to their moral and political studies. At the same time, however, it is obvious as well that any sociable life could not be abandoned, as it must have been necessary for a young Duke of such a high expectation to master sufficiently polite manners and social virtues. Although Smith was critical of the traditional style of Grand Tours,[4] he seems to be moderate enough to care about how Buccleuch should be given socialising experiences required of his status outside Paris, the most cosmopolitan city in Europe. Pursuing this second most important purpose of their Grand Tour, Smith and Townshend counted upon David Hume staying in Paris at the time. And it is highly possible that Hume above all had Colbert de Castlehill in mind, who was able to strongly support Buccleuch and Smith in terms of sociable and intellectual life, if they made a decision to go to France, but not Paris.

A Grand Tour, Supported by Colbert de Castlehill

Colbert was appointed as a Vicar-General in Toulouse by Étienne-Charles de Loménie de Brienne in January 1764,[5] which was less than two months before Baccleuch and Smith's arrival there. But, as probably his

[1] For more details, see Ueno (2023: 81–2).

[2] Corr., no. 76, letter from Townshend to Smith, 25 October 1763.

[3] In addition to my aforementioned article (Ueno 2023), see also Phillipson (2010: 184–5); Ross (1974: 185).

[4] WN V.i.f.36, 773–4. See also Ueno (2023: 79–81).

[5] See the Timeline on 'ColbertdeCastlehill.com'. https://colbertdecastlehill.com/timeline/

position was informally promised before this official appointment, it is likely that Hume already knew of Colbert's scheduled move from Paris to Toulouse when he was consulted about the plan of the young Duke's Grand Tour by Smith and Townshend. Although it is currently unknown exactly when Hume got to know Colbert, it is certain that they often met and contacted each other during their stay in Paris before Colbert went to Toulouse,[6] where he welcomed Hume's closest friend and his pupil at the beginning of March. As Andrew Moore points out as well, 'in Paris, Colbert moved in cosmopolitan, intellectual and literary circles'.[7] We know from Elizabeth Stuart's letter sent to Hume that 'Monsieur Hume' enjoyed that Parisian life in salons and other sociable spaces with Morellet, Prévost, the 'Rouergat' Raynal, Le Blanc, Galiani and Colbert.[8] It is reasonable (when considering our limited knowledge about Colbert's early career) to assume that Hume, recognising Colbert's intellectual and sociable talent, recommended Smith and Townshend to choose Toulouse for the Grand Tour's base if it should not be Paris, and that one of the main reasons for this is his knowledge of Colbert's move to Toulouse. Because Hume knew Colbert's sparkling activity in Parisian salons, he expected that this man of the world would help the little too rigorous Scot according to the French standard to enter into polite societies. Indeed, when Smith and Buccleuch had a short stop in Paris before reaching Toulouse, they were given a letter of recommendation to Colbert by Hume.[9]

David Dalrymple, Alexander Carlyle and other Smith's friends unconditionally acknowledged his scholarly distinctiveness, but they did not think that Smith was the best choice for the young Duke's trip to France, taking into account his French oral ability and social skills required in French high societies.[10] Perhaps, Smith himself (as well as his employer, Townshend) might have admitted this. In the early stage of Smith and Buccleuch's stay in Toulouse, therefore, Smith struggled hard to detect a

[6] Hume arrived in Paris in October, 1763, accompanying Lord Hertford.

[7] Moore (1988: 15). Parisian salons Colbert frequented include those of the Countess of Gacé and of Madame du Deffand, for the latter of whom he helped edit her correspondence with Horace Walpole many years later. See Alcouffe and Massot-Bordenave (2020: 61).

[8] Mossner (1954: 480); Bedier, Hazard and Martino (1949: 86, 99, 136).

[9] Moore (1988: 16); Campbell and Skinner (1982: 153).

[10] See Ueno (2023: 78–9).

good entrance for sociable life there. Typical of his (too) earnest character, he took very seriously the primary role as a Grand Tour tutor, namely to facilitate his young pupil to be introduced to French agreeable societies, but he appears to have recognised that it was indispensable to find a man of different character from the serious Smith for this mission. So long as Hume could not accompany the two Scots in Toulouse—apart from letters of recommendation from him—Smith who had not arrived in Toulouse yet could have anticipated that the originally Scottish clergyman introduced by Hume was one of the most reliable figures available in person in Toulouse. All the more because of Smith's expectation, however, he was first disappointed to find that the abbé Colbert was almost as much a 'stranger' in Toulouse as him. From the letter to Hume,[11] Smith's uneasiness can be observed. It was written on the 5th of July, already four months later since their arrival.

Smith's anxiety was eased considerably, however, after their excursion in Southwest France during 1764 summer, advised and accompanied by Colbert. One of its highlights was their visit to Bordeaux, in which they spent much time in the company of Isaac Barré (usually known as 'Colonel Barré'), Lord Shelburne's protégé, whose eloquence in the Parliament impressed Sir Robert Walpole so much. Ironically, Barré 'was soon to make a famous use of this eloquence during the discussion of stamp duty in February 1765 by sharply upbraiding Charles Townshend, who defended this duty imposed on North American settlers in exchange for the support they received from the British army'.[12] But this close connection between Barré and the Scottish visitor would be of great importance to think about the upcoming revolutionary period within the British Empire, since it shows that Smith, an author of the great book often linked with the cause of the American Independence, enjoyed conversation with such a wide variety of opinions concerning the imperial relations between North American colonies and the metropole.[13]

Another important encounter during their visit to Bordeaux is that with Marshal Richelieu, perhaps the most significant man in the region. Probably, the success to provide an opportunity of meeting the governor of Guyenne with the Duke of Buccleuch made Smith feel relieved, as he

[11] Corr., no. 82, letter from Smith to Hume, 5 July 1764.

[12] Alcouffe and Massot-Bordenave (2020: 180–1).

[13] Cf. Sato and Ueno (2023: par. 13–23).

apparently took it very seriously to have failed his mission to open up the door for the fashionable society during their first stay in Toulouse (from March to the beginning of July).[14] Even though intellectual life and cultivation for the young Duke was the primary end of this atypical Grand Tour for Smith and Townshend, it was obviously indispensable as well for the Duke to be presented to the high society of the French Kingdom, in which opportunities to master the most polite manner and art of conversation in Europe should be given for a man expected to be a British statesman with a cosmopolitan perspective. In terms of Smith's educational plan focusing on virtue ethics in particular, the Duke of Richelieu must have been an ideal figure for the Duke of Buccleuch to be introduced to. Richelieu was not only a man of courtly politeness or civility, but also the most remarkable example of the traditional *noblesse d'épée*. He was already a *légende vivante* when the visitors from Toulouse met. As soon as he arrived in Bordeaux as a governor of the province of Guyenne in 1755, he was welcomed as an almost royal or national hero,[15] and his other tremendous success in the Seven Years' War (1756–1763) added to his career incomparable military glory.[16]

In order to understand the gradual development of the two Scots' sociable life with help of Colbert de Castlehill, we have to mention their sojourn in Bagnères-de-Bigorre at last. After their meeting with Richelieu in Bordeaux, the three travellers moved to this thermal town located near the Pyrénées in mid-August. It was an ideal place to further the life of sociability Smith had badly wanted for the young Duke while in Toulouse. It is again in all likelihood that Abbé Colbert played an indispensable part in the two Scottish visitors' socialising in this French resort. Without his utmost support relating particularly to subtle communication in the French language, it could hardly have been imagined that Smith could manage to bridge the young Duke to men of ranks in France. Probably

[14] Alcouffe and Massot-Bordenave (2020: 169) shares this opinion: 'In Bordeaux, thanks to the meeting with the Duke of Richelieu, Smith fulfilled his first and main mission, in addition to his role as a teacher, that of introducing his student to men of quality'.

[15] Alcouffe and Massot-Bordenave (2020: 163).

[16] His fleet's victory and capture of Fort Mahon in July 1756 was so influential even to the negotiation of the Treaty of Paris in 1763, in which Lord Hertford and his secretary David Hume participated. Cf. Alcouffe and Massot-Bordenave (2020: 164–5). For the comparison between Richelieu and the Duke of Sully whose moral character Smith described in details, see Ueno (2022: 139–40).

because Smith himself thought that support from Humean connections would be essential for him and Buccleuch to succeed in the field of social practice, he did not hesitate to ask for every help available from this network. Nevertheless, it is also worth mentioning that Smith seems to have become better at socialising thanks to the unique environment of the spring town, quite different from that of Toulouse. For strangers like Smith and Buccleuch, it was much easier to get acquainted with other people in this type of resort than in Toulouse, where most members of the polite society were kind of fixed and already close to each other as settlers of the city (or their relatives). Of course, gatherings in Bagnères-de-Bigorre were exclusive from a viewpoint of class or hierarchy, but this was not a problem for these visitors accompanying the Duke of Buccleuch.

French sociability almost always accompanied relations between the sexes. And this may be a realm with which Smith was not very good at dealing, and probably at which Colbert de Castlehill was much better, who, already 'frenchified' in Paris, wrote to Hume just a few months after his arrival in Toulouse: 'Here I am [i.e. Toulouse], my dear cousin, less pleasantly occupied than when I was with the beautiful ladies of Paris, but that time could come again, this one will have to do now'.[17] As Alcouffe and Massot-Bordenave suggest, there is a possibility that the young Duke might have enjoyed such kind of sociability during their journey in the Southwest, and one of the possible cases that they mention in the monograph is the relationship with the Baroness de Spens. Interestingly, the Duke's aunt mentioned in her letter written on October 20th to Buccleuch[18] may be Lady Mary Coke (1727–1811),[19] whose letters and diary have been an almost unlimited source of gossip about the social elite of the Georgian era. Lady Coke was also famous (or infamous) among scholars on Adam Smith, since it is from her diary that the anecdote circulated by Lady George Lennox originates, an anecdote 'that has definitively

[17] Colbert (1764a), Letter from Abbé Colbert to David Hume, 4 March, 1764. Cited with the permission of the Royal Society of Edinburgh. I am grateful for their generosity, as well as for the kindness of Alain Alouffe, who showed me this unpublished correspondence.

[18] Alcouffe and Massot-Bordenave (2020: 191–2).

[19] Her sister was the Countess of Dalkeith, who, the mother of the Duke of Buccleuch, got married with Charles Townshend after the death of her former wife. Campbell and Skinner (1982: 174).

made Smith pass for the most distracted man on earth'.[20] The Baroness de Spens wanted the young duke to write a letter of recommendation for his aunt (probably Mary Coke) in favour of her cousins. If this anecdote was exaggerated (as is highly likely), it is also probable that the baroness, like Lady Coke, tended to think that Smith was a kind of peculiar and even eccentric man despite his extreme intelligence so that she did not count on Smith so much with something like a love affair. Instead, Abbé Colbert could be a figure one can rely on in this field. As mentioned in the aforementioned letter, the Baroness of Spens sent the duke her message through the abbé. It can be only for practical reasons, but at least it shows that the baroness, like many people who know him, trusted Abbé Colbert. As Alcouffe's monograph informs Smith scholars almost for the first time, it should be noted that Bagnères-de-Bigorre in the season was presented as a distinctive town that 'can compete for taste, abundance, wealth and luxury with Paris, all proportions kept' and 'is certainly much above this Capital, for the delights of life in whatever sense one understands it'. This is a quotation from *La coquette dupée par un religieux b***. et par un marquis*, a short story published in 1774 in a collection with an even more evocative title, *La Gazette de Cythère*, or *Avantures galantes et récentes*, sold in the main cities of Europe.[21] If an essence of sociability in the southern provinces of France, the land of Cythera or of 'heroes and heroines who rightly reaped the most glorious laurels in the field of love', lies in something like *galantrie*, the companion of Colbert de Castlehill was all the more required for the Scottish scholarly man and his young pupil.[22]

[20] This episode representing Smith as 'the most absent man that ever was' is that Smith was 'falling into discourse' so much that he mistakenly put into the teapot a piece of bread with butter instead of tea leaves and drank that 'tea'. Coke (1970: Vol. i, p. 141).

[21] Alcouffe and Massot-Bordenave (2020: 190).

[22] What could also be suggested here relying on Alcouffe's monograph is that Colbert and Buccleuch established a life-long friendship that allowed the former to *plaisanter* the duke in their correspondence, mentioning '*baisant le filles*' already having the double meaning 'to kiss' and 'to have sexual intercourse' (Alcouffe and Massot-Bordenave 2020: 56–7). In a letter sent to Buccleuch, Colbert wrote: 'I was six weeks between Paris and Toulouse […] I stayed in the various places along my route; I didn't travel like you, My Lord, in a good coach or in an English post-chaise, at your ease, eating good food and enjoying the girls' (Colbert 1766, Letter from Colbert to Henry Scott-Douglas, 18 September 1766). This kind of intimate relation between the two sounds contrastive to what one usually imagined about the Continental journey by Adam Smith, whose biographers 'have always presented him as a serious, rigorous character, amiable but little

Two Aspects of Abbé Colbert's Moral Character

After these successful journeys in the Southwest of France, Smith showed his changing mood in a letter to Hume written on October 21st. Grateful to Hume and the people introduced by him in this letter, Smith mentioned an episode regarding the letter of recommendation from the Duke of Choiseul, which played a significant role in their meeting with the Duke of Richelieu. This letter was given to the Duke of Buccleuch thanks to the efforts by Hume and Lord Hertford both in Paris. The episode is that Richelieu wrongly called Smith 'Robinson' because of Choiseul's mistake in the recommendation letter, and the way he introduced this reveals his good humour, which contrasts greatly with that gloomy or even melancholic tone of the previously quoted letter from Smith to Hume, written in early July, just before the summer journey. As Alcouffe says, 'Finally France was opening up to him and he could make new acquaintances'.[23] Smith's acquaintance with Richelieu also looks important to him as an Enlightenment intellectual because the Marshal is exactly the person Voltaire, Smith's hero, closely consulted in October and November 1761 about a religious persecution predicting the Calas case at which we shall have a close look later.[24] The Duke of Richelieu, as well as the Duke of Choiseul, were among supporters of Voltaire's intervention in the Calas Affair since 1762, so it is possible to say that the network Smith and Buccleuch were connecting largely consists of Voltaire's companions.

On the side of social life, Smith obviously relied on the Humean connection at whose centre was Colbert, rather than on Townshend. But, after the summer journeys, Smith and the Duke socialised relatively quickly and from this moment onwards would not live the life of travellers but that of two people inserted into the social life of the town, sharing

inclined towards female conquests' (Alcouffe and Massot-Bordenave 2020: 58). But this was a Grand Tour as well, and its aspect as 'a sentimental or sexual education' that should give young arstocrats 'a knowledge of the arts of love in the very physical sense of the term' may have been taken by Abbé Colbert rather than the Scottish professor.

[23] Alcouffe and Massot-Bordenave (2020: 170). Corr., no. 83, letter from Smith to Hume, 21 October 1764.

[24] It is not known whether Smith and Richelieu then talked about anything regarding Voltaire.

the daily life and residences of the 'Toulouse bourgeoisie and its aristocrats'.[25] One can find Smith's deep relief relating to the ordinary job as a Grand Tour tutor from the following message. It reveals that he finally got accustomed to that typically French sociability and idea of agreeableness, with his original disciplinary programme for educating Buccleuch maybe mitigated to a certain extent:

> Our expedition to Bordeaux, and another we have made since to Bagneres, has made a great change upon the Duke. He begins now to familiarize himself to French company and I flatter myself I shall spend the rest of the Time we are to live together, not only in Peace and contentment but in gayety and amusement.[26]

Having overcome his relatively weak side of sociable communication, Smith was now very active in his intellectual life with his pupils (that are correctly written in plural because the Duke's brother, Hew, joined the party after their second visit to Bordeaux in October). Although their first visit to Bordeaux may have been intellectually attractive compared to their previous stay in Toulouse,[27] their next excursion to Montpellier through the Languedoc Canal was a perfect opportunity to satisfy their intellectual curiosity. Smith was then allowed to be dedicated to his academic life, his main field, while teaching the Duke on the spot. The excursion to Montpellier was accompanied by Colbert again, whose intellectual virtues, as well as his sociable character and linguistic excellence, were probably recognised further.[28]

[25] Alcouffe and Massot-Bordenave (2020: 208).

[26] Corr. no. 83, letter from Smith to Hume, 21 October 1764. In another letter to Hume written a few weeks later (Corr. no. 84, 4 November 1764), to present his friend to Hume, Smith describes Urquhart de Cromartie as having good character compared to Hume himself, with a kind of French manner focusing on amiable rather than respectable virtues. See Rae (1895: 226–7).

[27] Rae (1895: 223); WN II.iii.

[28] His distinguished Latin ability must have attracted Smith, who paid special attention to the role of classics from Ancient Antiquity for the Duke's moral education. The classics in Colbert's inventories include many of those of great interest to Smith's education: 'Lucretius, Sallust, Horace, Plutarch, Livy, Cicero, Catullus, Seneca, along with Xenophon (Economique) and Mme. Dacier's translation of the Iliad and the Odyssey' (Moore 1988: 19). His inventories also include textbooks indicating his concern with not so much spiritual or ecclesiastical as practical knowledge necessary for a worldly improver, which is absolutely shared by Smith: *Physique des animaux*, *Police des grains*, *Amélioration des*

In contrast to this year of 1764, their stay in Toulouse in 1765 apparently looks less troublesome nor stimulating for Smith and Buccleuch if looking only at the very surface of the timeline of their Grand Tour. But it is actually not at all, as it was exactly in this year that the Calas affair came to a conclusion with the victory of the Enlightenment as an intellectual and practical movement for bettering the world. Despite the relative lack in evidence of Smith's simultaneous responses to the outcome of the affair,[29] there is no doubt that he was extremely interested in and excited by it staying in the very city, and it must have been Abbé Colbert who was the closest figure that was involved to what was happening in Toulouse after the reversing decision regarding this affair on 9 March 1765.[30]

Probably, in 1764, Smith and the duke accepted Colbert as an indispensable companion to their journeys, benefited chiefly by his amicable or amiable character in particular. As mentioned previously, yet struggling for finding the way to enter French aristocratic society, Smith's first impression about Colbert was that he was no less a 'stranger' in Toulouse than Smith himself so that Smith was not sure whether they could rely upon Colbert for their first mission Smith was not necessarily good at. Smith's recognition was not wrong then, but Colbert had a superior merit to socialise with others in polite society with his excellent French (and Latin in part),[31] thus distinctively helpful and useful for Smith and Buccleuch as 'strangers' to enter into French society. This would be the same even if Colbert might have kept his primary feeling as a stranger, in a sense, in the midst of the French. Without what was supplied by this sociable abbé's amiable character and his excellent art of conversation throughout the tour, it could not have been such a success.

Colbert's sociable character, perhaps cultivated by living an intellectual and physical border between the two nations, was not his only beauty,

terres, *Moyens de détruire la mendicité*, Boerhasse's *Method*. 'Colbert's prime aim was to be an efficient and informed 'Prélat administrateur', rather than a 'laboureur de diocèse', principally concerned with the purely spiritual needs of his flock' (Moore 1988: 20).

[29] It is more than likely that Smith eagerly paid attention to the Calas Affair, based on the fact that he had personal contact with a King's attorney general, Ruquet de Bonrepos, who was a key figure of the Affair, and that Smith brought back to Britain a pile of pamphlets and papers related to this event (perhaps commissioned by Townshend). See Alcouffe and Massot-Bordenave (2020: 131–47).

[30] Alcouffe and Massot-Bordenave (2020: 138–9).

[31] Alcouffe and Massot-Bordenave (2020: 64–5).

however. His other virtue seems to have appeared explicitly in 1765, and Smith and Buccleuch must have been impressed and influenced by his outstanding actions in relation to the aftereffects of the Calas Affair. Distinguished from his amiable or sociable nature which helped the two Scottish tourists during 1764, another remarkable aspect of Colbert's character was made explicit next year. This is what could temporarily be dubbed a 'Voltairian' aspect of the Abbé, and it may relate to a politically more radical dimension of the French Enlightenment, which led him and Loménie de Brienne (the latter of whom, Louis XVI's financial minister, was engulfed by the Revolution) to the centre of politics before and during the French Revolution.[32]

Abbé Colbert and Smith in 1765: A 'Voltairian' Intervention in the Public Issue

As lots of biographers have demonstrated, for Smith, Voltaire was the most outstanding hero of the French and European Enlightenment. It was difficult to suppose that Smith was not reminded of Voltaire's ongoing interventions to the affair in Toulouse when he discussed, probably in the autumn of 1763, with Townshend and Hume where to stay during their Grand Tour. In fact, about half a year after the victory of the social movement aroused by Voltaire's active Enlightenment, namely in October 1765, Smith and Buccleuch made a visit to Geneva in Switzerland, before moving to Paris (where they spent the rest of their tour until October 1766). Considering Smith's life-long admiration of Voltaire and the timing, there is very little doubt that one of the chief purposes of their detour was to meet Voltaire in Ferney.[33]

As is previously suggested, however, Smith's central moral character and its merits or virtues seem qualitatively distinct from Voltaire's active and aggressive character. Emphasised in his moral argument in the *Theory of Moral Sentiments*, the respectable virtues with a focus on self-discipline, firmness of the mind and a kind of Stoic tranquil insensitivity to hustle and bustle of the external world appeared to belong to his main moral character as well. Relating to these moral virtues, carefulness as a type of

[32] Alcouffe and Massot-Bordenave (2020: 61).

[33] Phillipson (2010: 189): 'The choice of Geneva as an appropriate if somewhat unusual city for a two-month visit suggests that Smith also had a hand in the planning of the tour'.

prudence was at the centre of Smith's character. He may have been almost the last person among the Enlightenment figures who attempted to carry moral subjects to public debate, tending to keep potentially politicised issues private as long as possible. Learning from Hume's bitter experience, who could not find an academic post in universities being suspected of atheism based on his metaphysical scepticism or agnosticism, Smith was very wary of expressing his theological-political opinions publicly.[34] This does not denote that he is too conservative to be counted as Enlightenment literati, but can be interpreted as showing that he was too careful a person to be part of an 'activist' Enlightenment, like Voltaire. Like Immanuel Kant, who declared that the essence of Enlightenment lies in the maxim of 'dare to know', Smith unconditionally agreed with the universal value of freedom of thinking, which is critical to human knowledge of truth. On the other hand, he prudently separated the freedom of expression from that of thinking, the former of which he was personally quite cautious of exercising or even mentioning. Probably like Kant again, Smith might consider that the extent to which freedom of speech or expressing one's opinion publicly could be somehow dependent on the historical stage to which an individual society belongs. He was thus not an active man of letters compared to Voltaire, who did not flinch at all from beginning 'pamphlet wars' for the Calas case, including publishing the *Histoire d'Elisabeth Canning, et de Jean Calas* in August 1762, and the *Traité sur la tolérance* in November 1763.

While Voltaire, who was incomparably skilful at working on the public opinion, found out his superior role in the *vita activa* rather than *vita contemplativa*, Smith tends to recommend the reading public (and his pupils) to reinforce their mental ability of not being too much influenced by external or worldly opinion. In this context, his recommended virtue is surely patience and firmness, rather than courage or daring to get involved in public dispute and turbulence. A consistent admirer of Voltaire, however, Smith seriously considered the importance of active interventions to public and political discourses for enlightening and improving the real world, perhaps after 1765, the year when he witnessed a series of events relating to Jean Calas staying in Toulouse. Although Smith seems aware of his moral merits being quite different from the

[34] Phillipson (2010: 133, 244–5). There are a few more episodes that show this aspect of Smith's character; see Campbell and Skinner (1982: 165; 239–44); Phillipson (2010: 242–6); Rae (1895: ch. 22).

Voltairian spirit, he showed his deep interest in such active citizenship and a certain type of moral character corresponding to it. This strong moral concern can be detected in the sixth edition of the *Moral Sentiments*, with Part VI demonstrating it in particular. Having not appeared in the first edition published in 1759, the part entitled 'Of the Character of Virtue' is a newly added part for the 1790 edition, and there can be found several 'Voltairian' subjects such as providence, deism and optimism, in which his experience of 1765 appears to be inscribed.[35]

He was in Toulouse on the very day of 9 March 1765, and he doubtlessly visited Voltaire in the autumn of the same year. This timing can be circumstantial evidence that suggests that Smith exchanged opinions about the Calas affair with Voltaire in Ferney or Geneva,[36] and their precious meetings would be one of the most critical sources of the insight developed in the later added part of Smith's *Moral Sentiments*, entitled 'Of the Character of Virtue'. However, Smith's 'Voltairian' experience was not limited to this opportunity that was more than half a year after March 9th. Although we have little direct evidence, it is highly likely that Smith observed an even more vivid 'Voltairian spirit' in Abbé Colbert's public engagement with a kind of sequel to the Calas affair.[37]

Colbert mentioned the Calas affair and the enduring fanatic mood obsessing most of the *Toulousains* with regret, in his letter to Hume in Paris, dated on 10 April 1765.[38] His surprise at the lay people's reaction to the news from the capital about the overturning judgement in favour

[35] TMS VI.i.9–16; VI.ii..1.20–22; VI.iii.11, 17–19, 48; VI.concl.2–7; cf. III.2.10–13.

[36] According to P. W. Clayden's *Early Life of Sammuel Rogers* (London, 1887), at one of their meetings Smith and Voltaire discussed 'the volatile relationships that were developing between the Court and the provincial parlements and Estates' (Phillipson 2010: 190). This is a topic closely associated with the Calas affair, because what Voltaire did in order to restore the honour the pitiful Huguenot and his family was essentially to stir the public opinion centred in Paris so as to influence the Court in Versailles, which had a contradictory interest to the Parlement of Toulouse. His basically positive opinion of the Kingship for the purpose of enlightening the society seems to be considerably shared with Smith. For the details of Smith's visit to Geneva, see Bonnyman (2009).

[37] During the first half of 1765, Smith and Buccleuch visited several places in Southern France such as Marseille and Arles, without any exact dates specified. But it is certain that they stayed in Toulouse in its largest part, and they were likely to keep in regular contact with Colbert, even when they were away from the city. See Ross (1995: 235).

[38] Colbert (1765b), letter from Colbert to Hume, 10 April 1765. See Alcouffe and Massot-Bordenave (2020: 142).

of Calas may possibly be interpreted as showing his relative lack of accurate knowledge about Toulouse and its popular culture. In this aspect, it is understandable and rather reasonable for Smith one year ago to be unsure whether he could entirely rely on the Abbé who was yet quite a stranger in Toulouse then. Indeed, with his breezy, relaxed manner like Hume's, what Colbert said to Hume one year ago (1764) could have sounded a little too optimistic to the careful and prudent Smith who had just arrived in this unfamiliar city: 'Si quelques anglais ou Ecossais vous demandent conseil où ils doivent aller pour leurs exercices: vous pouvez en toute sûreté leur recommander Toulouse. Il y a une très bonne académie et beaucoup de monde et de très honnêtes gens à voir ici'.[39] Nevertheless, Smith is not a cynical person who only remonstrates about seemingly imprudent or thoughtless judgement and action by a man of passion, but he admires Voltaire and what can be dubbed 'friends of humanity' who are passionately driven to fight against the *infâme* under a great moral cause of Enlightenment. And there is considerable possibility that Smith admired Colbert for his daring to make an active intervention in the city's political troubles brought about by the Calas affair, as will be illustrated below. Smith possibly took his philosophical activism as representing the Voltairian spirit of the French Enlightenment.

Only ten days before the victorious judgement by Versailles court rejecting the previous decision made by the parlement de Toulouse, Abbé Colbert wrote to Hume, indicating the unjust treatment of a city magistrate responsible for the false charge of Jean Calas in a different case:

> I was surprised to learn, my dear Cousin, that the court has forbidden Mr David Capitoul of Toulouse to punish him for the ill-treatment meted out to Colonel Forrester and General du Roure after their deaths.
> But the magistrate, Mr David, had no part in this extortion and if anyone should be punished, it is the king's people who are the only oppressors.
> This event caused a sensation here, because David is a great police officer and the only one who has brought some order to this very large city. It is believed that it was at the request of the English ambassador that the Court punished him in this way. It is quite right that those who oppress should be punished, but on this occasion the blow was aimed at the real

[39] Colbert (1764b), letter from Colbert to Hume, 22 April 1764.

> object. On the contrary, many Englishmen here have reason to praise Mr David, who has shown them a great deal of consideration.[40]

Without context, Colbert's advocacy of the capitoul David de Beaudrigue, the *infâme* worth being *ecrasé* in terms of his role in the Calas affair, might look to be not on the same line with the Enlightenment current symbolised by Voltaire. As is confirmed above, Colbert tried to clarify his unreserved critique of fanatic hostility towards the Huguenots shared by the majority of common people in Toulouse, but he was not entirely sure if his somewhat complex position regarding the treatment of David de Beaudrigue was mistaken as implying his counter-Enlightenment thinking or priestcraft as a vicar-general of the Gallican church, by Hume and his old friends in Parisian salons.[41] Colbert thus presented himself as an advocate of the capitoul in exactly the same cause for the Enlightenment as Hume and other Enlightenment intellectuals', clearly distinguishing his idea and practice from those of an enthusiastic crowd in Toulouse:

> The people here are so fanatic that you would be astonished; in spite of what has just happened, everyone believes Calas Father Guilty and it is useless to talk to them on this subject before reminding them to be wise and moderate, it will be necessary to destroy many establishments that have to do with religion and this Reformation can only come about little by little but it will finally be brought to an end.[42]

For Abbé Colbert, as Voltaire and other Enlightenment thinkers also recognised, the Enlightenment as a cultural improvement is a life-long project, particularly because it cannot simply be a certain type of democratisation that is just a linear process during which the public opinion of common populace is gradually overwhelming the pre-modern, hierarchical authority belonging to aristocrats.[43] As is shown by the last

[40] Colbert (1765a), letter from Colbert to Hume, 28 February 1765.

[41] '[...] ce que j'ai fait dans cette occasion a eu un motif pur; peut-être ai-je eu tort dans la forme. Je suis toujours prêt à me rétracter sur tout ce que j'ai pu faire en faveur d'un homme que je hais et que je méprise autant que je vous aime et vous respecte mon cher cousin' (Colbert 1764b, letter from Colbert to Hume, 22 April 1764).

[42] Colbert (1765b), letter from Colbert to Hume, 10 April 1765.

[43] See, for example, Doyle (2001).

quotation above mentioned, rather it is a long, historical course wherein the public opinions themselves would become gradually improved with the popular culture being refined as well.[44] When situating his own position in the midst of this Enlightenment and in opposition to popular fanaticism, his manner appears quite similar to Voltaire's expressed in Chapter 1 of his *Traité sur la tolérance*, in which his primary target is the superstitious culture of the madding crowd that urged the capitoul David and the Parlement to decide against the Calas family.[45] In order to compete with such mob obsessed by unrealistic imagination, which was, according to Voltaire, further stirred up by fanatic Feasts, Colbert emphasises the universal moral value of humanity and justice:

> Looking at Calas' death, the common opinion here is the most horrible effect of an outrageous fanaticism, I would be unworthy of your regard, my dear cousin, if I did not question myself on the subject and if I did not join with the cry of humanity to avenge the memory of an unhappy father on the author of his misfortune.

At the same time, it should also be worth noting that the Smithean or Humean idea of impartiality was focused on by the Abbé in order to justify his possibly controversial judgement for his friends in Paris most of whom were advocates of the Enlightenment. In the following passages from the same letter dated in April 1765, he tried to demonstrate that his position was neutral and impartial, saying that he had no vested interest or particular relation with David de Beaudrigue:

> Here is my request and the principle underlying my request, my dear cousin; I take no interest in this capitoul, I have never spoken to him, I have seen him only once and that by chance in the street, I hate the author of an event that dishonors this city and I rejoice at his disgrace. At the same time I must testify to his good conduct towards some Englishmen who are in Toulouse, but these particular actions will never blind me to the other side of his life. I couldn't deny him a testimony which I thought was due to him, he has a son worthy of a better father, he has parents here who are good people.

[44] Strategically, Voltaire depicts Paris as a city ruled by refined public opinion, and he criticises a rude popular culture in Toulouse based on this model. This is founded on the dichotomy between reason or philosophy and fanaticism. See Voltaire (2000: Chap. 1).

[45] Voltaire (2000: Chap. 1).

> These are the reasons for my conduct, by which you are surprised; I would have wished that the real culprits (and they are even meaner people than David) should have been punished for the case of Mr. Forrester and that the capitoul was accused for a real crime: the murder of Calas.
> If you think I should have denied him my testimony in a particular case, I would submit to your decision, but I hope you will be willing to distinguish an act (which I thought I had to do) of justice from an interest (which you might suppose me to have) in a man I hate..[46]

Here, Colbert underlined the significance of doing justice from a public and impartial point of view, no matter what relations one personally has with the person concerned. He presented himself as attempting to wipe out a false charge just in the same manner as the case of Calas, based on the universal and impartial idea of the rule of law. If he did not advocate David with the knowledge of the capitoul's innocence in this particular case, their critique of the prosecutors of Calas could not differ much from those zealots who made Calas a scapegoat. This attitude reminds us of Voltaire's cautious investigation at the early stage of his involvement in the Calas Affair. Voltaire was at first in favour of the judgement of the Parlement, at least until 22 March 1762,[47] and did not handle this matter with haste. Once he became convinced of the righteousness of Calas and his family after his careful examination, he no longer hesitated to publicly show his backing of them, claiming that the justice of humanity was absolutely on the side of the Calas family, so that potentially anyone would have felt obliged to commit oneself to the party of humanity, not to the *infâme*. In fact, the Voltairian spirit is usually connected with being a man of action or 'activist' for the case of the Enlightenment, who was demanding people to (openly) demonstrate in which position one would be: the party of humanity or the enemy of humanity. However, in spite of that aggressive maxim '*Écrasez l'infâme*', Voltaire equally values examining different, contradictory claims with impartiality in advance of showing one's particular position politically.[48] Furthermore, even after making an active commitment to the party or friend of humanity, he appears careful to present his argument with impartiality as much as possible, like his 'philosophical'

[46] Colbert (1765b), letter from Colbert to Hume, 10 April 1765.

[47] Alcouffe and Massot-Bordenave (2020: 136).

[48] Alcouffe and Massot-Bordenave (2020: 136–7).

historiography whose principle is to examine multiple evidence acquired from distinct sources. This 'philosophical' impartiality is incarnated by his writing strategy of the *Traité sur la tolérance*, whose main aim was to persuade those who had not yet taken a particular position with this case. In this sense, Colbert's framing of justice shown in the quotation above reasonably corresponds to another aspect of the Voltairian mind associated with the idea of impartiality.

Finally, we shall finish our discussion with another quotation from the same correspondence between Colbert and Hume, which exactly expresses what most people firstly associate the Voltairian ideal of tolerance with, and which might have enabled Smith to find a good example of the Voltairian spirit in Colbert:

> I believe with you, my dear cousin, that Capitoul David deserves all the indignation with which he is charged, and that the first perpetrator of the murder of an unfortunate father must be an object of horror for all honest people who have not been warned. But it is possible that a very bad man is nevertheless innocent of a particular crime attributed to him and for which he is punished. So I believe that if someone, out of ignorance of the facts, has attributed to this wicked man a crime he did not commit and had him punished for it, he must repair this wrong and do justice in this particular event. David had no part in the vexation of Messrs. Forester and de Roure, however Mr. de Florentin in the letter in which he announces his disgrace says it is to punish him for this conception. It was believed here that this punishment was as a consequence of the representations made to the court by the Ambassador of England.
> In this assumption, I believed, as the only one in a position to give an account of this affair, I ought to write to Milord Hertford and to give David, although I abhor him, the testimony due to innocence. At the same time, I deprived his Excellency of interceding for him, assuming that he had accepted that he was the author of this vexation..[49]

Here, Abbé Colbert seems to have behaved as if he followed the Voltairian maxim of toleration, according to which you should defend others' fundamental rights such as free speech, even if you criticise the

[49] Colbert (1765b), letter from Colbert to Hume, 10 April 1765. Cf. Alcouffe and Massot-Bordenave (2020: 141–2).

person for a different reason.[50] Actually, the saying commonly attributed to Voltaire, 'I may disagree with you, but I defend to the death your right to say it', is likely a later invention by Evelyn Beatrice Hall's work, *The Friends of Voltaire* (1906). It could be a little doubtful whether the real Voltaire owns such a character to do so.[51] Probably, this saying considered as representing the soul of Voltairian tolerance would even better suit Colbert de Castlehill, who decided—with worry, but courageously—to assist the capitoul David de Beaudrigue in his own false charge, not despite, but because of his solidarity with the 'cri de l'humanité'.

References

Abbreviations

Corr: Adam Smith (1977).
TMS: Adam Smith (1976a).
WN: Adam Smith (1976b).

[50] Academic freedom had been at the centre of debate in France particularly after Diderot and D'Alembert started to publish the *Encyclopédie* in the 1750s. Compared to Diderot, D'Alembert inclined to isolate the liberty of thought from religious and political controversies, responding chiefly to the criticisms by the *Journal des savants*. As Franco Venturi (1970: Chap. 3, 82–5) once argued, D'Alembert attempted to rebut and even suppress the Jésuites' (and his other enemies') criticism by recourse to the enlightened director of censorship, Malesherbes, requiring him to defend against what D'Alembert regarded as defamation or libel. While this liberal advocate of the *philosophes* had played a pivotal role in the publication of the first volume of the *Encyclopédie*, Malesherbes critically responded to D'Alembert, suggesting that D'Alembert should admit the freedom of press of his adversaries unless their explicit target was not his discourses but his personality or conducts irrelevant to the discourses concerned. Despite the fact that D'Alembert criticised Malesherbes's judgement in his letter sent to Voltaire in 1759, it appears to be not so much D'Alembert as Malesherbes who shared the Voltairian spirit that applies such freedom to enemies as well as friends in a universalist manner.

[51] Those who have attributed this quote to Voltaire, and spread it copiously under his name, base themselves on a letter dated 6 February 1770 written to Abbé Le Riche, while such a sentence nor even an idea does not appear there. In spite of this, the motto nonetheless illustrates his philosophy, as expressed in his *Questions sur l'Encyclopédie*: "I loved the author of the book of the *Esprit* (i.e. Helvétius). This man was worth more than all his enemies put together; but I never approved either of the errors in his book, or of the trivial truths he emphatically spouts. I took his side strongly when absurd men condemned him for these very truths." This footnote is indebted to Alain Alcouffe, to whom I am sincerely grateful.

Primary Sources

Lady Mary Coke (1970), *The Letters and Journals of Lady Mary Coke: 1756–1774*, (Ed.) James Archibald Home, Bath; Edinburgh: David Douglas [1889].

Seignelay Colbert de Castlehill (1764a), Letter from Abbé Colbert to David Hume, 4 March 1764. NLS MS 23,154.34; RSE Hume Calendar Ref IV, 34.

Seignelay Colbert de Castlehill (1764b), Letter from Abbé Colbert to David Hume, 22 April 1764. NLS MS 23,154.35; RSE Hume Calendar Ref IV, 35.

Seignelay Colbert de Castlehill (1765a), Letter from Abbé Colbert to David Hume, 28 February 1765. NLS MS 23,154.36; RSE Hume Calendar Ref IV, 36.

Seignelay Colbert de Castlehill (1765b), Letter from Abbé Colbert to David Hume, 10 April 1765. NLS MS 23,154.37; RSE Hume Calendar Ref IV, 37.

Seignelay Colbert de Castlehill (1766), Letter from Colbert to Henry Scott-Douglas, 18 September 1766. National Archives of Scotland, GD 224/2040/62/3.

Adam Smith (1976a), *The Theory of Moral Sentiments*, (Eds) D. D. Raphael and A. L. Macfie, Oxford: Oxford University Press; Glasgow edition. Reprinted, Liberty Fund (1982).

Adam Smith (1976b), *An Inquiry into the Nature and Causes of the Wealth of Nations*, (Eds) R. H. Campbell and A. S. Skinner, Oxford: Oxford University Press; Glasgow edition.

Adam Smith (1977), *Correspondence of Adam Smith*, (Eds), E. C. Mossner and I. S. Ross, Oxford: Oxford University Press; Glasgow edition.

Voltaire (2000), Le Traité sur la tolérance, (1765). Treatise on Tolerance and Other Writings, Cambridge Texts in the History of Philosophy, (trans.) Brian Masters, (ed.) Simon Harvey, Cambridge: Cambridge University Press.

Secondary Sources

Alain Alcouffe & Philippe Massot-Bordenave (2020), *Adam Smith in Toulouse and Occitania: The Unknown Years*, New York: Palgrave Macmillan.

Joseph Bédier, Paul Hazard, Pierre Martino (1949), (eds), *Littérature française*, Paris: Larousse.

Brian Bonnyman (2009), "Adam Smith in Geneva", in V. Cossy, B. Kapossy, and R. Whatmore (eds), *Geneva, an English Enclave 1725–1814*, Geneva, pp. 153–67.

Roy H. Campbell and Andrew S. Skinner (1982), *Adam Smith*, London: Croom Helm Ltd.; Routledge Library Edition (2010).

William Doyle (2001), *The Ancien Regime*, Second Edition, Studies in European History, Hampshire: Palgrave.

Andrew Moore (1988), *A Bishop of the Ancient Regime: Seignelay Colbert de Castle-Hill in the pre-revolutionary years*, Honors dissertation, University of Bristol.

Ernest C. Mossner (1954), *The Life of David Hume*, Oxford.

Nicholas Phillipson (2010), *Adam Smith: An Enlightened Life*, New Haven: Yale University Press; published in Penguin Books 2011.

John Rae (1895), *Life of Adam Smith*, London; New York: Macmillan & Co.

Ian Simpson Ross (1974), "Educating an Eighteenth-Century Duke", in (ed.) G. W. S. Barrow, *The Scottish Tradition: Essays in Honour of R. G. Cant*, Edinburgh.

Ian Simpson Ross (1995), *The Life of Adam Smith*, Oxford: Clarendon Press; Oxford University Press.

Hiroki Ueno (2022), "Adam Smith entre les Lumières écossaises et françaises", *Dialogue et Universalisme* 32(1):127–146.

Hiroki Ueno (2023), "Educating a Young Aristocrat during Grand Tour: Moral and Political Economy in Adam Smith", *The Journal of Scottish Philosophy*, 21(1):75–96.

Hiroki Ueno and sora Sato (2023), "Adam Smith and Josiah Tucker on Restructuring Empire", *La Revue d'études benthamiennes*, 24, "International Thought of the British Empire", Online since 30 August 2023.

Venturi, Franco (1963), *Le origini dell'Enciclopedia*, Piccola Biblioteca Einaudi.

CHAPTER 4

Adam Smith, Colbert of Castlehill, the Estates of Languedoc and the Diocesan *Assiettes*

Gilbert Larguier

Abstract The decision of the Duke of Buccleuch to embark on his Grand Tour in the aftermath of the Seven Years' War, with the south-west of the French kingdom as his destination, is an intriguing one. It is probable that David Hume, a friend of Adam Smith, arrived in Paris in the autumn of 1763, has recommended this choice as he was aware of the presence of Abbé Colbert de Catlehill, of Scottish descent. The letters of vicar-general granted to Colbert de Castlehill by Loménie de Brienne, who had been promoted to archbishop of Toulouse the previous year, were dated January 19, 1764. Smith arrived in Toulouse on March 3, 1764, when the archbishop was attending the annual session of the Estates of Languedoc

English revised by Andrew Moore.

G. Larguier (✉)
Université de Perpignan Via Domitia, Perpignan, France
e-mail: gilbert.larguier@wanadoo.fr

Université Toulouse Jean Jaurès, Toulouse, France

A. Alcouffe (ed.), *Seignelay Colbert de Castlehill (1735-1811)*,
https://doi.org/10.1007/978-3-031-75273-5_4

which Adam Smith attended the following year in Montpellier. One of the functions performed by the vicars-general of the Languedoc prelates was to assist them with the assiette of their diocese, which was an essential cog in the provincial administration. For almost twenty years, Colbert's main task was to monitor and even direct the work of the Toulouse diocesan assiette. This period proved to be an invaluable training ground for the future bishop of Rodez, who was to preside over the provincial assembly of Haute-Guyenne.

Keywords Colbert of Castlehill · Adam Smith · David Hume · Estates of Languedoc · Civil diocese · Assiette · Montpellier · Vicar General · Toulouse · Loménie de Brienne

Choosing the south-west of the Kingdom of France in the aftermath of the Seven Years' War for the Grand Tour of a young duke of Scottish descent promised to the highest functions in his country, and Toulouse in particular, has intrigued[1] many. This destination and the course of the tour, which did not conform to the usual practices of this type of aristocratic initiation, attracted attention not so much because of the personality of the pupil, the Duke of Buccleuch, as because of that of his mentor, Adam Smith. This trip, delayed because of the Seven Years' War, was not improvised. There are indications that David Hume, a friend of Smith's, was aware of this choice. On his arrival, he was welcomed by the Abbé Colbert of Castlehill, also of Scottish origin.

Note the following dates: David Hume arrived in Paris as secretary to the British embassy in the autumn of 1763; the letters of vicar-general granted to Colbert of Castlehill by Loménie de Brienne, who had been promoted to archbishop of Toulouse the previous year, were dated 19 January 1764; Adam Smith and his pupil arrived in Toulouse on 3 March 1764, but they were unable to meet the prelate, who had gone to Montpellier to attend the annual assembly of the Languedoc Estates. Adam Smith, Brienne and his vicar-general had in common that they were newcomers to Toulouse and the Languedoc. Another point in common:

[1] Alcouffe Alain & Massot-Bordenave Philippe, *Adam Smith à Toulouse et en Occitanie*, Toulouse, Éditions Privat, 2018.

the provincial assembly. Montpellier, where Smith was to go on the occasion of the next meeting of the Estates,[2] was one of the few escapades he allowed himself outside Toulouse, along with Bordeaux, L'isle de Noë and Bagnères-de-Bigorre. During his entire episcopate, the archbishop was very assiduous at the sessions of the assembly, being represented only twice. As for Seignelay Colbert, he was called upon to follow diocesan affairs closely.

Diocesan affairs should not be understood as *ecclesiastical*, but as temporal affairs. In this case those of the diocesan or civil diocese, a district essentially devoted in Languedoc to the distribution and collection of the Royal direct tax. The bishops presided over the tax base, or *assiette* of their diocese whose functions were not limited to this levy. Frequently, they delegated the care of temporal affairs under their charge to their vicars-general. A task that often remained in the shadows, which the example of Seignelay Colbert will partially shed light on.

Adam Smith and the Languedoc Estates

Smith's interest in the Languedoc Estates begs the question: how well did he know them? He was probably aware of their composition, the regularity of their annual assemblies, the distribution of taxes based on scrupulously observed tariffs and their well-established reputation in the field of public works. To what extent was he aware of the developments in the "*affaire du Vingtième*", a tax of 5% on all incomes instituted in 1749 by the Controller General Machault d'Arnouville? The Estates had vigorously protested against it on the grounds that it was established in an authoritarian manner in the middle of the peace and violated their privilege of "consent to taxation". The parliaments were also upset: the absence of prior registration tainted its legality in their eyes. The confrontation raised the question of the legitimacy of taxation and, more broadly, the capacity to reform the state. What better observatory than Toulouse to study the functioning of institutions and the relations between the state, the Estates and the parliaments[3]?

[2] Held from 1 December 1764 to 7 January 1765.

[3] Arch. dep. Haute-Garonne, 1B 4592. Devic Claude Et Vaissète Jean, *Histoire générale de Languedoc*, Paris, Vincent, 1730–1756, re-edited and continued until 1790 by Ernest Roschach, Toulouse, Privat, 1870–1904, 15 vols. XIV, col. 2261–2263.

Smith had a quick way of finding out about the provincial assembly: reading the minutes of its sessions. One point must surely have attracted his attention: the importance of public works, which had become the main subject of deliberations since the middle of the century. Contrary to the generally accepted idea, to which Arthur Young contributed a great deal with his *Voyages en France*, where he marvelled on the eve of the Revolution at the magnificence of the roads in Languedoc, which he attributed to the state—in this case the Estates —and to the tax levy,[4] it was not the royal power or the provincial assembly that were the sole omnipotent architects. The initiative came mainly from the dioceses. The Estates supervised and controlled more than they inspired.

When Smith arrived in Toulouse, Loménie de Brienne had just attended for the first time the Estates Assembly. From the outset, he occupied a prominent place. It was he who took the floor after the tax demands presented by the King's commissioners. Shortly afterwards, Brienne read a long report on a project aimed at rationalising the "*étape*", the service dedicated to the movement, housing and maintenance of troops in the Kingdom, which was burdensome for the communities placed on the "*chemin de l'étape*". It was an opportunity for him to insist strongly on the principles that inspired him: "the appropriateness of never departing, as far as possible, from the true principles of the administration of the states, such as: the solidarity of all the members of the political body; the harmony that must subsist between them in order to help each other; the balance that must be struck between all the parties in the contribution in general to all expenditure...".

These interventions, recorded in the minutes of the assembly, gave Smith access to first-hand information on the Estates of Languedoc, and a detailed understanding of the province's institutional and territorial architecture, as well as their control over diocesan *assiettes*.

In the Wake of Loménie de Brienne

In 1775, Abbé Colbert presided for the first time over the assembly of the diocesan assiette. This distinction marks an important stage in his career. Until then, it is difficult to document. It is necessary to go back to his beginnings in Toulouse. Brienne arrived in Toulouse on 19 August

[4] Young Arthur, *Voyages en France en 1787, 1788 et 1789*, translation by Henri Sée, Paris, A. Colin, 1931, 3 vols.

1763.[5] Seignelay Colbert accompanied him. The letters of vicar-general granted to him by the prelate, in which he is described as a priest of Moray in Scotland, are dated 19 January 1764. The link with Smith's trip to Toulouse is obvious.

The bishops maintained an average of six to eight, even up to ten like Dillon in Narbonne.[6] Becoming a vicar-general was almost an obligatory step for younger sons of aristocratic families who aspired to the episcopate. To do so, one had to be noticed or recommended, the choice being left to the prelates, hence the importance of networks of relations, the position of the candidates themselves and the influence of their protectors. It was a matter of personal capital, opportunity and even luck. The first, perhaps, Colbert was able to take advantage of, was the Parisian route through one of his uncles, who had already emigrated to France and to whom he was entrusted on the death of his father. The latter sent him to the Collège des Écossais, where he stayed for four years, then to the Collège d'Harcourt. There he showed excellent intellectual abilities, was nominated two years in a row for the general competition organised among the Parisian colleges and even won the "Prix d'honneur" in 1754. For these gratifying successes he was noticed by former students of the college, including Loménie de Brienne who had been a tutor there. So Brienne had known about his abilities for a long time.[7]

He was not ordained a priest until 1762.[8] In the meantime, even though he studied law in Reims, Colbert frequented the Parisian salons, where his origins were not the least of the qualities which caused him to be appreciated in literary circles, which were very Anglophile at the time. He established very solid relationships with the most prominent salonnières such as Madame de Rochefort and Madame du Deffand, a distant relative of Brienne. During this period, nothing is known about the means of subsistence of the young Scottish man without fortune.

At nearly twenty-seven years of age he took the plunge and entered the priesthood. His appointment as vicar-general followed closely. Adam

[5] *Les heures perdues de Pierre Barthès*, répétiteur à Toulouse .., Bibliothèque municipale de Toulouse, ms. 699 to 706.

[6] *La France ecclésiastique, 1782*, Henri Duchesne, Paris, p. 261.

[7] Alcouffe Alain & Massot-Bordenave Philippe, *Adam Smith..., op. cit*, p. 108.

[8] *Dictionary of Constituents*; *Halloran Scots College*, p. 354.

Smith's project was an unexpected opportunity for him. The circumstances were right. As soon as Hume arrived in Paris in the autumn of 1763 as secretary to the British embassy, Colbert had immediately approached him, as had the Archbishop of Toulouse. Had he already had the opportunity to correspond with him or did his compatriot status—Colbert had not yet been naturalised—operate as a sesame? We have noted the familiarity of tone in their epistolary exchanges in which they refer to each other as "dear cousin".[9]

Seignelay Colbert became the right man guiding the professor. Brienne was probably aware of another peculiarity of the abbé. He maintained relations with the Scottish aristocratic elites who remained faithful to their Jacobite sympathies and may have known Freemasonry through his father or one of his uncles.[10] The latter had been well established in Toulouse since the first lodge was founded in 1741 by the Irishman Richard de Barnewall.

Brienne already had several vicars-general. Among them was Barthélemy Chaumont de La Galaizière, probably the first one he attached himself to when he was elected to the see at Condom. He had had the opportunity to meet him in Rome in 1759. La Galaizière was the son of the chancellor of Lorraine during the reign of Stanislas Leszczynski—from 1737 to 1758—and of the sister of the future comptroller general of finances Orry. Brienne took him to Toulouse. Younger than Seignelay Colbert by two years, La Galaizière had a head-start in the vicariate general. He could already boast of good experience. His relations with the Court and the administration were also on a different scale, which was not without interest for Loménie de Brienne.[11]

He did not hesitate to use it in delicate circumstances. It is therefore not surprising that he entrusted him with the care of diocesan affairs. Unlike his predecessors, Brienne never presided over the annual

[9] Mossner Ernest C., *Hume and the French Men of Letters*, 1952, p. 228.

[10] His father had been a member of the *Saint John's* Lodge *of* Inverness. His uncle, Lachlan Colbert, was a member of the Royal Scots Regimental Lodge where he served.

[11] His elder brother, Antoine, briefly intendant in Montauban from 1756 to 1758, was then intendant of Lorraine and Barrois, and in 1777 intendant of Alsace; a second brother was first chaplain to the King of Poland Stanislas and then grand vicar of the bishopric of Toul.

assembly of the assiette.[12] This was not because he was uninterested in the temporal affairs of his diocese. Indeed, on several occasions he presided over meetings of the ordinary commissioners of the assiette charged between assemblies with examining the progress of work in hand, the requests of communities or authorising the syndic to borrow. At the beginning of his episcopate, he left the affairs of the diocese in the hands of the vicars-general who remained in Toulouse. From 1765 onwards, he entrusted them to the Abbé de La Galaizière. The latter presided over the annual assembly of the assiette without interruption until 1774 when he left Toulouse. In February, he had just been appointed by King Louis XV to the bishopric of Saint-Dié. This appointment brightened Colbert's horizon. It was clear that he had been struggling for ten years to find a place for himself. The letter written to his "dear cousin" Hume when Adam Smith arrived in Toulouse shows that he sensed his future condition, far from the Parisian mundanities:

> Here I am, dear cousin, less pleasantly occupied than when I act with the beautiful ladies of Paris, but that time may yet come again, it will be necessary to pass this one now.[13]

For the time being, his only job was to accompany Smith. He was in his company in Bordeaux, in Montpellier during the session of the Estates, and would be in Paris at the beginning of 1766 when the professor stopped off there on his way back. This was an opportunity for Colbert to rediscover the "belles dames" and the delights of the salons, particularly that of Madame de Rochefort.[14] For him, his mission to Smith did not constitute a radical break with his previous life. He stayed for many months outside Toulouse, frequented his compatriots and was able to spend several weeks in good company, meeting and talking with Madame

[12] Arch. dep. Haute-Garonne, 1C 961, 1C 962: 1755, François de Crussol duc d'Uzès; 1761, monseigneur Dillon.

[13] National Library of Scotland. Colbert will not cease to avail himself of his dense worldly relations. In a final exchange with Hume, he instructs him to say "well these things for me and my friends, tell them well that they neglect me much and do not keep me the fidelity they had promised me".

[14] 15 and 29 January, 5 February at Madame de Rochefort's; 17 February at the Marquis de Brancas'; 26 February at Madame d'Usson's, H. Walpole Paris Journals, pp. 295, 298, 300, 302, 309, Lewis Walpole Library, Yale University.

de Gacé, Walpole, the dukes of Saint Pierre and Saint Simon, Mirabeau, etc.

Until then, Colbert had hardly had the opportunity to make himself known in Toulouse. He remained largely a stranger there. He was not a naturalised citizen and his livelihood remained precarious. Without a well-defined status, the vicars-general did not enjoy an assured remuneration. This depended on their patron, at best a benefit that the patron had at his disposal. Colbert's integration was slow. He only obtained his letters of naturality in April 1767.[15] In November of the same year, he became Abbot of the Cistercian abbey of Val Richer in Calvados. The following year he married Paul d'Avessans de Saint-Rome to Gabrielle de Riquet de Lagarde, daughter of Riquet de Bonrepos.[16] For the first time in 1769—the only time before 1775—he signed the minutes of a meeting of the ordinary commissioners of the diocesan assiette.[17]

In a disenchanted letter to the Duke of Buccleuch in 1770, Colbert unabashedly exposed his situation:

> I am still in Toulouse in the same occupations, in the same habit, in the same room where you saw me, as fat as I was, with the same face as I had. I am working to govern a large diocese for another so that I can be given a small one to govern on my behalf. In the meantime, the king has given me a small abbey of two hundred louis to prevent me from dying of hunger. If I am made a bishop, my lord, I will invite you to my coronation and I will often raise my episcopal hands to heaven for your happiness.[18]

Colbert tried to establish relations in Toulouse, but as the years went by, fully committed to the episcopate, did he begin to lose hope? He was "working to govern a large diocese", he says. In what way? We do not observe it. La Galaizière held the leading role and did not intend to give up his position. Obviously, the position of dependence in which he found himself weighed on him. As for the abbey of which he had become abbot, it brought him more inconvenience than income. Decadent, it

[15] Arch. O/1/234. Original Ms., fol. 15r-16r. Document transmitted by Madame Françoise Launay.

[16] *Dictionnaire biographique, catalogue sur les pensionnaires de l'académie royale de Juilly*, 1651–1828, p. 461.

[17] Arch. dep. Haute-Garonne, 1C 975, fol. 115–116v°, 25 October 1769.

[18] Toulouse, 17 June 1770.

had only six monks left. The abbey's income had dwindled. The accounts were confused. The monks proved to be "difficult". There were lawsuits. Reluctant to take legal action, Colbert refused to prolong the dispute, and at the end of 1768 told the director general of the commissaries of Lisieux that he would rather sacrifice his interests than undertake another trial.[19] Less than a month later he announced to him: "I will no longer meddle in giving any orders for the affairs of my abbey. From now on he would leave his management to his uncle Alexandre Colbert[20]". It was at this time that the former law student composed *Elements of the Law of Nature and Natural Morals,* published in Basel without imprimatur under the patronymic "Baron de C**". An exercise in overcoming the dissatisfactions of everyday life?

With no hope in Toulouse as long as La Galaizière was there, Colbert had little alternative but to be in Brienne's service. In a fit of temper, he had declared that he no longer wanted to deal with Val Richer's affairs. He kept up an assiduous correspondence with Mr Boudard, director of the commissaries of Lisieux. This correspondence is useful, not so much for the details it contains as for the places from which Colbert wrote, which allows us to follow his peregrinations. At the beginning of 1771, he was in Montpellier for the session of the Etats de Languedoc. During the month of March, he stayed in Narbonne with Brienne. On April 6, he writes from the Parc aux Dames abbey,[21] on June 7 from Massy.[22] In October, he is in Paris, rue d'Anjou, with the archbishop. He stayed there until the end of November when he planned to visit his abbey, but had to give up because he "could not make any fixed plans".[23] The following year he lived almost permanently in Paris, still burdened by the business of his abbey. It was there that he stayed most often until 1774, except for a few weeks in the summer spent in the Château de la Chapelle belonging to the family of the Controller General Orry, near Nogent-sur-Seine, or in the Château de Brienne.

At the end of 1773, in a letter to the director of the commissaries in Lisieux, Colbert began to talk about his return to the South. This

[19] Arch. dep. Calvados, F 5045, 2045/6, 11 December 1768.

[20] *Ibid*, F 5045/0239, 1 April 1769.

[21] Abbey located near Dury, in the south-east of the present-day department of Oise.

[22] Current department of Essonne.

[23] All this is in file F 5045 of the Calvados Arch. dep.

was slow to materialise. It was postponed until the following February.[24] Only at the end of September, from Sainte Assise, did he become more specific with the president Du Bourg with whom he had continued corresponding.[25] At the beginning of November he was still only in Montereau but announced his presence the following month in Montpellier for the annual session of the Estates.[26] Return slow to take shape, embarrassed by money worries. He urged Mr Boudard on several occasions to send him some.

As can be seen, uncertainty transpires from Colbert's correspondence. In Toulouse, however, La Galaizière, who had been less assiduous since the autumn of 1773, had other colleagues, notably Charles-Antoine-François de Beaumont d'Autichamp, with whom he was very close, deputise for him at the meetings of the *commissaires ordinaires de l'assiette*.[27] Since the summer of 1774, the epizootic—the rinderpest—which started in Turkey in 1769, was active in Flanders and the northern provinces of France in the following years, and was raging in Béarn, Gascony, southern Guyenne, and was getting dangerously close to Languedoc.[28]

[24] Arch. dep. Calvados, F 5045, Ph 0125/6/7; 0258/9.

[25] 27 September 1774: "I am leaving next Tuesday with my archbishop for Fontainebleau, Brienne, Montpellier and Toulouse, where I shall be at the end of December", Arch. mun. Toulouse, sub-series 5 S; Doucet-Seiden, Christine, "La présidente Du Bourg: diffuser et mettre en pratique ses lectures. Réflexions à partir d'un exemple toulousain", in Brouard- Arend Isabelle & Plagnol-Dieval Marie- Emmanuelle (dir.), *Femmes éducatrices au siècle des Lumières*, Rennes PUR, 2007, pp. 75–92.

[26] 4 November 1774, Letter to the bursar Boudard, Arch. dep. Calvados, F 5045/ 0264.

[27] He presided over all of them between 25 November 1773 and 22 November 1774. In *the Procès-verbal of t h e general assembly of the clergy of France held in 1772* Beaumont d' Autichamp, priest, canon of the church of Paris, vicar general of the diocese of Toulouse, is carried like being deputy by the second order of the proxy of Paris (p. 7). Chaumont de La Galaizière, also deputy with the assembly, is member of the office of the common expenses in company of Beaumont d' Autichamp.

[28] *Histoire générale du Languedoc*, ed. Éd. Privat, 1904, t. XIV, pp. 1231–1262; Dronne, Michel, *Bertin et l'élevage français au XVIIIe siècle*, thesis, Alfort, 1965; VALLAT, François, "Les épizooties en France de 1700 à 1850", *Histoire et Sociétés rurales*, 2001/1, vol. 15, pp. 67–115; *IDEM*, *Les bœufs malades de la peste. La peste bovine en France et en Europe (XVIIIe– XIXe siècle)*, PUR, 2009.

From Dependence to Responsibility

In the first half of November, the Intendant of Languedoc, Saint-Priest, taking up the provisions of the Council's decree of 31 January 1771 for the northern provinces previously affected, had issued orders to preserve Languedoc from the plague. He recommended limiting the movement of livestock, reporting suspicious cases to municipal magistrates, slaughtering sick animals and disinfecting contaminated stables. He asked his subdelegates to consult with the diocesan syndics. On 15 November, the syndic general Montferrier also asked them to inform him of the places where the troops soon to be sent could be housed. A plan was being drawn up. The idea was to establish a cordon sanitaire along the Garonne from Saint-Gaudens to the Tarn and then to the Aveyron. The extent of the territory to be monitored, the number of roads and waterways to be controlled, the dispersion of the habitat, the sinuous layout of the limits between Languedoc and Guyenne as well as the absence of a natural border made the task delicate.

The Estates had not yet met. Their session opened on 1 December. It was of course question of the epidemic, the cordon sanitaire to be set up and the order of the *Contrôleur général* to kill all the animals which appeared to be attacked. Then, as the intendant proposed to compensate the owners, the assembly decided to advance the necessary funds "to be counted later with the king".[29] Before the end of the session, on 25 December, Loménie de Brienne addressed a long letter to the priests of his diocese. "Who better than you can convince them..." [this refers to landlords], he told them, urging them to dissuade them from resorting to ineffective remedies and to keep him informed of the livelihoods of rural families affected by the scourge. He reserved the right to "provide for the needs of the unfortunate" and announced that he would soon be coming to Toulouse.

The plan of action that had been drawn up required good coordination between the intendant, the commander-in-chief of the province and also the Parliament of Toulouse, as the execution of the ordinances was suspended on their registration. As for the Estates, after their separation on 9 January they could not decide anything before their next assembly. They did not have an "intermediate commission" empowered to act in the

[29] Minutes of the Assembly of States.

meantime on their behalf. This condemned the diocesan base to impotence, as any decision, any loan or commitment of expenditure, in order to become enforceable, had to receive their authorisation. The diocese of Toulouse was in the front line, the most exposed to the plague. The correspondence that has come down to us, as well as the minutes of the assemblies of the assiette in 1775 and 1776 and the intermediate meetings of the ordinary commissioners, gives a fairly good account of the way the epizootic was experienced on the spot.[30]

At the end of December, the syndic of the diocese Besaucèle became impatient. The decree of the parliament authorising the execution of the orders was delayed. The promised troops had begun to arrive, but in insufficient numbers.[31] The archbishop, expected, stayed a few weeks. On 8 February, he attended a meeting of the ordinary commissioners. Colbert presided over the next one, on 22 April. The assembly of the assiette held on 22 May did not show any feverishness. The first measures aimed at monitoring and limiting communications, which had been reduced during the winter, seemed to contain the epidemic. It expressed in strong terms "its admiration and gratitude towards the prelate benefactor of its people" as well as its thanks to the baron of Cadignan in charge of commanding the troops of the cordon sanitaire.[32] On 7 June, Colbert, replying to a letter from Madame du Deffand, wrote to her again: "the cattle disease has not yet been eradicated in our cantons [...] our harvests have the best appearance in the world".[33] The same day, however, from Auch where he was, Baron Cadignan sounded the alarm:

> "The disease is back in full force everywhere, and the most energetic measures must be taken before it is too late. The archbishop must be informed as soon as possible".[34] On 19 July, before the ordinary commissioners of the diocese, his words were even more dramatic: there was no more time to lose, all the animals in the infected stables, whether sick or still apparently healthy, had to be slaughtered, otherwise, in eight days,

[30] *Ibid*, 1C 963, fol. 233 *ff*, 1C 964, fol. 24 *ff*, 1C 976, fol. 80–89.

[31] Arch. dep. Haute-Garonne, 1C 839, letters of 21 and 24 December 1774. Jean-François de Besaucèle, former principal lieutenant of the *sénéchaussée* and presidial of Carcassonne, former capitoul of Toulouse.

[32] *Ibid*, 1C 963, fol. 237.

[33] Yale University, Walpole Collection.

[34] *Histoire générale du Languedoc*, t. XIV, *op. cit*, p. 1245.

it would no longer be possible to save the plain of Revel and the Black Mountain, from there the mountains of Auvergne and even the whole kingdom where the plague will not fail to spread.

The area had no natural borders behind which to take shelter, except for its main rivers. Above all, nothing would be possible without the goodwill of the owners. Without the assurance of immediate compensation, they would never agree to sacrifice their animals. The unprecedented nature of this intervention can be seen, as the diocesan administration had no decision-making power. Impressed, the commissioners thought that they should "rise above the rules of prudence and circumspection which have always characterised their administration" and commit themselves to paying two thirds of the price of the healthy animals to be slaughtered on the spot, the other third having been promised previously at the last assembly of the states. The receiver of the diocese agreed to advance the funds at 5% interest. Abbé Colbert was instructed to send the deliberation immediately to the archbishops of Narbonne and Toulouse and to ask them to use their credit with the King to obtain the reimbursement of the advances made by the diocese.[35]

Since the Spring, Seignelay Colbert had been "governing for someone else" the diocese, as he had hoped to do in the past, an opportunity for him, given the circumstances, to demonstrate his administrative abilities. Was he the inspiration behind the proposal made by the syndic or, carried away by the urgency of the situation, did he agree to it? The receiver's agreement to advance the funds suggests that it had been agreed beforehand. One question, however, was there any chance that this initiative would be endorsed by the Estates? It was in the spirit of Brienne's letter to the priests of the diocese and Colbert could claim proximity to him. But the government, the intendant and even the syndic general Montferrier, far from Toulouse, did not measure the gravity of the situation.[36]

In Montpellier, the epidemic was thought to be exaggerated. An instruction given to the Count of Périgord ordered him, in order to stop the contamination, to move all the infected cattle to the left bank of the Garonne in order to create a protection zone. The diocesan commissioners were moved and managed to convince him of the folly of the project. It would only spread evil. The subdelegate of Toulouse, on the

[35] Arch. dep. Haute-Garonne, 1C 976, fol. 82–83.

[36] *Ibid*, 1C 839, letter from syndic general Montferrier to Besaucèle, 8 August 1775.

other hand, announced that he had received orders from the intendant not to pay the promised third of the healthy animals. The news could destroy the confidence of the owners, who were now hostile to allowing their livestock to be sacrificed. Meeting on 18 August, the commissioners deliberated on paying the full price of the slaughtered animals. But the cost appeared to be quickly become impossible to bear. The receiver was worried. On 26 September, it was decided to suspend the compensation. The expenditure already amounted to 103,929 livres 6 sols.

Colbert had to work hard throughout the period, effectively assisted by the syndic Besaucèle who, in addition to his syndicate duties, managed the temporal affairs of Brienne.[37] Colbert and Besaucèle also remained in constant contact, even when the vicar-general was away from Toulouse for a few days at the château de Bonrepos, as at the end of August 1775, when he set an example by attending the slaughter of the cattle and visiting the neighbouring communities with the Marquis de Caraman.[38] Having become close to Baron de Cadignan, whose vigilance he appreciated and whose advice he listened to, Colbert shared with him the feeling that the defence against the epidemic was not only the business of the diocese and the province of Languedoc, but that of France. Hence his impatience with the procrastination, his alarmist letters to the counts of Moncan and Périgord,[39] and the initiatives taken in agreement with the syndic. He remained in contact with Loménie de Brienne who approved their action.[40] This was in keeping with the reputation the Archbishop held dear. In the face of the plague, it was necessary to help but also to honour the commitments made. At the end of the year, Colbert went to the assembly of the Estates in the place of Brienne. Before it broke up, the assembly committed itself to paying the expenses caused by the pandemic up to 1,200,000 livres.

[37] Tournier Clément, *Le mesmérisme à Toulouse,* suivi de *Lettres inédites sur le XVIIIe siècle d'après les Archives de l'Hôtel du Bourg*, Toulouse, Imp. Saint-Cyprien, 1911, letter from Abbé Colbert to the President of the Bourg, 27 June 1774, pp. 100–102.

[38] *Ibid*, 1C 839, his letters to him always begin with 'My dear syndic'.

[39] *Ibid*, 1C 839, *Histoire Générale du Languedoc*, t. XIV, p. 1149. The count of Moncan marshal of camp, commander in Languedoc, the count of Périgord, commander in chief of the province.

[40] *Ibid*, 1C 839, 24 August 1775, letter from Colbert to Besaucèle.

The minutes of the assiette of 1776, which are highly complimentary of Colbert,[41] emphasise his determination and the zeal he had shown throughout the previous year. His persuasion of the Estates and his credit had produced the best effect. The vicar-general was presented as the saviour of the diocese. Let us not be fooled. If he had not held the pen himself, Colbert knew the terms of the deliberation, ready before the assembly took place. Circumstances had allowed him to play an unprecedented role and to impose himself.

From then on, Colbert took the first place at the diocesan assiette, presided over its annual assembly and did not leave it to anyone else to convene the ordinary commissioners, except when he represented the archbishop who was unable to attend the Estates.[42] The after-effects of the epizootic were fading. Let us only point out, because it is a characteristic of this assiette, the difficult relations maintained with the town of Toulouse. They had been tense during the epizootic because of a supply situation that had become permanently uncertain. The agreement on the work projects to be carried out and their realisation from the guarding to the diocesan territory also remained problematic.

To what extent was Colbert able to influence the relationship between the diocesan assiette and the capitouls in charge of the city's affairs? The latter jealously guarded against any encroachment on their territory and their freedom of action. One is surprised, however, when one learns the identity of the diocese's creditors, at the low level of participation by Toulouse society in the financing of the public works it was planning. More than two thirds of the funds borrowed between 1775 and 1780 came from charities, the "bouillon des pauvres" of the parishes, the general hospital and the women's religious houses of the city. The proportion, if we add the loans granted by clergymen in their personal capacity, amounted to more than 80%.[43] The laity, on the other hand, did not participate much. No name is known however among the lenders, no noble or parliamentary. In the neighbouring dioceses, the participation of charities, hospitals and women's religious houses in the loans made

[41] *Ibid*, 1C 964, fol. 23 *ff*.

[42] Thus in 1777, Arch. dep. Haute-Garonne 1C 976; Arch. dep. Calvados, F 5045, 0290/1/2.

[43] Arch. dep. Haute-Garonne, 1C 803, 804. Bouillons des pauvres des paroisses de la Daurade, du Taur, de Saint-Sernin, de Saint-Étienne. The bouillon of the sick poor of the parish of Saint-Étienne lent 53,120 livres during these five years.

by the dioceses for public works is everywhere important. It is higher in Toulouse. The explanation probably lies in the number of these in the city and in the abundance of funds from donations they had at their disposal.

We have little information on Colbert's relations with Toulouse between 1775 and 1780. He continued to receive 1,200 livres each semester from the abbey of Val Richer, for which always thanked the director of the commissioners in Lisieux. The only traces are his efforts to bring John and Nicolas Barnewall, sons of Count Richard de Barnewall—"father of Toulouse masonry", by founding the *Saint-Jean* lodge on 2 December 1741—closer together and his continued exchanges with Presidente Du Bourg. Richard de Barnewall, of Irish origin, and his younger brother, who had emigrated to France, had agreed to make the elder Nicolas their sole heir following his marriage to Marthe Henriette Daguin, daughter and sister of a mortar president. The younger son claimed his father's share of the estate. The Abbé Colbert and the Baron de Puymaurin intervened. A transaction was concluded on 10 May 1779.[44] As for Presidente du Bourg, an open-minded person who hated intolerance, she had been seduced by the illuminist current of Freemasonry and became one of the only women initiated into Cohen's Chosen.[45] No definite conclusions can be drawn from these meagre clues, President Du Bourg, for example, did not share his wife's inclinations in this area. They simply suggest his assiduous and trusting association with the parliamentary milieu of Toulouse and his loyalty to his British roots.

On 14 June 1779, Colbert presided for the last time over the assembly of the diocesan assiette, on 6 April 1780 over a meeting of his ordinary commissioners. On the 24th, he arrived in Paris, three days later he visited Madame de la Vallière, who was staying with Madame du Deffand. He dined in good company with her on several occasions, at least until August.[46] He was consecrated bishop of Rodez on 22 April of the following year.

[44] *Ibid*, 3E 6486, fol. 111–124. All this according to Michel Taillefer, *La Franc-maçonnerie toulousaine…*, *op. cit.* p. 18 *sq.*

[45] Taillefer Michel, *op. cit.* and Dousset-Seiden Christine, art. cit.

[46] Mme Du Deffand, *H. Walpole Paris Journals*, pp. 459, 460, Lewis Walpole Library, Yale University.

Conclusion

Seignelay Colbert reached his goal. His was a curious journey, both singular and representative. He arrived from Scotland as a teenager, endowed with good abilities, he had the talent to make himself noticed, which opened the door to the Parisian salons and enlightened circles, and he knew not to be forgotten. As soon as he could, he would not rest until he appeared again. Without fortune, without support, except for those he knew how to attract, he was lucky enough to be distinguished by a prelate of the future and to enter his service thanks to Smith's trip to France.

However, he did not escape the uncomfortable condition of vicar-general, uncertain and entirely dependent on his patron. This condition often remains obscure and poorly documented. We know very little, for example, about Loménie de Brienne's other vicars-general. The example of Colbert, precious in this respect, sheds at least some light on this.

The diocesan base, partly due to Brienne's long absences from Toulouse, enabled him to stand out at the Estates of Languedoc, in front of the representatives of the royal power, the intendant and the commander-in-chief of the province, and to prove his ability to "govern a diocese" in rare circumstances. He is served by events.

The diocese of Rodez welcomed an experienced prelate, well versed in the institutions of a "Pays d'état". Colbert was in fact called upon to administer more than a "small diocese", since he also became President of the Provincial Assembly of Haute-Guyenne.

CHAPTER 5

An Eighteenth-Century Man Envisaged: An Analysis of a Moral Treatise by Seignelay Colbert of Castlehill

Timothy R. Day

Abstract Perhaps influenced by his long association with Adam Smith, whose teaching in Glasgow included *Lectures on Jurisprudence* (1762–1763), Seignelay Colbert of Castlehill published a treatise in 1770, *The Elements of the Law of Nature and Natural Morals*, which Timothy R. Day has examined. Colbert's treatise is a characteristic representation of a typical Enlightenment trend of thought, which would become quite dated only a few decades after the beginning of the nineteenth century. Such a treatise produced by a Catholic clergyman shows that the influence of the philosophes, to whom Colbert refers in his work, reached its peak in the second half of the eighteenth century. This influence can be seen

T. R. Day
Central Michigan University, Mount Pleasant, MI, USA

T. R. Day (✉)
Wichita State University, Wichita, KS, United States
e-mail: day1tr@cmich.edu

A. Alcouffe (ed.), *Seignelay Colbert de Castlehill (1735-1811)*,
https://doi.org/10.1007/978-3-031-75273-5_5

in the writings of Colbert, who places himself in the sphere of philosophy [one can speak of the Catholic Enlightenment]. Colbert's treatise focuses on the role of man in the natural order of things, presenting the objects of his study to those who have the natural right to maintain peace and concord between nations. Sometimes abstract, Colbert's treatise nevertheless attempts to give a technical basis to his ideas on human nature. Colbert's treatise is valuable as a historical document because its contents bring a certain clarity to an increasingly complex discourse on the Enlightenment.

Keywords Enlightenment · Counter-enlightenment · Deism · Natural Law · Catholic association · Philosophes · Eighteenth-Century Catholicism · *Gegenaufklärung* · Aristocratic order · Progressive thought

Introduction

Seignelay Colbert de Castlehill (1735–1811) is an intriguing figure in the history of modern France. As a Catholic bishop, he became a member of a French ecclesiastical establishment with a long tradition of wielding influence and power in pre-revolutionary society. This fact would not be particularly notable without several other features that distinguished Colbert's position in French society, which was punctuated by his involvement in the French Revolution and his move to Britain in the Revolution's aftermath. His birth in Scotland and his familial ties there also provide some transnational distinction.[1] There is no doubt that Colbert would have remained an obscure historical figure, like so many of his contemporaries, were it not for the course of revolutionary events in his lifetime. He is chiefly remembered for playing a decisive role in providing episcopal support for the revolutionary aspirations of the commoners in the Estates-General in the crucial early stages of the French Revolution. He is also remembered for having refused the oath to the Civil Constitution of the Clergy, thus rejecting subsequent revolutionary reforms imposed on the Gallican Church during the 1790s and

[1] Alain Alcouffe and Phillipe Massot-Bordenave, *Adam Smith in Toulouse and Occitania: The Forgotten Years* (2020). See Alcouffe's and Massot-Bordenave's book for the details on Colbert's Scottish connections.

early 1800s.[2] The end of Colbert's career, which he devoted to upholding the Catholic sectarian network known as the Petite Église, is a good representation of the pivot in French society from the Ancien Régime to the post-revolutionary context of laïcité.[3]

While it is impossible to ignore this revolutionary history in hindsight, this present article analyzes a moral treatise that Colbert published before the Revolution in 1770 entitled *Les Élémens du Droit de la Nature et de la Morale naturelle*. It was also published before Colbert became the Bishop of Rodez in 1781, taking the place of his mentor Lomenie de Brienne. By itself, Colbert's treatise is both impressive and bemusing for its length and circuitous logic. It is therefore necessary to review the pre-revolutionary intellectual climate in France to better understand the rationale behind the publication of this specific work. It is also necessary to frame Colbert's ideas in the context of certain historiographical concepts on the French Enlightenment with reference to key social and religious developments in eighteenth-century France.

Seignelay de Colbert de Castlehill's treatise, which begins with an appeal *Aux nations civilisées et policées de l'Europe*, pursues a rational connection between morality and its communal manifestations. Colbert applies this rational connection to civil societies composed of individual humans who possess the ability to employ their faculties to bring about morally desired ends. Colbert frames his thesis in juxtaposition to the hard sciences, which he claims have an adequate degree of evidence to support their systematic application. In contrast, he notes that the sciences of "natural right" and "moral right" are based on widespread assumptions. Colbert therefore seeks to systematically explore a "new route" to demonstrate the moral basis of civilization.[4]

[2] Andrew Moore, "A bishop of the Ancien Regime," (1988), 8–9. See this dissertation for the details of Colbert's pre-revolutionary life and career.

[3] C. S. Phillips, *The Church in France, 1789–1848: A Study in Revival* (1929; repr., 1966), 153. On the post-revolutionary religious and intellectual shift, C. S. Phillips writes, "Under the shock of a common misfortune a *rapprochement* between clergy and *noblesse* had been effected from both sides. The former had shed its liberalism, the latter its skepticism."

[4] All full-length quotes from Colbert's work in French are the author's translations. These original French quotes can be found in the French version of this edited volume: Timothy Day, Aperçu d'un homme du dix-huitième siècle: analyse d'un traité de morale de Seignelay Colbert de Castlehill (2022), 115–132.

Although Colbert writes about God in relation to the existing moral and physical order, he uses unmistakably Enlightenment-influenced terms to describe God, terms such as the Supreme Being, the Creator Being, Providence, and the Supreme Divinity. Nevertheless, the focus of the treatise remains squarely on "the nature of man." Colbert claims that established moral truths can be ascertained without dwelling upon their apparent acceptance across nations. Colbert further claims that it does not matter if moral truths are understood within "human hearts," or if they are revealed in God's commandments; he asserts that the "philosophic spirit" of the eighteenth century demands that these truths be discovered in nature and in the associated order that humans follow in their actions. Thus, Colbert envisages human nature, allowing for God as a "first occupant," as possessing the capacities to fulfill a natural moral law. Sharing the benefits of these capacities with others, according to Colbert, is the key to maintaining a state of innocence. The human interplay between morality and the natural order must take the form of recompenses or punishments. Adverse effects arrive especially when humankind does not systematically apply its faculties to objects that are developed with a proper utility in mind. Conversely, when properly applied, these objects serve as signs of peace, happiness, and flourishing in the present life.[5]

The Social and Religious Dynamics in Pre-Revolutionary France

We can learn more about Seignelay de Colbert's ideas by taking a closer look at the author himself and the social and religious dynamics of French society in the decades immediately preceding the French Revolution. A detailed consideration of these dynamics raises several questions, most

Colbert uses the name Monsieur le Baron de C. in the treatise's title, referred to as Colbert in the footnotes hereafter. Monsieur le Baron de C. « *Aux Nations civilisées et policées de l'Europe*» in *Les Elémens du Droit de la Nature et de la Morale Naturelle* (Basel, 1770), iii–v.

[5] Ritchie Robertson, *The Enlightenment: The Pursuit of Happiness, 1680–1790* (2021), 18–19. Robertson writes, "A dimly imagined happiness might exist beyond the grave, but the prospect could not compensate for the shortcomings in this life…Enlighteners wanted to attain it before death. To them, happiness was not, as it often is in present-day discussions, simply a subjective state…it meant attaining the preconditions for personal happiness, including domestic affection, material sufficiency and a suitable degree of freedom."

notably: Why would a cleric of the Roman Catholic Church such as Abbé Colbert write a treatise infused with language and reasoning that appear alien to the traditional teachings of the Church? Did Colbert view himself as representing eighteenth-century Catholicism with this writing? Given the directed nature of his arguments and exhortations, did Colbert view his important ecclesiastical position as a help or a hindrance in reaching a wide stratum of elites across Europe? Colbert's life journey may have had modest origins, but once accepted into the higher echelons of French society, he clearly took advantage of the opportunities this afforded to make his own contribution to Enlightenment culture. As the authors of "The French Enlightenment Network" note, "The preponderance of aristocrats thus highlights the alliance between gens de lettres and gens du monde that appears to lie at the heart of the French Enlightenment network."[6] Colbert's writing reveals a comfortable attitude when addressing high society. Indeed, his writing is devoid of those social and religious exigencies that would come to characterize the post-revolutionary context.

Colbert's writing shows that he hoped it would have an overall positive effect by appealing to the ruling classes in distinct civil societies in a European setting. The topics and language that Colbert employs reveal a preoccupation with social order and the interests that uphold this order. This preoccupation is also reinforced by Colbert's repetitious style, which comes across as one trying to subdue the reader with systemic logic. Even Colbert's title displays this repetitious approach, which describes the nations he addresses not only as *civilisées*, but also as *policées*; these words are nearly synonymous in English, where *policées* might be translated as "ordered" or "governed" in this context.

Colbert's ideas were clearly not considered radical in the latter stages of the Enlightenment, even if they were propagated by a prominent member of the high clergy. "Most of the radical writers, along with the clergy, government and monarch," remarks S. J. Barnett, "also accepted that the Church was necessary to promote an 'acceptable' social peace: without the public assertion of post mortem rewards and punishments, what value would oaths have had?"[7] Indeed, the efforts of both religious

[6] Maria Teodora Comsa et al., "French Enlightenment Network," (September 2016): 512.

[7] S. J. Barnett, *The Enlightenment and religion: The myths of modernity* (2003), 59.

and lay persons to create an atmosphere of social and scientific progress were typical in Western countries of the time.[8] Colbert's treatise is far from a traditional pastoral letter, so he apparently believed that it was within his purview to reach beyond his confessional diocesan audience to a network of transnational elites.[9] The attempt to reach wider audiences can be viewed as part of a secularizing tendency that increasingly took hold over the course of the eighteenth century. Regarding religious texts, Ralph Gibson notes:

> In principle, books were subject to government authorization; the proportion of religious titles in the authorization lists fell from a third in the 1720s to a fifth in the 1750s, and a tenth on the eve of the Revolution...the absolute number of religious books increased, but other categories increased faster, particularly those of literature, science, and the arts...It seems, however, quite clear that during the second half of the eighteenth century the educated lay (male) elite lost its taste for religious literature; novels, plays, and political works began to take over.[10]

While explicitly Christian literature still circulated widely, it was joined by a wide range of works with more worldly preoccupations, which included secularized forms of philosophy that were most prominent in France. It was not so much that Colbert's treatise represented eighteenth-century Catholicism, but rather that the demand for philosophical works created a ready market for opportunistic writers to fulfill. Additionally,

[8] Alexander Dick, "Moderate Enlightenment and Religious Controversy in Eighteenth-Century Scotland," (Winter 2017): 507. This appears to have been the case in Scotland as well. Dick describes the moderate influence of the Protestant clergy during the Scottish Enlightenment in the realms of morality and practical scientific application.

[9] Alain Alcouffe and Phillipe Massot-Bordenave, *Adam Smith in Toulouse and Occitania: The Forgotten Years* (2020), 62. The authors note, "The last paragraph of the letter tells us that despite his lack of means, Abbé Colbert was nonetheless anxious to appear in the Parisian salons or at least not to be forgotten. In Paris, he frequented the Countess of Gacé, a member of the upper ranks of the French nobility close to the Matignon family."

[10] Ralph Gibson, "Catholicism under the *ancien régime*," "The warning lights of dechristianization," "The causes of dechristianization," in *A Social History of French Catholicism, 1789–1914* (1989), 1–14. Gibson's introduction provides a synopsis of research which has pointed to a relative decline in French Catholicism during the latter half of the eighteenth century, though religious practice remained high in absolute terms and in certain regions.

whether one belonged to a priestly order or to a lay Catholic association, an emphasis on promoting the general welfare and fulfilling civic obligations began to take root in Colbert's time.[11]

While the broad topics addressed may appear presumptuous on the part of Colbert, this literary approach makes more sense in light of the changes in public discourse that had developed in France since the latter half of the seventeenth century. The origin of this discourse was elitist in temperament and was driven in large measure by high churchmen themselves or those educated by the ecclesiastical establishment. In "The Fabrication of the Philosophe: Catholicism, Court Culture, and the Origins of Enlightenment Moralism in France," Damien Tricoire describes the late seventeenth-century debates among the Jansenists, Jesuits, and Rigorists over the adaptation of ancient pagan philosophy to a modern, Christian context. He writes, "Philosophy was meant to enhance religion: it opened the way to an understanding of God's greatness through the study of nature. It also taught the existence of God and his unity; many pagan philosophers had discovered these principles through reason alone. In modern times, therefore, philosophy was not only useful, but was also necessary for religion."[12] Tricoire identifies the Jesuits as the primary agents adopting this position, and although it was never wholly accepted (especially by the Jansenists), the Rigorists eventually established philosophy as an acceptable vehicle for the moral improvement of society. Through this formative intellectual period, the Catholic Church held unrivaled influence at the French Royal Court, which served as a focal point for debates of crucial national and international importance. While the philosophic shift became more humanistic in the eighteenth century, Catholicism in France was, indirectly in the least, involved in the dialectic process that gave rise to the more distinctly Enlightenment-influenced discourse recognizable in Colbert's treatise.

[11] David Garrioch, "Man is Born for Society," (Spring 2017): 108. Garrioch's article focuses on the development of Catholic lay confraternities in Paris and Milan during the eighteenth century. He notes their gradual secularization, especially in France in the latter half of the eighteenth century. Garrioch notes, "As religious associations, of course, they encouraged Christian charity and stressed mutual consideration and concern, in the present world and in the afterlife. This operated both within the confraternity, whose members were supposed to have a particular responsibility for each other and, more broadly, within the wider urban community and indeed the whole Catholic world."

[12] Damien Tricoire, "The Fabrication of the Philosophe: Catholicism, Court Culture, and the Origins of Enlightenment Moralism in France," (2018): 459.

The Distinctiveness of Enlightenment Thought in Eighteenth-Century France

We must next consider the French intellectual culture of the eighteenth century that facilitated the writings of a personage such as Colbert de Castlehill. It is fair to say that Colbert's ideas would be quite out of place for a committed Catholic writer who lived during the seventeenth century, as well as for one who lived during the nineteenth century. What was unique therefore about the literature in eighteenth-century France? It was in France that the Enlightenment reached its apogee under the influence of the philosophes, whose writings sought to challenge traditional Catholicism's stewardship of interpretive thought.

The distinctiveness of Enlightenment thought arose from a series of intellectual movements that influenced each other and became immersed in what has been called an "entangled history" by Jeffrey D. Burson.[13] Burson's articles on the subject detail some intransigent methodological and contextual issues that have, somewhat ironically, complicated the progress of Enlightenment scholarship. Burson's main points critique interpretations of a unitary Enlightenment on the one hand and of a "balkanization" on the other. While Burson's points are well taken, they downplay emphases in Enlightenment thought which contributed to a relative stasis in the dialectical process in the immediate pre-revolutionary context in France. According to Burson, "Even with the best intentions, attempts to construct a unitary metanarrative often result in the writing of contrary perspectives out of the Enlightenment, even where such perspectives arguably have their place."[14] It is not necessary, however, to dwell on counter-narratives in this respect. For example, Lars O. Erickson explores the general format of many Enlightenment-era works in *Metafact: Essayistic Science in Eighteenth-Century France*. Erickson writes:

> The essay usually does not belong to a discipline; but when it does, it speaks from an unorthodox position in order to express ideas that have no other enunciative structure...As part of an attack on the established views of nature, philosophers used it to vulgarize new ways of examining

[13] Jeffrey D. Burson, "Entangled History and the Scholarly Concept of Enlightenment," (Winter 2013): 3–9.

[14] Jeffrey D. Burson, "Reflections on the Pluralization of Enlightenment and the Notion of Theological Enlightenment as Process," (2012): 525.

> the physical world. The popular approach stressed individual discovery over authoritarian delivery...This mode promotes individual discovery as it demotes authoritarian interpretation and it appears in nearly all the essays of the eighteenth century.[15]

Out of this entangled history, it is therefore possible to delineate an Enlightenment tradition of thought that, in the process of going mainstream in the eighteenth century, caused a noticeable polarization of intellectual life around its principal ideas and its modes of delivery.

Though he includes some pointed critiques, Colbert's writing lacks any polemical edge against the movements of rationalism and natural philosophy. Hence, his work cannot be considered as belonging to the Counter-Enlightenment. Nor can Colbert's writing be seen as contributing to the rise of modern Christian apologetics, which responded to the neo-pagan currents of the eighteenth century.[16] Colbert's lack of both the polemical and apologetical strains of thought is important for properly situating his own ideas in the broader context of the Enlightenment.[17] In "The Counter-Enlightenment: Historical Notes on a Concept that Historians Should Avoid," James Schmidt explains the development of these distinctions, which entered the American lexicon via German theological debates. Referring to the German Counter-Enlightenment term *Gegenaufklärung*, Schmidt writes:

> To take but one example : in 1906, an article in the Munich journal Hochland employed the term not to refer to religious opponents of the

[15] Lars O. Erickson, *Metafact: Essayistic Science in Eighteenth-Century France* (2004): 45.

[16] This is not to say that the deists did not have their own polemics. As Peter Gay notes, "At least the deist wing of the Enlightenment had every right to claim that its polemics were designed not to destroy, but to purify religion...the philosophes subdued or exercised awe before Power or even before the grand regularity of nature." *The Enlightenment: An Interpretation, The Rise of Modern Paganism* (1966): 122.

[17] Jeffrey D. Burson, (2012): 528. Burson's work addresses various issues regarding the classification of different types of Enlightenments, such as the Catholic Enlightenment or the Religious Enlightenment. Burson's propagation of Theological Enlightenment seeks to resolve some of these issues by focusing on the Enlightenment as a process. Accentuating some of the difficulties involved, he writes, "Nevertheless, it remains impossible to bisect the Enlightenment into national or confessional variations without risking the disregard of the cosmopolitanism so self-consciously dear to philosophes, clerics and statesmen throughout eighteenth-century Europe."

> Enlightenment but instead as a way of designating materialist critics of religion…Down to the closing decades of the nineteenth century we can still find German writers laboring to defend what they regarded as a "true enlightenment" grounded on religious faith from various secular imposters.[18]

Much has been written about the French context with regard to the existence, or lack thereof, of any religious sentiment among the principal philosophes and encyclopedists. The enduring controversies over the religiosity of the French Enlightenment have in many ways reflected the controversies among the Enlightenment figures themselves. D. C. Potts and D. G. Charlton note:

> Despite his bitter anti-clericalism (which, for a short period in the 1760s, became a violent attack on Christianity and even on the person of Christ), Voltaire thus maintained belief in God and a universal morality against the atheist materialists. The same was true of the third great figure in the philosophe movement, Jean-Jacques Rousseau (1712–78). He shared many of the views that the philosophes had in common, and he contributed to the Encyclopédie, but his relationship with the philosophes was uneasy and he finally became convinced that they, as well as the common enemy, the Church, were persecuting him.[19]

The other figure in question here was Baron d'Holbach, whose strident atheism cannot be considered to have represented conventional Enlightenment thought. Nevertheless, the anti-clericalism of the French philosophes remained strong, although they drew on an older tradition of anti-clericalism in this regard. For clergymen such as Colbert, their aim was to integrate the Enlightenment's more popular ideas into an

[18] James Schmidt, "The Counter-Enlightenment: Historical Notes on a Concept Historians Should Avoid" (Fall 2015): 84.

[19] D. C. Potts and D. G. Charlton, *French Thought since 1600* (1974): 29.

acceptable social and religious paradigm.[20] These controversies over religion have, therefore, demonstrated the lasting influence and high stakes surrounding the ideas of the Enlightenment.[21]

Earlier in the Enlightenment, the debates between the Ancients and Moderns revealed some nuanced contours in the elitist struggle to promote moral renewal. Even in this earlier stage of the Enlightenment, the diffusion of ideas on experience, sense data, and the scientific method rendered ancient philosophy less tenable in the public sphere. As Peter Gay notes, "In the combat between the Ancients and the Moderns which agitated poets and philosophers at the end of the seventeenth century, the victory of the moderns was secured far less by literary than by scientific arguments."[22] It is easier to declare "the victory of the moderns" from our contemporary vantage point; it remains difficult to argue otherwise given the obsession for constructing supposedly "new" systems of morality during the eighteenth century. However, there was always an underlying tension against this supposed victory of modernity, which was symbolized by the influence of the Encyclopédie. In *Contemporary Reactions to the Enlightenment*, Cyril B. O'Keefe remarks:

> There is no doubt that the Encyclopédie with all its emphasis on factual knowledge, with its accent on the practical and the technical, with its exposition of a wholly empirical and positivistic philosophy, caught the fancy of the thousands who read it. And yet this work, and the whole movement which it symbolized, while they stirred up boundless enthusiasm,

[20] Ritchie Robertson, *The Enlightenment: The Pursuit of Happiness, 1680–1790* (2021): 18. On this sensitive balance, Robertson writes, "And the campaigns waged by some Enlighteners against the Churches—as well as the campaigns often undertaken within the Churches by believers who wanted to reconcile the doctrines of Christianity with the demands of common sensewere intended to demolish the falsehoods that kept people in unhappy intellectual immaturity and social subjection."

[21] Colin Heydt, "The Problem of Natural Religion in Smith's Moral Thought" (January 2017): 73. Heydt writes, "Adam Smith is one of the philosophers whose views on the relation of morality to religion have been very actively debated. It is accepted that Smith had unorthodox personal religious beliefs. The crux of the debate, however, is whether or not the God of natural religion is essential, in one or more ways, to Smith's moral theory."

[22] Peter Gay (1966): 310.

also raised serious misgivings about the outcome of the movement if the radical philosophes were to assume complete control.[23]

It was therefore left to establishmentarian figures such as Colbert to complement the ideas of the philosophes in his writings to reinforce the existing order.[24]

It would take until the nineteenth century for the social sciences to be properly established, but the efforts of thinkers such as Colbert to understand human motivations in scientific terms certainly helped lay the groundwork. This is because much of Enlightenment thought reflected positivist beliefs in humankind's freedom to rationally apply their faculties and to achieve beneficial results. As Robert Niklaus declares, "And in spite of the determinist belief of many of the philosophes, it is the constant awareness of this personal freedom so manifest in practice that enabled them to step into new pastures and to lay the foundations of much progressive thought in the nineteenth and twentieth centuries."[25] It would be mistaken, however, to construe all such "progressive thought" during the Enlightenment as fundamentally inimical to the aristocratic order.[26]

[23] Cyril B. O'Keefe, *Contemporary Reactions to the Enlightenment (1728–1762)* (1974), 94.

[24] Colbert, « Aux nations civilisées» in « Les Élémens du droit», xii–xiii. Colbert states, "I also ask, GREAT AND NOBLE ONES OF EUROPE, the protection & benevolence of your Lordships for this essay, which I venture to publish on the State, the Rights, the ends & the natural duties of man…RACE OF DEMI-GODS, POWERFULLY BORN OF ORDER, SUPPORTS AND ORNAMENTS OF THRONES, your heredity possession of this high rank, & your peaceful enjoyment of this high fortune will only appear more merited & more just, after the publication of this Work."

[25] Robert Niklaus, *A Literary History of France: The Eighteenth Century, 1715–1789* (1970): 389.

[26] Maria Teodora Comsa et al., op. cite (September 2016): 529. The authors note, "The considerable involvement of the state and of social elites in the French Enlightenment network is surprising, as it challenges a certain self-aggrandizing narrative about (and by) the philosophes…As our study reveals, the philosophes were just the tip of the Enlightenment iceberg: they could count on the eager attention and support of a large number of officials, high and low, many of whom were active participants in the intellectual polemics of the day (as witnessed by the substantial overlap between the "government" and "letters" networks)."

Colbert de Castlehill's Treatise as Enlightenment Contribution

Much like the *Encyclopédie*, Colbert de Castlehill's treatise includes a *Discours préliminaire*, which follows the introduction *Aux nations civilisées et policées de l'Europe*. After these long introductory chapters, Colbert dedicates the rest of his work to detailed analyses of the themes, terms, and concepts thus presented. The main body of the treatise is further divided into chapter sections with headings that specify the topic under examination. There do not appear any footnotes throughout the work or a bibliography at the end, but there is an appendix with a comprehensive list of terms with corresponding pages and sections. Colbert's writing is dense and often repetitive, yet it is also precise and carefully thought out and constructed. Colbert makes clear to the reader that the treatise he produced was a long-term project which took much dedication to bring to fruition.

In the *Discours préliminaire*, Colbert further explains the underlying principles for putting his ideas to paper. He does this by dividing the chapter numerically into 37 different bullet points, each one addressing specific aspects of his thoughts but building upon a general and successive logic. The logic behind each point tends to come back to the themes of natural order and morality from a humanist perspective, though Colbert does assert the importance of divine revelation in certain passages.[27] As Lester G. Crocker observes, "In their defense of Natural Law as the origin of our moral experience, most apologists took care to emphasize the necessity of Revelation as a completion and corrective to the intuitively perceived moral law which characterizes man as a rational animal."[28] But this is only one aspect of Colbert's list of acceptable and critical attributes to employ. After dispelling with supposedly unreliable recourses to truth, Colbert declares:

> The known Accuracy of Experience & its modesty, as well as the fidelity of the reports of Reflection & Combination, whenever they are enlightened by experience, attracted my confidence ; I decided to take Experience

[27] For Colbert's treatment of divine revelation, see Colbert, « *Discours préliminaire*» in *Les Élémens du droit*, xxxiv–xxxvi.

[28] Lester G. Crocker, *Nature and Culture: Ethical Thought in the French Enlightenment* (1963; repr., 2019), 19.

> with Reflection & Combination for my WAY, & Meaning, with Understanding & Taste, its auxiliaries, for my GUIDE, by rejecting the illuminations of painting, comparison, hypothesis & fiction, & the distorted suggestions of the Imagination, although it also employs Reflection & Combination, as does Meaning.[29]

Here we can see the influence of Enlightenment thought conveyed through Colbert's usage of language which aims to provide certitude to his social analyses and to cast doubt on other perceived methods of analysis. Colbert uses these guides to ponder the individual's place in "Universal Nature." Through these various intellectual exercises, Colbert connects the individual's pursued "ends" to a grand design in a rationalistic manner.

Colbert then identifies five different "societies" that an individual must take part in to fulfill an adequate communal role. The first of these is a *société générale de l'espéce humaine* and the second is "that with which men have to inhabit the same country in order to find under the natural law their respective well-being and to share the same fate."[30] The third society is family or blood relations, and the fourth is "that of friends or servants."[31] The fifth society that Colbert specifies is *la Politique*, or "that of men who inhabit the same country, participate in the same rights and goods, following, outside of the natural law, the same written law, and are protected by the same government."[32] When describing the communal obligations that bind these societies together, Colbert stresses the operative words *volontairement* and *librement*. Interestingly, Colbert also references "Mr. Puffendorf and other moralists,"[33] who he claims:

[29] COLBERT, « *Discours préliminaire*» in *Les Elémens du Droit*, xxv.

[30] Colbert, ibid, xix, xx.

[31] Colbert, ibid, xxi.

[32] Colbert, ibid, xxi.

[33] Detlef Döring, "Samuel von Pufendorf (1632–1694)," in *Dictionary of Literary Biography, Volume 168: German Baroque Writers, 1661–1730*, trans. Gunther Holst, ed. James Hardin (1996), 330. Döring states, "Samuel von Pufendorf is among the most significant German examples of the polyhistor, a type prevalent in the scientific world of the seventeenth century. He achieved an international reputation, above all, as a proponent of a secularized theory of natural law, a concept that greatly influenced the philosophy of law in the Age of Enlightenment."

> were right to limit themselves to saying that man was by his nature permanently and simply sociable, and not associated; but they were then wrong to count for nothing his independent state and his duties in this state, and not to clearly mark the different occasions when the sociable becomes associated, with his duties in each association; in a word, not to explain the fixed state as well as the mobile state of man, with his fixed and mobile duties.[34]

Curiously, Colbert says that he cannot go into much detail on the changing nature of human society and so he highlights society's unchanging characteristics instead. He states, "It suffices for me, after having rapidly clarified these principles of the State and of social duty, to observe that all these societies are equally founded or based on the rule of Law and the Moral law which I have designated as natural."[35] He further states that, "those, who are in the case of showing themselves to be members of these societies, and by the Order established therein, or because of their individual interest...it is not possible to reverse the nature and order of the things which establish them; this nature and this order are neither accidental, nor additive, nor fake."[36] In this way, Colbert illustrates the morality of an agreeable interchange between individuals who, although they each have their own goals, can contribute to a shared society by means of association.

Colbert also makes clear that he does not offer the legal perspective of *Politiques & des Jurisconsultes*; rather, he treats his subject matter only as a *Philosophe & Moraliste*.[37] This philosophical approach is evident throughout Colbert's work, which lacks a definite recourse to legal precedents, procedures, or canon law. Consequently, Colbert's interest lay in, "the principles which must serve as preliminary and as key to this subsequent association of man, to these particular positive laws, and to these duties, following the maxim of the School *ubi definit Ethicus, incipit Juriperitus*."[38] Thus, according to Colbert, it is necessary to define the ethical basis behind the natural order of things before beginning to set down juridical precepts. Colbert finishes his preliminary discourse by

[34] Colbert, op. cite, xxiv–xxv.

[35] Colbert, ibid, xxv.»

[36] Colbert, ibid, xxv.

[37] Colbert, ibid, xli.

[38] Colbert, ibid, xli.»

underscoring his claim that the real consequences that arise when individuals and associations eschew morality, even those holding differing beliefs and interests, prove the existence of an overarching law and order that, as far as we can tell, binds humanity together. Colbert returns to these themes in the next portion of his treatise, which he divides into five books and numerous smaller chapters.[39]

Colbert's Philosophical Moralism in *Cinq Livres*

Colbert opens his *livre premier* by noting three inter-related components of man: the physical, the intellectual (or *esprit*), and the moral. These components are further segmented by Colbert into features which constitute an integral whole and give man *une certaine realité* and the qualities of *un personnage*. Colbert describes each human domain with its own faculties, effects, and laws, and that each operates differently but not altogether independently. Colbert asserts, "It is relative to these points of view or aspects, that we weigh the man." He continues:

> If it were possible that a man existed who brought together only two of these principles, without joining the third, the moral principle, for example, and who did not show forth the tendencies of humanity on suitable occasions, paternal or filial love, and other affections that constitute the moral man, this being would not be a man, he would be a fraction of one at most, and if he showed only opposing tendencies, we would say that he was unnatural, of another species, we would call him a monster.[40]

With this quote, Colbert envisions humanity as having a certain civility that is inextricably social, with particular reference to the moral nature of man. Colbert even tries to compare the three components of which he speaks to mathematics and *des trois dimensions de la grandeur materielle*.[41] Colbert's reasoning is that any one dimension can only be considered an abstraction in the real world, just as his allusions to facets of human nature can only be understood as part of the reality of the whole.

[39] These "books" more so resemble chapters and these "chapters" more so resemble sections; together, they comprise 227 pages in total.

[40] Colbert, *Livre premier*, in *Les Elémens du Droit*, 3.

[41] Colbert, ibid., 6.

In his *livre second*, Colbert focuses on human motivations, or what he describes as passive or active movements emanating from the human heart. More precisely, Colbert writes of *le système du cœur*, in which the *substance* and the *base* consist of its *science morale*.[42] Colbert connects these motivations to external objects, to which the fulfillment of human desires must conform according to *l'Orde de la Nature & de l'Humanité*.[43] Colbert explains:

> My goal here is to demonstrate, that the morality of men would be defective and imperfect, if it only required this occupation from each, this corporeal work for them to accomplish it, & external deference to propriety which results from it. Man has an inward existence and a Morality exists that is related to it. The nature & order of things, and the situation of man even in a state of Nature, and away from his social connections, still require him to practice a Morality which is relative to his inward existence, to this moral faculty, that here I call *honor*, which directs itself towards the Moral Order as towards its object, & which has its own rewards.[44]

In this explanation, Colbert highlights the interlocking meanings of his claims. He reinforces the notion that mere physicality does not suffice to confer an ethical framework upon human desires. These desires must align with man's inward sense of morality and they must become actualized in relation to objects that yield beneficial results. Colbert makes it clear that these same principles are evident in social relations when individuals practice them in the context of a wider society.

Conclusion

There has rarely existed broad scholarly consensus on any given subject in the history of ideas. This is true regarding the eighteenth-century Enlightenment, which has generated much controversy among scholars over the essence of Enlightenment thought. These controversies are important because they seek to contextualize the intellectual shift the protagonists of the Enlightenment exerted on the Western philosophical tradition. Outside of the realm of academic debate, however, the view of

[42] Colbert, *Livre second*, in *Les Elémens du Droit*, 79.

[43] Colbert, ibid., 86–88.

[44] Colbert, ibid., 90.

the Enlightenment as a singular philosophical movement has remained a strong force in popular imagination. There are, in fact, good reasons for the persistence of this view, whether the Enlightenment's influence is perceived in positive or negative terms. This is because the Enlightenment consisted of some identifiable philosophical features that were popularized during the time period, especially by the French encyclopedists and the thinkers of the Scottish Enlightenment. Of these features, as we have seen, the idea we may call divine naturalism was particularly influential. This idea may be equated in many respects to deism, or what Ludwig Feuerbach later termed "religious naturalism."[45] This line of thinking derives spiritual inferences from the study of naturally occurring systems and, crucially, connects these inferences to the study of human relations. It is this idea that comes through mostly strongly in Colbert's long moral treatise *Les Élemens du Droit de la Nature et de la Morale naturelle*. Although Colbert makes clear on certain points that he was not promoting deism in his treatise, he largely employs the language and rationale of deistic thought. While it is difficult at times to follow Colbert's logic, his treatise is structured in such a way as to give the reader a chance to digest each part in measure. It is apparent that Colbert took great care in his writing to give each plausible vantage point adequate attention. One such vantage point is indeed Christian, but this is certainly not the main focus of the treatise. The main focus of the treatise is ultimately on the connection between the subservient nature of mankind to natural law and morality. Just as Christianity had been used to justify the existing order in previous centuries, the ideas popularized in the eighteenth century could be used to serve the same purpose. This appears to be the strategy Colbert undertook in his treatise, which was published in a climate of increasing radicalism and secularism during the latter stages of the Enlightenment.[46] As far as we can tell, Colbert was confident in the moral order that he outlines in his treatise to steer humanity toward

[45] Ludwig Feuerbach, *The Essence of Christianity* (1854): 102. Feuerbach notes, "The admiration of Providence in Nature…is nothing else than the admiration of Nature, and therefore belongs merely to naturalism, though to a religious naturalism…It is true that religious naturalism, or the acknowledgement of the Divine in Nature, is also an element of the Christian religion…But it is by no means the characteristic, the Christian tendency of the Christian religion."

[46] Jeffrey D. Burson, "Reflections on the Pluralization of Enlightenment and the Notion of Theological Enlightenment as Process," (2012): 529. Burson notes, "With a religious Enlightenment that emerged as a house divided against itself, and careening

peace and cooperation. Overall, Colbert's ideas embody a critical juncture in the pre-revolutionary context that reflected the pervading influence of the philosophes.[47] This is evident from the terminology Colbert's treatise employs, its relational logic, its moral emphases, and the unitary and comprehensive worldview it attempts to convey.

References

ALCOUFFE, Alain. *Seignelay Colbert de Castlehill (1735–1811): Un évêque entre Lumières écossaises et Contre-Révolution.* Toulouse: Presses de l'Université Toulouse 1 Capitole, 2022.

BARNETT, S. J. *The Enlightenment and religion: The myths of modernity.* Manchester and New York: Manchester University Press, 2003.

BURSON, Jeffrey D. "Entangled History and the Scholarly Concept of Enlightenment." *Contributions to the History of Concepts* 8, no. 2 (Winter 2013): 1–24.

BURSON, Jeffrey D. "Reflections on the Pluralization of Enlightenment and the Notion of Theological Enlightenment as Process." *French History* 26, no. 4 (2012): 525–537.

C., Monsieur le Baron de. *Les Élémens du droit de la nature et de la morale naturelle.* Basel, 1770.

CHARLTON, Donald G. and Denys C. Potts. *French Thought since 1600.* London: Methuen, 1974.

COMSA, Maria Teodora, Melanie CONROY, Dan EDELSTEIN, Chloe SUMMERS EDMONDSON, and Claude WILLAN. "French Enlightenment Network." *The Journal of Modern History* 88 (September 2016): 495–534.

Crocker, Lester G. *Nature and Culture: Ethical Thought in the French Enlightenment.* 1963; repr., Baltimore, Maryland: John Hopkins University Press, 2019.

DAY, Timothy. « Aperçu d'un homme du dix-huitième siècle: analyse d'un traité de morale de Seignelay Colbert de Castlehill. » In *Seignelay Colbert de Castlehill (1735–1811): Un évêque entre Lumières écossaises et Contre-Révolution.*

towards a desacralization of both monarchy and Catholic Church in France, the Enlightenment of both the high-brow philosophes and the often more radical underground could emerge as a third wave of secular reformers."

[47] Andrew Moore, op. cite (1988), 18. As Moore's dissertation notes, "Like Boisgelin, Dillon, Brienne, or his predecessor as Bishop of Rodez, Champion de Cicé, Colbert belonged to that group of churchmen...who were penetrated with the values and concepts propounded by the 'philosophes': a spirit of critical examination, a belief in reason, tolerance and individualism, a desire to deal, through reforms, with those phenomena limiting 'the greater happiness of all mankind': ignorance, disease, crime, and poverty."

Edited by Alain Alcouffe. Toulouse: Presses de l'Université Toulouse 1 Capitole, 2022.

Dick, Alexander. "Moderate Enlightenment and Religious Controversy in Eighteenth-Century Scotland." *The Eighteenth Century* 58, no. 4 (Winter 2017): 507.

Döring, Detlef. "Samuel von Pufendorf (1632–1694)." In *Dictionary of Literary Biography, Volume 168: German Baroque Writers, 1661–1730*. Translated by Gunther Holst. Edited by James Hardin. Detroit, Washington D.C., London: Bruccoli, Clark, Layman, Gale Research, 1996, 328–337.

Erickson, Lars O. *Metafact: Essayistic Science in Eighteenth-Century France*. Chapel Hill: U.N.C Department of Romance Languages, 2004.

Feuerbach, Ludwig. *The Essence of Christianity*. Translated by Marian Evans. London: Chapman, 1854. Internet Archive.

Garrioch, David. "Man is Born for Society." *Social Science History* 41, no. 1, Special Issue: European Civil Society (Spring 2017): 103–109.

Gay, Peter. *The Enlightenment: An Interpretation, The Rise of Modern Paganism*. New York and London: Norton & Company, 1966.

Gibson, Ralph. *A Social History of French Catholicism, 1789–1914*. London and New York: Routledge, 1989.

Heydt, Colin. "The Problem of Natural Religion in Smith's Moral Thought." *Journal of the History of Ideas* 78, no. 1 (January 2017): 73-94.

Moore, Andrew. "A bishop of the Ancien Regime." Honors diss., University of Bristol, 1988.

Niklaus, Robert. *A Literary History of France: The Eighteenth Century, 1715–1789*. London: Ernest Benn Limited, 1970.

O'Keefe, Cyril B. *Contemporary Reactions to the Enlightenment (1728–1762): A Study of three critical journals: the Jesuit Journal de Trévoux, the Jansenist Nouvelles ecclésiastiques, and the secular Journal des Savants*. Genève and Paris: Librairie Slatkine & Honoré Champion, 1974.

Phillips, Charles S. *The Church in France, 1789–1848: A Study in Revival*. 1929; repr., New York: Russell & Russell, 1966.

Robertson, Ritchie. *The Enlightenment: The Pursuit of Happiness, 1680-1790*. New York, NY: Harper Publishers, 2021.

Schmidt, James. "The Counter-Enlightenment: Historical Notes on a Concept Historians Should Avoid." *Eighteenth-Century Studies* 49, no. 1 (Fall 2015): 83–86.

Tricoire, Damien. "The Fabrication of the Philosophe: Catholicism, Court Culture, and the Origins of Enlightenment Moralism in France." *Eighteenth-Century Studies* 51, no. 4 (2018): 453–477.

Waterman, A. M. C. *Political Economy and Christian Theology Since the Enlightenment: Essays in Intellectual History*. Houndmills, Basingstoke, Hampshire and New York, N.Y.: Palgrave MacMillan, 2004.

PART II

From Rodez to Versailles

CHAPTER 6

Bishop Colbert de Castlehill in the *Nouvelles Ecclésiastiques*

Julien Béchard

Abstract Julien Béchard has researched the articles devoted to the episcopacy of Mgr Colbert de Castlhill by *Les Nouvelles Ecclésiastiques*, the Jansenist weekly published from 1728 to 1803. The Jansenists had many grievances against the French episcopate in the eighteenth century. They accused the first order of exercising despotic power over the second-order clergy and the lay faithful as a whole. The bishops were neglecting their role as defenders of the faith, allowing incredulity to grow throughout the kingdom, and making pacts with the Church's enemies, the Philosophers. Although Gallican, the episcopate was in continual conflict with the Jansenists and parliamentarians in order to defend the Church's interests, notably the independence of its jurisdiction. The first opposition newspaper, Nouvelles Ecclésiastiques, relayed this pejorative view of the episcopate to a wide audience, showing the evils of the Unigenitus bull for

English revised by Andrew Moore and Timothy R. Day.

J. Béchard (✉)
Institut Catholique de Vendée, La Roche-Sur-Yon, France
e-mail: j-bechard@ices.fr

A. Alcouffe (ed.), *Seignelay Colbert de Castlehill (1735-1811)*,
https://doi.org/10.1007/978-3-031-75273-5_6

the Church and exposing the persecution Jansenists suffered at the hands of ecclesiastical authority. The episcopacy of Mgr Colbert de Castlehill did not escape the harsh analysis of the Jansenists. For Les Nouvelles, the episcopacy of the bishop of Rodez was merely a continuation of that of Mgr Loménie de Brienne, archbishop of Toulouse from 1763 to 1788, one of the bishops most criticized by the newspaper. Both were accused of despotism and complacency towards the doctrine of the Philosophes. This paper focuses on the Nouvelles Ecclésiastiques' analysis of the person and episcopacy of Colbert de Castlehill, in two sheets dating from 1784 to 1789.

Keywords Colbert of Castlehill · Loménie de Brienne · Champion de Cicé · Jansenism · Philosophers · Episcopate · Canon law · Clergy

The Enlightenment century witnessed a real relentlessness against the French episcopate by the *Appelants*.[1] Initially, this substantive was used to designate a group of ecclesiastics, later extended to include lay people, who opposed the Apostolic Constitution *Unigenitus Dei Filius*, published on 8 September 1713. This papal bull condemned the work by the Oratorian Pasquier Quesnel (1639–1719), *Réflexions morales*,[2] in the form of 101 propositions extracted from the work. The Constitution plays a central role in the religious and political history of eighteenth-century France. It gave rise to a flurry of new ideas, conflicts and controversies that destabilised the Church from within, as well as the royal authority.

A friend of the Great Arnauld,[3] Father Quesnel is considered by his opponents and by historians to be the leader of Jansenism at the end of the seventeenth century.[4] As soon as the bull was published, fifteen bishops, including Cardinal de Noailles, Archbishop of Paris, rejected

[1] We have kept the French spelling because the Appel phenomenon was particularly prevalent in France. The term also exists in English: Appellants. Cf. "Appellants", in *The Oxford Dictionary of the Christian Church*, Oxford University Press, 1997, p. 93.

[2] P. Quesnel, *Le Nouveau Testament en françois, avec des Réflexions morales sur chaque verset pour en rendre la lecture plus utile et la méditation plus aisée*, Paris, André Pralard, 1693. BNF, cote: A-6398.

[3] Antoine Arnauld (1612–1694) was the leader of Jansenism in the seventeenth century.

[4] L. Cognet, *Le jansénisme*, Paris, P.U.F., coll. « Que sais-je ? », 1961, p. 96.

the condemnation. Then, in 1717, four bishops[5] filed a notarised deed at the Sorbonne calling for a general council to judge the relevance of the Roman document. They were quickly followed by around thirty prelates, universities, chapters and religious congregations, and soon by some members of the Paris Parliament. This was the birth of the Cause of the Appeal, supported by the *Appelants*. This substantive was claimed by those concerned, who preferred it to Jansenist. Despite the publication of the bull *Pastoralis officii* in 1718, which excommunicated those who refused to accept the *Unigenitus*, and the submission of cardinal de Noailles, the *Appelants* persisted in their cause.

Doctrinally, they were supported by a group of theologians from the Saint-Magloire oratorian seminary in Paris, where Pasquier Quesnel himself had taught before his exile to Holland. Acquiescent to the Cause of the Appeal, they developed little or no theological theories on morality and spirituality as in the seventeenth century, but rather sought to defend the teachings of the Jansenists of the *Grand Siècle*, particularly as transmitted by Pasquier Quesnel. In their view, the *Unigenitus* bull was the consecration of doctrinal errors in the Church, which had been going on since medieval times. On the contrary, the Jansenists of the previous century would have tried to restore the ancient teaching and practices of the so-called primitive Church, judged to be more in line with the teaching of the Gospel. In the context of conflict with the episcopate, which forced the acceptance of the bull, these *Appelants* continued the efforts of their predecessors by developing ecclesiological theses, very close to richerism, and reflected on the relationship between Church and State, particularly in the area of the delimitation of spiritual and temporal jurisdictions. The question of the rights of parish priests, as opposed to those of bishops, is central to this ecclesiology.

The *Appelants* were soon joined by members of parliament who were offended by proposition 91 of the Bull. This was opposed to the following quotation from the *Réflexions morales:* "even the fear of an unjust excommunication must never prevent us from doing our duty. One never leaves the Church even when it seems that one has been banished by the wickedness of men, when one is attached to God, to Jesus Christ, and to the

[5] They were Bishop Jean Soanen (1647–1740), bishop of Senez, Bishop Charles-Joachim Colbert de Croissy (1667–1738), bishop of Montpellier, Bishop Pierre de La Broue (1669–1720), bishop of Mirepoix, Bishop Pierre de Langle (1698–1724), bishop of Boulogne.

Church itself by charity.[6]" The Gallicans could not accept this condemnation, which reversed "the work of the legists who had done so much to free temporal power from all Roman tutelage[7]". With this proposal, the Bull reaffirmed that the subjects of an excommunicated sovereign no longer had to obey him and that the Pope had temporal power over kings. The public prosecutor Henri François d'Aguesseau (1668–1751) warned of the danger of this condemnation of a doctrine "which was truly that of France itself and which it had so often opposed to the threats of the popes[8]". The parliaments thus took up the cause of the part of the clergy opposed to Rome's interference in the affairs of the Church in France and in the internal politics of the monarchy. As soon as the *Unigenitus* Bull and the *Pastoralis officii* bull were published, the Parliament of Paris, followed by other parliaments, entered the fray. The conflict came to a head in the years 1720–1730, when the royal declaration of 4 August 1720, which ordered observance of the bull, and that of 24 March 1730, which made the bull a law of the realm, were forcibly registered in parliament.

The ecclesiastical appellants were continually vexed in their ministry by an episcopate that wanted to force them to accept the *Unigenitus*. To defend themselves, they hired lawyers who supported the Cause of the Appeal. In their memoirs, they contribute to doctrinal developments in ecclesiology and the relationship between temporal and spiritual jurisdictions, in favour of the temporal. In the 1720s, the Appelants realised that Rome and the monarchy would never agree to convene a general council to rule on the *Unigenitus* bull. They changed their strategy and decided to involve the general public in the Cause of the Appeal by means of public testimony. When the *Appelant* bishop, Bishop Soanen, was condemned at the Provincial Council of Embrun in 1727, the *Appelants* sought to "address the faithful directly through the distribution of writing specially conceived for this purpose[9]". The

[6] *Table raisonnée et alphabétique des Nouvelles Ecclésiastiques depuis 1728 jusqu'en 1760 inclusivement*, première partie, 1767, p. XXIII.

[7] M. Cottret, *Histoire du jansénisme,* Paris, Perrin, coll. « Pour l'Histoire », 2016, p. 153.

[8] Quoted by R. Taveneaux, *Jansénisme et politique*, Paris, Colin, coll. « U », 1965, p. 134.

[9] C. Maire, *De la cause de Dieu à la cause de la Nation. Le jansénisme au XVIIIe siècle*, Paris, Gallimard, coll. « Bibliothèque des Histoires », 1998, p. 379.

Nouvelles Ecclésaistiques ou mémoire pour servir à l'histoire de la constitution Unigenitus[10] are reinvested for this purpose. This newspaper had existed since 1713, but appeared irregularly. After Bishop Soanen's conviction, the *Appelants* decided to use it as a propaganda tool, "a key part of the strategy of appealing to the public [to revolt against the *Unigenitus* bull][11]". The journal became a weekly and appeared regularly from 1728. It went underground after being banned by the Archbishop of Paris, Bishop Vintimille du Luc (1655–1746), in 1732. It quickly became the leading newspaper for political and religious opposition in France. Among other things, the weekly presented current religious events linked to the *Unigenitus* bull, to show its harmful consequences. Although it claimed to reflect public opinion, it was actually the cause of the protest movement.

The *Nouvelles* was the product of a steering committee subject to the "spiritual authority of successive leaders[12]". The editors-in-chief were initially members of a core group that developed around the theologians of Saint-Magloire, who were the theorists of the second wave of Jansenism in the eighteenth century, then by their spiritual sons. After the expulsion of the Jesuits in 1764 from the Kingdom of France, two members of the Jansenist party dominated the steering committee of the *Nouvelles Ecclésiastiques*: Bon François Rivière, also known as Pelvert (1714–1781), and Gabriel-Nicolas Maultrot (1714–1803). Their ideas were relayed in the weekly and religious events were read and interpreted through their lens. Pelvert distinguished himself in his fight against the Enlightenment, while Maultrot defended the divine institution of the parish priests and criticised the policy of the French episcopate, which he described as despotic. During the episcopate of the Bishop of Rodez, the Jansenist struggle against the French episcopate was mainly focused on defending the rights of the lower clergy and fighting against the doctrines of the Philosophers, with the Roman bull no longer arousing passions.

Bishop Colbert de Castlehill did not escape the fate reserved for the episcopate by the *Nouvelles*. The newspaper approaches the episcopate of the bishop of Rodez as an extension of that of Bishop Loménie de

[10] We have used copies of the collection of the Institut Catholique de Toulouse, published in Utrecht. Cote: J324.

[11] C. Maire, *op.cit.*, p. 124.

[12] Ibidem.

Brienne (1727–1794), one of the bishops most flayed by the *Nouvelles*.[13] The prelate of Toulouse was described as an intriguer, more concerned with affairs outside his diocese than with its administration. He strongly supported the Sulpicians and their Molinist doctrines, thus demonstrating his anti-Jansenism. Colbert de Castlehill's predecessor, Bishop Champion de Cicé (1735–1810), was hardly appreciated by the newspaper,[14] participating in Bishop Loménie de Bienne's intrigues to serve the interests of his order. The bishop of Rodez could not therefore escape the harsh analysis of the Jansenists. We find a treatment of his episcopate in two sheets. The first, dates 10 December 1784, reports on the diocesan synod of the archdiocese of Toulouse, convened by Bishop Loménie de Brienne in 1782. In this context, the newsletter refers to a letter from Bishop Colbert de Catlehill announcing a pastoral visit in preparation for the meeting of a diocesan synod in the diocese of Rodez. The second sheet, dated 21 August 1789, deals more explicitly with his ministry during 1788 and early 1789.

We will highlight two aspects of Bishop Colbert de Castlehill's episcopate: a despotic episcopal policy and complacency towards the doctrines of the Philosophers.

In order to better to shed light on the presentation bellow, we propose to expand on the treatment of the Jansenist journal regarding Colbert's predecessor, Bishop de Cicé, and Bishop Loménie de Brienne, archbishop of Toulouse.

A Critique of the Despotism of Colbert's Episcopate in the Line of Maultrot

The *Nouvelles Ecclésiastiques* provide little information about Colbert de Castlehill's episcopate but highlight aspects that were relevant to the editorial line of the weekly. What the journalist first highlights, in line with Maultrot's thinking, was the despotism of Colbert's government.

[13] The *Nouvelles* devoted seventeen articles to Bishop Loménie de Brienne between 1768 and 1787. As articles directly concerning his episcopate, we can cite: *Nouvelles Ecclésiastiques*, 1771, p. 189; 1768, pp. 68 and 173; 1769, p. 180; 1783, p. 165; 1784, pp. 84, 141 and 197; 1787, p. 20.

[14] The bishop is dealt with in an article when he was still grand vicar of the diocese of Auxerre in *Nouvelles Ecclésiastiques*, 1765, p. 72, and mentioned in another article during his episcopate in Rodez, in *Nouvelles Ecclésiastiques*, 1778, p. 143.

The newspaper reports two examples of abuse of authority. The first example, an "act of despotism of which there are few examples[15]", took place during 1788. A Capuchin religious defended four magistrates of the presidial of Rodez, who had refused to exercise their function in accordance with the edicts of 8 May 1788 (judicial reform). Since the edicts had not been registered by the Parliament of Toulouse, the magistrates refused to take them into account by virtue of their oath to judge only cases in accordance with the laws duly registered in parliament. The reminder of the duty to respect an oath taken by the Capuchin provoked an outcry against him, forcing the bishop to take exemplary disciplinary measures. The journalist claims, though, that the prelate had sided with the Capuchin. However, "although peaceful in character[16]", he "did not have the courage to resist [the] repeated solicitations [of the Capuchin's opponents][17]". This act, described as despotic, was therefore the result of a weakness of character.

The second example concerns the drafting of an episcopal letter that exempted lay faithful from the obligation to abstain from meat three days a week during lent. We will return to this document in the second point of this communication. The journalist, considering this decision as unjustified, deplores that Bishop Colbert de Castlehill did not consult his chapter, and adds: "Bishops must govern in common with the priests of the Diocese, and not with strangers. The 2nd Order will sooner or later assert its imprescriptible rights, and they will have to be returned to them, despite any objections[18]".

In these words, we see the doctrine of Gabriel-Nicolas Maultrot. When he took the helm of the Jansenist movement in the late 1770s, he steered the movement towards defending parish priests in conflict with their bishop, at a time when episcopal authority was being reasserted. The weapon of Maultrot and his colleagues was the *Consultations.* A real battle against the episcopate was waged, expressed in the defence of parish priests. The eclipse of the parliamentary movement made it unnecessary to have recourse to the ecclesiology of witness to the Truth, which favoured a secularism that was the driving force behind parliamentary action in

15 *Nouvelles Ecclésiastiques (N. E.),* 1789, p. 136.

16 Ibidem.

17 Ibid.

18 Ibid.

spiritual matters. To defend second-order ecclesiastics, the canon lawyer used the doctrines of Edmond Richer and the Paris school (early seventeenth century) with theologians such as Jean de Gerson, Jacques Almain (1480–1515) and Pierre D'Ailly (1351–1420). In *Consultation pour les curés du diocèse de Lisieux*,[19] Maultrot denounced a plot by the episcopate to silence the parish priests and impose strict observance. The aim is not to abolish the parish office, but to strip them of the rights attached to their office. The canonist demonstrates the divine institution of parish priests, instituted by Christ himself as are bishops. In *Consultation*, he sets out to demonstrate the divine origin of the parish office and the authority of the diocesan synod. Referring to canon 6 of session 23 (De Ordine) of the Council of Trent,[20] he concludes that those in the ecclesiastical hierarchy are all of divine institution. They have all received the right to govern from God Himself. Parish priests and priests are the successors of Christ's apostles and not of the seventy-two disciples, the latter having been "entrusted with the same office[21]" as the apostles. Maultrot also bases himself on chapter 10 of the Gospel according to Saint Luke[22] and on the Tradition of the Church, with authors such as Theodulf and his Capitulary (797). He based on the Catechism of the Council of Trent, which "speaks of the Priesthood as comprising the Episcopate and the Priesthood; and of Bishops and Priests as interpreters and envoys of God to teach his law [...]. [Jesus-Christ] sent Apostles and Disciples throughout the world; and likewise let Priests, clothed with the same power as them, be sent forth every day[23]".

[19] *Consultation pour les curés du diocèse de Lisieux, à l'occasion du Mandement de M. l'Évêque de Lisieux, du 20 décembre 1773, et de son Instruction Pastorale du 13 avril 1774.* It was signed by Maultrot, Vancquetin, Viard and Camus. The document was censured by a Conseil d'État ruling dated 26 November 1775, as 'tending to disturb the order and harmony that should reign between the first and second orders of the clergy'. cf. *Arrest du Conseil d'État du Roi, qui supprime une brochure intitulée: Consultation pour les Curés du diocèse de Lisieux, etc.* BNF, cote: F-21191 (50).

[20] "If anyone says that there is not in the Catholic Church a hierarchy instituted by divine disposition, composed of bishops, priests and ministers, let him be anathema" (Canons on the sacrament of Holy Orders, canon 6, session 23).

[21] *Consultation pour les curés du diocèse de Lisieux*, p. 23.

[22] Luke 10, 16: "Whoever listens to you listens to me, and whoever rejects you rejects me."

[23] *Consultation pour les curés du diocèse de Lisieux, op.cit.*, p. 27.

The newspaper's view of the bishop is not more positive when he announced in an episcopal letter the holding of a synod, which would meet after a pastoral visit. To understand the nature of the comments made by the Jansenist weekly, it is worth remembering that Gabriel-Nicolas Maultrot attached great importance to the question of this institution. According to him, parish priests have the right to participate in the government of a diocese, a participation that is even more evident at the meeting of the diocesan synod. In this assembly, which is necessary for a non-despotic government of a diocese, the parish priests can judge with the bishop. The bishop cannot take any decision without consulting the parish priests at the synod. These same parish priests have deliberative vote in the synod and council, even on doctrinal matters. Maultrot thus opposed the bishops to the divine right of parish priests and the authority of the diocesan synod. In *Les droits du second ordre, défendus contre les apologistes de la domination épiscopale*, the lawyer defines the government of the diocese as follows: "If we absolutely want the Diocese to be a Monarchy, it will be an aristocratic Monarchy. The Bishop is Monarch if you like, but must govern with the advice and consent of the Priests. The law is published under his name but formed in the assembly of the Priests. The same applies to all matters important to the general good of the Diocese. It is the episcopal authority that regulates and decides them, but after deliberation in the assembly of Priests.[24]"

The problem with this future synod was the purpose of the assembly, which the newspaper directly quotes from the episcopal letter mandate: "to propagate there the path already traced by that great archbishop, our master and model[25]". The "great archbishop" was Bishop Loménie de Brienne, Archbishop of Toulouse, of whom the Bishop of Rodez was one of the great vicars before taking the episcopal see of Rodez. Brienne convened a diocesan synod in 1782, which the *Nouvelles* had already given a mixed review of.[26] When the prelate's mandate appeared, the *Nouvelles* hurried to renew the report on the synod of Toulouse in order to give an idea of what the synod of Rodez might be like. The one in

[24] G.-N. MAULTROT, *Les droits du second ordre, défendus contre les Apologistes de la domination Episcopale ou Réfutation d'une Consultation sur l'autorité législative des Évêques dans leurs Diocèses, publiée en 1775 en faveur de M. de Condorcet, évêque de Lisieux, contre les Curés de son Diocèse*, 1779, pp. 445–446. Bibliothèque de Port-Royal, cote: BPd968.

[25] *N. E.*, 1784, p. 197.

[26] *N. E.*, 1783, p. 121.

Toulouse partly met the expectations of the lower clergy regarding the increase of the *portion congrue*, which had long been demanded by the congruists. However, the archbishop did not consult the priests on the new measures. "M. de Brienne was alone his entire synod. It was he who planned and dictated everything [...] The ecclesiastics, parish priests and others [...] were put aside, they were not consulted.[27]" The journalist thus fears that the same thing would happen for the synod of Rodez. Nevertheless, as we know, Bishop Colbert de Castlehill ultimately did not convene a diocesan synod in his diocese.

An Episcopate Marked by the Influence of Incredulity and the Philosophers

A second criticism that emerges in these two articles was Bishop Colbert's connivance with the doctrine of the Philosophers and their disciples. In another article,[28] the journalist deplores the fact that the works of the Philosophers, with Voltaire as their leader, pushed their admirers, at best, to a relaxation of morality, or at worst, to commit acts of impiety and debauchery. We can see here the repercussion of Pelvert's statements,[29] a disciple of the theologians of Saint-Magloire, who distinguished himself in a fierce fight against the Philosophers, with the *Nouvelles* constituting a channel for spreading his ideas.

In addition to the indirect criticisms towards the behaviour of the Grand Vicars, who did not live "in the decency that is appropriate to their state[30]", it is the episcopal letter, mentioned earlier, that was strongly attacked, with the journalist taking the liberty to make remarks and an analysis of the episcopate of Bishop Colbert de Castlehill.

This document allows the consumption of meat three times a week during lent, due to a harsh winter that damaged the crops and weakened the health of the population in the diocese. The journalist first rejects the bishop's official intentions, using testimonies from priests in

[27] *N. E.*, 1784, p. 201.

[28] *N. E.*, 1781, p. 116.

[29] Pelvert is notably the author of *Lettres sur la distinction de religion naturelle et de religion révélée et sur les opinions théologiques*, 1769; *Examen approfondi des difficultés de M. Rousseau de Genève contre le Christianisme catholique*, 1770; *Lettres où l'on examine la doctrine de quelques écrivains modernes contre les incrédules*, 1776.

[30] *N. E.*, 1789, p. 135.

the diocese who said that the winter did not have as harmful consequences as the prelate had claimed.[31] By the end of the eighteenth century, the practice of granting dispensations from the obligations of abstinence by bishops was well established, when circumstances so required. In cases of begging, poverty, illness, fatigue, work or travel, a dispensation could be requested for a just cause, provided that alms were substituted for the fast.[32] However, these priests thought that the dispensation granted was not based on a just cause. Some of the parish priests of the diocese were so convinced of the weakness of the bishop's argument that they refused to publish the order. At that time, compliance with canonical requirements was a criterion of fidelity to Christ and submission to the Church.[33] For these priests, the episcopal order was not based on a just cause. Thus, in this episcopal act, Bishop Colbert was not demonstrating his fidelity to Christ and submission to the Church. That is why "good people said to each other: Is he Catholic? Is he a Christian?[34]"

The reason why the bishop may have allowed a relaxation in discipline is that "irreligion [which] is making frightening progress, especially since it has slipped into the Sanctuary (through the negligence of the first pastors [bishops])[35]". The journalist adds another "powerful", reason: "it is in order to be a little less blameworthy (in the eyes of men) in the intemperance of his guests and servants. It is very unfortunate that such complaints can be made about a bishop[36]". The bishop was accused of letting irreligion and the practices that resulted from the doctrine of the Philosophers spread. Worse, he would himself be taking part in these practices. He would encourage laxity in morals and discipline, which were very serious ills for the Jansenists. Moreover, in a leaflet from 1769, we think that we are able to recognise the prelate in the criticism of a grand vicar of Bishop Loménie de Brienne, who would have supported a troupe

[31] *Ibidem*.

[32] E. VANCADARD, « Carême », *Dictionnaire de théologie catholique*, Paris, Letouzey et Ané, t. 2, 1905, col. 1724–1750.

[33] J.-F. GALINIER-PALLEROLA, « Peut-on manger avec plaisir et sans péché ? La gourmandise dans les sermons catholiques français du XVIIIe siècle », *Lumières*, n°11, 1er semestre 2008, pp. 47–56.

[34] Ibidem.

[35] Ibid.

[36] Ibid.

of actors established at the Collège Royal[37] in Toulouse. The bishop of Rodez would thus have submitted to the spirit of the world, endangering the salvation of Christ's faithful in his diocese through his pastorals.

Bishop Colbert de Castlehill's episcopate followed in the footstep of his predecessor, Bishop de Cicé, and his «master and model[38]», Bishop Loménie de Brienne. This concludes our work on developing the treatment of the *Nouvelles* about these two figures. This will give us a better appreciation of the spirit of the Jansenist journal and shed light on the above discussion.

Bishop Champion de Cicé

The *Nouvelles Ecclésiastiques* devotes two articles to Bishop Champion de Cicé. The first article, dated 24 April 1765, deals with the Abbé de Cicé, the vicar-general of the diocese of Auxerre, who allegedly attempted to corrupt witnesses in favour of a priest of the diocese who was described as a "fanatic", that is, showing excessive anti-Jansenism and pro-Bullism.

The second article, dated 4 September 1778, mentions the action of Bishop de Cicé, then Bishop of Rodez since 1770, at the General Chapter of the Celestine Order. The prelate was sent by the Commission of Regulars to the chapter as a commissioner of the king to preside over it. This commission was created by the monarchy following a request from the Assembly of the Clergy in 1766. Louis XV formed the Commission of Regulars to force religious congregations to reform and to examine their financial situation. The commission decided to suppress nine religious orders, including the Celestines, and to close several abbeys. The most influential member of the commission was none other than Bishop Loménie de Brienne, who acted as the commission's rapporteur.

The General Chapter of the Order in 1778 was the last in its history. During the chapter, the majority of the capitulants voted for the suppression of the Order, preferring secularisation rather than reform. Bishop de Cicé was accused of having manipulated the vote because he pushed a Celestine for the election to the Generalate, Father Camille-Marie Saint-Pierre, who was in favour of this decision. The latter allegedly pressured his confreres to obtain the vote for secularisation. At the end of

[37] *N. E.*, 1769, p. 180.

[38] *N.E.*, 1784, p. 197.

the chapter, a *lettre patente* from King Louis XVI and a papal decree suppressed the order in the same year, after nearly five centuries of existence. The buildings were quickly sold by the clergy. The *Nouvelles* thus accused the Commission of Regulars of being a means for the high clergy to recover the property and benefits of the regulars in a context of financial crisis. The numerous suppressions of religious congregations, orchestrated by Loménie de Brienne, provoked strong criticism, forcing the dissolution of the commission in 1780.

Bishop Loménie de Brienne

We have noted seventeen articles dealing with Bishop Loménie de Brienne in the *Nouvelles Ecclésiastiques*.

The prelate is first described as placing his trust in disreputable subjects. Thus, he publicly honoured the superior of the diocesan seminary in Toulouse, a Sulpician named Mr Calvet,[39] who was zealous for the good of the diocese. In 1768, the archbishop had entrusted the direction of the seminary to the Society of Saint Sulpice, to the great displeasure of the journalist we examined.[40] This support was said to be due to the fact that the superior himself financed the extension of the seminary, adding a hundred more rooms to the building. Moreover, the Archbishop decided during his diocesan synod in 1784 to entrust the Sulpicians with the direction of the new minor seminary in Toulouse. In general, the *Nouvelles Ecclésiastiques* points out the increasingly important role that the archbishop granted to the Sulpicians in the diocese, as these clergymen were perceived as primary anti-Jansenists.

However, there were congregations that did not benefit from the prelate's favours. Thus, the Congregation of Saint Maur did not find favour in his eyes. During a somewhat heated exchange with the superior general of the institution, the prelate "said bitterly: What is your congregation after all? Jansenists and rascals[41]".

Thus, Bishop Loménie de Brienne was a convinced anti-Jansenist. In an article dating from 1774,[42] the journalist analyses his criticisms of

[39] *N. E.*, 1784, p. 84.

[40] *N. E.*, 1768, p. 68.

[41] *N. E.*, 1778, p. 205.

[42] *N. E.*, 1774, p. 69.

the Churches of Holland, which were opposed by the Archbishop of Utrecht. However, like other dioceses, he adopted the Paris Breviary for his diocese. His episcopal letter for the breviary was praised by the journalist,[43] who pointed out that the bishop had been accused of Jansenism by the Sulpicians.[44]

Finally, he is also described as a schemer in favour of his interests. For instance, there is the case of the General Chapter of the Celestines Order in Paris[45] where the prelate allegedly disregarded the law in the way he intervened in the chapter. His intervention was due to the conflict that had arisen between two factions within the chapter: those in favour of reforming the order and those who preferred the secularisation of the members. The former claimed that the chapter had been conducted in an irregular manner. Instead of convening a Special Chapter after invalidating the General Chapter, the prelate decided to hear the opinion of each religious in secret, rather than letting them confront each other. The journalist says that the assembly resembled a Confessional Tribunal, rather than a deliberating chapter. This intervention in Paris is to be compared with another criticism: the constant and long absence of the prelate from his diocese, which prevented him from properly governing it.[46] According to the *Nouvelles*, he was always occupied with other affairs elsewhere in the kingdom and left the care of Toulouse's affairs to his grand vicars, who were ignorant and frivolous ecclesiastics, unable to think or speak about religion.

Conclusion

The episcopacy of Bishop Colbert de Castlehill can be read through the prism of the doctrines of the Jansenist party, in particular the lawyer Gabriel-Nicolas Maultrot and the theologian Bon François Rivière also known as Pelvert. The bishop was seen as a despot who overstepped the rights of the lower clergy and was sympathetic to the doctrines of irreligion, but without the *Nouvelles* being able to prove his true connivance with the Philosophers. Although the French episcopate was regarded as

[43] *N. E.*, 1771, p. 189.
[44] *N. E.*, 1768, p. 200.
[45] *N. E.*, 1778, p. 144.
[46] *N. E.*, 1784, p. 141.

decadent by the Jansenists, the inspirers of the journalist that we have quickly commented on did not reject the episcopate as such. Maultrot defended the rights of priests while recognising the legitimate existence of the Catholic hierarchy. What was being fought against were behaviours and a conception of the episcopate that, according to him, were in disagreement with the ancient tradition of the Church, where priests enjoyed their full rights. The catastrophe of the *Unigenitus* bull would be to have indirectly reinforced the episcopal power, this same episcopate filled with errors and schismatic towards the true Church of Christ.

CHAPTER 7

The Rallying of the Clergy to the Third Estate in June 1789 and Its Consequences

Guy Astoul

Abstract Guy Astoul examines the attitude of the clergy in May-June 1789. Since the first meeting of the Estates-General on May 5, 1789, the clergy had been deeply divided on the question of voting by order. 19 ecclesiastics, including some bishops, were the first to join the Third Estate, on June 16, and the very next day they associated themselves with the proclamation of a National Assembly. This changeover was decisive in the oath taken in the Salle du Jeu de Paume on June 20. Due to the closure of the Salle du Jeu Paume, the session of June 21 took place in the Church of Saint-Louis, where 145 deputies of the clergy entered, led by Jérôme-Marie Champion de Cicé, Archbishop of Bordeaux, Jean-George Lefranc de Pompignan, Archbishop of Vienne, Jean-Baptiste de Lubersac, Bishop of Chartres and Seignelay Colbert de Castlehill, Bishop of Rodez. These prelates recognized the need for reform, and Lefranc de Pompignan was even elected president of the National Assembly on July

English revised by Andrew Moore.

G. Astoul (✉)
FRAMESPA (UMR 5136—Université Toulouse Jean Jaurès), Toulouse, France

A. Alcouffe (ed.), *Seignelay Colbert de Castlehill (1735-1811)*,
https://doi.org/10.1007/978-3-031-75273-5_7

3. This paper analyzes the extent to which this rallying was decisive in the evolution of events at a time when tensions were crystallizing between the upper and lower clergy. These tensions are linked to a deep sense of inequality, which is leading to divorce and a desire for profound change. Many clerics later regretted their commitment to the Revolution, notably Seignelay Colbert de Castlehill.

Keywords Colbert of Castlehill · Estates General · National Constituent Assembly · Lower clergy · High clergy · Abolition of feudal rights · Nationalization of clergy property · Civil Constitution of the Clergy

At a time of alarming financial crisis, Louis XVI appointed the Archbishop of Toulouse, Monseigneur Loménie de Brienne, as Controller General of Finances, in April 1787. He proposed tax measures that immediately provoked debate and tension. The rejection of new taxes was general and revolt was in the air. In the Dauphiné, an Assembly of the three orders met after a riot.[1] It called for a meeting of the General Estates and adopted a symbolic measure: the doubling of the number of representatives of the Third Estate. This Assembly was chaired by Jean-Georges Lefranc de Pompignan, the Archbishop of Vienne, who petitioned the King to adopt such a reform for the meeting of the General Estates. In March 1789, when the cahiers de doléances were being drafted, the clergy was deeply divided, and some were already adopting points of view that distanced them from the traditionalists. Prelates of good birth, such as Jérôme-Marie Champion de Cicé, the Archbishop of Bordeaux, Seignelay Colbert de Castlehill, the Bishop of Rodez, or Jean-Georges Lefranc de Pompignan, whose name has been mentioned, were ready to accept profound reforms and wanted to see the Church renewed. A letter from the Bishop of Rodez to the Count of Barneval on 14 March 1789 reveals the ferment of spirits and the hopes raised by the meeting of the General Estates.

> We are at present here in all the agitations which must naturally precede this great event. In the course of the next week, we will have made our elections in Rouergue and we will have written the cahiers de doléances.

[1] The "day of the tiles" in Grenoble, 7 June 1788.

> It is a great revolution which will take place. I have no doubt that it will turn out well, and I desire it more than I can express to you.[2]

Although the Bishop of Rodez, like the other clergymen, remained resolutely attached to the Christian religion, they were aware of the dysfunctions of a Church and a centralised state that were far removed from the concerns of the people. Ready to debate the issue, they not only wanted the General Estates to be convened, but also intended to demand profound changes from the King. The involvement of the clergy on the side of the liberals and patriots broke with tradition and forced the King to make concessions far removed from the recommendations of his entourage.

The sources for this period are infinitely rich[3] and the bibliography is immense. Paradoxically, the role of the clergy has been minimised, apart from the involvement of two strong personalities: Abbés Grégoire and Sieyès, who belonged to the Third Estate... It is worth asking to what extent the commitment of this first order was decisive in the course of events in June and July 1789; to ask what the consequences of this rallying were, which led to a "great fracture" within the clergy; to ask, finally, how and why the gap between the patriotic deputies and those of the clergy continued to widen.

At the first meeting of the General Estates in Versailles on 5 May, the question of voting by order or by head was not settled. Of the 1,177 deputies, the Third Estate accounted for half and its deputies wanted a vote by head and a plenary session, a change that the nobility and the clergy rejected, demanding to remain separate for the verification of their deputies' powers. On 6 May, the deputies present at this first order meeting opted for the *status quo* by only 19 votes (133 to 114). The Abbés Sieyès and Grégoire, determined to get closer to the Third State, gathered around them priests wishing to reform the political institutions as well as the functioning of the Church. They were joined by liberal prelates, so that the clergy was deeply divided at the beginning of June 1789, while the question of voting by order or by head was still not settled within the General Estates. In the session of 6 June in the

[2] Gaston MARTIN, "Les élections aux États généraux dans le Sud-Ouest. Some unpublished documents" *La Révolution française: Revue historique*... 1928, p. 236.

[3] Most of the documents concerning the deliberations of the assemblies have been digitised, but it is not always easy to access them...

Commons, the presentation of the rules of the Assembly was interrupted by the arrival of a deputation of the clergy, composed of two Bishops, that of Nîmes, Pierre-Marie-Magdeleine Cortois de Balore and that of Autun, Charles-Maurice de Talleyrand and of six priests. The Bishop of Nîmes, their spokesman, read a decree in which the members of the clergy agreed to accede to the King's request by being ready for a "conciliation" between the three orders.

At the first order meetings, several of the 60 bishops and archbishops were in favour of rapprochement and a common assembly. Two actively participated in the discussions and were "ready for many". In a report to the papacy, the Apostolic Nuncio, Antonio Dugnani, referred to Champion de Cicé's commitment.[4] The Archbishop of Bordeaux had been very involved, since the Assembly of Notables in 1787, in the negotiations conducted to resolve the financial difficulties of the Royal Treasury.

Considering themselves as the deputies of the communes and, as such, as the representatives of the people, the deputies of the Third Estate invite, on June 10, the two other orders to join them for the verification of the powers. On the 12th, three priests from Poitou, including Jacques Jallet, a well-known Jansenist,[5] joined them. Four days later, 19 other clergymen, including Abbé Grégoire, sat with the Third Estate. They contributed to the acceleration of events. On the 17th, all the deputies of the Third Estate decided to constitute a National Assembly charged with giving a Constitution to the Kingdom. During the meeting of the Clergy, on June 19, the liberal camp confronted the conservatives led by Cardinal de La Rochefoucauld. By virtue of the internal vote that was then organised, 135 ecclesiastical deputies vehemently refused to rally to the communes and 127 were ready to do so. Twelve clerics hesitated and expressed reservations. They finally agree to rally, thanks to Jérôme-Marie Champion de Cicé who made a convincing speech that day, and especially thanks to the Archbishop of Vienne who contributes by his charisma to

[4] *The Lost Honour*... p. 183 and note 21 mentioning the source: Arch. sec. Vatican, Nunz. Di Francia, S 573.

[5] Dale Kenneth VAN KLEY, *Les Origines religieuses de la Révolution française, 1560–1791*, Paris, Seuil, "Points", 2002. This historian places great emphasis on the influence of Jansenism on the clergymen present at the National Assembly.

the massive rallying of the clergy.[6] The list of 149 clergymen who "voted for joint credentials in the General Assembly Hall appears in *Le Journal des États généraux*.[7]

The next day, the showdown began when the King closed the Hôtel des Menus-Plaisirs, the usual meeting room of the Third Estate. Massed in front of the closed door, the deputies of the communes decided to go to the nearby Salle du Jeu de Paume. There they unanimously swore an oath not to separate until they had given the kingdom a constitution. This hall being closed. The session of Monday 22 June took place in the church of Saint Louis where the Assembly met. According to Marmontel, "the Archbishops of Bordeaux and Vienne, the Bishop of Chartres and the Bishop of Rodez at the head of one hundred and forty-five deputies of the clergy came forward.[8]" As a convinced monarchist, he evokes, in an ironic and irritated way, the joy and the applause which accompanied the entry of the four prelates quoted: Jérôme-Marie Champion de Cicé, Jean-George Lefranc de Pompignan, Jean-Baptiste de Lubersac and Seignelay Colbert de Castlehill. The number of these deputies, which varies according to the sources, represents well over half the members of the First Order.[9] Another Bishop signed on 19 June and joined in this solemn entry into the church: that of Coutances, Ange François de Talaru de Chalmazel.[10] Lefranc de Pompignan was designated as spokesman by his fellow clerics. He declared: "Gentlemen, we come with joy to execute the decree taken by the majority of the deputies of the Order of the Clergy to the General Estates". This meeting which has today for object only the

[6] François CADILHON, *L'honneur perdu de monseigneur Champion de Cicé*, Bordeaux, Fédération Historique du Sud-Ouest, 1996. This work insists on the role of the archbishop of Bordeaux during this meeting and minimises the role of Jean-George Lefranc de Pompignan, writing that he was "only a simple guarantor". However, it is a fact that he played a central role in this period...

[7] [Online at Gallica], p. 188. *Le Journal des États généraux convoqués par Louis XVI* was written by Étienne Le Hodey de Saultchevreuil and appeared three times a week. It compiled all the reports, motions, deliberations and speeches of the sessions of the Assembly. The newspaper ceased publication in 1791.

[8] Jean-François MARMONTEL, *Mémoires*, Paris, Mercure de France, 1988, p. 659.

[9] Michel WINOCK, *1789, L'année sans pareille*, Paris, Perrin, Tempus, 2004, pp. 113–114.

[10] He is cited by the *Journal des États généraux* and by Michel Péronnet, "Nos Seigneurs du clergé de France en 1789", *Dix-huitième Siècle*, 1988, n° 20, p. 124. Many historians speak of 7 prelates, but the sources do not mention them.

common checking of the powers is the signal, and I can say, the prelude, of the constant union which they wish with all the orders and particularly with that of Messieurs the deputies of the Communes. The President of the Assembly, Bailly speaks about "a day of happiness for the Assembly" and rejoices by evoking "the temple of the religion become the temple of the fatherland".

Surely these clergymen must have forgotten that the traditional distinction between the orders for the meeting of the General Estates placed them in the same privileged position as the aristocrats. If it was easier for parish priests close to their parishioners to join the Third Estate, the five prelates who accompanied them showed bravery and boldness. Some gained a reputation as prelates won over to Enlightenment ideas and embraced the economic modernisation advocated by the Physiocrats. Colbert of Castlehill was one of these. They all were won over by the spirit of the Enlightenment and were convinced of the discredit of their Church and the injustices of its operation. Their awareness undoubtedly led them to question a whole set of traditions and practices by taking the measure of discontent with the clergy as well as with royal policy. For Lefranc de Pompignan, the evolution is more complex, since he was fiercely opposed to the new ideas, which earned him the dislike of Voltaire as much as his brother.[11] No doubt he was shaken by the protests of a parish priest in his archdiocese, Henri Reymond, who fought against the privileges and defended the rights of the lower clergy and the increase of the "portion congrue.[12]" While he had sent a pastoral letter to the parish priests of his diocese on 15 July 1788, reminding them of "the obedience due to the royal power,[13]" his appointment as president of the assembly of the Dauphiné Estates led him to contest the projects of Loménie de Brienne and to agree with the demands of the representatives of this province. Very close to the monarchist Mounier, Pompignan appends his signature, in Spring 1789, to a memorandum refuting the apology of the privileges made by the deputies of the nobility and some prelates: "*Réponse*

[11] Guy ASTOUL, 'Jean-George Lefranc de Pompignan et son engagement politique', paper at the Colloque *Chrétiens contre philosophes: autour de Loménie de Brienne*, May 2016, forthcoming.

[12] Albert REY, *Henri Reymond (1737–1820)*, Paris, L'Harmattan, 2014. Later, this constitutional bishop refers to 'the trust of the archbishop' in a memoir quoted in full on p. 18.

[13] [Online in Gallica].

des députés de la province de Dauphiné aux états généraux, au nouveau mémoire intitulé "Mémoire pour une partie du clergé et de la noblesse de Dauphiné.[14]" This was not the first time he had criticised the attachment of the wealthy to their benefits and privileges. Opposing the 'managerial' drift of the episcopate, he protested against those administrative functions which "masks and disguises the bishop.[15]" He reproached his fellow bishops for being too attached to their titles and privileges and wished that they would be more faithful to the evangelical virtues, as expressed in numerous "cahiers de doléances" (registers of grievances).

If the 149 deputies of the clergy solemnly committed themselves to the deputies who had taken the oath of the Jeu de Paume and definitively sealed the reunion of the three orders in the National Assembly, as it was henceforth called, Abbé Grégoire was far from reassured when he wrote his "*Lettre*" to his fellow deputies of the lower clergy in the General Estates. He denounced the collusion of the high clergy with the aristocracy and asked all parish priests to support the Third Estate without discussion, considering that "the torch of religion must light up our zeal, and it is in the name of religion that part of the clergy, the minority of the Nobility and the Communes will rally around their king under the flag of the fatherland.[16]"

At the royal session on 23rd June, Louis XVI, urged on by his court entourage, reaffirmed privileges in his speech and rejected any accommodation with the Assembly. The first article of his declaration states: "The king wants the old distinction of the three orders of the State to be preserved in its entirety [...] (He) declared null and void the deliberations taken by the deputies of t h e order of the Third Estate on the 17th of this month". His threatening speech towards the Assembly of the Commons was very badly received by the deputies of the Third Estate who refused to comply with the monarch's injunctions or to leave the chamber. On June 24, Lefranc de Pompignan presided over the Assembly with Bailly at his side and the majority of the clergy, in particular of the low clergy, took part in this meeting. That day, the carriage of Le Clerc de Juigné, the archbishop of Paris opposed to the rallying, was

[14] Bnf, Lb39-1896 [Online in Gallica].

[15] *Lettres à un évêque sur divers points de morale et de discipline concernant l'épiscopat*, published by M. Emery (S. n. d'éditeur), Paris, 1802.

[16] Henri GREGOIRE, député du clergé, *Nouvelle lettre à MM. les curés, députés aux États généraux*, [s.n.], 1789, p. 39.

pelted with stones in the streets of Versailles. Pursued, the Archbishop was rescued by Seignelay Colbert, whose commitment was acclaimed by the crowd, which he succeeded in calming down, according to witnesses.[17] Obviously, the threats posed by the summoning of royal troops around Paris had the effect of strongly mobilising the people, who were disappointed by the dismissal of Necker and anxious to protect the National Assembly. The hostile demonstrations multiplied. Aware of the risks of a popular uprising, the eminent members of the high nobility (The Dukes of Orleans, La Rochefoucauld and Luynes) agreed to join the Assembly where they were enthusiastically welcomed. The last prelates who had refused to join up until then were worried about the pressure exerted by the people and some of them changed their minds.

June 27 was the decisive day. The King addressed the privileged orders. A letter was sent to Mgr de La Rochefoucaud in which he "commits his faithful clergy to reunite without delay with the two other orders" and in another missive sent to the Duke of Luxembourg, he called on the nobility to do the same. The three orders were then reunited when these "gentlemen of the clergy and nobility were received by the Assembly with great applause". For President Bailly, this "must be a day of rejoicing and joy" and he declared that "the National Assembly is going to occupy itself, without distinction and without respite, with the regeneration of the kingdom and public happiness.[18]" Close to Bailly, Pompignan played the role of moderator, and on 27 June he succeeded in convincing the people, mobilised in support, not to enter the meeting hall. Concord seemed to reign, even if the recalcitrant minority had not said their last word.

Their spokesman, Cardinal de La Rochefoucauld, wanted to read out in the session of 2 July, a "protest which he said was that of the majority of his order". Pompignan opposed him by accusing him of having drafted

[17] Claude-François Beaulieu, *Essais historiques sur les causes et les effets de la révolution de France: avec des notes sur quelques événemens et quelques institutions*, Paris, Maradan, 1803. Quoted by Thiers.

[18] *Archives parlementaires (A.P.) de 1787 à 1860*, 1ère série, t. VIII, Paris, 1875, A.P. Tome VIII, p. 189.

a protest which was "false and abusive". In a tête-à-tête with the cardinal he had "un choc furieux... de paroles.[19]"

On 3 July, the Duc d'Orléans was elected President of the National Assembly[20] in place of Bailly and was widely applauded. However, he refused to assume this function and asked for a new vote. Jean-George Lefranc de Pompignan was then elected with 700 votes out of 793 voters.[21] He warmly thanked the deputies and concluded his speech[22] by saying: "What is left for me to desire if not to cast my last glances at the regeneration of France and to bury myself in the restoration of our common homeland". In his *Memoirs*, Bailly speaks about "the general satisfaction which burst out" following his very applauded intervention; he testifies to the connivance which exists then between the clergy and the Third State within the Assembly. For all that, uncertainty remained. The threats posed by the royal troops called to surround Paris energised the people. On the evening of July 8, the King met the President of the Assembly in order to reassure him on his intentions. The next day, the National Assembly proclaimed itself a Constituent Assembly, definitively sealing a break with the Ancien Régime and a desire to change the laws of the kingdom. On 14 July, the people of Paris took the Bastille, the symbol of monarchical absolutism, and forced the king to give in and recall Necker, whom he had dismissed a few days before. The Revolution spread to all the provinces, the people armed themselves by forming militias and attacking castles. On the night of 4 August, the Assembly decreed the abolition of the feudal system and privileges. In the following days, the laws implementing this decision were drafted. On August 7, the King called upon four deputies of the Assembly as ministers of his government. Pompignan was appointed "Ministre de la Feuille", responsible for ecclesiastical appointments, and Champion de Cicé became Keeper of the Seals, responsible for legal matters. The assembly unanimously applauded a message from the King who called for appeasement: "The choice which

[19] Les *bulletins des correspondances réunies du clergé et de la Sénéchaussée de Rennes,* Rennes, Vatar, t. 1, 1789, [On line]. Some details on the internal debates of the first order. "a furious clash... of words"

[20] A position held for 15 days.

[21] *Archives Parlementaires,* t. VIII, p. 186. The debates of the Constituent Assembly are presided over by Jean-George Lefranc de Pompignan until July 14.

[22] *Bulletins des correspondances réunies du clergé et de la sénéchaussée de Rennes*, quoted above, p. 199.

I make, in your assembly even, announces to you the desire which I have to maintain with it the most constant and the most friendly harmony".

The abolition of tithes decided on 4 August gave rise to a debate in which Seignelay Colbert participated. On the evening of 10 August, he "spoke for a long time afterwards on the two questions of the purchase of the '*dixmes*' and the ownership of clergy property. He spoke as a man convinced that the property of the clergy was necessary for the maintenance of religion, the decency of worship and the relief of the poor. But his speech was made in against a disorderly ferment. Sieyès, who spoke next, was very reluctant to abandon the tithes. His fully argumented speech, which was taken up by the *Moniteur Universel,* was not well received. "The noise, the tumult, the brouhahas which rose from the Communes interrupted it several times" as the *Journal de Paris notes*.[23] He believes that despite all its faults and injustices, the system of tithes should not be abandoned. In his opinion, "The law must guarantee all property. It guaranteed this one like all the others, and in truth this one was worth no less than any other". He adds that if the tithe is no longer necessary, it must be redeemed in the same way as seigneurial rights. Thus, "the tithe being correctly placed among the class of properties that are legitimate in truth, but harmful to the public good, it must be extinguished as one extinguishes these kinds of property, that is to say, by offering an indemnity". He adds: "The repurchase must be agreed by mutual consent between the communities and the tithe holders, or regulated at the most moderate rate by the assembly.[24] The next day, the clergy decided to rely on "the justice of the Nation". The articles of the law were written by stipulating that the tithes "are abolished, except to provide for the means of providing in another way f o r t h e expenses of divine worship, for the maintenance of the ministers of the altars, for the relief of the poor.[25]..."

After the adoption of the law on the abolition of ecclesiastical tithes, Colbert had a "mandement" published in application of article XVII of this law stipulating that: "the National Assembly decrees that in memory

[23] *Tableau des opérations de l'Assemblée nationale d'après le Journal de Paris*, tome 1, p. 245 for the two interventions. This newspaper has the advantage of taking an interest in the atmosphere of the debates, which the *Moniteur Universel* which is then taken over by the *Archives parlementaires*.

[24] *Archives Parlementaires de la Révolution Française*, 1875, t. 8, p. 387.

[25] *Tableau des opérations de l'Assemblée nationale*, t. 1, p. 246.

of the great and important deliberations, which have just been taken in for the happiness of France [...] it will be sung, in thanksgiving, a Te Deum in all the parishes and churches of the kingdom. In his letter, Colbert wrote: "It was not enough for this august and generous assembly to tear away abuses which had been growing for centuries, in the shadow of the authority of Justice, of Religion itself; it was not enough for it to annihilate privileges consecrated by time, but which had become odious by their extent and multitude; it was not enough to open up the career of honours to talent and virtue..., it was not enough finally to put the title of citizen above all titles and the Law above all exceptions: animated by the enthusiasm for the good..., the worthy representatives of the Nation have renounced rights that seemed unquestionable, and this unprecedented sacrifice has not cost any effort.[26]" Was he satisfied or was his humour wry ? He did not intervene afterwards in the debates that led to the civil constitution of the clergy. No doubt he realised that the General Estates intended to put an end to the injustices that the Church had supported for too long without it being possible to stop these changes, even if he feared their excesses.

As Michel Péronnet notes, the political and institutional influence of the episcopate gradually collapsed during the summer of 1789. For these prelates, who were used to ruling with authority, even coercion, the test was harsh. In the space of a few months, the bishops had not only lost their attractive revenues, but above all their complacency had distanced them from their flock for too long. "They who were the *sanior pars* of the first order of the kingdom are now only a derisory minority in an assembly deliberating according to the principle of the *major pars*.[27] Many had chosen to refuse all innovation, to defend traditions tooth and nail. Those who, like Colbert, Pompignan or Champion de Cicé, the Keeper of the Seals, believed in a moderate monarchy gradually lost all control over the course of events. Above all, many patriotic clerics adopted revolutionary positions, as two recent books demonstrate. Rita Hermon-Belot has

[26] Quoted by Andrew Moore in his memoir, pp. 128–129, after Pierre Benoît, *Le vieux Rodez*, Rodez, 1912.

[27] Michel PERONNET, "Nos Seigneurs du clergé de France en 1789", *Dix-Huitième Siècle*, 88 20, pp. 119–132. Part of a thematic issue: L'année 1789.

studied the work of Abbé Grégoire[28] and Jean-Claude Meyer the revolutionary commitment of two southern constitutional bishops:[29] Antoine Pascal-Hyacinthe Sermet and Paul-Benoît Barthe. These three ecclesiastics never denied their attachment to the Christian religion, but they approved of the Revolution, considering it as "this great change that the hand of God h a s just operated in this kingdom.[30]" Convinced of the need to reform the royal state, they supported the upheavals of August 1789, glorifying the abolition of feudal rights and privileges or the Declaration of the Rights of Man and the Citizen. They considered them to be the result of a Christian policy[31] tied to evangelical precepts, in favour of justice, equality and fraternity. They were very critical of the way the Church operated, especially the system of commend, under which tithes were used to pay for purely honorary functions.[32] For these clerics, who wanted a profound change, selling Church property to meet the needs of the State or to help the poor in no way contradicted the dogmatic foundations of Catholicism. They intended to put an end to the contempt of a high clergy whose abuse of authority and distance from the faithful they condemned; they wanted to build a more just and humane society in a spirit of charity where a new Church would have its full place.

Colbert seemed resigned to playing second fiddle. He was appointed commissaire de la salle des séances (quaestor) and it was in this capacity that he took part, on 12 October, in the committee responsible for finding a place where the National Assembly could be transferred to Paris. He was a member of the committees for the regulation and extinction of begging in 1790.

[28] Rita HERMON-BELOT, *L'abbé Grégoire, la politique et la vérité*, Paris, Seuil, 2000.

[29] Jean-Claude MEYER, *Deux théologiens en Révolution*, Les Plans-sur-Beix (Suisse)-Paris, Parole et silence, 2011.

[30] This is what Sermet wrote, quoted by Jean-Claude Meyer, p. 142.

[31] Rita Hermon-Belot discusses the Jansenist foundations of the political views of patriotic priests such as Abbé Grégoire and Abbé Lamourette. Their ideas are based on The "immense antidespotic and even democratic Christian culture" found in their speeches, cf. pp. 218, 128–129.

[32] Loménie de Brienne received 126,000 livres in annuities, an enormous sum which almost corresponded to his income as archbishop of Toulouse, as abbot of Moissac, even though this abbey had been secularised since the beginning of the seventeenth century...

Following the adoption of the Declaration of the Rights of Man and the Citizen,[33] a solution had to be found to the financial difficulties of the Royal Treasury. In order to bail it out and remedy the impending bankruptcy, the idea of nationalising the property of the clergy arose. From then on, the reorganisation of the Church of France was considered indispensable. Such a project led to a new definition of the relationship between the Church and the State. This debate became the major concern of the Constituent Assembly when an ecclesiastical committee was set up at the end of August.

The clergy, initially enthusiastic about the reforms of the Constituent Assembly,[34] became deeply divided on the question of the nationalisation of Church property and the reorganisation that should follow. In the discussions, the patriotic clergy who wanted a profound change approved the sale of Church property to meet the needs of the State or to help the poor, considering that this did not contradict the foundations of Catholicism.

Confiscating patrimonial wealth belonging, essentially, to the faithful, was justified by considering that it belonged to the nation and that its management was a matter for its representatives. This was stated by Talleyrand in a landmark speech: "These properties have been given to the Church. Now, the Church is the assembly of the faithful, and is the assembly of the faithful in a Catholic country anything other than the Nation[35]? On 13 October 1789, Jean-Louis Gouttes, parish priest of

[33] Voted on 26 August 1789 by the National Assembly: the text adopted was largely inspired by Champion de Cicé.

[34] In *L'Église catholique et la Révolution française*, t. 1, *Le pontificat de Pie VI et la crise française (1776–1799)*, Paris, Hachette, 1946, André Latreille summarises the state of mind prevailing among the clergy when he writes: the Revolution "began, in France, in an atmosphere of agreement and harmony between the Church and the Nation".

[35] Second speech by Talleyrand of 2 November 1789, "Sur les biens ecclésiastiques" in *Orateurs de la Révolution française*, p. 1563, quoted by Jean-Claude Meyer, p. 117.

Argelliers[36] in the Lower Languedoc region, took to the podium of the National Assembly and analysed the situation realistically:

> But is it for the clergy to give up their property to the State? Is it in the interest of the State to strip the clergy of all property and to pay them in money? Would it not be more appropriate to leave to the ministers necessary for religion, and especially to the pastors, funds of sufficient product to provide for their needs and to help the poor? [...] .

He insisted on his idea of giving land to parish priests to enable them to live, as he did not believe that the state could pay clerics through taxation. He remained sceptical about the capacity of public finances to pay for such expenses, and others, such as the Abbé Grégoire, shared this view. The debates resume at the end of October. Talleyrand wanted the sale of the property of the clergy and Mirabeau exclaimed "Religion belonging to all, it is necessary for that reason only that its ministers should be remunerated by the nation". Worried for their future, the deputies of the clergy wished for reforms less radical than the nationalisation of the property from which they drew their income. During these debates, they got into the habit of sitting on the right side of the President of the Assembly, thus definitively establishing the right-left divide in the Chamber. All their speeches on 30 and 31 October, particularly those of Abbé Maury or the very long harangue by Boisgelin de Cucé[37] did not change anything. On

[36] Born in Tulle (Corrèze) on 21 September 1739, he left the army to take up the ecclesiastical state. He was initially a parish priest near Bordeaux before being appointed to Argelliers (today in the Hérault). Elected on 27 March 1789 as a deputy of the clergy to the General Estates for the *sénéchaussée* of Béziers, he was one of the first to call for the reunification of the three orders and, on 19 May 1789, he proposed, in a meeting of the clergy, the abandonment of all the privileges of his order in the matter of taxes. On 31 October, he supported Talleyrand's motion proposing the sale of the clergy's property; he then made a much-applauded speech in which he mocked the wealth of the clergy. In April 1790, he was elected president of the Assembly to replace M. de Virieu. The following July, he voted for the civil constitution of the clergy. Elected constitutional bishop of Saône-et-Loire (1791), he replaced M. de Talleyrand in Autun, who had resigned. As he protested against the suppression of religion and the Terror, he was denounced and arrested by decree of the Committee of Public Safety, Put on trial on 6 Germinal Year II, he was sentenced to death and executed in Paris on 25 March 1794. Speech in *Archives Parlementaires de la Révolution Française*, 1875, t. 9, pp. 431–434.

[37] Jean de Dieu-Raymond de Boisgelin de Cucé, archbishop of Aix, elected deputy of the clergy to the General Estates, votes for the abolition of privileges and the equal distribution of taxes. He defends the right of property of the clergy in his *Discourse on the*

2 November 1789, under the presidency of Armand-Gaston Camus,[38] by 568 votes to 346, the National Assembly placed the property of the Church at the disposal of the nation. All religious institutions, in turmoil, became dependent on the State. On 13 February 1790, the contemplative orders were dissolved and only clerics involved in teaching or charitable works were spared. In the name of a reaffirmed Gallicanism, all these reforms were undertaken without reference to the Pope or, at least, he was presented with a fait accompli, without any negotiation.

Henceforth, it was necessary to undertake a reform of the religious system and to draft what was called the Civil Constitution of the Clergy. Two prelates took part in the Ecclesiastical Committee: Boisgelin de Cussé archbishop of Aix, and Bonal, Bishop of Clermont. They were surrounded by three priests and the canon law expert Durand de Maillane. The first draft they presented on 23 November was judged to be too moderate, although it was imbued with Gallicanism. The project was rejected. The committee was then modified and enlarged. It was composed of a majority of patriots who were in favour of the reforms; the two prelates decided not to take part anymore, while most of the bishop deputies showed themselves more and more hostile to the fact that the Church and the clergy were now too dependent on the State.

The final text of the "*plan d'organisation du clergé*" proposed by the Ecclesiastical Committee was discussed from 29 May 1790 by the Constituent Assembly. Jean-Baptiste Treilhard made a presentation of it, which was much applauded. The debates opposed the patriotic deputies to those who had already committed themselves in October against the nationalisation of the property of the clergy and who were then supported by most of the bishops.

Voted on 12 July, the Civil Constitution of the Clergy completely reorganise the functioning of the Church, which freed itself from the tutelage of Rome, affirming a radical Gallicanism and putting an end

property of the ecclesiastical goods by M. the archbishop of Aix, Paris, 1789. He advocated moderation...

38 Armand-Gaston Camus, born on 2 April 1740, was a lawyer, elected in Paris as a deputy of the Third Estate to the General Estates. President of the assembly from 28 October 1789 until 11 November, he voted for the nationalisation of the clergy's property. He contributed to the drafting of the Civil Constitution of the Clergy and voted for it. He also had the annates paid to the papacy abolished and pushed for the annexation of the Comtat Venaissin.

to the Concordat of 1516. The Constitution recognise the Pope's "primacy" over the Church of France but denied him "jurisdiction" over the affairs of the clergy. The text suppressed small dioceses and keeps only 83, corresponding to the departments. All clerics were to be elected and paid like other state officials. The state expected from them unquestioning loyalty, as was expected from its lay officials. Bishops were responsible for giving canonical institution to parish priests, and metropolitan bishops (the former archbishops) to bishops without their receiving the pope's unction. Finally, the remuneration of members of the clergy was precisely defined so that parish priests and vicars enjoyed a much better situation than under the Ancien Régime. As early as 13th July, an *Adresse au clergé de Saint-Lo*[39] was read at the tribune by their deputy. Favourable to the decisions of the assembly, these priests wrote: "We will be the organs of religion and liberty" and in a more exalted, way "we will revive these golden centuries of Christianity that the luxury of our days so willingly relegated to fables". This led to the passing of a law requiring clerics to take an oath on 27 November 1790. Mirabeau considered this oath requirement unnecessary when he realised that it would constitute a major obstacle and lead to schism. According to him, it would be sufficient not to impose it by decreeing "the universal vacancy of ecclesiastical appointments" and by submitting them all to an election.[40] His intervention changed nothing to the vote. The oath became a bone of contention that deeply divided the clergy. Numerous ecclesiastical deputies hesitated, and, for the majority, the bishops were hostile the oath's implementation, except for Talleyrand. S. Colbert finally gave up and explained his choice in a letter addressed to the clergy of the diocese of Rodez,[41] on 8 January 1791. In this letter, he expressed at length the reasons that led him to refuse to take the oath. He explained his refusal and made a long analysis of the decisions of the National Assembly by reproaching it for the fact that he was a member of the National Assembly, reproaching him for making the Church dependent on the political authority. He writes: "The Civil Constitution of the Clergy removes, grants, divides, reunites,

[39] Address of the clergy of Saint-Lo (To day in the Calvados).

[40] Michel Winock, *La grande fracture 1790–1793*, Paris, Perrin, Tempus, 2014, pp. 26–27.

[41] Tolosana, digital library of the Toulouse universities, the letter is digitized from the copy Res 34777/2, of the Bibliothèque universitaire de l'Arsenal (SCD Toulouse 1), available online.

limits, extends, suppresses and re-establishes at the whim of men, and of administrative and political assemblies, these same spiritual powers, and this without any intervention of the Church [...]". But he urged his clergy to call for calm and not to support the violence of their parishioners.

Pope Pius VI's reaction was slow in coming. As he said later, his main concern was not to make matters worse by rushing. Louis XVI sought an accommodation with him, but he was inclined to follow the advice of his ministers, the Keeper of the Seals, Jérôme-Marie Champion de Cicé, and the Archbishop of Vienne, Jean-George Lefranc de Pompignan, Minister of the Benefices, then Minister without Portfolio when appointments to ecclesiastical benefices were suspended on 9 November 1789. Although historians' opinions differ, they advised him to approve the decisions of the Assembly, judging it necessary to approve it in order to guarantee social peace. In a letter known to Lefranc de Pompignan, the Pope wrote to the King on 9 July 1790 "We must tell you with firmness and fatherly love that if you approve the decrees concerning the Clergy, you will mislead your entire Nation, you will precipitate your Kingdom into schism". The next day, he sent writs that were delivered to the King on 23 July, asking him to reject the constitution. These documents arrived too late, because the civil constitution of the clergy had been adopted on 12 July 1790, and Louis XVI had officially announced his decision to approve the decree, which he promulgated on 24 August. It was only on 10 March 1791 that the Pope sent the brief "*Quod Aliquantum*", a brief strongly condemning the royal decree and comforting clerics hostile to the oath.

The Revolution was committed to reforming a church that was much criticised in the "cahiers de doléances", which contained detestations of tithes, of demands for an increase in clerical revenues, of the constraint of a minimum parish service, and anger at the privileges of the high clergy. The many parish priests elected to the General Estates were very angry with their hierarchy and resolutely set out to challenge the Ancien Régime. By subjecting the Church to the State, the deputies believed they were putting an end to the profound injustices and dysfunctions of the institution. After the demand for an oath to the Constitution, the patriots rejected all the moderates who were ready to accept reforms, precipitating them into the camp of the counter-revolution. More seriously, the schism took root in France, where two churches were confronting each other: one that remained faithful to tradition and attached to the refractory clergy was now illegal; the other, the official church that respected the law, was considered schismatic by the papacy and sometimes violently rejected.

In a letter addressed to the Duke of Buccleuch on 21 October 1792, from Cossey, near Norwich, Colbert evoked his resentment by recalling that he had been forced to leave France like most of his colleagues, led by Champion de Cicé:

> They have put us in the awful alternative of either disgracing ourselves by an oath contrary to our principles or losing our lives. Fleeing has been our only resource and today everything is lost for us, except our honour. [...] Whatever may happen, we shall persist in our principles and we shall never bow the knee to the present idols of France.[42]

In *Mémoires affrontées*,[43] Valérie Sottocasa analyses "the shock caused by the oath and its consequences". She notes that in 1791, popular demonstrations were linked to the religious policy of the Constituent Assembly, but they have too often been considered as hostility to the Revolution. Above all, it was a refusal to accept changes that called into question traditions and practices, and this refusal led the Catholic faithful, no doubt in spite of themselves, to support the refractory clergy. Whether one speaks of a "break" like Roger Dupuy, a "fracture" like Michel Winock[44] or a rupture, whatever the case, the Church had indeed become the main factor in the divisions of the French....

[42] Alain ALCOUFFE & Andrew MOORE, "The correspondence of Bishop Seignelay Colbert of Castlehill and the Duke of Buccleuch, p. 15.

[43] Valérie SOTTOCASA, *Mémoires affrontées. Protestants et catholiques face à la Révolution dans les montagnes du Languedoc*, Rennes, Presses Universitaires de Rennes, 2006.

[44] In *La grande fracture*, he quotes Roger Dupuy who "speaks of a break, as early as May 1790", in Brittany...

CHAPTER 8

Colbert of Castlehill's Social Thinking as Shown by His Work on the *Comité de mendicité*

Jean-Baptiste Masméjan

Abstract Jean-Baptiste Masméjan recalls that Seignelay Colbert de Castlehill was constantly preoccupied with the treatment of the indigent. Initially vicar general in Toulouse, he served in this capacity under Archbishop Loménie de Brienne. Loménie de Brienne chaired a commission on begging at the request of the Controller General of Finance, Turgot, which, although short-lived, was an ambitious liberal project. As bishop of Rodez and president of the provincial assembly of Haute-Guyenne, Colbert de Castlehill set out to provide local relief by establishing charity workshops and supporting charitable foundations. Elected as a deputy of the clergy to the General Estates, it was only natural that he should find himself a member of the Begging Committee, which he joined as vice-president. However, it seems that this enlightened prelate was torn

English revised by Jennifer Morag Henderson.

J.-B. Masméjan (✉)
Law History, University of Nantes, Nantes University, France

A. Alcouffe (ed.), *Seignelay Colbert de Castlehill (1735-1811)*,
https://doi.org/10.1007/978-3-031-75273-5_8

between the new ideas of assistance and the defense of the Church's interests. The Bishop of Rodez remained committed to the protection of Church property and the role of the clergy in providing assistance. Nevertheless, his involvement with the Committee has been consistent. Most of his work focused on hospital issues and the treatment of incurable patients.

Keywords Colbert of Castlehill · Begging Committee · French Revolution · Public assistance · Enlightened prelates · Constituents · Indigent relief · National Constituent Assembly · Social reforms · Larochefoucauld-Liancourt

The Revolution was accompanied by a resolutely optimistic political will regarding the treatment of begging and the care of the sick poor. The Constituents' ambition was to put an end to the misery that they believed was indissociable of the social life of the Ancien Régime and that was still present at the beginning of the revolutionary period. Indeed, the Comité de mendicité, or Committee on Begging, on the basis of data reported by the *départements* (departments[1]), estimated the percentage of indigents in the population at 11.6%.[2] The revolutionaries wanted to put an end to this endemic misery. Fingers were pointed at royal power and the dysfunction of charitable institutions. The destitute were seen above all as victims of the laws and shortcomings of the state. The regenerative ambition of the deputies was accompanied by an unparalleled freedom to make changes in this area. As representatives of the sovereign nation, they wanted to carry out a series of reforms aimed at guaranteeing relief to all citizens and putting an end to the vicissitudes of the Ancien Régime with regard to the reduction of begging and the health treatment of the poorest. It was for these purposes that the Committee on Begging began to take shape at the end of January 1790.[3] It was charged with proposing

[1] Ed. Note: The department was the level of government under the national level created on 22 December 1789.

[2] Christine DOUSSET, "Statistique et pauvreté sous la Révolution et l'Empire", *AHRF*, n° 280, 1990, p. 173.

[3] *Infra*. On the morning of 23 January, the President invited the deputies to nominate four members from among themselves to form a committee to recover the funds for

the establishment of new legislation on public assistance for the indigent. Its remit was wide-ranging: it intended to ensure both the care of the sick poor in towns and the countryside and to remedy begging.

Colbert de Castlehill was elected deputy for the clergy of the *sénéchaussée*[4] of Rodez and was fully supportive of the committee's ambitions. He was, in fact, the instigator of charitable works within his diocese[5]. Moreover, the works in his personal library show his interest in these issues. He was one of those enlightened prelates who contributed to the start of the Revolution. The bishop of Rodez was one of the 148 deputies of the clergy who joined the Third Estate on 19 June 1789.[6] His participation in the political revolution carried out by the deputies of the Third Estate thus gave him a certain popularity.

However, this active role is not reflected in the National Assembly, as he is rarely recorded as speaking. This does not mean that he was inactive. He was a member of three committees created under the Constituent Assembly: those dedicated to research, to regulation and finally the committee on begging, which he joined on 17 March 1790 and of which he was vice-chairman.[7] No doubt his long experience as president of the provincial assembly of Haute-Guyenne gave him a certain legitimacy, although we do not know the process of designation.[8] Indeed, the

the poorest people and to find ways to ensure their subsistence. The creation of this Committee was in response to a massive press campaign and public demand for the National Assembly to address this key issue. However, as Alexandre Tuetey and Camille Bloch point out, the genesis of the Committee was more the result of a situational need than a long-standing political project. Camille BLOCH, Alexandre TUETEY, *Procès-verbaux et rapports du Comité de mendicité de la Constituante,* Paris, Imprimerie nationale, 1911, pp. IX–X. On the origins of the Comité de mendicité, see our publication: Jean-Baptiste MASMÉJAN, "Le Comité de mendicité mandaté par la nation: vers une harmonisation de la politique d'assistance des valides (1790–1791)", *Cahiers Jean Moulin,* No. 2.

[4] Ed. Note: The *sénéchaussée* is the area of jurisdiction of a seneschal.

[5] On Colbert de Castlehill's social work as de Brienne's vicar general, see Andrew MOORE, *Seignelay Colbert de Castlehill in the pre-revolutionary years, A Bishop of the Ancien Regime*, Dissertation in History, University of Bristol, 1988, p. 95. See also *below*.

[6] Edna LEMAY et al., *Dictionnaire des Constituants: 1789–1791*, Oxford, Voltaire Foundation, 1991, vol. 1, p. 230.

[7] For a quick retrospective of his various speeches and actions under the Constituante, see Castlehill's entry on Colbert in Ibid. pp. 229–230.

[8] On 14 April, the result of the election of the various commissioners responsible for the question of the extinction of begging was announced by the president of the National Assembly: Cretot, 70 votes; Guillotin, 70; David, priest, 67; the abbot of Bonnefoy, 33;

minutes of the province of Haute-Guyenne testify that he had to deal with issues relating to the relief and treatment of begging.[9]

Colbert de Castlehill was not among the first four members appointed by the National Constituent Assembly at the end of January 1790.[10] He joined later because of the extent of the work to be done within the Committee. Thus, on 17 March 1790, the Assembly decided to elect six new deputies, including the bishop of Rodez.[11]

Before the addition of these new members, it was decided on 26 February 1790 that the members of the Begging Committee would work separately to establish the basis and plan of their work in view of the multiplicity of tasks and would therefore be divided into sections. On 26 April 1790, these were organised, and Colbert de Castlehill was part of the 2nd section relating to the sick poor, which included, among others, the famous doctor Guillotin, Thouret[12] and de Virieu.[13] The minutes of the session of 9 June 1790 reveal that the mass of documents collected by the Committee in order to establish a new legislation would be processed, as far as the documents on provincial hospitals were concerned, by the bishop of Rodez. On 3 September 1790, a refinement between the different sections was carried out, with Colbert de Castlehill maintaining a role related to what had been initiated on 20 April. His

the bishop of Oléron, 29; the bishop of Rodez, 23. Camille BLOCH, Alexandre TUETEY, *Procès-verbaux et rapports du Comité de mendicité de la Constituante, op. cit,* p. XI. Moreover, the formation of the office was carried out on 19 April 1790, although we do not know how the appointment was made. Ibid., pp. XXIV–XXV.

[9] See, for example, the report of 5 December 1786 of the Bureau du bien public. *Procès-verbal des séances de l'assemblée provinciale de Haute-Guyenne tenue à Villefranche dans les mois de novembre et décembre 1786,* Paris, Crapart, pp. 220–233.

[10] The four members are the Duke of La Rochefoucauld-Liancourt, the Abbé d'Abbécourt (Simonnet de Coulmiers), Massieu, parish priest of Cergy, and Prieur, deputy of the Third Estate of Châlons-sur-Marne. Ibid., p. X.

[11] Thus, in the minutes of 1er April 1790, we find the following six deputies: the bishop of Oléron, Guillotin, the bishop of Rodez, Decretot, Bonnefoy, David, and two substitutes: de Virieu and Barère de Vieuzac. *Ibid,* p. XI.

[12] Michel-Augustin Thouret was the brother of the famous deputy of the Constituante. He was a doctor with a great knowledge of the hospital environment of his time, which explains his recruitment by the Comité de mendicité. A brief bibliography is available in *Ibid.* p. XVI.

[13] Ibid., session of 26 April 1790, pp. 21–23. Virieu is deputy of the nobility of Dauphiné. He was also a member of the Committee on Subsistence on 19 June 1789. Ibid., p. XVI.

work concerned both relief for the poor in the countryside and relief for the infirm, alongside the same Guillotin, Thouret and de Virieu.[14]

The work of the Committee on Begging and its doctrinal imprint are inextricably linked to its president, Larochefoucauld-Liancourt,[15] which explains why he is credited with the authorship of the various reports issued. Elected deputy of the nobility of the bailliage of Clermont-en-Beauvaisis to the General Estates, he was also president of the Committee on Taxation and a member of the Committee on Alienation. His life was marked by philanthropic activities. Under the Ancien Régime, he was, for example, the founder of the farm-school and the vocational school of Liancourt, associated with the Maison philanthropique de Paris.[16] We also owe to him the particularly broad remit of the Committee. Indeed, Bailly, the mayor of Paris, requested the support of the Assembly in order to contribute to the subscription that he had opened for the benefit of the needy. Refusing to support this city in particular to the detriment of all the others, the National Constituent Assembly declined this request, but decreed on 21 January 1790: "*that there is no need to deliberate on the letter written to its President by the mayor of Paris; and however, wanting all the donations that all its members are willing to make in favour of the poor of this capital to be used in the most advantageous way, has decreed that four commissioners will be appointed to receive them, and to hand over the sums that come from them to the municipality, responsible for regulating their use and distribution; and the same commissioners will be responsible for presenting the Assembly with views on the means of eliminating begging.*"[17] The last part of the decree is directly attributable to Larochefoucauld-Liancourt, who, at the time when it was question of designating the commissioners in charge of collecting the donations of the deputies, opposes a taxation of the representatives of the nation.

[14] *Ibid*, pp. XXVI–XXVII. Colbert de Castlehill was in charge of questions relating to "Relief for the poor in large towns", alongside Guillotin, Périsse du Luc and Thouret; "Relief for the poor in the countryside", alongside Guillotin, de Virieu and Thouret and finally "Relief for the infirm" alongside Guillotin and Thouret. *Ibid*, session of 3 September 1790, p. 127.

[15] For a biography of Larochefoucauld-Liancourt, see Ferdinand DREYFUS, *Un Philanthrope d'autrefois. La Rochefoucauld-Liancourt, 1747–1827*, Paris, Plon Nourrit et Cie, 1903.

[16] Camille BLOCH, Alexandre TUETEY, *Procès-verbaux et rapports du Comité de mendicité de la Constituante*, *op. cit*, p. XIII.

[17] Ibid., p. IX.

He successfully proposed the aforementioned amendment so that these commissioners could seek ways to put an end to begging.[18]

Most of the reports are associated with Larochefoucauld-Liancourt's name, which tends to obscure the role played by other members of the Committee.[19] Moreover, knowledge of Colbert de Castlehill's social thinking seems difficult to determine as most of the Committee's archives have disappeared.[20] Among the mass of documents at our disposal are the minutes of meetings, correspondence and, of course, the various reports and draft decrees. It is clear from reading them that Colbert de Castlehill's actions were more focused on technical points than on doctrinal and political ones. In our opinion, this cannot be explained solely by the prominence given to the Chairman of the Committee on Begging. The most plausible hypothesis is dissension over the policy of assistance to be adopted, although this is not clear from his interventions in the Committee on Begging. Studying the thinking of the bishop of Rodez, which we will try to understand through a series of clues, sheds light on the political differences on the question of assistance for the poorest.

So, how does Colbert of Castlehill's involvement reflect the issues surrounding the treatment of destitution under the Constituent?

Although the political position of the Bishop of Rodez within the Committee confined him to a rather minor role (I), his action and expertise demonstrated his desire to transform the treatment of destitution within the Kingdom (II).

(1) A position giving a marginal political role to the Bishop of Rodez

The prominent position, occupied by the president of the Committee on Begging, Larochefoucauld-Liancourt, is not simply the result of his personality. He was politically in line with the direction taken by the Constituent Assembly with regard to the treatment of the clergy and begging. The difference between the president and the vice-president

[18] Ibid., p. IX.

[19] Ibid., p. XLV.

[20] Apart from traces of the minutes of the Comité de mendicité transcribed by Alexandre Tuetey and Camille Bloch, the only surviving reference is F^{16} 936 in the National Archives. On this point, see Guy THUILLIER, *Un observateur des misères sociales: Leclerc de Montlinot (1732–1801),* Paris, Comité d'histoire de la sécurité sociale, 2001, p. 277.

seems explicit in this respect. Larochefoucauld-Liancourt was a fervent defender of the central role that the state should play in providing relief. This position is reflected in the various reports and projects proposed by the Committee.[21] It can be seen in the thorny issue of the abolition of privileges, including the tithe, and the making available of clergy property to the nation. On 10 August 1789, although we do not have the precise content of his speech, Colbert of Castlehill seems to have expressly opposed the abolition of the tithe and the future sale of the Church's patrimony. According to him, the income of the clergy and its patrimony are necessary for the exercise of Catholic worship as well as

[21] The Committee agreed, as regards the method of distribution of relief funds, that the total mass of funds should be administered by the nation. Consequently, it was considered no longer appropriate for hospitals and other charitable institutions to enjoy their own income. They therefore asked that their assets be disposed of. On this question, see in particular the third report of the Comité de mendicité entitled: "Bases constitutionnelles du système général de la législation et de l'administration des secours" (Constitutional bases of the general system of legislation and administration of relief), by Larochefoucauld-Liancourt, which was read to the Committee on 3 September 1790. This report is reproduced by Camille BLOCH and Alexandre TUETEY in *Procès-verbaux et rapports du Comité de mendicité de la Constituante, op.* cit. The abolition of tithes was not the subject of political criticism, but was instead seen as an opportunity for the nation to take charge of assistance, Ibid. p. 360. The report is particularly explicit about this claim: "We shall say that it is for the Nation alone to explain this word, because it is its duty and interest to give to public relief the direction and application most useful to the wish of humanity, to the prosperity of the State, to the improvement of the morals of its inhabitants; and we shall say finally that by distributing them in this way, that by assigning them to the truly needy, wherever they are, the Nation preserves, defends, and extends the rights and property of the poor, far from violating them. To all of these truly constitutional reasons, and necessarily consequent upon all of the principles that have guided you up to this point, we will add others which, although less essential, are still of some weight. A large part of the revenue of hospitals is reduced by those of your decrees which have destroyed tolls, the right of banality and above all tithes". Ibid., p. 361. The end of the report also presents a draft decree. Article 11 of the draft decree provides that: "The endowments and subscriptions which will be made in the future for the benefit of the poor and which will not contravene the laws of the kingdom, will be followed in all their intention, during the space of fifty years and always during the life of the donors or subscribers. The names of the subscribers or donors shall be engraved on one of the walls, in the most conspicuous place of the main establishment". Article 22 is also explicit on this point: "As a consequence of the preceding provisions, the goods whose income is today destined for the maintenance of hospitals, houses of charity, the goods governed by the hospital orders, the funds allocated to the sick homes and other establishments of the same kind, under whatever denomination, are declared national goods, and all the provisions of the laws relating to the aforementioned goods will be common to them: the question on the goods assigned to the order of Malta remaining adjourned".

for the poorest.[22] The Paris newspaper is more precise about the content of the Bishop of Rodez's remarks. It is reported that: "*M. L'évêque de Rodez spoke for a long time afterwards on the two questions & of the redemption of the tithes & of the property of the Clergy. He spoke as a man persuaded that the goods of the clergy are necessary to the maintenance of religion, to the decency of the worship & to the relief of the Poor; but some of these maxims did not seem national enough, & from this moment it was difficult to appreciate what this Prelate said, because he always spoke in the middle of a tumult which absolutely stifled his voice.*"[23] Thus, as early as the summer of 1789, Colbert of Castlehill rejected the abolition of the tithe and the arguments of the patriots, a position he maintained throughout the Constituent Assembly, in contrast to the doctrine forged by the Committee on Begging. Although the committee, like his peers appointed by the sénéchaussée of Rodez, wished to reform the tithe,[24] the bishop of Rodez certainly have feared the social consequences of its abolition, even though this tax, which had been widely misused, only allocated a meagre portion for the benefit of the indigent.[25]

However, the *status quo* remained on these two points concerning national property and tithes dedicated to the poor.[26] Article 8 of the

[22] We do not have a precise transcript of what the bishop of Rodez said on this point. The parliamentary archives simply report that: 'M. Colbert de Seignelay, bishop of Rodez, speaks of the property of the clergy as being essentially necessary for the maintenance of religion and the decency of worship, and as being the property of the poor'. A. P., t. VIII, session of 10 August 1789, p. 387.

[23] *Journal de Paris of 12 August 1789*, n°224, pp. 1009–1010.

[24] Andrew Moore points out that 'tithing, however, was defended as long as it was devoted exclusively to the payment of the congruent portion'. In this respect, the author believes that 'it is unlikely that Colbert would have objected to these principles'. Andrew MOORE, *Seignelay Colbert de Castlehill in the pre-revolutionary years, A Bishop of the Ancien Régime*, *op. cit*, p. 126.

[25] According to Dupont de Nemours, the share of the tithe devoted to the assistance of the poor was 15 million out of a total amount estimated at more than 100 million. This is why the speaker proposes to increase this amount following the abolition of the tithe. A. P., t. IX, séance du 26 septembre 1789, pp. 151–152. On this question, see Pierre-Henri GOUTTE, "Économie et transitions: l'œuvre de Dupont de Nemours au début de la Révolution française 1789–1792", *in* Jean-Michel SERVET (ed.), *Idées économiques sous la Révolution (1789–1794)*, Lyon, PUL, 1989, pp. 145–234.

[26] Mathieu Arnoux specifies that at the end of the debates in August 1789, "the role of the tithe in the maintenance of the secular clergy, teaching and assistance, will be recognised *in fine* by the Assembly, which subsequently charged the Tithe Commission with setting up assistance for the poor at the same time as proceeding to abolish the levy".

decree of 20 April 1790 states that: "*Are and remain excepted, for the time being, from the provisions of article 1er of the present decree*[27]*, the order of Malta, the fabrics, the hospitals, the houses and establishments of charity and others where the sick are received; the colleges and houses of institution, study and retreat, administered by ecclesiastics or by secular bodies, as well as the houses of nuns occupied with the public education and the relief of the sick; which will continue, as in the past, and until otherwise ordered by the Legislative Body, to administer the goods, and to collect, during the present year only, the tithes which they enjoy; except to provide, if necessary, for the following years, for the compensation which the order of Malta could claim, and to provide for the needs which the other establishments would experience by the deprivation of the tithes.*"[28] A decree of 23 October 1790 extended the deferment of the property of hospitals.[29] The same applies to another decree of 5 April 1791, which provides for their maintenance until 1er January 1792.[30]

It is true that among the immense diversity of charitable institutions within the kingdom, some were dependent on the tithe which provides for their functioning.[31] However, the point raised here is not self-evident in the writings of the bishop of Rodez. In the introduction to his *Projet d'un traité de paix générale et perpétuelle entre les différentes puissances chrétiennes de l'Europe,* Colbert de Castlehill refers to the importance of the Church in terms of moral instruction, but does not explicitly mention

Mathieu ARNOUX, "Pour une économie historique de la dîme" *in* Roland VIADER (ed.), *La dîme dans l'Europe médiévale et moderne,* Toulouse, PU du midi, 2010, pp. 145–159.

27 Article 1 of the decree states: 'The administration of property declared by the decree of 2 November last to be at the disposal of the nation will be and remain, from this year, entrusted to the departmental and district administrations, or to their directorates, under the rules, exceptions and modifications which will be explained'. Jean-Baptiste DUVERGIER, *Collection complète des lois, décrets, ordonnances, règlements, avis du Conseil d'État,* Paris, A. Guyot & scribe, 1834, t. I, pp. 154–155.

28 Ibid., pp. 154–155.

29 Adolphe de WATTEVILLE, *Législation charitable,* Paris, Alexandre Heois, 1843, p. 3.

30 Ibid., p. 8.

31 On this issue, see Alan FORREST, *La Révolution française et les pauvres,* Paris, Perrin, 1981, pp. 72–73. See also Louis TRÉNARD, "L'idéologie révolutionnaire et ses incidences" *in* Jean IMBERT (ed.), *La protection sociale sous la Révolution française,* Paris, Association pour l'étude de l'histoire de la sécurité sociale, 1990, p. 164.

its temporal role in providing assistance.[32] Moreover, the issue of public relief is not immune to the modernity of Colbert de Castlehill's thinking. In addition to the *Moyens de détruire la mendicité (Means of eradicating begging)*, which was part of his personal library—a work which had a great impact on public opinion by giving pride of place to new ideas[33]—the Bishop of Rodez was the instigator of a charity workshop, a work of assistance through labour, which testifies to the avant-garde nature of his social thinking.[34] Through the various offers of free work that he intended to create for the benefit of the destitute, Colbert de Castlehill was fully in line with the spirit of the end of the eighteenth century,

[32] Its author makes the temporal role of the Church explicit: "The purpose of this institution or establishment of a religion and *hierarchy*, as political and purely human, is to instruct the citizens from their infancy, as I have just said, in the most essential truths, in wisdom, and in the law of justice, or in mutual innocence; To teach them the application of these to the different occupations and situations of life; to persuade, exhort, and excite them by its natural sanctions to confirm themselves in them, and this by virtue of the sole natural and essential authority of their political ministry".

The purpose of this institution, as Divine and Christian, is to instruct the citizens also in the essential dogmas of the faith, in the law of mercy, of beneficence, of Christian charity, and to exhort them to submit to this faith and this law by the actions attached to it, to administer the sacraments, and to celebrate the mysteries and public worship with the proper decency, by the assistance alone of which the citizens profess and manifest to each other their submission to these two laws, and personally contract, and it must be assumed voluntarily, the obligation to conform to them. Seignelay COLBERT OF CASTLEHILL, *Projet d'un traité de paix générale et perpétuelle entre les différentes puissances chrétiennes de l'Europe, précédé d'explications préliminaires*, 1782, pp. 43–44.

[33] The work of which he was the owner was the *Summary of the memoirs which competed for the prize awarded in 1777 by the Academy of Sciences, Arts & Belles Lettres of Châlons-sur-Marne and whose subject was, the means of eradicating begging in France, by making the beggars useful to the State without making them unhappy*, Châlons-Sur-Marne, Seneuze, 1779.

[34] According to Andrew Moore, in 1789 Colbert of Castlehill proposed "the foundation of a 'charity workshop for the extinction of beggary', which would provide work for those who were able to do so 'at the same time as the genuinely needy were assured of relief commensurate with their needs'. This establishment was not to survive the advent of the Revolution, once it had lost the support of the Church; on 13 November 1790, the secretary of the association sadly noted: 'the office has consumed the little funds it had left'. Andrew MOORE, *Seignelay Colbert de Castlehill in the pre-revolutionary years, A Bishop of the Ancien Regime*, *op. cit*, p. 111.

favouring a liberal conception of assistance to the able-bodied through work rather than coercive measures.[35]

Furthermore, it seems that the Bishop of Rodez had enlisted the services of Regnier,[36] a former military doctor, who was the author of several pamphlets aimed at reorganising and rearranging the Hôtel-Dieu de Paris. Regnier paints a harsh picture of the treatment of patients in this establishment.[37] He also vilified the nuns who provided relief there on the grounds that they hindered the improvement of the treatment of patients and the rationalisation of the operation of the establishment.[38]

Despite his closeness to the propagators of the new ideas, Colbert de Castlehill remained torn between them and the defence of the interests of the Church as the conflicts became more and more intense. He was a signatory of *the Exposition sur les principes de la Constitution civile du clergé,* but also of the letter written by the bishop deputies to the National Assembly in response to the Pope's Brief *Quod Alicantum,* in

[35] On this question, please refer to our research work: Jean-Baptiste MASMÉJAN, *L'assistance par le travail à l'aune du traitement de l'indigence au XVIIIe siècle. Idées et institution- l'exemple lyonnais*, PhD law thesis, Université Lyon III, 2021.

[36] Regnier is the author of a *Project for a Hospital for the Sick or Hôtel-Dieu, in which the sick, each lying alone in a bed, would receive the best help with the least possible expense, divided into three parts* London and Paris, 1776. It seems that he is a secretary of the bishop of Rodez. Indeed, a copy of this work in the National Library specifies in manuscript that the author is "M. Regnier, secrétaire de M. l'évêque de Rodez Colbert de Castlehill, rue Saint-Benoît, 28". Maurice TOURNEUX, *Bibliographie de l'histoire de Paris pendant la Révolution française,* Paris, Imprimerie nouvelle, 1900, t. III, p. 342. Moreover, correspondence reveals that a certain Regnier is Colbert's secretary in a letter of 5 June 1786 concerning the purchase of fire pumps.

[37] Regnier is in line with his contemporaries on this issue. See, for example, the gloomy picture painted in the *Encyclopédie* in the *verbo* "Hôtel-Dieu", which in reality concerns only that of Paris. *Encyclopédie ou Dictionnaire raisonné des sciences, des arts et des métiers,* article Hôtel-Dieu (Hist. mod.), vol. VIII, 1765, pp. 319b–320a. The *Dénonciation des principaux abus de l'Hôtel-Dieu de Paris (Denunciation of the main abuses of the Hôtel-Dieu of Paris) to the General Assembly of citizens* was presented to the Committee in the session of 30 April 1790. In addition, Regnier himself submitted his *Project for a hospital for the sick or Hôtel-Dieu, in which the sick, each lying alone in a bed, would receive the best possible help with the least possible expense.* Camille BLOCH, Alexandre TUETEY, *Procès-verbaux et rapports du Comité de mendicité de la Constituante, op. cit,* p. 25. On the potential influence of Regnier's work, particularly on the Neckers, see Camille BLOCH, *L'assistance et l'État en France à la veille de la Révolution,* Paris, Alphonse Picard, 1908, p. 227.

[38] REGNIER, *Projet sur la nécessité de construire hors de la ville un Hôtel-Dieu commode et spacieux, op. cit,* p. 9.

which the disposal of the clergy's property for the benefit of the nation was deplored.[39]

This point of view is explained in a more personal way in his *Mandement et ordonnance de l'évêque de Rodez on the subject of the election of M. de Bertier*: "*Did our oppressors want to debase in advance those whom they were preparing to deprive, and after this despoilment do they seek to make us odious, so that our ruin may be more agreeable to the multitude? Our wealth was the pledge of the service of our temples, of the splendour of worship; they were also the patrimony of the poor and the resource of the state in its urgent needs, for they were never refused to the fatherland when it called for help: We were only the custodians, the guardians and the dispensers, we neither gave nor delivered this sacred deposit, but force majeure took hold of it and we did not resist it; we offered the sacrifice of it to the author of all goods, and today we have no other regret than that of no longer being able to support the weak, to relieve the needy and to alleviate the disasters of the unfortunate man.*"[40] Thus, the bishop of Rodez could not but feel torn between defending the Church of France and the orientation taken by the Committee on Begging on the question of assistance.

He could not but be reluctant to accept the wishes of the chairman of the Committee on Begging, who sought to ensure that charities were placed under supervision. However, this does not mean that Colbert of Castlehill was opposed to state interference in these matters. Although we do not know the content, he wrote a report for the Committee on the relief to be provided in the départements, implying a desire for a degree

[39] "We claimed against their alienation, and we dare to say what we were made to feel: how much more useful it would have been for the State to seek resources in the offerings of the clergy, than to alienate all its goods; and if our loss had not been sworn to, the churches of France would still be the centre of the charities on which misery was fed, and the most assured resource for the State. And when the decree was passed, which stripped us of all our possessions, our silence made it clear how inaccessible we were to all the temporal interests, the enjoyment of which had attracted hatred and envy to us. We have not disturbed with a single word, with a single complaint, the course of the operations founded on the mortgage of the goods which have been taken from us. *Exposition des principes sur la constitution civile du clergé, par les Évêques députés à l'Assemblée nationale, suivie de La lettre des mêmes évêques, en réponse au bref du Pape, en date du 10 mars 1791 et de la lettre de M. l'archevêque d'Aix, en réponse au bref de sa sainteté le pape Pie VII, en date du 15 août 1801,* Paris, Le Clere, 1801, pp. 139–140.

[40] *Mandement et Ordonnance de M. l'évêque de Rodez (Seignelay-Colbert de Castlehill) au sujet de l'élection de M. de Bertier par les électeurs du département de l'Aveyron, en qualité d'Évêque du même département*, 1791.

of state interventionism.[41] This should be taken into consideration when discussing the degree of possible divergence between the president and the vice-president of the Committee.

Thus, the ambition of the bishop of Rodez in social matters is measured against the role he gives to the clergy in matters of assistance. Although his doctrinal imprint seems weak due to political disagreements with the president of the Comité de mendicité (Committee on Begging),[42] the fact remains that his experience proved very useful.

(2) Expertise for the Committee on Begging: the search for a rationalisation of assistance

Although his influence on the Committee was probably limited, the Bishop of Rodez was very active. Colbert of Castlehill was the author of a number of missives in response to requests and other work received. He was never the only signatory.[43] His interest in financial matters was certainly valuable in understanding the documents received by the Committee on Begging. Colbert de Castlehill took on the task of studying Duvillard's project to establish a provident fund or the Lafarge tontine, created in 1791.[44]

[41] The minutes of the session of 12 May 1790 state that: "The bishop of Rodez proposed the question of knowing on what basis it would be proposed to the National Assembly to make the first distribution of relief given in a permanent manner to the departments, and, by them, to the districts, and from the districts to the municipalities. Camille BLOCH, Alexandre TUETEY, *Procès-verbaux et rapports du Comité de mendicité de la Constituante*, *op. cit*, p. 38. In addition, on 19 November 1790, "M. de Rodez again read out the address to be sent to the departments, inviting them to receive relief workshops for workers in the capital who are without work, and left a copy of the memorandum addressed to the directorate of the department of Seine-et-Marne by the municipalities of Pringy and Saint-Fargeau-sur-Seine". Ibid., p. 191.

[42] It seems that Larochefoucauld-Liancourt, like the great nobles who renounced their privileges, showed a certain distance from the national party. However, it appears that his ideas on assistance linked him to this current. On Larochefoucauld-Liancourt's political position, see François FURET, Denis RICHET, *La Révolution française*, Paris, Fayard, 2010, p. 63. Concerning Colbert de Castlehill, he was a member of the club des Impartiaux from 1790 and later of the club des monarchiques. Edna LEMAY et al., *Dictionnaire des Constituants: 1789–1791*, *op. cit*, pp. 229–230.

[43] Transcriptions are made by Camille BLOCH, Alexandre TUETEY, *Procès-verbaux et rapports du Comité de mendicité de la Constituante*, *op. cit*, pp. 141–143.

[44] On November 12, 1790, Duvillard brings to the Committee the calculations which it had just carried out with a view to establishing a provident fund. It is said that "M. de

It was above all on health issues that his action was the most consistent. The bishop of Rodez, aware of the difficulties inherent in providing relief in the countryside—the latter generally suffering from major shortcomings in this area—read out a report on relief for the sick in the countryside and a second one on assistance for the sick.[45] In this way, he certainly contributed to the draft decree explained in the fourth report of the Committee on Begging by Larochefoucauld-Liancourt. It is stated in the introductory remarks that four-fifths of the sick in the countryside do not have access to the help they need because of institutional deficiencies and the lack of personnel.[46] The project also provides for the placement of doctors paid by the state, who will deliver free relief to the poor.[47]

The contribution of the bishop of Rodez was not limited to the sick of the countryside, but also to the institutions of the largest city in

Rodez was in charge of the examination of these calculations". Ibid., p. 183. In addition, on 17 November 1790, it is reported that 'MM. de Cretot and de Rodez have been appointed commissioners to examine the project of M. Lafarge'. *Ibid*, p. 189. According to Andrew Moore, 'It seems that his speciality was in the field of finance, particularly that of taxation, a subject with which he would be particularly concerned when he was appointed President of the Provincial Assembly of Upper Guyenne. Andrew MOORE, *Seignelay Colbert de Castlehill in the pre-revolutionary years, A Bishop of the Ancien Regime*, *op. cit*, p. 101. On the Lafarge tontine, see Guy THUILLIER, *Une ténébreuse affaire: la Caisse Lafarge (1787–1892)*, Paris, Comité d'histoire de la sécurité sociale, 1999.

[45] The bishop of Rodez read out a report on relief for the sick. Camille BLOCH, Alexandre TUETEY, P*rocès-verbaux et rapports du Comité de mendicité de la Constituante*, *op. cit*, p. 135. In addition, on 6 November 1790, he made a report on the relief to be given to the sick.

[46] "The poor inhabitant of the countryside, thus usually left to his own resources, was, to be sure, in many parts of the kingdom, assisted by charities, by particular alms: but alms, particular charities are always partial, incomplete, uncertain. The charity which dictates them undoubtedly makes the friends of humanity who spread them highly esteemed, but in the very places where they are more abundant and more constant, they depend on the free will of these benefactors, and in no case do they exempt society from its duties. Moreover, it is quite impossible for them to be general; and one can boldly state that more than four-fifths of the inhabitants of the countryside, deprived of any assistance in their illnesses, are doomed to all kinds of misery as a result. Also, a higher proportion of mortality than it should be, frequent relapses for those who do not succumb, premature old age, infirmities, and numerous accidents add to the all too certain chance of misfortune and human misery in the countryside". Ibid., Fourth Report of the Committee on Begging, p. 392.

[47] See the transcript of the draft decree on rural relief. Ibid., pp. 399–400. On the establishment of doctors and surgeons in the countryside, Ibid., pp. 394–395.

the kingdom. He wrote a number of reports on the charitable structures in Paris. He presented a report on the Hòtel-Dieu, the Hôpital de Saint-Louis, the Hôpital de Sainte-Anne, the Charité, the Hôpital des Convalescents, the Maison Royale de Santé and the Hospice de Saint-Sulpice.[48] He then produced a second report on the administration of the Incurables.[49] Of this work, the report on behalf of the Committee that followed was written by Larochefoucauld-Liancourt alone. However, as Camille Bloch and Alexandre Tuetey point out, although the president of the Committee seems to be the real author, it seems undeniable that the bishop of Rodez certainly provided valuable information concerning the above-mentioned establishments.[50] The information given by Colbert de Castlehill contributed to the evaluation of each of these charitable works. Firstly, their origins are presented, as well as their development, the way in which treatment was provided to the sick and, finally, the reforms that needed to be carried out in order to improve their operation. What emerges systematically is the criticism of overcrowding and its disastrous consequences: high mortality, spread of contagious diseases, etc. In the wake of Regnier, proposals are made to reduce the number of patients hospitalised, and a desire to rationalise the management of hospitals appears. Above all, considerations of hygiene predominated: living conditions and insalubrity were vigorously denounced. Criticism of the Hôtel-Dieu highlighted most clearly the dissatisfaction with conditions. In fact, in line with enlightened opinion under the Ancien Régime, the institution was accused of not taking proper care of the sick because of

[48] Ibid., session of 15 October 1790, p. 145.

[49] Ibid., session of 10 November 1790, pp. 180–181.

[50] As Alexandre Tuetey and Camille Bloch note, "The three parts of the report on the visits made to the hospitals in Paris are printed under the name of La Rochefoucauld-Liancourt. He is probably the real author of this report and its two sequels, since it was he who reported to the Committee on these visits (pages indicated if necessary). But we also see in the minutes that it was the bishop of Rodez who reported to the Committee on the Hôtel-Dieu, the hospitals of Saint-Louis, Sainte-Anne, Charité, Convalescents, the Maison Royale de Santé, the hospice of Saint-Sulpice, and the Incurables. As the first report is devoted to the Hôpital Général and the visits Liancourt reported on concern the various houses that made it up, there is a good chance that he is right to be credited with this report, as is the case with the two sequels which are devoted to the Quinze-Vingts, the Petites Maisons and the Trinité. But there is reason to presume that at least the participation of the bishop of Rodez in the other suite concerning the Hôtel-Dieu, the houses of the Brothers of Charity, the parish hospices, etc., must have been great. *Ibid,* pp. XLIII-XLIV.

overcrowding and poor treatment. The Committee, vilifying the exorbitant size of this health structure, favoured the dissemination of smaller establishments and, above all, home help.[51]

* * *

Thus, Colbert de Castlehill's participation in the Committee on Begging highlights the political issues surrounding the assistance of the indigent. Although his position seems to have given him a rather marginal role, the fact remains that the opposition reported between the defenders of a conception centred on state intervention and the promoters of the Church did not constitute such a strict rupture as it might seem. The bishop of Rodez was one of those enlightened prelates concerned with rationalising and organising assistance so that everyone could benefit, including those in the countryside.

[51] Assistance at home was unanimously welcomed by enlightened opinion. On this question, see Louis TRÉNARD, "L'idéologie révolutionnaire et ses incidences", *op. cit.* pp. 171–172.

CHAPTER 9

Colbert and Debertier Tested by the Revolution

Bernard Fixes

Abstract Bernard Fixes presents the reactions of two priests from Rouergue at the turn of the year 1792. Colbert had left full of hope to participate in the Estates-General after having been elected as a representative of the clergy of Rouergue. His attitude was to change when the Civil Constitution of the Clergy and the obligation to take an oath were implemented, even if we do not know exactly how it evolved from the end of 1789 to the spring of 1792. Colbert was soon to adopt a hard line, as can be seen from his letters to the priests of his diocese. Bernard Fixes explains the context in Rouergat and establishes the position of the priests who were faced with an agonising choice by the Constituent. It is very likely that the position of their bishop influenced their decisions. The massive refusal of the priests, which had far-reaching consequences, illustrated the divorce between the Church and the Revolution.

English revised by Timothy R. Day. Abridged from the French (https://books.openedition.org/).

B. Fixes (✉)
Parish Priest of Bozouls, Bozouls, France

A. Alcouffe (ed.), *Seignelay Colbert de Castlehill (1735-1811)*,
https://doi.org/10.1007/978-3-031-75273-5_9

Keywords Colbert of Castlehill · Civil Constitution of the Clergy · Rodez · Claude Debertier · Episcopal Election · Diocese of Rodez · Constitutional Church · Schism · Concordat of 1802 · Revolutionary France

The limited scope of this paper does not allow us to make an exhaustive study of the diocese of Rodez under the episcopate of Colbert, nor of the position of the priests in the face of the Civil Constitution of the Clergy, which was undoubtedly the main event.

We have therefore chosen, after recalling some data concerning Colbert, to focus on his position with regard to the Civil Constitution and his disagreements with Claude Debertier shortly after the latter's election as constitutional bishop of Rodez. It was not without interest to see the clash of two ecclesiologies and two men around the Civil Constitution and the vacant see of Rodez. This clash led to a painful and profound fracture in the Church of Rouergue, which was to lead to schism with the refusal by the "small Church" of the Concordat of 1802. This refusal was encouraged at the beginning by Colbert.

We will not go back over Colbert's formative years and his position as grand vicar to Loménie in the archdiocese of Toulouse. We will only recall that he was appointed bishop of Rodez by the King on 2 April 1781, replacing Mgr Jérôme-Marie Champion de Cicé, who had resigned on 3 March to join Bordeaux, the see for which he himself had just been appointed.

Cicé's succession was not the easiest given the personality of the resigning prelate and the incessant activity he had shown in his diocese since his appointment in 1770. His role as president of the Provincial Assembly of Upper Guyenne, created by Necker in 1779, and where he was to reveal brilliant administrative qualities which could give him hope of a ministerial career of the first rank, demanded solid qualities from his successor. It is not impossible, given Cicé's long-standing links with Mgr Yves-Alexandre de Marbeuf, who then held the "feuille des bénéfices", that he himself, if not chose his successor, at least expressed a decisive opinion....

With less splendour, but a certain similarity in approach, Colbert was also to show his gifts in the administration of the diocese and the province. More present in his diocese than his predecessor—as the register of priestly ordinations, where the name of the consecrating prelate is always mentioned, seems to testify—he was particularly concerned with the training of the clergy and the organisation of studies in the colleges of Rodez and the seminaries of Laguiole, Saint-Geniez and Villefranche—notably by launching a survey in 1784.

At the Provincial Assembly, "*he calmed*", according to Lavergne, "*by his conciliatory character, the irritations of people whom his predecessor would perhaps have irritated, which did not prevent him from showing on occasion an unshakeable firmness*".[1] This was clearly seen in the conflict which pitted him against the intendant Meulan d'Ablois in 1782. *Mr. Intendant*, The bishop defended himself: "*Mr. Intendant seems to be accusing us of spreading concern about the shortage... It is not from the government that we must receive our instruction. The general principles which come to us from education and local knowledge, the government needs us to acquire... Are the men who govern us gods? Do they have no need of knowledge and instruction on objects remote from them? Can they know the needs of the people, if they forbid those who represent them the means of learning about them and depicting them?*[2]" This was the day after the poor harvest of 1781.... The same year, he was concerned about the danger that the populations of Quercy and Rouergue were running from the floods, and launched a large number of projects of a social nature—the creation of child-birthing classes in each chief town of election, the resolute pursuit of the project of repairing the land register, which was in opposition to many interests, care for livestock....

It is therefore not surprising that the bishop was elected as a representative of his order to the Estates-General pursuant to the order made on 26 February 1789 by the lieutenant-general of the *sénéschaussée* of Rodez, Joseph-François de Séguret, summoning the electors of the three orders to the church of the royal college of the town for the election of deputies to the Estates on 16 March 1789. The Rouergue was divided into two *sénéchaussées*—that of Millau, in whose jurisdiction Rodez was located, and that of Villefranche. It seemed interesting to us to follow the electoral operations more closely. Although very precise on these days regarding the procedure and the voters, the minutes of the sessions held in Rodez

[1] Lavergne, Léonce de - *Les assemblées provinciales sous Louis XVI*, éd. Lévy, Paris, 1879, page 85.

[2] *Op. cit.* page 89.

and Villefranche do not give us the votes obtained by the deputies[3] sent to the Estates-General. They merely state that Colbert was elected deputy of the clergy on the first ballot on 23 March. According to Servières, writing at the end of the nineteenth century, and reporting a tradition, the result was uncertain for a long time[4] and the bishop would have preceded the Abbé Malrieu by only one vote, a prior parish priest of Lebous and professor at the royal college who was considered to be less liberal than him. Gautier Louyriac reports in his memoir[5] that Colbert had previously set out a programme in which he advocated improving the lot of vicars and parish priests, founding an honourable pension for infirm or elderly priests and saying that he paid particular attention to ecclesiastical education. Perhaps on this occasion he won the decisive vote or votes?

The next day, 24 March, in Villefranche, the assembly, presided over by the bishop of Vabres, Jean de la Croix de Castries, elected Abbé Malrieu in the third round and, on the 25th, it was a great vicar of Colbert, Jean-Chrysostome de Villaret, future bishop of Amiens and Alexandria, who was elected in the second round. If the election testifies to the good opinion of the Rouergat clergy on Colbert—all the candidate bishops were not elected—it also reveals some reservations. The very good score of a parish priest in Rodez, narrowly missing out on election against the bishop in the first round, and his success in Villefranche on the second day against one of Colbert's closest collaborators, illustrates the dynamic survival of richerist ideas in the Rouergue clergy. I would be more dubious than Gautier Louyriac about the fading of Jansenism in a diocese which was marked by the combative episcopate of La Vove de Tourouvre and the bitter debates around Unigenitus and the anti-Jansenist oath. These affairs had left traces that were not easily healed. The proof is that Debertier, summoned in his last days to retract his constitutional oath, refused to do so but affirmed his retraction of the oath he had had to take to be ordained a priest, an oath that guaranteed his adherence to the Form. This vote may have also sanctioned a certain distance from the bishop, whose "*absence*" was deplored in the cahiers de la noblesse et du Tiers

[3] The elections of 1789. Procès-verbaux. Society of Letters, Arts and Sciences of Aveyron.

[4] E. de Barrau, *1789 en Rouergue*, Rodez, Vve Carrère, 1873, p. 375.

[5] Gautier Louyriac, "Le diocèse de Rodez à la fin du XVIIIe siècle. Part I Sous l'épiscopat de Mgr Seignelay-Colbert (1781–1789)", master's thesis, Université Jean Jaurès.

de Villefranche, while at the same time requesting the application of the canons "*concerning the residence and visitation of bishops in their diocese*". It could also be that his known closeness to Brienne and his liberal ideas put him at a disadvantage in the eyes of some who were more familiar with Malrieu's reputation for rigour and his status as a theologian.

The deputies of the Third Estate to the Estates-General proceeded to form themselves into Communes and then into the National and Constituent Assembly. Colbert, having been one of the first bishops[6] to join it at the session of 22 June, made him very popular with the people. His first votes placed him among the liberals of the Assembly and it was not until the vote on the Civil Constitution of the Clergy that he was thrown into opposition to the Revolution.

If there is one event that has profoundly marked the history of France and that of the Church, it is the Civil Constitution of the Clergy. Its consequences have continued to be felt in the political and religious life of the country to this day. Voted on 12 July 1790, the Civil Constitution of the Clergy was sanctioned by the King on 24 August. The Archbishop of Bordeaux, Colbert's predecessor in the see of Rodez, Jérôme-Marie Champion de Cicé, had contributed to this decision. The debate continued at that time not only in the Constituent Assembly but throughout the country, where supporters and opponents clashed, sometimes violently.

This passion was fuelled by the silence of Pope Pius VI, which gave free rein to all interpretations. However, one document, published on 30 October, emerged from all the literature generated by the event. It was the *Exposition des principes sur la Constitution civile du clergé* written by the influential archbishop of Aix, Boisgelin, who had, from the opening of the debates on 29 May, denied the Assembly the necessary competence to legislate on spiritual matters. If they had made themselves scarce during the discussion, the bishops were now expressing themselves. Thirty signatures, including that of the bishop of Rodez, Colbert, who had hitherto been known for his liberal stance, supported the document and thereby demonstrated the distance of the most conciliatory prelates from the religious policy of the Assembly. The tone was not yet one of rupture but of a firm warning. Nothing acceptable could be done "*until the Church had manifested her wish by the voice of her visible head, or until the canonical*

[6] With the archbishops of Vienne and Bordeaux, the bishop of Chartres, in Albert MATHIEZ, *Les grandes journées de la Constituante*, Paris, 1913, page 8.

forms had been observed…". And the bishops concluded by placing "*their trust in the response of the successor of St Peter, who, placed in the centre of the Catholic universe and of communion, must be the interpreter and organ of the universal Church*[7]". Sent to the bishops who were not deputies, the Exposition received almost unanimous approval. The only ones to refuse it were those who were to take the oath a few months later. Talleyrand, Savine and Gobel had not associated themselves with the step of sending. Brienne and Jarente, not elected, did not adhere to it. In his correspondence with Bernis, the ambassador of France to the Holy See, Boisgelin was conscious to express himself in the name of the episcopate of France: "*I did not want to let a sentence remain, an expression which the bishops did not approve. I can say that they signed every line.*" The exhibition also received the signatures of deputies of the second order, including Villaret and Malrieu.

At first, the Assembly had not demanded an oath to the constitution. The first oath required was on 24 July from priests who wanted to be able to receive the Nation's salary, following the nationalisation of the clergy's property on 2 November 1789. It was not until the Voidel report, following the critical wait-and-see attitude of the bishops, that a decree was passed on 27 November 1790 "*obliging (…) within a week of this publication, (…) the bishops (…) and parish priests whose sees and cures have been preserved (…)* to solemnly swear, in the name of the Nation, to the following conditions*) to solemnly swear, if they have not already done so, to watch over the faithful of the dioceses and cures entrusted to them, to be faithful to the nation, to the law and to the king, to maintain with all their power the constitution decreed by the National Assembly and accepted by the king*" (Art. II).

"*The bishops and the parish priests shall take the above-mentioned oath on a Sunday, at the end of mass, (…) in the presence of the municipalities, the general councils, the communes and all the faithful.* (Art. III).

"*If they fail to take the above-mentioned oath within the specified period, the said bishops and parish priests shall be deemed to have renounced their offices, and their replacement shall be provided for, as in the case of a vacancy…*"[8]

[7] Exposition of the principles on the Civil Constitution of the Clergy by the deputy bishops—Annex to the session of 30 October 1790.

[8] Parliamentary archives from 1787 to 1860 for the first series (1787–1799) Volume XX. From 23 October to 28 November 1990, Perseus, Generic file.

It is not without interest at this stage of events to reread the letter sent by Boisgelin to Louis XVI in response to a request for advice, dated 1 December "*One hopes in the unanimous opposition of the clergy of France. There are forty thousand parish priests: what will be the small proportion of those who are not held back by fear? It is thought that the people would be on the move for religion; that would be a great evil. There is nothing that the bishops should not do to prevent it, and this evil will not happen, because it concerns questions which are beyond the reach of the people. There are two principles which the clergy must never lose sight of: 1° that religion must not be mixed up in political discussions; 2° that the Church must do, for fear of a split, all that it can do*[9]". This is a remarkable letter from the pen of one of the most listened-to personalities of the French clergy, one of those to whom Colbert felt closest. It is reasonable to assume that the two prelates were more or less on the same ground between those who were prepared to accept the constitution as it stood and those who opposed any concessions. The king must not have been very far from these two men who, after waiting in vain for a reply from the pope, had to resolve to give his constitutional sanction to the decree on 26 December 1790, giving it the force of law, pressed by an increasingly impatient public. The next day, Abbé Grégoire went up to the rostrum of the Assembly to take the required oath, followed by fifty-one deputy priests, and, on the 28th, the very recent bishop of Autun, Talleyrand.

In Aveyron

The law was to be published in the department of Aveyron on 3 January 1791, the day before the day set as the deadline for ecclesiastical deputies to take the oath.

We must report here in its entirety what Servières writes in his *Histoire de l'Église du Rouergue*, published in 1874, on a testimony of the Abbé Malrieu: "*The last deadline for the taking of the oath was fixed at 4 January 1791. The bishop of Rodez was going to take it and was preparing a letter for his diocesan staff. Abbé Malrieu has run to his hotel. The prelate is lying down and the servant is defending his door, because Seignelay must leave the following day for Rodez. Abbé Malrieu, by dint of insistence, finally reached him, and explained to him the seriousness of the act he was about*

[9] Abbé Lavaquery, "le Cardinal de Boisgelin" (1732–1804), Paris, Plon, 1921, (1er vol. pages 114 and 115).

to perform. You are," he said, "the successor of holy bishops and the head of a holy clergy, and in one fell swoop, you are going to obscure this glory. This motto of which the city of Rodez is so proud: Rutena fidelis Deo et Regi, Rodez faithful to God and the King, you are therefore going to disown it! It will thus be said that a Colbert will lose the beautiful diocese of Rodez. My lord, get up and leave at once for England. To this sharp apostrophe, the bishop answered nothing, he buried his head in his bed, and, the next day, he left for England instead of heading for Rouergue. Abbé Malrieu, asked by the venerable Doctor Marion how a bishop "as pious as Mgr Colbert" could have conceived such a project, replied that he had been led to this decision by his secretary[10] ».

This testimony cannot, in our opinion, be accepted without examination. On the one hand, it contains at least one inaccuracy since we know that Colbert did not leave France on the date indicated. We have evidence of his presence in Paris during February and March 1791 and the letter to the Duke of Buccleuch dated 21 October 1792 "was probably written shortly after Colbert's arrival in England", says Alain Alcouffe who published it with Andrew Moore.[11] Moreover, we have seen him close to Boisgelin who, despite his efforts at conciliation, showed an unequivocal attitude at the decisive moment. Colbert was also quick to publicly express his opinion on the Civil Constitution in a letter to his clergy, which we must quote since we have mentioned the suspicion raised about his determination. "*What advice can I give you in this moment of distress, if not the one I have chosen myself? What other rule of conduct can I indicate to you than that which is justified by the principles of the Church, transmitted by her in the monuments of her doctrine and tradition (...)?*

The moment is approaching; prepare yourselves for it by prayer; be penetrated by a sense of your duties; remember your vocation; remember that we are travellers on earth, that we must not cling to its perishable goods; that we must suffer for the sake of justice; that persecution is a means which God uses to purify his sanctuary (...).

You will be notified of the decree of the oath: it is up to you to examine your conscience. The fate of your whole life will probably depend on the choice you make. If you refuse, you will be expelled from your property and left to

[10] A. B. Servières, *Histoire de l'Église du Rouergue*, Rodez, Vve Carrère, 1874, page 551.

[11] Alain Alcouffe & Andrew Moore, 'La correspondance de Seignelay Colbert de Castlehill et du Duc de Buccleuch' in Études Aveyronnaises.

humiliation and poverty. Another will take your place and take over your people (...).

If your parishioners who esteem and love you think of defending you, use all the credit you have on their minds to soften and appease them. In a word, let us bless those who persecute us, and let us console ourselves by thinking that we are suffering for justice (...) let us be like lambs that are tied up and sacrificed, but that do not resist[12]". It seems that this is rather the truth of a man who only reluctantly resigned himself to becoming a refractory to the law and for a long time believed that he could find a conciliatory formula likely to be accepted by the King, the Church and the Nation, at the risk of appearing timid in the eyes of those who were more resolute in their opposition.

Does the episode reported by Malrieu not reflect this difference in temperament and bear witness to a persistent misunderstanding between the two men? This is the hypothesis we propose to explain the contradiction observed, a hypothesis which does not seem to contradict the subsequent evolution of the two men. Having become superior of the Concordat seminary, Abbé Malrieu could hardly have understood the resolute opposition to the Concordat of priests who claimed to be followers of Colbert and could have been tempted to play on their suspicions about the character of a prelate whose conciliatory spirit could have led him to be accused of pusillanimity. In the absence of more reliable information, we will leave it at that, pending further documentation on this episode.

The first priests we find taking the oath in the diocese are two brothers, the parish priests of Muret and Calmont de Plancade, Jean and Raymond Long, on Sunday 16 January. Curiously, Claude de Bertier, parish priest of Laguiole and future constitutional bishop, waited to take the oath until 6 February, but this delay should not be blamed on him because he organised, with Benoit Dasnières, his former colleague and principal of the college in Rodez, conferences on "the legitimacy of the Civil Constitution" at the same time as he consigned with him a "Letter of a priest to his fellow-member on the Civil Constitution" of which the Society of the Friends of the Constitution voted the impression on January 15 and 19 before addressing public congratulations to him for "*the courage which he*

[12] Copy of the Letter written by Monsieur l'Évêque de Rodez to Mgr, Curé & Vicaire forain de son Diocèse, (in Paris on 8 January 1791).

showed in his eagerness to swear submission and fidelity to the Civil Constitution of the clergy." The municipality of Laguiole must have been less eager than its pastor to organise the oath ceremony.

To tell the truth, it does not seem that the new authorities of the department and the communes were moved by a devouring zeal. It is only on Sunday February 13 that the clergy of Rodez were called to take the oath and still the members of the club of the Friends of the Constitution planned "*to go to the ceremony to protect the swearers...*" which augured the feelings of the ruthénoise population! Undoubtedly the example of Millau, where the mayor Bouzès had been forced to resign following a real riot, where "*a considerable number of women and children of all ages*" had invaded the town hall and where two hundred active citizens had signed a petition asking for the suspension of the decree on the Civil Constitution of the Clergy, on 25 January, aroused legitimate fears among the supporters of the oath. Serious disorders were also reported in Clairvaux, Entraygues, Espalion, Estaing, Flavin, Ginolhac, Laguiole, Laissac, in Nayrac, in Saint-Geniez and Trémouilles... and there circulated, as in Saint-Jean de Clauzelles, on January 29, petitions "*begging to keep (their pastor) away from this fatal day when he must be challenged to make this horrible oath, the mere idea of which has thrown alarm into all hearts and trouble into all the consciences of Roman Catholics, (begging) to instruct the gentlemen of the department and the Assembly, if necessary, that they are very willing to make all sorts of sacrifices rather than separate themselves from the religion of their fathers, the only one which can lead them to the happiness of the future life*".

The opponents were to receive considerable support with the resignation of Louis de Bonald, president of the departmental directoire, dated the day the oath was to be taken at the chief town. Bonald unambiguously explained the reasons for his resignation: "(...) *I owe to the faith that I profess another tribute than an equivocal absence or a timid silence. (...) I would prevent the decisions of the head of the Church, defy the unanimous opinion of its pastors, dishonour my religion by placing priests between conscience and interest, between perjury and degradation! I would say to them: "Swear, or renounce your functions", "your livelihood", as in other times men were told: "Believe or die! No, no, gentlemen, humanity as much as religion revolts at this thought*[13]". This resignation was to lead to others, that of the public prosecutor of the Séguret department in particular.

In the meantime, on 13 February, only the clergymen wishing to obey the oath had presented themselves to take it, "*at the end of the mass of the cathedral parish*" before the mayor Arsaud, the prosecutor of the commune Dasnières, himself subject to the oath, and the general council of the commune. If the parish priest Alazard had shied away, his two vicars were present, soon to be followed by professors at the royal college: Galan, sub-principal; Fabre, professor of philosophy; Louchet, a tonsured professor who was to play an important role in the fall of Robespierre; the chaplain of the Hôtel-Dieu; and Abbé Viala, chaplain to Colbert. The notable absence of Charles Carnus, professor of philosophy and physics at the college, who had made a name for himself with Louchet by climbing into a hot-air balloon on 6 August 1784, and that of Abbé Malrieu, a former professor of philosophy who had recently been elected deputy, should be noted. In Villefranche, the parish priest did not appear; the third vicar read the decree before taking the oath without restriction. He was followed by the second and third vicars who added restrictions to their oaths "*formally excepting those objects which may depend on the spiritual power*". Millau had given an unequivocal answer with the refusal of all the parish priests and vicars of the town and district. We were on a border region with the Protestant country.

Largely according to the districts, this massive refusal took on the appearance of a major disavowal of the new religious policy in Rouergue, worrying authorities and partisans about the oath whose bitterness one can perceive in the explanations of the parish priest of Laguiole, future constitutional bishop Debertier: "*A thing affects me and disturbs my rest: it is to see a number of my confreres, very zealous moreover and very pious, blindly following false impulses and dictated by an ill-founded fear - to incur the disgrace of a nation which wants to be and will be profoundly religious; to make themselves forever odious to peoples to whom their lights and their piety were useful - and to turn, without wishing to do so, the weapons of religion against religion itself. (...) I consider myself fortunate that true principles have confirmed me in the judgement I had long made of a law whose wisdom is disputed, and which I had regarded as the restoration*

[13] A. C. Sabatié, *Debertier, évêque constitutionnel et le clergé de Rodez*, Rodez, 1912, pages 44, 45.

of religion ... God grant that such a beautiful work, which I believe to have come from his hands, may succeed![14]

This letter is interesting in that it expresses the intimate feelings of the man who was to lead the Constitutional Church of Aveyron at a time when he was still unaware of it, and it is reasonable to think that it expresses the position of many of those who adhered to the Civil Constitution.

This is a valuable testimony, especially as these priests took a "pure and simple" oath to obey the law... For them, it was not a question of renouncing any of their former loyalties but of living out what they considered to be a restoration of religion. It was a return to a more stripped-down Church that could not help but remind them of the original Church, as the persecuted Jansenists had also wanted to restore it. This was an exalting moment for them because it was lived in close union with the Nation, itself in the process of regeneration.

On 21 February, the authorities noted the vacancy of the episcopal see due to the refusal of its incumbent to take the oath. This set in motion a process whose consequences were beginning to be felt.

In a letter to Colbert dated 14 March, the Abbé de Grun, the vicar-general, gave an account of events a few days after Pius VI's brief, *Quod aliquantum*, condemning the Civil Constitution: "*The week we have just spent has been very stormy.... The electors have been called for next Sunday, the 20th of this month. I spoke to several from the countryside; they appeared to me in good dispositions and with the intention of complying with your letter written to the department; but I believe and I fear very much that the great number will be to appoint (...)*[15]".

On 20 March, the meeting of the electoral assembly that was to carry out the episcopal election was held in the cathedral.

The session was opened with a speech by Nogaret, who testified to the existence of a resistance which was echoed in the *Gazette nationale* in its issue of 7 April.

"There is perhaps no department where patriots have had more to do with fighting fanaticism than this one ...

Almost all the electors, on their way to Rhodez, were assailed by fanatical priests who had posted themselves on their paths, and who, after having

[14] A. C. Sabatié, *op. cit.* pages 42, 43.

[15] A. C. Sabatié, *op. cit*, page 61.

sought to sound the alarm about the fate of religion to them, filled their pockets with libels against the National Assembly and the new constitution it had decreed.[16] (...).

The voting process could then begin. Of the 320 members present and the 700 expected, 173 voters elected the parish priest of Laguiole, Claude Debertier, as president.

At the end of the first two rounds of voting on 22 March, an absolute majority could not be reached... It was by a simple majority of 221 voters that the parish priest of Estaing, Albouy, was elected in the third round. Born in 1735, doctor in theology, member of the AA,[17] Amans Albouy was ordained as a priest in 1761 and became parish priest of Estaing in 1777. In his district, exceptionally, no priest refused the oath.

However, after thanking the assembly for its confidence, Albouy stated that he was "*mortified at not being able to respond to it (...) This is not a disapproval of the civil constitution of the clergy; I have always made and continue to make the case for it.*[18] *I would be delighted if my health and my talents allowed me to take advantage of the benefits which it provides for the clergy of the second order*. Back in Estaing, Albouy and his two vicars retracted "*absolutely*" the oath they had taken before a notary on 13 February (...) which they "*want and claim to be regarded as null and void*[19]" (...).

Having taken note of Albouy's resignation, the assembly elected, without surprise, on 23 March, by 156 votes, the parish priest of Laguiole and superior of the seminary of this town, Claude Debertier.[20]

Proclaimed bishop of the department of Aveyron, Debertier was to receive the canonical investiture of Sermet, the metropolitan of the south, and to be consecrated in Paris by Gobel on 1 May 1791.

Born in Clermont on 22 May 1750, Claude de Bertier had joined the diocese of Rodez at the age of ten to attend the royal college with the hope of succeeding his uncle Benoit-Pantaléon de Bertier, parish priest

[16] *Gazette Nationale*, 7 April 1791, page 54, reprinted 1841.

[17] Ed. note: The AA [Association of Friends] was a secret society inside the clergy.

[18] A. C. SABATIÉ, *op. cit*, page 79.

[19] Rétractation de serment faite devant notaire à Estaing et enregistrée par le "sieur Bestier," à Espalion, le 18 avril 1791, quoted by A. C. SABATIÉ, *op. cit.* pages 82, 83.

[20] It is from this moment that Claude de Bertier abandons his particle to be called Debertier.

of Flaujac. After brilliant studies, the young man was ordained deacon by Mgr de Cicé and sent to Mende to receive the priesthood in the first week of Lent 1775.

His uncle having died and another candidate having been preferred by the prior, Debertier was appointed professor at the royal college. He lived there for four happy years but resigned to apply for the parish of Coubisou where Colbert was to come and appoint him parish priest of Laguiole on 10 February 1783. He was to keep '*a father's heart*' for this parish, as he wrote to one of his former parishioners in 1808. The bishop's choice reflected his confidence in a priest who, as superior of the seminary of this town, was also called upon to exercise a real moral authority over one of the richest and most dynamic regions of the diocese... that of the mountains. In this task of formation, Bertier knew how to give *the* best of himself, "*supervising the teaching very well*". This was also reflected in his moral ascendancy, which explains both the choice of the oath made by the majority of the priests in the districts of this region... up to the Lot valley... and its influence beyond.

The latter had made his feelings known shortly before in a letter dated 13 February.

"*In showing zeal for the constitution and for the civil constitution of the clergy (...) I did only what I believed to be the duty of every citizen, of every Christian, of every priest and of every pastor. (...) I sought the truth with all the uprightness of my heart, and when I thought I saw it, I fought to embrace it against all the opposition that arose. My oath taken on the 6th of this month is proof of my feelings. Far from repenting, I congratulate myself on it every day. (...)*".

This letter is interesting. It expresses the intimate feelings of the man who would be called upon to lead the Constitutional Church of Rouergue at a time when he was still unaware of it, and it is reasonable to think that it also expresses the position of many of those who adhered to the Civil Constitution.

On 21 April, the day that Debertier arrived in Paris, Colbert signed a curious "*Agenda for the time of the schism*[21]" which was intended as a directory for bishops and parish priests. We do not know whether this notebook, found in the diocesan archives of Aveyron, was widely

21 "Agenda pour le temps du schism", 60 articles for bishops, 32 for parish priests, given in Paris on 21 April 1791, manuscript, 38 p. Diocesan archives, Colbert collection.

distributed. It is a real organisational plan for a Church forced underground. Sixty articles concern the bishops, thirty-two the parish priests. From this thick document, we will retain only a few provisions. Title two obliges "*parish priests*", in the event that the administrative bodies notify a bishop to stop exercising his functions, "*not to recognise the authority of any bishop other than himself, as long as the Church has not withdrawn his mission and transferred it to another.*

The same obliges their flock "*not to recognise any other bishop or parish priest than the one the Church has given them, and not to take part in any irregular elections which could only result in intruders*".

In anticipation of difficult times, "*and being necessary to provide each day for the government of the diocese, and for the spiritual needs of the people, it seems expedient to entrust temporarily to all the parish priests and vicars serving parishes, annexes or branches which would remain faithful to the legitimate bishop, the powers to confess throughout the diocese, even those in religious vows and to absolve from sins and censures reserved to the bishop, to give their parishioners the dispensations on marriage impediments which are retained by the laws and practice of the Church, to allow in their parishes the use of eggs during Lent, and to perform all other acts of daily practice. These powers would be given until 1rst January 1793, except to renew them then, if the good of religion requires it. Each parish priest and the curate who will be given these powers will keep a register of all the acts which he will do by virtue of the said powers, and he will give an account of them to the bishop or to his grand vicars, as often as it will be possible for him to do so in order to maintain the unity of the government and of authority in the diocese*".

If "*the prudence of each bishop will determine the wisest conduct to be maintained in each diocese, with regard to sworn priests*" (art. 29) … "*all the laws of the Church forbid any communication in divinis with intruder priests, and consequently to hear their masses, to attend the divine offices celebrated by them, to receive from them Easter communion, to receive their visits as pastors in times of sickness, and all other religious acts…*" (art. 31).

In this document, Colbert shows astonishing foresight as to future events at a time when persecution was not yet the order of the day, even if major disturbances continued to agitate the Rouergue, attesting to the exasperation of the people and their resistance, particularly the women.

It was a woman who, in Millau, had read a letter to the Cordeliers from Colbert, dated in Paris (4 August) and bearing the words: "*If the ministers of error set traps for you, refuse to accept their perfidious insinuations... Pray for them, and keep charity and peace towards them*".

On 6 May, the day on which the priest of Bousquet was prosecuted for having circulated a libel against Debertier, the directoire of the department "*informed of all the seditious manoeuvres practised by the enemies of the public good and especially by priests refractory to the law*", affirms "*to have to take all the precautions and to employ all the means of rigour which the law determined, to prevent the disorders and to stop the progress of fanaticism.*

(...) it [the Directoire] decides that

1° *Within a week, elections will be held to replace parish priests who have died, resigned or refused to take the oath.*
2° *The authorities shall be required to denounce and prosecute all priests who show themselves to be rebellious to the law.*
3° *All those who, having been replaced, interfere in their former functions will be punished*".

These were not vain threats since on May 11, proceedings have been engaged against M. Alazard, priest of Rignac, guilty of having spoken against the constitution in the catechism. The same day "*the Society of the Friends of the Constitution has been moaning for a long time about the ravages caused by the inflammatory writings spread with profusion in our department. It has learned with the greatest sorrow that the town of Rodez and the neighbouring countryside were flooded with so-called pastoral letters which have no other aim than to cause trouble in consciences and to arm the citizen against the citizen.* And, as proof of what she advances, she sends to the directoire of the department" *a copy of the regulations addressed to the nuns of our department. This work is attributed to Colbert, the former bishop of Rodès.*

The latter did not remain inactive and, the following day, 12 May, a letter from Mgr de Colbert states "*by the grace of God and the authority of the Apostolic See bishop and count of Rodez*", after having deplored "*abuses... which had reached their peak... which had degraded morals, weakened the springs of government and tired the obedience of the people*", abuses which "*had introduced themselves even into the sanctuary and had altered its austere discipline, and heard the cry of France calling loudly for reform*". Astonished, Colbert wonders: "*But was it necessary to overthrow the institutions themselves to correct their vices?*"

"*Was it by the annihilation of principles that it was possible to restore their strength and bring them back to their primitive purity?*"

This is followed by a vigorous denunciation of the Civil Constitution, "*that strange law*" which "*carries the suppression of fifty-three dioceses... violates the absolute distinction between spiritual and civil power*" and this denunciation is reiterated as a leit-motiv: "*We will not take the oath... because it tends to the overthrow of the hierarchy, it violates the rights of the Pope, the bishops and the good priests... because it would be to applaud the destruction of episcopal authority, subject to the decisions of a council of priests... for this would be to confuse the power of order and jurisdiction; the civil power cannot give spiritual powers... for the civil power cannot dissolve monastic vows, abolish religious orders... for this would be to approve the destruction of chapters and other ecclesiastical institutions...* This is also followed by a vigorous denunciation of Debertier, "*this reckless priest... who, trampling on the laws of honour and the priesthood, enters like a thief into the house of the father of the family and prepares to ravage his inheritance, after having driven him out by force!*" and the solemn affirmation according to which "*there can be no other bishop of Rodez today than the one whose place you have usurped*"... "*You will find, perhaps, some banned or crazy, infamous ecclesiastics, some apostate monks or others of the same kind, who have been the opprobrium of the Church and who today deserve to be its rejects? These are the worthy companions you deserve to have: do not wait for others to come along!*[22]".

The letter concludes with a declaration of the nullity of a "*schismatic election*" and of all acts arising from it.

The situation could not have been clearer. It is not necessary to see in this coincidence of dates the effect of chance, but we can well see the fact that approached the moment where the elected bishop was to be installed, who his adversaries called "*the intruder*" or "*the bishop of straw*". Welcomed on the 14th in the city of Rodez by a large gathering of people in which the patriotic societies stood out, Debertier, surrounded by his clergy, took possession of the cathedral on the 15th of May and took "*the*

22 Seignelay Colbert de Castlehill, *Mandement et ordonnance épiscopale de M. l'évêque de Rodes au sujet de l'élection faite les 20 mars de M. Debertier... au diocèse de Rodez, par MM. les du département de l'Aveyron, en qualité d'évêque du même département*, 12 mai 1791, éd. Brille, 48 p.

civic oath to watch over the faithful entrusted to his care, to be faithful to the nation, to the law and to the king, and to uphold with all his power the constitution decreed by the National Assembly and accepted by the king".

Was the man whose election had been declared schismatic by Colbert going to be able to impose his authority on a reluctant clergy and a mostly reserved, if not hostile population who were forbidden in the same writ to "*communicate with the intruding bishop or with the priests, deacons and sub-deacons known to be of his communion*".

A denunciation sent from Mur-de-Barrez on 14 May by the administrators underlines the concern of the local authorities confronted with the reactions of the clergy and the faithful who remained loyal to Colbert. "*We see, Messieurs, with the greatest sorrow a hypocritical coalition prepared by the high clergy, favoured by the Easter confessions and supported especially by the retraction of the priest of Estaing. We fear that it will spread to the other cantons, with all the more reason as we learn every day of a few recantations by our public officials.* The local administrators considered taking coercive measures while stressing a certain impotence: "*Our patriotism*", they write, "*would need to be supported by force in case of resistance and we do not dare to answer to you for it, so much so that the cause of religion, adroitly presented by the priests, has shaken the confidence of the People and their obedience to the laws*". Revolutionary rhetoric did not prevent a certain lucidity. The administrators of Mur-de-Barrez, close to their compatriots, were well aware of the ongoing divorce between the People and the Assembly on religious issues. And if the conspiracy thesis is a comfortable explanation, and moreover not very original in those times, it makes it possible to account for the fracture that appeared in the social body. How can we explain, if not by a "hypocritical coalition" of the privileged class attached to defending their privileges under the cover of religion, this first and serious crack in the national consciousness, which had been almost unanimous until then? This unanimity would have to endure, and those who evaded it could only be plotters attached to the defence of an old order and therefore no longer having a place in the nation. The door was open to all terrorist excesses… and the measures of proscription, which were not yet on the agenda of the Assembly, already appear to be in germ in this militant logic.

The rest of this story is beyond this scope, it is the story of the Revolution.

PART III

A Scottish Bishop of the Gallican Church Exiled in London

CHAPTER 10

'Our Countryman, the Bishop of Rodez': Seignelay Colbert of Castlehill and the Scottish Mission

Clotilde Prunier

Abstract Abbé Colbert de Castlehill entered the Scots College, Paris in 1747. He did not come home to Scotland to serve the Mission once he had completed his studies, but rather remained in France where he eventually was consecrated Bishop of Rodez in 1781. Unlike his uncle, Abbé Alexander Colbert, who had strong links with influential members of the Scottish Catholic community, he seems to have had very little contact, if any, with the Scottish Mission until 1790. By then, however, John Farquharson, the Rector of the Scots College, Douai, had established a

This is an abridged version of the original French text. I have substantially revised the 'Paris' section to take into account documents that I had not been able to consult due to travel restrictions during the Covid-19 pandemic.

C. Prunier (✉)
Centre de Recherches Anglophones (CREA) EA 370, Université Paris Nanterre, Nanterre, France
e-mail: cprunier@parisnanterre.fr

A. Alcouffe (ed.), *Seignelay Colbert de Castlehill (1735-1811)*,
https://doi.org/10.1007/978-3-031-75273-5_10

connection with Colbert who, alongside another member of parliament, Merlin of Douai, actively supported the Rector's endeavours to preserve the Scots College, Douai from the worst effects of the French Revolution. Two years later, the now refractory Bishop of Rodez was again called on to help the Scottish Mission in its attempt to resolve its dispute with Alexander Gordon, Principal of the Scots College, Paris at a time when events in France threatened the very existence of that establishment. This chapter first seeks to explore the role the Bishop of Rodez actually played in those two major crises for the Scottish Mission which ultimately failed to secure its Scots Colleges in France, then examines the nature of his relationship with the Scottish Mission during his exile years in Britain.

Keywords Seignelay Colbert · Scottish Mission · Scots College, Paris · Scots College, Douai · Merlin of Douai · French Revolution · John Geddes · Principal Alexander Gordon · Highlands of Scotland

'Mr Colbert' was first mentioned in Scottish Catholic correspondence in the 1730s, but this was Abbé Alexander Colbert, Seignelay Colbert's uncle, who had close links to the Scottish Mission, having been educated at the Scots College in Paris. When Seignelay Colbert studied in his turn at the Scots College, George Innes recorded the progress of 'little Colbert' to distinguish him from his uncle and until the latter's death in 1782, Seignelay Colbert was referred to as Abbé Colbert's nephew.

The relationship between the Scottish bishops and Seignelay Colbert seems to have begun at the time of his ordination to the bishopric of Rodez in 1781. In the next thirty years, it fluctuated considerably. Three phases emerge—first from 1781 to the outbreak of the French Revolution, then from 1790 to 1792, and finally from the Bishop's flight from France to his death in London. Though only eight letters written by Colbert and four drafts of letters addressed to him have been traced so far in Scottish Catholic correspondence, documents held by various repositories in Scotland and on the continent attest to the existence of both written and oral exchanges between the Bishop of Rodez and the Scottish Mission.[1]

[1] These are mainly the Blairs Letters (BL) and Colleges Abroad: Paris (CA1) in the Scottish Catholic Archives collection now held by the University of Aberdeen, the third

From Colbert's Consecration to the French Revolution

Alexander Gordon, the Principal of the Scots College at Paris, immediately acquainted the Procurator of the Scottish Mission at Edinburgh of Colbert's consecration which, it was hoped, would afford the Scottish Mission new opportunities to further its interests in France.

John Geddes, who had just been appointed Coadjutor to the Vicar Apostolic of the Lowland District of Scotland, stopped over in Paris in April 1781 on his way back from Spain, where he had served as Rector of the Scots College at Valladolid, but did not meet Colbert, which the rector of the Scots College at Douai, Robert Grant, deeply regretted because Colbert's 'friendship and protection might be of real service in many occurrences.'[2] Unlike his coadjutor, Bishop Hay, the Vicar Apostolic for the Lowland District, met the Bishop of Rodez when he stayed a few weeks in Paris a year later, as is clear from a letter he wrote from the French capital:

> I find that it is perfectly in vain to think of recovering suspended funds, but as I found the Bishop of Rhodez very much inclined to do all he can for us, I have given him at his own desire a full state of the Case, & he has promised to use his Interest to see if he can procure any thing by way of favour. It will be next Winter before he can act any thing in it, because he must go soon to his Diocese where he will remain all the summer, but both his uncle & Mr Innes are to keep him in mind at his return & see if anything can be got done.[3]

This letter points to the fact that Abbé Colbert was regarded as the necessary conduit between the Scottish Mission and his nephew the Bishop of Rodez. Unfortunately, he died soon after, which came as a severe blow to the Mission, dashing their hopes of securing the Bishop of Rodez's good offices by his uncle's means. Robert Grant, however, did not abandon the

volume of 'Scritture Riferite nei Congressi Scozia' at the Archivio Storico de Propaganda Fide in Rome (hereafter APF, SC Scozia) and the documents confiscated from the Prior of the Carthusians in Paris, Dom Felix de Nonant held by the Archives Nationales in Paris (hereafter AN).

[2] Aberdeen University Library, Scottish Catholic Archives, Blairs Letters (hereafter SCA, BL), Robert Grant to John Geddes, 1 November 1781.

[3] SCA, BL, George Hay to John Geddes, 1 June 1782.

plan altogether: 'I understand that Prelate's great and principal concern is for our College of Paris, where he had a part of his education, and I could wish it extended to all. I propose seeing him when he comes to the Capital which will probably be towards the end of next month. He has it much in his power to render us essential service without taking Sixpence from his pocket.'[4]

The only other mention of the Bishop of Rodez in Scottish Catholic correspondence in the 1780s is to be found in a letter from the Principal of the Scots College in Paris to Bishop Geddes in August 1784 in which he let his correspondent know that he had forwarded his letter to Colbert. Geddes might have written to Colbert about his cousin, James Cuthbert, who had just arrived at the Scots College in Douai where he was to be a boarder for the next five years before travelling back to Canada with his father, James Cuthbert, seigneur of Berthier.[5] While Colbert's links with Catholic clergy in Scotland were tenuous, he did not hesitate to entrust his young cousin to the Scots College in Douai where he enjoyed preferential treatment. Indeed, John Farquharson, who succeeded Robert Grant as Principal of that College, gradually got rid of all fourteen boarders who stayed in the College in 1784 with the exception of James Cuthbert who, from late 1786 to 1789, remained the only lodger not meant to become a priest.

The Vicar Apostolic of the Lowlands, Bp Hay, and his coadjutor, Bp Geddes, were persuaded that Colbert, more than any other French bishop, was not only able to assist them, but also most willing to do so. Their conviction stemmed from the fact that he was a Scot and had studied at the Scots College in Paris. Though Scottish Catholic clergy routinely referred to 'our countryman, the Bishop of Rodez,' Colbert's nationality was a moot point. Colbert was indeed born in Scotland, but he left his native country as a young boy and became a member of the French clergy on completing his studies. Colbert's distance from his native country was both geographical and linguistic. His brother Lewis wrote him in English, but in 1783 he sent him 'Lowth's Grammar written

[4] SCA, BL, Robert Grant to George Hay, 20 December 1782. Alexander Innes was the Prefect of Studies at the Scots College, Paris.

[5] James Cuthbert, seigneur of Berthier, was Protestant, as was his son when he first arrived at Douai. On his return to Canada, he renunced his Presbyterian faith to be received into the Catholic Church, much against his father's wishes. SCA, BL, John Farquharson to George Hay, 5 July 1790.

by the Bishop of London & which [he] recommend[ed] to [his brother] for correcting [his] English.'[6] In 1790, the Principal of the Scots College, Douai enjoined Bp Hay to address a letter of thanks to Colbert, adding that the letter could be drafted in English: 'I shall translate it, if necessary, for in French I correspond with him, as I'm afraid he has forgotten in a great measure his Mother tongue.'[7] As a matter of fact, Scottish bishops always made use of English in their correspondence with Colbert, even though he only dropped French for English in 1799. While he had adopted French as his language of choice, he did not relinquish the reading of books in English. Besides an English Grammar and an English-French dictionary, there were in the two trunks sent to Cahors in 1783 quite a few so-called 'English' books of which six were in fact Scottish.[8] The catalogue of the library Colbert left behind when he went into exile lists a substantial number of 'English' books which evince his interest in the Scottish Enlightenment, Jacobitism and, more generally, Antiquities.[9] One may be surprised to find a Gaelic translation of Tuberville's Abridgement of Christian Doctrine among Colbert's books but there are hints in his correspondence with the Duke of Buccleuch that he had at least a rudimentary knowledge of Gaelic. In the first letter he wrote to the Duke from Britain in 1792, he recounted how his 'tartan-clad countrymen' who had come to England for a cattle fair 'were greatly surprised to hear someone they did not know speak Gaelic' and more amazed still

[6] Archives départementales de l'Aveyron, G84, Lewis Cuthbert to Seignelay Colbert, 4 June 1783.

[7] SCA, BL, John Farquharson to George Hay, 5 July 1790.

[8] Archives départementales de l'Aveyron, État des Livres et autres Effets de Mgr L'Evêque de Rodez Contenus dans deux Malles adressées à Caors pour L'Attendre à L'Evêché, 1783. The six works were: *Critical Dissertations on the Origin, Antiquities, Language, Government, Manners and Religion, of the Ancient Caledonians...* by John MACPHERSON, Francis HUTCHESON's *An Inquiry into the Original of Our Ideas of Beauty and Virtue*, George BUCHANAN's *The History of Scotland*, Allan RAMSAY's *Scots Songs*, David HUME's *Philosophical Essays* and *The History of the rebellion in 1745 and 1746*.

[9] 'Catalogue des Livres de la Bibliotheque de Colbert Evêque Emigré' MS 142 (1795), https://bvmm.irht.cnrs.fr/resultRecherche/resultRecherche.php?COMPOSITION_ID=13944.

when they discovered he was 'a French bishop.'[10] This letter unequivocally shows that Colbert identified as a French bishop. To be sure, his recent exile and the events that led to it could not fail to heighten his sense of belonging to the Church of France. However, in 1790 he had already set forth the distinct natures of his links with both countries when he mentioned 'the attachment and gratitude [he felt] for the country of his birth,' feelings which his 'adoption by another people' could never obliterate.[11] Scotland was his native land (patrie) but he was now French by adoption and that was precisely what led Scottish bishops to regard him as the ideal instrument to champion their interests when he became the Bishop of Rodez—his Scottish birth would act as an incentive to work for the good of the Scottish Mission, but it was his 'adoption' by France which put him in a position to do so effectively. For all their talk of Colbert's potential usefulness, Scottish bishops seemed to have allowed their links with him to lapse after his uncle's death. Insofar as the connection was essentially transactional, it comes as no surprise that it waned when the Mission was in no need of his stepping in. The relationship was revived in the aftermath of the French Revolution as its repercussions on the Scots Colleges in Paris and in Douai afforded Colbert opportunities to assist the Scottish Mission.[12]

1790–1792: the Scots Colleges in France in Turmoil

The earliest item extant from the epistolary exchanges between the Scottish Mission and the Bishop of Rodez is the draft of a letter written on 18 August 1790 to acknowledge his endeavours on behalf of the Scots College, Douai whose Principal, John Farquharson, fought hard

[10] Alain ALCOUFFE & Andrew MOORE, 'La correspondance de Mgr Seignelay Colbert de Castlehill, évêque de Rodez et duc de Buccleuch,' *Études Aveyronnaises*, 2020, pp. 342–363 (p. 350, p. 356).

[11] SCA, BL, Seignelay Colbert to the Scottish Bishops, 20 October 1790.

[12] When historians mention Colbert in their work on the Scottish mission, which is relatively rare, it is mainly in the context of the difficulties faced by the two Scots Colleges in France. See, for example, J. F. S. Gordon (ed.), *The Catholic Church in Scotland from the Suppression of the Hierarchy Till the Present Time*, Glasgow, John Tweed, 1869; M. G. Rapport, 'A Community Apart? The Closure of the Scots College in Paris During the French Revolution, 1789–1794,' *Innes Review*, Spring 2002, pp. 79–107; Michael Rapport, 'Loyal Catholics and Revolutionary Patriots: National Identity and the Scots in Revolutionary Paris,' *Journal of Irish and Scottish Studies*, September 2008, pp. 51–71.

to preserve both the students and the College itself from the effects of the French Revolution.

In January 1790, Farquharson turned to the Bishop of Arras, Mgr de Conzié, whose support he did not doubt. Still, he suggested that Conzié might exert himself even more to protect the College if Bp Hay and Bp Geddes wrote a letter to him. He provided the model of a letter in French to spare his superiors the effort of drafting it. They expressed their hopes that the establishment had 'nothing to fear' from the French nation under whose 'protection' it had been founded for the benefit of Scottish Catholics who had borne the whole charge of it but if 'contrary to all expectations,' the College was threatened in any way, they 'wholly relied on' Conzié's protection to avert danger.[13] In his answer, dated 2 April 1790, the Bishop of Arras professed to do all in his power to ensure that the College felt, 'as little as possible the effects of the baneful Revolution' currently under way in France, insisting that religion still held sway in his bishopric.[14] However, a few months later, Farquharson wrote that the 'Bishop of Arras dare[d] not appear in his Diocese' and that 'any further application to our B. of Arras w[ould] be deemed bordering on treason.'[15] As early as Spring 1790, Farquharson had realised the wind had turned. In the letter he sent to Bp Hay on 5 July 1790, he let him know that 'since Easther [he was] in close correspondence with the B. of Rodez & with another celebrated Deputy,' that is to say Merlin of Douai. He acquainted his superiors of all the steps he took on the advice of both Merlin of Douai and the Bishop of Rodez, who was also a member of the National Assembly. He had first drawn up 'with the advice' of the Bishop of Rodez a memorial on behalf of the Scots College, Douai which was 'presented and enlarged upon' by the Bishop of Rodez himself to the Comité Ecclesiastique on 29 May, then in June addressed another memorial to the Comité des pensions 'to save if possible our pension of 2000tt upon the Royal treasury' which was 'given in and fully seconded by [his] friend our Douay deputy [Merlin].' Meanwhile, a decree enjoined all foreign ecclesiastical establishments to give in a list of their moveable and immoveable property. Farquharson looked on it as 'a bad omen the

[13] SCA, BL, George Hay and John Geddes to the Bishop of Arras, 25 February 1790.

[14] SCA, BL, Bishop of Arras to Bishop Hay and Bishop Geddes, 2 April 1790.

[15] SCA, BL, John Farquharson to George Hay, 28 October 1790; John Farquharson to John Geddes, 1 November 1790.

B of Rodez wanted in vain an exception for those who had nothing from France,' such as both the Scots Colleges in France, though he tried to convince himself Merlin and the Bishop of Rodez were not mistaken when they endeavoured to reassure him about the fate of the College. He ended his letter urging the Bishops to send him 'a joint letter of thanks for his Lordship of Rodez: he has greatly shown himself our friend in this critical period, and a letter from you [...] may make him exert himself still more.'[16] In August, Farquharson kept the Scots Agent in Rome abreast of the latest developments and begged him 'to engage his Eminence [Cardinal Antonelli, Prefect of Propaganda Fide] to thank the B of Rodez for his spirited exertions in behalf of our National houses.'[17]

At their annual meeting in August 1790, the bishops complied with the Principal's demand. They explicitly established a connection between the hope his promotion in 1781 had elicited and their present letter of thanks:

> Our Joy on [the Occasion of your promotion] was truly very sincere on account of our great Esteem and Regard for Your Lordship; We also rejoiced on our own account and on that of these poor Missions; because we were well assured from Your humane, beneficent Dispositions, and from Your Attachment to this Country that You would embrace every Opportunity of promoting the Interests of Religion here. Our Hopes in that respect have been fully answered by Your charitable and strenuous Exertions in favour of our national College at Douay, of which its Principal Mr Farquharson has not neglected to inform us.
> Although we did expect these Exertions from Your Zeal for Religion and Your Love to Scotland, which had the Honour to give You Birth; yet we do not think ourselves the less obliged to You, and we return You most hearty thanks in our own Name and in that of the whole Nation, which will never forget this Your patriotic Behaviour.[18]

This letter was sent to Farquharson who passed it on to Colbert, alongside a memorial in French (whose model was provided by Farquharson) signed not only by all three Scottish bishops but also by the heads of the greatest Scottish Catholic families. They reminded the National Assembly

[16] SCA, BL, John Farquharson to George Hay, 5 July 1790.

[17] SCA, BL, John Farquharson to John Thomson, 4 August 1790.

[18] SCA, BL, Bishops MacDonald, Hay and Geddes to the Bishop of Rodez, August 1790.

that 'the Scots College, Douai, founded by Mary Stuart in 1580 owed all its property to the liberality of the Scottish nation' and that it was to be regarded as a 'trust placed under the protection of France' and therefore exempted from any measure which might subject 'all Colleges in France to a general system of reform' or 'change the nature of their property or amalgamate several of them or bring them all under a new plan of French national education.'[19]

This memorial was presented to the National Assembly on 27 September 1790 by the Bishop of Rodez who answered the Scottish Bishops' letter four weeks later, days before the decree 'relating to the foreign ecclesiastical establishments in France' was passed on 28 October, stating that they would all 'continue to enjoy as they had hitherto done the property they or their nation had paid for with their own money' as he hinted in his letter:

> You have deigned to thank me for the care I took of the Scots College, Douai. In this, I was only fulfilling what I will always look upon as one of my most sacred duties. Be in no doubt that I will always watch over the interests of that precious establishment and I find solace in the belief that they are not in danger in spite of the terrible crisis which has already brought about so many unexpected events in this country. The members of the Committee established to handle ecclesiastical affairs and the National Assembly itself have acknowledged that the establishments founded in France by foreigners with their own money must not be placed at the disposal of the French nation and that if illustrious fugitives who fell victims to the troubles in their countries were welcome in France, which afforded them an asylum, this act of hospitality and humanity gives no right to the Sovereign of the people who received these foreigners to seize the goods they may have brought with them. Therefore, the National Assembly will not infringe the rights of the Scots, English and Irish Colleges which France has not endowed in any way. These Colleges will be exempt from the provisions of the decrees which have put in its hands the property of the Church as well as that of other public establishments in this kingdom. I am not afraid to give you most positive and reassuring assurances that it will be so and when it is formally decreed and this incontrovertible principle applied to particular cases as they shall arise I will not fail to let you know. It will afford me a new opportunity to express, as I do today, the

[19] SCA, BL, Bishops MacDonald, Hay and Geddes and the Heads of the Greatest Catholic Families in Scotland to the National Assembly, 1790 (with a letter from John Farquharson).

> sincere respect and attachment with which I have the honour to be, your Most Reverend Lordships, your most obedient humble servant.[20]

If it was ever written, this second letter is not extant but Farquharson suggested to Bp Hay that as soon as he received it, he should send a further letter of thanks to Colbert because 'hitherto he ha[d] been remarkably friendly, and [they] may have further need of his interest.' It is noteworthy that in this letter, Farquharson revealed that Merlin was 'not quite so confident of success at least in some respects, as the good Bishop' but that on his advice he had 'made fresh application' to recover the suspended pension of 2000 tt.[21] As he was wont to do Farquharson, who was now in possession of a copy of the decree, wrote two almost identical letters on 1 November—the one for Bp Geddes in Scotland and the other to the Scots Agent in Rome, John Thomson. He renewed his call for the latter to 'engage Cardinal Antonelli to write a letter of thanks to the B: of Rhodez for his friendly interposition in our behalf' and indicated that as a result of Merlin's efforts, the pension had indeed been recovered.[22] What is striking in those two letters dated 1 November is the way Merlin of Douai is referred to. Whereas in July Merlin was a nameless 'Celebrated Deputy,' in November he was named to Bishop Geddes and presented in slightly more detail—Merlin was 'an acquaintance of [his] from this town who is much considered, was lately president.' Though he was 'a leading member of the prevailing party, [he had] warmly espoused [their] interest.'[23] Farquharson added in his letter to Thomson that Merlin, 'a particular acquaintance of' his, had 'been of immense service' to the Mission.[24] By late November, Merlin had unmistakably superseded Colbert. Just as he had been quick to understand that the Bishop of Arras could no longer be of any use to him, Farquharson realised that Colbert's 'weight' in the Assembly was on the wane. Though he was 'very much obliged to him' for all his endeavours on behalf of the Scots College in Douai, he was aware that in the last resort it was to Merlin he owed the positive outcome of the steps he took: 'the B of

[20] SCA, BL, Seignelay Colbert to the Scottish Bishops, 20 October 1790.

[21] SCA, BL, John Farquharson to George Hay, 28 October 1790.

[22] SCA, BL, John Farquharson to John Thomson, 1 November 1790.

[23] SCA, BL, John Farquharson to John Geddes, 1 November 1790.

[24] SCA, BL, John Farquharson to John Thomson, 1 November 1790.

Rhodez employd his interest, which I fear is not great: our success is principally owing to Mr Merlin's exertions [...]. [H]e has been of the greatest service to us, nay, I am assured, without him, my petition would not have been regarded.'[25]

Farquharson's opportunism did not prevent him from having great respect for Colbert—his episcopal status gave him indisputable legitimacy even after he was replaced with a constitutional bishop in the spring of 1791. Farquharson set about drafting a new constitution for the Scots College in Douai which he hoped would enable it to weather the upheavals brought about by the French Revolution in public education. He imparted the broad outline of his plan to the Vicar Apostolic of the Lowland District in order to get his approval and gave him the list of the people he wished to have on the Board, among whom Merlin 'without whose concurrence we can do nothing' and whose opinion on his plan he intended to ask for. Farquharson urged once more Bp Hay to write to Merlin and to the National Assembly, but also to the Bishop of Rodez 'intimating to the latter what [sic] you approve or disapprove my plan and requesting his seconding my endeavours.'[26] Hay complied with Farquharson's demands on 7 May; he copied Farquharson's model of a French letter to Merlin and penned a letter in English to the Bishop of Rodez which was similar in content. Whereas he informed Merlin that Farquharson had been advised to seek both his and Colbert's advice, he made no mention at all of Merlin in his letter to Colbert, however, and voiced his fears in a more open manner:

> After the Interest you took lately in our affairs was crowned with the wished for Success, we had no thoughts of being obliged so soon to have recourse again to your protection. But the design of new modelling the general plan of Education in all the Colleges with you allarms us exceedingly [...]. We therefore find it necessary to make another application to the National Assembly, & have communicated our thoughts on that subject to Mr Farq[uharso]n whom we have desired to consult with you in a particular manner in his proceedings. We make no doubt but your zeal for the good of your Country of which we have already had such experience, will exert itself on this occasion, no less important than the former, &

[25] SCA, BL, John Farquharson to John Thomson, 26 November 1790; SCA, BL, John Farquharson to John Geddes, 29 November 1790.

[26] SCA, BL, John Farquharson to George Hay, 21 April 1791.

> absolutely necessary to secure the good effects of what you have already done for us.[27]

In late July, Farquharson let Bp Hay know that the letter sent to Merlin had the desired effect—'much flattered with the attention paid him,' Merlin had 'charged himself with delivering the [Vicar Apostolic's] letter to the N. Assembly'; on the other hand, the letter to Colbert had not been delivered because he had 'long ago left Paris.'[28] The same fate awaited Cardinal Antonelli's letter of July 1792 and that of the Scottish bishops in August 1792, which were both intended to thank Colbert for supporting Bp Geddes while he stayed in Paris from 23 December 1791 to 20 April 1792.

Paris

The difficulties facing the Scots College, Douai arose exclusively from the French Revolution. The same cannot be said of the crisis which shook the Scots College, Paris. For almost a decade, the relationship between the Scottish Mission and the College's Principal, Alexander Gordon, had been fraught. There is no need to give an exhaustive account of the various factors of this latent conflict. The uneasiness between the bishops and the Principal proceeded from their divergent views on whether the Mission had a legitimate right to interfere in the running of the College whose Superior was officially the Prior of the Carthusians. It was in fact managed by the Principal who by 1789 also acted as Procurator. Those quarrels resulted in the bishops' no longer sending boys to the College. As a retaliatory measure, the Principal withheld some of the funds the Mission so sorely needed. This internecine strife came to a head at the time of the French Revolution as the abolition of religious orders left a void at the top; the Prior of the Carthusians, Dom Felix of Nonant, still strove to fulfil his role at the head of the College, but his situation was precarious. He was depicted as a kind-hearted but weak man and some correspondents claimed he was a mere puppet in the hands of Principal Gordon, who was the effective head of the College. Further, the Revolution generated disagreements between the Prefect of Studies, Alexander Innes, and

[27] SCA, BL, George Hay to the Bishop of Rodez, 7 May 1791.

[28] SCA, BL, John Farquharson to George Hay, 25 July 1791.

the Principal who had engaged in manoeuvres to gain absolute control over the College and its property, including its precious archives, which he seemed intent on selling in the hope of settling the College out of France. With a view to defeating the Principal's purpose, the Vicars Apostolic and the heads of the greatest Scottish Catholic families appointed Bishop Geddes their representative in France in August 1791 and granted him full power to treat with the Prior of the Carthusians, the National Assembly or anybody else that he may need to negotiate with to secure the property of the Scots College, Paris and, more generally, the interests of the Scottish Mission in France.

In early September, before he left for France, Bp Geddes wrote to the Scots Agent in Rome to seek on his behalf the help of Cardinal Antonelli who in turn appealed to Cardinal Zelada, Pius VI's Secretary of State, who then informed the Pope's internuncio in Paris, Abbé Salamon, that Geddes was on his way to Paris to try and save the Scots Colleges in France. Zelada entreated Salamon to assist Geddes so as to ensure his endeavours were brought to a successful conclusion. Salamon assured him that he would help Geddes to the utmost of his ability.

Geddes arrived at Douai on 22 November 1791. He stayed there about a month then left for Paris which he reached on 23 December. Two weeks later he wrote to Bp Hay: 'The Bp of Rhodez, I am told, is privately in Paris; but I have met with nobody as yet, who knows where he lodges.'[29] That was the first mention of Colbert in the epistolary exchanges regarding the troubled situation at the Scots College, Paris and there is no indication that he was initially meant to play a part in the Mission's attempt to solve the problem. Geddes eventually met the Bishop of Rodez on 9 February. Since his arrival at Paris, Geddes had paid a number of visits to the British Embassy to meet the Ambassador, Lord Gower, and his wife, Lady Sutherland, who was a Scot. Colbert also frequented the Embassy and it was on one of his visits there that he heard Geddes was in the French capital. He then asked Abbé Salamon to bring Geddes to his place. Geddes, who 'had inquired at many Persons for the Bp of Rodez in vain' was delighted to meet him at long last.[30] In the diary he kept while in Paris, 'Account of a Journey made in the Years 1791, 1792,' Geddes simply noted in his entry for 9 February that he

[29] SCA, BL, John Geddes to George Hay, 5 January 1792.

[30] SCA, BL, John Geddes to George Hay, 13 February 1792.

had been to see Colbert with Abbé Salamon, but he gave a more detailed account of the episode in a letter to Bp Hay a few days later. On the other hand, Salamon made no mention of it in his correspondence with Cardinals Antonelli and Zelada. Though he was well-disposed towards Geddes, Salamon found it as difficult to get in touch with him as it had been for Geddes to trace Colbert. Contact was made through John Baptist Walsh, the Irish Superior of the Lombard College, who took Geddes to Salamon's on 25 January, over a month after his arrival at Paris.[31] Geddes's first weeks in the French capital seem to have been rather difficult and he summed them up in a cursory manner in his journal before embarking on a proper diary punctuated by the innumerable visits he paid to the various protagonists of his attempt to put an end to the conflict with the Principal. Between 25 January and 18 April 1792, Geddes either called or was called on by Salamon about 25 times. He did not elaborate on these visits, except to mention that Salamon, 'who was very friendly,' took him on a number of occasions to the Prior of the Carthusians' or 'to dine with M. Le Maire.'[32] The social nature of their interactions is confirmed by Salamon who informed Cardinal Zelada that he had regularly taken Geddes 'to dine with [his]friends]' to ensure his stay in Paris was agreeable.[33] They last met when Salamon handed Geddes his passport 'seen by the Municipality' before he departed for Douai. Between 9 February and 19 April 1792, Geddes and Colbert met about 15 times and Geddes's contemporary diary suggests that they usually engaged in 'long conversations' about the College's affairs whether they were on their own or joined by other people. This is corroborated by the 'Account of a Journey to Paris made by Mr John Geddes Bp of Morocco In the end of the Year 1791 About what regarded the Scotch College there' which Geddes dictated to Paul MacPherson sometime between August 1792 and July 1793 'from the original Letters, and other Papers; from what [Geddes] wrote at the time, or ha[d] quite fresh in [his] memory.'[34] In that later

[31] APF, SC Scozia, vol. 3, f. 430, Abbé Salamon to Cardinal Antonelli, 30 January 1792.

[32] SCA, CA1/22/1–2 'Account of a Journey Made in the Years 1791 and 1792'.

[33] *Correspondance secrète de l'Abbé de Salamon [...] avec le cardinal Zelada (1791–1792)*, Paris, Plon, 1898, p. 342.

[34] SCA, CA1/22/3 'Account of a Journey to Paris Made by Mr John Geddes Bp of Morocco In the End of the Year 1791 About What Regarded the Scotch College There,' n° 1.

narrative, Geddes hardly ever dated events, but gave a more circumstantial account of some meetings and inserted abstracts (in English) of important documents. On 9 February, the Bp of Rodez seemed 'to be very desirous to be of service to his country & [Geddes] on this occasion' and 'expressed a wish, and hopes of effecting a reconciliation between' Geddes and the Principal.[35] Further, Geddes noted that he 'found him favourable' to the Mission in its dispute with the Principal, which gives the impression that he felt the need to ascertain Colbert's support. This, added to the fact that Colbert was unaware of the Mission's rift with the Principal and of Geddes's coming to Paris, demonstrates that there had been no prior discussions with Colbert on the means to resolve the deepening crisis. The Principal of the Scots College, Douai, John Farquharson, may have suggested to Geddes while he stayed in that town to turn to the Bp of Rodez for assistance. At any rate, when Geddes wrote to him that he had at long last been able to meet Colbert, Farquharson answered: 'I'm happy you have found out the worthy B. of Rodez, and trust you'll not fail to thank him in the most cordial terms for his spirited exertions on behalf of this house: this Shop & I in particular have very great obligations to him, and nothing will afford me greater pleasure than to see him restored to his Bishopric, where I'm told he's adored.'[36]

Bp Geddes initially hoped to settle the dispute through one-on-one meetings with Principal Gordon but these conversations ended in deadlock. As early as late December 1791, Alexander Gordon had suggested to the Prior of the Carthusians that if they failed to reach an agreement while 'on their own, [...] the vicar general of the Bp of Paris, Abbé Floirac, and the visitor of the Carmelites, Abbé Rigaud' should be invited to join them.[37] By the time Geddes resigned himself to such a conference, Alexander Gordon, 'exasperated' by Geddes's 'insignificant and honeyed talk,'[38] first declined the offer then accepted it under conditions.

He put a categorical veto on the College's Prefect of Studies, Alexander Innes, and Abbé Salamon, the two persons Geddes had chosen to attend

[35] SCA, CA1/22/3 'Account of a Journey ... In the End of the Year 1791,' n° 51.

[36] SCA, BL, John Farquharson to John Geddes, 22 February 1792.

[37] AN T//583/1 cotte treize n° 8, Alexander Gordon to the Prior of the Carthusians, 27 December 1791.

[38] AN T//583/1 cotte treize n° 22, Alexander Gordon to the Prior of the Carthusians, 26 January 1792.

their conference as the counterparts of the two clerics named by the Principal.[39]

Geddes insisted he needed Alexander Innes, whom Gordon regarded as a 'cantankerous man,' to act as his interpreter. He looked on Gordon's 'motives' to reject Abbé Salamon's presence as 'frivolous'[40] and clarified that Salamon was 'not to assist at our Meeting as exercising any Papal jurisdiction; but as a Person to whom [Geddes was] recommended, and in whom [he] confide[d].'[41] In order to vindicate himself, the Principal, who had visibly kept abreast of the developments in French politics, put forward arguments that were far from being as 'frivolous' as Geddes claimed. He first wrote that he needed to reflect on the proposal to assess 'whether he [could] consent, without endangering either [him]self or the College, to a conference in presence of M. Salamon. We need to be careful how we act as decrees regarding the university of Paris, of which we are a part, are about to be adopted. At such a critical juncture, we cannot lay ourselves open to criticism on account of a matter so trivial in itself as the presence of M. Salamon.'[42]

Then, a week later, he wrote to the Prior to account for his final veto:

> Wise people whom I have consulted with have assured me that the presence of this chargé d'affaires [M. Salamon] may have dangerous consequences for both the College and me in present circumstances, most of all now when it is known that the Pope is about to anathematize the constitutional clergy of this kingdom. You must realize that this piece of news, which I have had on good authority, must make us cautious since anything that relates to the court of Rome is necessarily bound to give umbrage to the powers that be. I asked a third party to sound out the directors of the department of Paris on this point and the response was by no means encouraging.[43]

[39] AN T//583/1 cotte treize n° 26, Alexander Gordon to the Prior of the Carthusians, 5 February 1792.

[40] SCA, CA1/22/3 'Account of a Journey ... In the End of the Year 1791,' n° 50.

[41] SCA, BL, John Geddes to Alexander Gordon, 20 February 1792.

[42] AN T//583/1 cotte treize n° 27, Alexander Gordon to the Prior of the Carthusians, 7 February 1792.

[43] AN T//583/1 cotte treize n° 28, Alexander Gordon to the Prior of the Carthusians, 14 February 1792.

On 14 February, Gordon, Geddes and Colbert dined together at the Scots College. The 'conversation of almost three hours' between the three men may have been instrumental in Geddes and Gordon reaching an agreement on Colbert's involvement in the Conference. In a letter to the Prior of the Carthusians, Gordon asserted that on that occasion the Bishop of Rodez had 'not been as supportive of Geddes's claims as he might have hoped.'[44] As for Geddes, he left different accounts of the meeting, but they all point to his being 'well pleased with the Bp of Rodez.' In the letter he sent to Bp Hay on 29 February, Geddes asserted that Colbert 'was entirely on our side.'[45] In the 'Account' dictated to Paul Macpherson, Geddes reiterated that Colbert had maintained that all he 'required was very reasonable.' However, he acknowledged that Colbert had 'objected only to my expression of *Principally* with regard to the College being destined to Educate Missionaries, whereas he thought the Foundation papers made it *Equally* for Clergymen & seculars; tho' he owned, that considering the state of our Country, the Superiors ought to give the greatest encouragement to those young men who seemed to have a vocation to the church.'[46]

The major bone of contention between the Scottish Mission and the Principal was his insistence that he could act independently of the Vicars Apostolic in Scotland, in particular when it came to his plan of selling the College. On that point, the Bishop of Rodez squarely sided with Geddes: 'he strongly asserted [that the Bishops in Scotland] had an inherent right to be consulted on such matters. On this subject he and the P^l^ had a long contest; but the P^l^ was evidently confuted and much perplexed.' As is clear from this statement, Gordon and Colbert did most of the talking and Geddes noted that 'the good Prelate said enough for me; and pleaded my cause extremely well.' That evening, Geddes and Colbert left the College together and on their way home Colbert 'consented to be present at the Conference,'[47] which led Geddes to agree to the Principal's veto and dispense with Alexander Innes and Abbé Salamon once he 'got [him] to

44 AN T//583/1 cotte treize n° 29, Alexander Gordon to the Prior of the Carthusians, 18 February 1792.

45 SCA, BL, John Geddes to George Hay, 29 February 1792.

46 SCA, CA1/22/3 'Account of a Journey ... In the End of the Year 1791,' n°52.

47 SCA, CA1/22/3 'Account of a Journey ... In the End of the Year 1791,' n°52.

allow the presence of the Bp of Rodez whom on several accounts [he] looked upon as the most proper auxiliary [he] could have.'[48]

Eventually, the Conference took place on 22 February in the room of the Prior of the Carthusians in the presence of Bp Geddes, the Principal, the Prior, Abbé Floirac, Abbé Rigaud and the Bishop of Rodez. Though the latter was not originally intended to participate in the Conference, Geddes had come to see him as an essential ally of his, as his nervousness while waiting an hour for him to eventually arrive indicates.

The Bishop of Rodez was assigned the thankless task of drawing up an account of the meeting in part from the notes taken by Gordon and Geddes, but 'principally from his own recollection.'[49] The 'Result of a Conference which took place on 22 February in Paris' opened on summaries of Geddes's claims on behalf of the Scottish Mission and of the Principal's answers, then listed the eight articles agreed on as a result. The fourth article supported the Mission's view that it was 'contrary to the Statutes, that the whole administration of the College should be in the hands of one person and that it would seem proper, that the P^{r} of the Carth^{s}, as chief Sup^{r} should name, in the usual way, a Procurator to be associated in the administration according to the custom of the House.'[50] However it added that 'the Prior may pay what regard his wisdom shall suggest to him to Mr Gordon's observations on the actual state of the College' in a clear attempt to placate the Principal, whose own account of the result of the Conference on that point was perceptibly different as he first maintained that it was merely a custom that the two offices should not be held by the same person and 'that those reasons which have induced the present Prior to depart from that custom are good & valid.' He reluctantly accepted that as the Scottish Mission was bent on not letting him having the

> sole management of the College, the Pr ought to pay deference to this desire, the [Vicars Apostolic] persisting in it after having maturely considered before God whether or not the reasons on which this desire is

[48] SCA, CA1/22/3 'Account of a Journey ... In the End of the Year 1791,' n°53.

[49] SCA, CA1/22/3 'Account of a Journey ... In the End of the Year 1791,' n°58.

[50] AN T//583/1 cotte treize n° 32, 'Resultat d'une Conférence qui a eu lieu à Paris le 22 février1792.' This and the following quotations are taken from SCA, CA1/22/3 'Account of a Journey ... In the End of the Year 1791,' n°58, which is a faithful account in English of the original French document.

> grounded are sufficient for authorizing the additional burden which the nomination of a Procurator would occasion to the College at a time when its income is considerably diminished.[51]

The fifth article exonerated the Principal from any sinister motive in attempting to sell the College and stated that 'though they thought the uneasiness of the Catholics in Scotland when they heard of this project was very natural, yet they could not join in it themselves.' One of the reasons adduced was that 'the first and most sacred duty of the Principal & other Superiors of the College would always hinder their executing any Plan regarding the sale of the goods moveable or immoveable belonging to this Establishment without first concerting it with the heads of the Mission who would be essentially interested in such an operation.' In the original version of the Bishop of Rodez's 'Result of a Conference,' this was immediately followed by an article which put all in mind that it was 'of the utmost importance for the good of the College & of Religion that a perfect harmony subsist between the Suprs of this Establishment, & the Heads of the Mission' and hinted that both sides were at fault for the breakdown of concord: 'the [Vicars Apostolic] ought to send the number of youths that the House can maintain; and [...] the administrators of the College should send to the Mission the yearly sum of 274 tt that arise from Mr Lewis Innes' Foundation according to his intention.' The concluding article wished 'that this College, of such importance to Religion & Humanity flourish more & more; and that all misunderstanding cease between the persons interested in it.' These two articles offered a much toned down account of the conversation compared to that drafted by Gordon whose final point was that 'the diffidences conceived with regard to the P^{l} ought to be considered as ill-founded, unless the persons who have imbibed them, show the contrary by positive facts well proved; and that until then, it is their interest as well as their duty not to manifest these suspicions by word or action, if they cannot banish them entirely from their minds.' On 6 March, Geddes wrote to Bp Hay that he had been given a copy of the 'Result of the Conference' which was 'the

[51] CA1/24/4 'Resultat d'une Conference a la Chartreuse de Paris sur les affaires du College des Ecossois, redigé par M. Gordon, Principal du College.' This and the following quotations are taken from SCA, CA1/22/3 'Account of a Journey ... In the End of the Year 1791,' n°57, which is indeed an 'almost literal translation of Mr Gordon's account of the conference'.

substance of what passed and was agreed on at our Meeting on Ash Wednesday, and it is well expressed by the B. of Rodez.'[52] In fact, on first reading the 'Result,' Geddes noticed an omission, which he asked the Bp of Rodez to correct. This led to the insertion of a supplementary (sixth) article on what should happen if the Prior of the Carthusians could no longer fulfil his role as Superior of the College: 'we are of opinion, that no new arrangement can be settled without consulting the [Vicars Apostolic] in Scotland. In any sudden emergency, the Superiority would fall of right to the Archbishop of Paris as Diocesan.' Geddes was understandably pleased with the 'Result of the Conference' as it unambiguously affirmed that the Principal could neither act independently of the Vicars Apostolic in Scotland nor have the sole management of the Scots College, which were the main points he sought to establish on behalf of the Scottish Mission. As was to be expected, Gordon came to a completely different conclusion. While all other participants in the Conference subscribed the 'Resultat,' Gordon refused to do so and wrote on 13 March a 'long Letter of Eight quarto Pages to show, that the Bp [of Rodez] was mistaken.'[53] Colbert answered the Principal on 4 April and wrote to the Prior the day after, having given Geddes an opportunity to read both letters before they were sent. He was visibly affronted by the censure of the Principal which he methodically addressed, sometimes with scathing comments:

> You complain that my account of Mr Geddes's statement is inaccurate […]. Your attention must have been distracted if you did not hear Mr Geddes's complaining in the manner I have reported in the 'Resultat…' […]. Are the Vicars Apostolic of Scotland not entitled to become alarmed and to voice their fears when they learn through the papers or through private letters that a plan was set on foot to sell the funds of the College, as well as its moveable and immoveable property, without their participation and without their knowledge? […] Surely, Sir, the Vicars Apostolic and the Catholics of Scotland have a right to oppose such a plan […]. [Both you and the Prior of the Carthusians] must justify your administration to them. Were you to refuse to do so and claim to dispose without their concurrence of a property of which you are only the temporary administrators, you would turn yourselves into despots or proprietors and would of course fail

[52] SCA, BL, John Geddes to George Hay, 6 March 1792.

[53] SCA, CA1/22/3 'Account of a Journey … In the End of the Year 1791,' n°63.

> to abide by the rules of justice and good faith; but you are not capable of such dereliction of duty […].
> It is most unfortunate that good intelligence and mutual trust do not prevail between you and the Heads of the Mission. Still, it seems to me that nothing is clearer and simpler than the nature of the relationship which exists between them and you. They are not seeking either to interfere with your administration or to usurp the functions which the founders exclusively reserved for the Prior of the Carthusians […] but, in a word, they want the College to be as useful to students and to religion as can naturally be expected. Your acknowledged justice and the feelings of honour and loyalty by which you are distinguished will not allow you to deny satisfaction to the apostles of your native land […]. I would have expected Mr Gordon to show an eagerness worthy of him to meet such demands and to set to his successors a model of accuracy and zeal which it is essential to the College, Religion and Scotland they should follow ever after.[54]

In the letter he wrote to the Prior of the Carthusians on 5 April, Colbert was even more supportive of the demands made by Geddes who was about to leave Paris and was particularly keen to see the Prior appoint a Procurator as soon as possible, but the Prior was irresolute and constantly vacillated between contradictory injunctions. Geddes noted in his diary that on 18 March he 'spoke to him strongly' and that as a result he 'promised to follow the Advice of the B. of Rodez, Messrs Floirac and Rigaud.'[55] A week later he went to see Colbert who in his turn 'promised […] to use his utmost Endeavours, in the course of this Week, to get the Prior to name Mr Alex^r^ Innes Procurator, however averse Mr Gordon may be to that measure.'[56] However, both Rigaud and Floirac advised the Prior against appointing Alexander Innes so that by the end of that week, Colbert let Geddes know that he had persuaded the Prior to appoint Henry Innes, rather than his brother Alexander. Henry Innes, who used to be the Procurator of the College, had renounced his position in order to become chaplain to a Catholic family in England. In the letter Colbert wrote to the Prior on 5 April, he seemed to accede to the Principal's wish by explicitly advising him against appointing Alexander Innes on account of the Principal's inflexible opposition to such a move and suggested he

54 SCA, BL, Seignelay Colbert to Alexander Gordon, 4 April 1792.

55 SCA, CA1/22/2 Continuation of the Account of a Journey Made in 1791 and 1792.

56 SCA, BL, John Geddes to George Hay, 26 March 1792.

should first attempt to convince Henry Innes to take up his former position at the Scots College. He was not oblivious to the predicament the Prior would be faced with if Henry Innes declined his offer:

> It is to be hoped he will accept of the position [...] but were he not to accept of it, what ought you to do? [...] If one Mr Innes declines the position, how not to offer it to the other Mr Innes who does not decline but whom Mr Gordon dislikes? Such a circumstance could be embarrassing if it came to pass, but it is to be hoped it will not. At any rate, your heart and your principles will instruct you to act according to the rules, not to be unfair to anyone and to arrange everything the best you can. It is in your own feelings directed by grace that you will always find your true resource, whatever may happen.[57]

As expected, Henry Innes refused to take up his former position as Procurator, plunging anew the Prior into the throes of indecision. He turned once again to the Bishop of Rodez whose answer, written on 6 May 1792, probably betrayed his weariness in the face of the Prior's dithering, but also his reluctance to get too involved in a process he knew was fraught with pitfalls and whose responsibility should lie exclusively with the Prior. Still, Colbert offered to help the Prior reach a final decision, should he seek his advice then: 'The first thing to decide is whether it is timely to appoint a Procurator. This decision will depend on the state of income and expenditure [of the College]. Then you will make your choice and once it is done, I will be only too pleased and obliged to give you my opinion on it, if you ask for it.'[58]

After he left Paris, Geddes was kept abreast of the unfolding events by Alexander Innes who, in two letters sent in May 1792, wrote to him that 'Pr^{l} Gordon [was] impolite to [the] Pr^{r} of Carth. & [the] B. of Rodez.'[59] Geddes elaborated in the 'Account' he dictated to Paul MacPherson: 'Th P^{l} had written to the Bp of Rodez, requiring that the Bp should meddle no more in the affairs of the College; but [...] the Bp had said, he would

[57] AN T//583/1 cotte treize n° 34, Seignelay Colbert to the Prior of the Carthusians, 5 April 1792.

[58] AN T//583/1 cotte treize n° 41, Seignelay Colbert to the Prior of the Carthusians, 6 May 1792.

[59] SCA, CA1/22/2 Continuation of the Account of a Journey made in 1791 and 1792.

pay no regard to such a requisition; but would do all in his power to bring matters to a proper state.'[60]

On 8 May 1792, the Prior signed a copy of the College's accounts for the years 1788, 1789 and 1790 delivered to him by the Principal and had it carried by Alexander Innes 'to the Bp of Rodez, that he might make his observations on them, [the Prior] being still determined to follow his advice in whatever concerned the College.'[61] Colbert examined very closely the accounts, as is clear from the observations he sent to the Prior, some of which were passed on to Geddes by Alexander Innes, in particular concerning conflicting statements about an annual sum of 274 tt which Geddes had claimed was withheld from the Mission by the Principal while the latter had actually stated it among the expenses of the College. Colbert wondered whether Geddes had voiced 'a complaint lacking in substance.'[62] Though in May Innes requested Geddes to 'let [him] know how matters [stood],' Geddes did not clarify this point, leaving his correspondent to write again on 20 June, quoting at length from the Bishop of Rodez's observations. In the 'Account,' Geddes mentioned that Colbert had pointed out this discrepancy but did not provide any explanation for it, underscoring rather the underlying criticism of the Principal's rule of the College:

> [The Bishop of Rodez] adds, that these acco^ts^ had been given in by the P ^l^alone, whereas according to the Statutes they ought to have been given by the Proc^r^ in the presence of the P^l^. Hence he infers the necessity of naming one for the Place of Proc^r^. And as he had lately read the Statutes, he subjoins, that it was still more essential to reestablish the Discipline of the House according to these Statutes, w^h^, it appeared, were not at all observed: wherefore, in the actual state of ye College, it was very far from answering the end of its foundation.[63]

[60] SCA, CA1/22/3 'Account of a Journey ... In the End of the Year 1791,' n°74.

[61] SCA, CA1/22/3 'Account of a Journey ... In the End of the Year 1791,' n°76.

[62] SCA, BL, Alexander Innes to John Geddes, 20 June 1792.

[63] SCA, CA1/22/3 'Account of a Journey ... In the End of the Year 1791,' n°79. This was an almost literal translation of the Bishop's observations quoted in Alexander Innes's letter, which makes it all the more striking that Geddes chose not to enlarge on the issue of the 274 tt.

In his 20 June letter, Alexander Innes imparted to Geddes that 'the Bp of Rodez [had] been in the Country for some time & [would] remain there till the late decree concerning the deportation of priests be determined.'[64] The day after Innes penned this letter, the Prior of the Carthusians wrote to Abbé Salamon, urgently requesting a one-on-one meeting with him so that he could advise him on the course to take since the Bishop of Rodez 'who seemed so keen at the beginning, now seem[ed] very lukewarm or indifferent.'[65] Salamon enclosed the Prior's letter with his own to Cardinal Antonelli and made sure that the Prior's remark did not go unnoticed: 'Your Eminence will see from the Prior's letter that the Bishop of Rodez, a former student at the Scots College, who seemed at the beginning to show some interest in it has now almost completely abandoned it. As for me, I can assure your Eminence that I will never abandon it and will ever show the same zeal for it.' It should be noted that Salamon took liberties with the original text—while the Prior stated that Colbert 'seemed so keen at the beginning,' Salamon played down his role and went so far as to say that he had 'abandoned' the Scots College. On 30 July, in another letter to Cardinal Antonelli, he exposed his plan of action to get Alexander Innes, whom the Prior had by then appointed Procurator, properly settled in case the Principal should remain opposed to his appointment: 'without needing [the assistance of] the Bishop of Rodez or Abbé Wals [h], I will go and see the English Ambassador to have him speak earnestly to Gordon; if that fails, I will take him to court.' In his two letters to Cardinal Antonelli Salamon hinted at his antipathy for Colbert, but he was more explicit in the letter he wrote to Cardinal Zelada on 24 April 1792. Strangely enough, in his correspondence with the Secretary of State, Salamon never brought up Colbert in the context of his endeavours to support Geddes's enterprise in Paris, but rather gave vent to his dislike of the Bishop of Rodez while touching on an unrelated episode:

> The Coadjutor of Sens is very mortified and complains bitterly against the Pope having included him in the Brief though he has not sworn the civic oath and I have just learnt that the Bishop of Rodez has presumed to write to Rome to corroborate this assertion and have his Holiness believe that

[64] SCA, BL, Alexander Innes to John Geddes, 20 June 1792.

[65] APF, SC Scozia, vol. 3, f. 437, Prior of the Carthusians to Abbé Salamon, 21 June 1792.

> he was misled. Since the Bishop of Rodez wants to be talked about, I will let Your Eminence know his true colour.
> This prelate is one of those ever vacillating beings trying to be all things to all men. He is ambitious, convinced of his transcendent merit though in fact very mediocre, very attached to the Loménies even after their downfall [...]. Since the Revolution, he has behaved in a very equivocal manner and he certainly would have sworn the oath had he not been prevented from doing so by his fellow clergymen sitting with him in the Constituent Assembly.[66]

It is therefore not unreasonable to query the reliability of Salamon's judgement on Colbert, all the more so as he had a propensity to inflate his role in the Scottish Mission's attempt to resolve its conflict with the Principal of the Scots College, painstakingly recounting in great detail all the steps he had taken to support Geddes. Alexander Innes and Bishop Geddes corroborated Salamon's intense activity on behalf of the Mission. However, as a general rule, Salamon was not mentioned independently of Colbert. For instance, in a letter to John Thomson, Alexander Innes referred to the 'friends Bp Geddes [had] left [him in Paris] particularly the Bp of Rodez & Monsr Salamon.' Similarly Geddes let Cardinal Antonelli know how helpful both Salamon and the Bishop of Rodez had been. Though at first he had insisted on Alexander Innes's and Salamon's presence at the Conference, Geddes then noted that their 'Absence was well made up by the Presence of the Bishop of Rodez.'[67] Geddes was grateful to Colbert for his exertions on behalf of the Mission, and more particularly for drawing up the 'Resultat' and for his strongly-worded rebuttal of the Principal's criticisms. Further, during Geddes's sojourn in Paris, Colbert had lent him unflinching support in his attempt to get the Prior to act decisively and appoint a Procurator for the Scots College. That is probably the reason why on his leaving Paris Geddes made the Prior promise that he would not undertake anything material concerning the College without seeking the advice of the Bishop of Rodez and the consent of the Scottish Mission.[68] In spite of his four-month stay in Paris, Geddes seemed unaware of Salamon's ill will towards Colbert. Indeed,

[66] *Correspondance secrète de l'Abbé de Salamon [...] avec le cardinal Zelada (1791–1792)*, Paris, Plon, 1898, p. 402.

[67] SCA, BL, John Geddes to John Thomson, 19 March 1792.

[68] APF, SC Scozia, vol. 3, f. 423, John Geddes to Cardinal Antonelli, 30 April 1792.

he was persuaded that it was the conjoined activity of both men which would eventually enable the Mission to weather the crisis that threatened the Scots College, Paris, as is clear from the letter of thanks the bishops sent to Salamon in August 1792. They first expressed their deep gratitude to him, then called on him, 'together with the Bishop of Rodez, to continue to help the Prior with [his] advice and to support Mr Innes, the Procurator.'[69]

A few days earlier, the bishops had written a similar letter of thanks to Colbert. However, they set forth in a more explicit manner why they were grateful to God 'for raising up so powerful a Protector to defend our just Claims in such critical circumstances':

> The clear and distinct account, which your Ld^{p} gives in the Resultat, and still more explicitly in your answer to Prin^{l} Gordon's letter, of the rights which belong to us relative to that College; gives us the most agreeable satisfaction. Your Ld^{p} has now shown the just line of distinction, for which we sincerely thank you. Far be it from us to entertain a thought of passing that line, or of encroaching in the smallest degree on what belongs to the Prior's Jurisdiction, but we certainly wish to know what our just rights are; that we may be able to make such use of them as our Duty may require on any proper Emergency.[70]

While the Bishops were content to wish that the Holy See 'would show or maybe [...] had already shown its gratitude' to Salamon for his 'charitable conduct' in dealing with the College's affairs, their hopes for the Bishop of Rodez, and more generally for his adopted country, were much more ambitious: 'we trust in our good God, that after having purged his barnfloor & tried his true Servants, he will again restore his vineyard to its former Splendour, & our generous & much esteemed friend to the peace of the Government of his beloved flock for his & their comfort & sanctification.'[71] Their wish was not granted. On 27 August, Alexander Innes imparted to John Thomson, who had sent to him Cardinal Antonelli's letter of thanks to be forwarded to Colbert, that it was 'a considerable time since [he had] seen him or known where he [was] & [he could] not

69 SCA, BL, Scottish Bishops to Abbé Salamon, 30 August 1792.

70 SCA, BL, Scottish Bishops to Seignelay Colbert, 20 August 1792.

71 SCA, BL, Scottish Bishops to Seignelay Colbert, 20 August 1792.

discover it in the present situation of Things.'[72] That same day, he wrote to John Geddes: 'he is just under the lash of the late decree of deportation for all the Paroch. Clergy. I wish he had gone with you to Scotland in the beginning of summer.'[73] In late September, John Farquharson informed John Geddes that he had not 'been able to learn as yet, whither or not, the good B of Rhodez [had] escaped'[74] while the Duke of Buccleuch tried to learn of Henry Dundas the whereabouts of Colbert:

> I am anxious to know if the Bishop of Rodez is at London. He was a very particular friend of mine in France & I have a great regard for him. His name is Colbert with us Cuthbert. You may have an opportunity of finding him out if he is in England. It would give me great pleasure to be of any service to him, he is a worthy sensible man.[75]

Less than a month later, Colbert answered the letter he had just received from the Duke from 'Cossey, near Norwich.' He was to spend the remainder of his days in Great-Britain.

Exile

There is no way of ascertaining whether Colbert contemplated exile as early as Spring 1792, but by then he already planned to visit Scotland in the summer according to what Geddes wrote on 26 March to Bp Hay, who had observed in an earlier letter that the Bishop of Rodez's friends in Scotland 'long[ed] to hear from him.'[76] However, Geddes added: 'this you need not as yet mention. Then, at all events, he is to return to his Diocess.'[77]

[72] SCA, BL, Alexander Innes to John Thomson, 27 August 1792.

[73] SCA, BL, Alexander Innes to John Geddes, 27 August 1792. The 'décret sur la deportation des prêtres réfractaires' passed by the National Assembly on 26 May 1792 was vetoed by Louis XVI in June. However, it was implemented as soon as the King was imprisoned on 10 August with the Commune establishing lists of refractory priests to be arrested.

[74] SCA, BL, John Farquharson to John Geddes, 26 September 1792.

[75] The National Archives, HO 42/21/7, f. 718, Duke of Buccleuch to Henry Dundas, 27 September 1792.

[76] SCA, BL, George Hay to John Geddes, 12 March 1792. SCA, BL, John Geddes to George Hay, 26 March 1792.

[77] SCA, BL, John Geddes to George Hay, 26 March 1792.

On his return from Scotland in November 1793, Colbert wrote to the Duke of Buccleuch that if order was not restored, precluding him from being 'a bishop in France,' he would be 'a farmer in Scotland.'[78] Nevertheless, the Bishop of Rodez's exile in Britain is associated with London rather than Scotland,[79] even if he made regular visits there, at least until 1806. There is little direct evidence of the relationship between the Bishop of Rodez and the Scottish Mission after 1792—three short letters in English from Colbert, two of which were letters of recommendation addressed to his 'dear friend' Bp Hay in 1799 and 1801. The remaining one was an answer to William Rattray, a priest officiating in Edinburgh, who had urged him to contribute to the subscription opened for the building of a new chapel in the Scottish capital in 1802. All these letters were sent from London, where he met Bp Hay when he stayed there in June 1794.[80] His name was mentioned by some correspondents, in particular John Chisholm, the Vicar Apostolic of the Highland District, but those instances are relatively rare in view of Colbert's frequent visits to Scotland.

In August 1793, Paul MacPherson acquainted Bp Geddes that Colbert, whom he had met in London on his way to Rome, was about to set out for Scotland and that he had given him 'a Letter of recommendation to De Bernis.' He added: 'He is a sensible man; and much your friend, which is a circumstances [sic] agreeable to me.'[81] He gave no hint that Colbert might call on Bp Geddes, then at Scalan, but wrote in a separate letter to Bp Hay in Edinburgh that he would 'probably see the Bp of Rodez' the following week.[82] Colbert himself let the Duke of Buccleuch know that he had left Edinburgh at the end of August to spend

[78] Alain ALCOUFFE and Andrew MOORE, 'La correspondance de Mgr Seignelay Colbert de Castlehill, évêque de Rodez et duc de Buccleuch,' *Études Aveyronnaises*, 2020, pp. 342–363 (p. 357).

[79] See Dominic Aidan Bellenger's chapter in this volume.

[80] SCA, BL, George Hay to John Geddes, 11 June 1794. Hay wrote that the following day, Colbert was to introduce him to the Bishop of St Pol de Léon, whom Bishop Geddes had already met on 27 May 1792 in London on his way back to Scotland from France. On the purpose of this meeting, see Dominic Aidan Bellenger, p. 229.

[81] SCA, BL, Paul MacPherson to John Geddes, 14 August 1793.

[82] SCA, BL, Paul MacPherson to George Hay, 15 August 1793.

the month of September 'in the North.'[83] Though they may not have had an opportunity to meet that summer, Geddes still regarded Colbert as a friend who might be able to assist the Mission. When Charles Erskine, the papal envoy to London who was himself of Scottish descent, stayed a few days in Scotland over Christmas 1793, he requested Hay to 'draw out a full state' of the Mission affairs and send it to him in London. In turn, Hay asked his coadjutor for 'a scroll of the chief things to be laid before' Erskine,[84] which he duly did. He advised Hay to insist on the repercussions of the difficulties faced by the two Scots Colleges in France, starting with an even more acute shortage of priests. This was the context in which Geddes noted: '[Erskine] will either have seen, or you should take care that he do see the Bp of Rodez.' Geddes further observed that Hay should 'let him know, how much [they] were obliged and may as yet be obliged to Abbe Salomon, agent for the Holy See at Paris.'[85]

On 23 September 1793 John Chisholm, the Vicar Apostolic for the Highland District who was then stationed at Fasnakyle, wrote to Hay: 'B Cuthbert is just now not far from this place but I do not know if I can see him.'[86] Judging by the letter Chisholm sent to Hay in January 1794, the two bishops did meet. Distressed by the lack of priests in the Highlands, Chisholm confided to his Lowland counterpart:

> When I saw B Cuthbert he told me he had in view to procure one [priest] for Inverness and the vicinity of it before the french revolution. By the accounts I had receiv'd of his present circumstances I thought myself authoris'd to observe to him that I hop'd he had not drop't that Scheme. I have had no accounts of him since he went to London. his Brother is rich & has an estate near Inverness while he resides himself in the west Indies and offer'd him the half of it. incase you saw any opportunity either by Correspondence or Conversation (for he meant to return by Edinr to Castlehill if excluded from France) I wish you would use your influence to promote this good scheme he had formerly in contemplation.[87]

[83] Alain ALCOUFFE and Andrew MOORE, 'La correspondance de Mgr Seignelay Colbert de Castlehill, évêque de Rodez et duc de Buccleuch,' *Études Aveyronnaises*, 2020, pp. 342–363 (p. 356).

[84] SCA, BL, George Hay to John Geddes, 27 December 1793.

[85] SCA, BL, John Geddes to George Hay, 31 December 1793.

[86] SCA, BL, John Chisholm to George Hay, 23 September 1793.

[87] SCA, BL, John Chisholm to George Hay, January 1794.

Five months later, Chisholm returned to this topic in another letter to Hay: 'B. Cuthbert is to come to the vicinity of Inverness this Summer I am told. I hope you'll see him in his way & remember what I have written before.'[88] There is no indication that Hay did broach this matter with the Bishop of Rodez, either in writing or in person. Besides, it is doubtful that Colbert was either able or willing to go through with such a plan. When in 1803 he was called upon to contribute towards the building of a new chapel in Edinburgh he declined to do so on account of his lack of means: 'I wish that I my self were in a condition to help your efforts and concurring to the laudable undertaking you have formed for the glory of God and the good of your faithful flock. I'll answer then as St Peter… *Non est mihi aurum neque argentum.*'[89]

It is quite clear from the letters Chisholm wrote in the 1790s that what he first and foremost craved from the Bishop of Rodez was financial support to meet the cost of one or possibly more extra priests. It would seem that he did get his wish, but in a somewhat unexpected manner—Colbert himself officiated on the isle of South Uist, whose population was mainly Catholic. At any rate, that is the conclusion that can be drawn from a passage in a letter sent in June 1803 by Charles Maxwell, the Procurator of the Mission, to Paul MacPherson, the Scots Agent at Rome: 'you know that Mr Austin, and Mr Alexr McDonald from Uist went off last year with the emigrants to America. – the French Bishop who is now in Uist in Mr Alex[r] McDonald's place, and Mr John McDonald in Ardnafueran were both desirous of going over this year but I understand they have given up all thoughts of it for this year at least.'[90] Maxwell did not name Colbert but, as James McGloin observed,[91] that French émigré bishop can be no other than Seignelay Colbert, Bishop of Rodez. Strange as this hypothesis may seem, it is nevertheless plausible. Colbert spoke Gaelic. That was a *sine qua non* condition to officiate in South Uist, which is why a priest from the Lowland District could not be sent to the Hebrides. Further, finding priests to be stationed in Uist was a particularly arduous task in the

[88] SCA, BL, John Chisholm to George Hay, 5 May 1794.

[89] SCA, BL, Seignelay Colbert to William Rattray, 9 January 1802.

[90] SCA, BL, Charles Maxwell to Paul MacPherson, 8 June 1803.

[91] James McGloin, 'Some Refugee French Clerics and Laymen in Scotland, 1789–1814,' *Innes Review*, 1965, pp. 27–55 (p. 28).

years 1802–1803. Two priests emigrated with members of their respective flocks in 1802, as Maxwell pointed out in his letter, leaving Ranald MacEachan as the only priest to serve the whole island. He died in Spring 1803, much to the dismay of his bishop, who wrote to Maxwell in April that he was at his wit's end to find a replacement for him. That was the context in which Maxwell mentioned the presence of a French bishop in Uist in early June. Maxwell may have had this information from John Chisholm as they were in regular correspondence, though none of John Chisholm's extant letters for this period refer to Colbert's presence in Uist. Ultimately, even if the Bishop of Rodez did alleviate the shortage of priests in Uist, it can only have been for a very short period of time. On 16 April 1803, he wrote a letter from London where he was back at the latest on 25 August, when he sent to Major Cuthbert in Georgia details on their common ancestry. While Colbert's presence in Uist that summer is plausible, though not proven, it is far more difficult to form an opinion on his supposed desire to emigrate to Canada. There definitely was a branch of the Cuthbert family settled in Canada with whom Colbert was in touch, at least in the 1780s as he was instrumental in getting James Cuthbert to board at the Scots College, Douai, but he did not seem to have any contact with the Seigneur de Berthier after he left France for London. The letter Colbert sent to Major Cuthbert in Georgia in August 1803 made it clear the two men did not know each other and there was no hint that Colbert might travel to North America.[92] This is not evidence enough to rule out this hypothesis, but unless some new sources are uncovered, it seems unlikely that Colbert intended to emigrate.

Alongside the dispute between the Mission and the Principal of the Scots College, Paris, Colbert's hypothetical stay in South Uist is probably the most often mentioned episode in Colbert's dealings with the Scottish Mission. It also seems to enable some authors to pass negative judgment on Colbert, the émigré bishop (rather than the pre-exile Bishop of Rodez). In his biography of Bishop Hay, J.A. Stothert merely noted that clergymen accompanying members of their flocks in successive waves of emigration had made the lack of priests even worse and as a result there was 'an Emigrant French Bishop discharging the onerous duties of a Missionary in the remote Island of Uist. It is not surprising to learn

[92] J. G. B. Bulloch, *The Cuthberts, Barons of Castlehill and Their Descendants in South Carolina and Georgia*, 1908, pp. 29–35.

that he too, was desirous of seeking better fortunes in the Far West.'[93] Stothert did not find fault with Colbert—he went so far as justifying, partly tongue in cheek, the bishop's urge to forsake his heavy toil.

Twentieth-century commentators have been less charitable. In his 1963 article on Abbé Nicolas, James McGloin lamented the fact that Colbert had 'utterly failed' to 'provide some leadership' to the refugee clergy in Scotland.[94] Two years later, in his article on 'Some Refugee French Clerics and Layman in Scotland, 1789–1814,' McGloin derided as 'worthless' the 'claims of the Cuthberts of Castlehill to royal origin.' He hinted that Colbert had not always been respectful of the London Vicar-Apostolic's authority, 'exceed[ing] any possible lawful jurisdiction' by issuing letters 'giving faculties and jurisdiction to all French priests in exile' and concluded his account of Colbert thus: 'In Scotland (so far as we know) he exercised no authority over French emigrés but he cultivated his alleged relationship to Scottish noble families.'[95] In 1970, Peter Anson published *Underground Catholicism in Scotland 1622–1878*, a classic account of the post-Reformation Roman Catholic Church in Scotland.[96] Anson had manifestly little time for Colbert. He quoted at length from Geddes's account in his diary of his endeavours to locate Colbert and of their first meeting in Paris, but remained surprisingly silent about the role played by the Bishop of Rodez, failing to comment on the quotation. Again, when he wrote about Bp Hay's meeting in 1794 with the Bp of St Pol de Léon to discuss whether French priests could be enticed to come and settle in Scotland, he omitted to let his readers know that Colbert was instrumental not only in the two men's meeting but also in convincing Bp Hay that it might benefit the Scottish Mission. Conversely, when Anson broached the subject of the refractory bishops exiled in London who refused to resign their sees at the time of the Concordat in 1801, he painted an unflattering picture of Colbert which he concluded with these scathing, but unsubstantiated, comments: 'apparently without the authority of Bishop Chisholm, Vicar-Apostolic of the

[93] J. F. S. Gordon (ed.), *The Catholic Church in Scotland*, p. 437.

[94] James McGloin, 'The Abbe Nicolas,' *Innes Review*, 1963, pp. 10–29 (p. 11).

[95] James McGloin, 'Some Refugee French Clerics and Laymen in Scotland, 1789–1814,' pp. 28–29.

[96] For eighteenth-century Scottish Catholicism, it was superseded by Christine Johnson's *Developments in the Roman Catholic Church in Scotland 1789–1829*, Edinburgh, John Donald, 1983.

Highland District, the deposed Bishop of Rodez extended his travels to the Western Isles, with the vague idea of leading colonies of emigrants to Canada. It was a task for which he was quite unsuited.'[97] In 1991, Kathleen Toomey relied on such statements by Anson to claim that Colbert 'sought refuge in Britain where he became a thorn in the side of the vicars apostolic both in England and Scotland by granting faculties to exiled French priests.'[98]

When it has not ignored Colbert altogether, Scottish historiography has passed a harsh judgment on him, but is this verdict justified? Ultimately, the last word on it must be left to the Scottish Mission. It may well be that, from the mid-1790s on, Vicars Apostolic in Scotland, especially Bp Chisholm, came to have mixed, if not wholly negative, feelings about the Bishop of Rodez in view of his failing to fully support his embattled colleagues in Scotland, but no material evidence of it has yet come to light. What the available sources for the period 1790–1794 unambiguously testify to, on the other hand, is how grateful the Mission, starting with Bp Hay and Bp Geddes, felt towards their 'Countryman, the Bishop of Rodez.'

[97] Peter F. ANSON, *Underground Catholicism in Scotland 1622–1878*, Montrose, Standard Press, 1970, p. 222.

[98] Kathleen TOOMEY, Emigration from the Scottish Catholic bounds, 1770–1810 and the role of the clergy, PhD, University of Edinburgh, 1991, p. 217 note 95.

CHAPTER 11

The Emigration Route Across the Channel of the Bishop of Rodez Colbert de Castlehill: A Network Woven in Occitania and in the Sorbonne

Patrick Ferté

Abstract Patrick Ferté has attempted to reconstruct the network of relationships that underpin the period of Colbert's exile. Across the Channel, whether in Scotland or London. This network was forged well before the Revolution in four converging centres of friendship (1) with his first mentors, the bishop of Chartres, Lubersac, his character witness, and his patron in Toulouse, Loménie de Brienne, and above all in his diocese of Rodez since 1781; (2) with the liberal La Rochefoucauld family, particularly the Duchesse d'Enville and her nephew the Duc de Liancourt, followers of Turgot and Adam Smith; (3) at the Sorbonne, through some

English revised by Andrew Moore. Slightly abridged from the French (https://books.openedition.org/).

P. Ferté (✉)
University of Toulouse-Jean Jaurès, Toulouse, France

A. Alcouffe (ed.), *Seignelay Colbert de Castlehill (1735-1811)*,
https://doi.org/10.1007/978-3-031-75273-5_11

of his fellow students but above all through his professors, some of whom were from Rouergue and whom he later met again in London; (4) his British connections also played a major role, due to his Scottish origin, but Ireland was just as decisive in this instance. These four focal points, segmented to clarify the presentation, are most often intertwined: Some of the Irish refugees he met or ordained in Toulouse or Rodez became professors at the Sorbonne before fleeing to England or Dublin (to the Catholic College of Maynooth); others were from his Rouergat flock who themselves obtained a chair at the Sorbonne and/or a position as chaplain or confessor to the royal family. The fact remains that these four hotbeds, which formed a solid network, shared the same ideology and converged towards exile, usually in London.

Keywords Brienne (Loménie de) · Edgeworth de Firmont · La Rochefoucauld-Liancourt · Toulouse · Maynooth · Sorbonne · Mgr de Lubersac · Abbé Anglade

The cardinal of La Rochefoucauld, archbishop of Rouen, found it necessary to flee Paris after the carnage of September 1792 during which he lost 3 nephews, the bishops of Beauvais and Saintes massacred in the Carmes prison and the duke of La Rochefoucauld (Louis-Alexandre) stoned to death in Gisors[1]; he managed to reach Boulogne-sur-Mer and embarked on 20 September 1792 for Dover while his grand-nephew, the Duc de Liancourt,[2] president of the Comité de Mendicité with Seignelay Colbert de Castlehill, bishop of Rodez, as vice-president, withdrew first to Rouen before reaching Le Crotois where he had difficulty finding a boat to England and took refuge with Arthur Young. Seignelay Colbert, a commensal of the La Rochefoucauld family, may have taken a similar route: he had family and friendly ties in Boulogne-sur-Mer, whose bishop, Mgr Asseline, was very early on one of the leaders of the insurrectionist front and was even considered for a long time with Colbert as a leader

[1] D. Vaugelade, *Louis-Alexandre de La Rochefoucauld, 1743–1792, un aristocrate au service de la science*, Éditions de l'Amandier, 2014.

[2] To distinguish him from his cousin the Duke Louis-Alexandre de La Rochefoucauld, whom we shall call the Duke of L. R., we shall call François-Alexandre de La Rochefoucauld-Liancourt simply 'Liancourt'.

of the *Petite Église*. Above all, Mgr Asseline, whose grand vicar is a Toulouse native, the Abbé de Mongazin, elected deputy of Boulogne to the General Estates, was previously a professor at the Sorbonne alongside two Rouergat colleagues, the Abbé Dièche and the Abbé Anglade. The latter, once ordained to the priesthood by Seignelay, fled like his bishop to England and then to Ireland. There he joined the Catholic seminary of Maynooth set up thanks to Moylan, an Irishman who had graduated from Toulouse, and where several Sorbonnian colleagues of Anglade and Asseline were already in place, themselves linked to the networks of the bishop of Rodez as shall be see.

This trajectory is therefore possible; unless Colbert did like the Abbé Edgeworth de Firmont, chaplain to Louis XVI on the scaffold and to his sister Mme Elisabeth, another Irishman also educated in Toulouse with his friend the Moylan. Edgeworth went to join the Count of Artois in Scotland by way of the crossroads of Lower Normandy, via Bayeux and the Channel Islands: Colbert was Abbot of Valricher in the diocese of Bayeux (suffragan of Rouen) as was Mgr Dillon (Abbot of Saint-Etienne de Caen) and as was Edward Booth, Dillon's Vicar General in Narbonne who was Abbot of Ardennes[3] in Caen for 25 years (1765–1790). However, the vicar general of Bayeux was a Rouergat, the Abbé d'Albignac de Castelnau, who became bishop of Angoulême (1784), then insermenter, and was part of the anti-concordat bloc in London alongside Colbert. Above all, Colbert had Franco-Scottish relatives, settled near Bayeux, in Vaux-sur-Seulle, Magny-en-Bessin and Vierville-sur-Mer, the Drummonds of Melfort and the Grants of Vaux, whom he met again, with Dillon, in London, where he celebrated the marriage of one of their daughters to... a relative of Brienne[4]! In his *Historical Memoirs*, Charles Grant devotes more than 400 pages to proving the antiquity of his Scottish nobility, originating from Inverness like Seignelay, the installation of a Grant branch in Normandy as early as 1359, and his alliances with "the Melforts, Perys, Seignelay Colberts, Morins [of Litteau], and finally the Grants of Scotland and Normandy"; and to quote in several places our bishop of Rodez his distant relative, since, he argues, "the Grants have contracted several alliances with the House of Colbert Seigneley (*sic*),

[3] A. Sabarthès, *Arthur-Richard Dillon, Dernier archevêque de Narbonne (1763–1806)*, Narbonne, 1943, pp. 48–49.

[4] On 18 February 1793 and on 26 December 1793 Ch. Grant, *Historical, Political, Military*, etc. *Memoirs of the House of Grant...*, 1796, pp. 335–336, 356–357.

descendant of the barons of Castlehill in Scotland as is notified by a certificate of Mr. Bishop of Rhodèz Seigneley Colbert of his name, which is in the hands of the viscount Grant de Vaux[5]".

Whatever the precise route by which Seignelay arrived in London, which remain matter for conjecture, after this simple introductory overview of the interweaving of the links to be examined, an attempt will be made to establish more precisely all his links with the prelates emigrated across the Channel, links woven sometimes well before the Revolution between 3 or 4 poles of acquaintance, first in Occitania (Rodez, Toulouse, Narbonne), then Paris-Versailles (the court, the hotel of La Rochefoucauld and the Sorbonne), and finally across the Channel (Ireland, England and Scotland), whether in the shadow of Brienne and Mgr Dillon, in the circle of La Rochefoucauld, but also within that of Mgr Lubersac, bishop of Chartres, or in liaison with the Sorbonne professors and other chaplains of the royal family who were, very often, Rouergats and therefore his diocesan family.

To expose the skein of all these links woven before the Revolution by Seignelay, and renewed in exile, the historian is spoilt for choice. Which first piece of the puzzle to choose? An arbitrary choice must be made. First the network surrounding Colbert in many ways, the influential circle of the Dukes of La Rochefoucauld, before following the tracks of the prelates Lubersac and Dillon, and finally listing all the abbés of the Court and the academics, very often Seignelay's diocesans. All these leads converge across the Channel, whether in London, Scotland or Ireland.

[5] Ibid., p. 337 note; see also pp. 94, 95, 449, 452, 454. The intimate archives (not consulted) of Charles Grant de Vaux, a distant relative of Colbert, are held in the William L. Clements Library at the University of Michigan Ann Arbor; they may contain further traces of his contacts with the bishop of Rodez.

The Liberal Circle of La Rochefoucauld

A beginning can be made with a first liberal household, the philanthropic aristocratic family of La Rochefoucauld[6] (the Duke Louis-Alexandre,[7] his mother the Duchess of Enville[8] and his cousin Liancourt[9]), whether in their Parisian residence, in La Roche-Guyon or in Liancourt. It serves to establish links between Colbert de Castlehill, Toulouse and/or Rodez and British tropism, as these liberal nobles, keen on economics and the Enlightenment, were fervent Anglophiles: they were all followers of Turgot and were guests of Adam Smith, Arthur Young, the Abbé Morellet, a fellow student at the Sorbonne of Loménie de Brienne, and of Seignelay himself.

Before evaluating this, let us note that Brienne, Seignelay's first mentor, was related to the La Rochefoucauld family since a very long time. The author of the famous *Maximes* had indeed married in 1628 a daughter of André de Vivonne and Marie-Antoinette de Loménie de Brienne (1594–1638). They were the parents of François VII duc de La Rochefoucauld, grandfather of the duke Alexandre de La Rochefoucauld (1690–1762): The latter was the father of the Duchess of Enville and the grandfather of the Duke de Liancourt, who will reappear again in the company of the Bishop of Rodez, whether at their property in La Roche-Guyon or in their Parisian hotel.

It should also be noted that, before becoming bishops, Dillon and Brienne were together vicars general of the archbishop of Rouen, Mgr de Saux-Tavannes, who liked to stay with the La Rochefoucaulds at La Roche-Guyon.[10] When Mgr de La Rochefoucauld succeeded Saux-Tavannes in the see of Rouen (January 1760), he extended Brienne's stay in Pontoise, and Dillon and Brienne, who had each become bishops, then remained honorary canons of Rouen, Brienne had been abbot of St-Ouen

[6] S. Fasquelle, *Les La Rochefoucauld*, Paris, 1992.

[7] D. Vaugelade, *Louis-Alexandre de L. R., op. cit.*

[8] D. Vaugelade, *Le salon physiocratique des La Rochefoucauld animated by Louis Élisabeth de La Rochefoucauld, duchesse d'Enville (1716–1797)*, Paris, Publibook, 2001; see also Michèle Crogiez ed, *Correspondance de la duchesse d'Enville*, Éd. de l'Oeil, 2016.

[9] J. Ferdinand-Dreyfus, *La Rochefoucauld-Liancourt (1747–1827), un philanthrope d'autrefois*, Paris, Plon, 1903.

[10] See one of the letters quoted by P. Chevallier, "Une promotion épiscopale sous Louis XV (1752–1753)", *RHMC*, 1959, 6–3, p. 221 sq.

de Rouen since 1787 and of St-Wandrille since 1785, and the duke of Liancourt, nephew of the archbishop, was governor of Rouen just before his exile.

Brienne was in fact the nephew of the Marquise du Deffand[11] as she assures us in one of her letters to Walpole. Also "his salon [was] naturally open to the Briennes, his relatives; they met the Broglies, the Beauvaus, the Choiseuls, La Rochefoucauld, etc., as well as Montesquieu, D'Alembert, Marmontel, Condorcet, Condillac and other philosophes[12]". All these genealogical and/or relational links are useful to explain the frequent visits of Brienne and his protégé Seignelay Colbert, whether in the salon of Mme du Deffand or in that of the La Rochefoucauld family led by the Duchess of Enville, her son the Duke of La Rochefoucauld and her nephew the Duke of Liancourt. Through this liberal aristocratic network, the young Seignelay was very early exposed to the ideas of the Encyclopedists. Mme d'Enville, who was nicknamed "the mother of the Enlightenment", was a friend of the Physiocrats, Turgot, Condorcet and Voltaire, whom she particularly helped in the Calas Affair, by getting the two daughters of Jean Calas released, etc. It was at this time that Colbert arrived in Toulouse as vicar general of Brienne... Let us also note that, on 3 June 1781, when he was given possession of the bishopric of Rodez through the intermediary of his procurator, Canon Viguier de Grun, Colbert is reported as "currently in Paris, lodged at the Hôtel de Brienne in the rue St-Dominique, parish of St-Sulpice"[13].

To demonstrate more positively the link between La Rochefoucauld and Colbert, as well as his involvement in the first reforms of 1789–1791, the list of members of the Comité de Mendicité can be consulted, whose "competences were to be extended thanks to Liancourt" to the point that "the revolutionary crisis would make him one of the essential organs of the [Constituent] Assembly", along with the Comité des Recherches. La Rochefoucauld-Liancourt was a hyperactive philanthropist, a physiocrat haunted by the failing economy and the social woes that consisted

[11] Loménie de Brienne's paternal grandmother was the half-sister of Anne Brulart, the mother of Mme du Deffand.

[12] L. Dutil, "Philosophie ou religion, Loménie de Brienne, archbishop of Toulouse", *Annales du Midi*, 1948, 61-1-2, p. 44. See also letter from Mme du Deffand to Abbé Barthélemy of 11 May 1768.

[13] Société des Lettres, sciences et arts de l'Aveyron, fonds Girou Bedel de Buzareingues (now SLA-GBDB).

essentially in his eyes in the lack of work for the people, poverty and the appalling condition of hospitals: like his cousin the Duke of La Rochefoucauld, with whom he was brought up in La Roche-Guyon, he was an intimate of Louis XVI, whom he frequented very often as Grand Master of the King's wardrobe (since 1783), especially during the early work of the Constituent Assembly, of which he was president from 18 July to 2 August 1789. He is well known for his reply to the King who asked him if the Parisian riots were a "revolt": "no, Sire", he answered, "it is a revolution".

When, on 26 April 1790, the *Comité de Mendicité* (Begging Committee) appointed Liancourt as its president, it was the bishop of Rodez who was appointed vice-president[14]: both were linked at the time by the same economic and social, if not political and religious progressivism (Liancourt and his cousin were not bigots, and were undoubtedly deists) and were working on the said committee to give concrete expression to a right to work guaranteed by the state[15] and to set up a public hospital assistance system.[16] A militant for national solidarity, Liancourt wanted to include "imperiously" in the Declaration of the Rights of Man and of the Citizen "the right of every man to his subsistence". Colbert may have recognised in this voluntarism of "public beneficence" a secularised, nationalised and rationalised form of one of his own episcopal missions of charity towards those whom Dufourny, echoing Abbé Sieyès, called the "Fourth Order" or "the sacred order of the unfortunate".[17] There is no doubt that he gave his blessing to his president and sincerely applauded when Liancourt declared on 12 June 1790: "No State has considered the poor in the Constitution. It has always been thought to

[14] C. Bloch, A. Tuetey, *P.-v. et rapports du Comité de mendicité de la Constituante (1790–1791)*, Paris, Imprimerie nationale, 1911.

[15] According to the wish of the Chevalier de Jaucourt in D. Diderot, d'Alembert, *L'Encyclopédie*, art. "Mendiant" [political economy], t. 21, pp. 482–483.

[16] J.-B. Masméjan, 'Le comité de mendicité mandaté par la Nation: vers une harmonisation de la politique d'assistance des valides (1790–1791)', *Cahiers Jean Moulin* (online), no. 2.

[17] M. Grenot, *Le souci des plus pauvres. Dufourny, la Révolution française et la démocratie*, PU Rennes, 2020 [online], pp. 81–108.

give charity to the poor, but never to assert the rights of the poor man over society and those of society over him.[18]

Liancourt knew Seignelay Colbert well before the Estates-General, whether through all his stays at the La Rochefoucauld mansion, through his protector Brienne, through the minister Choiseul (who cherished Liancourt like a son), or by Turgot, whom Liancourt knew from his stewardship of the Limousin (1761–1774) and who, with his fellow student Brienne, was in charge of the Commission des Réguliers[19] (1766), or even through Abbé Raynal (a diocesan of Colbert's) and/or Adam Smith. At the Assemblée des Notables (1787), the Bishop of Rodez was privileged to be convened with many of his acquaintances, including Archbishops Dillon and Brienne, the Count of Choiseul and the Duke of La Rochefoucauld.[20] Several of Colbert's letters also mention a stay "at Chantelou par Amboise" at the home of the widow Choiseul, where the Duc de Liancourt and Loménie de Brienne were regulars.[21]

The Begging Committee of the Constituent Assembly followed a first attempt with the Begging Commission created by Turgot, who entrusted the task to his fellow student and colleague at the Sorbonne (1748–1752), Loménie de Brienne, then Archbishop of Toulouse, who energetically invested himself in this task and in 1775 wrote a "Report on begging" which "lays the foundations of a social administration well ahead of its time[22]". Although the effort was cut short by the dismissal of Turgot (May 1776), it was thus not by chance that, 15 years later, the idea was revived during the Constituent Assembly, under the presidency of Liancourt, nephew of the Duchess of Enville, who had taken

[18] Archives parlementaires de la Révolution Française, 1ère series (1787–1799), Paris, P. Dupont, 1883, 16, pp. 182–184.

[19] P. Chevallier, *Loménie de Brienne et l'ordre monastique (1766–1789)*, Paris, Librairie philosophique Vrin, 1959–1960.

[20] P. Chevallier ed, *Journal de l'Assemblée des notables de 1787 par le comte de Brienne et Étienne Charles de Loménie de Brienne, archevêque de Toulouse (Bureau de Monsieur et Bureau du comte d'Artois)*, Paris, Librairie Klincksieck, 1960.

[21] See, for example, his letter of 7 September 1783 (SLA-GBDB).

[22] G. Thuillier, Comité d'histoire de la Sécurité sociale, "Aux origines de l'administration sociale: le rapport sur la mendicité de Loménie de Brienne en 1775", 14 February 2003, online.

in Turgot at Chatel-Guyon after his disgrace,[23] and that the Bishop of Rodez was chosen as vice-president, he who had learnt much as vicar general of Brienne….

Since possible links are being sought with emigration to England, other than the obvious appeal of his native country, it can be noted that the main testimonies on the close links between the liberal circle of La Rochefoucauld and Seignelay, whether before or during the Revolution, come from English authors, for example, Adam Smith or Arthur Young, themselves commensals of both!

In the Wake of Adam Smith and Arthur Young

P. Massot-Bordenave, A. Alcouffe, A. Moore[24] have studied effectively the links between Adam Smith and Colbert de Castlehill during the Grand Tour of the Duke of Buccleuch and his tutor Smith in the South of France between Bordeaux, Toulouse, Montpellier and Bagnères, from March 1764 to the end of September 1765. It will not be necessary to return to this subject except to highlight several connections between the La Rochefoucaulds and the work of Adam Smith that show the ideological affinities.

The Duc de La Rochefoucauld, like his cousin Liancourt, discussed liberal political economy with Adam Smith on many occasions; better still, he twice undertook the abortive project of translating Adam Smith's *Theory of Moral Sentiments*, but preceded by the Abbé Jean-Louis

[23] Turgot, *Œuvres de Turgot et documents le concernant*, VI, *Turgot dans la retraite (1776–1783)*, n° 238, letter to Voltaire (July 1776), Paris, F. Alcan, 1923.

[24] Ph. Massot-Bordenave, 'L'influence des Écossais sur l'Assemblée provinciale de Haute-Guyenne, à la fin du XVIIIe siècle, en Quercy Rouergue', *Études aveyronnaises*, 2010, pp. 345–360; of the same, *Relire la fabrique d'épingles. Vers une théorie de l'économie sociale et solidaire*, Éditions Larcier, 2013, pp. 207–230; A. Alcouffe, Ph. Massot-Bordenave, *Adam Smith à Toulouse et enOccitanie*, Toulouse, Privat, 2018; A. Alcouffe & A. Moore, *Smith's Encounters in Occitania—March 1764-October 1765, 31st Annual Conference of the Eighteenth-Century Scottish Studies Society Networks of Enlightenment*, Eighteenth-Century Scottish Studies Society, July 2018, Glasgow [HAL].

Blavet,[25] he gave up on completing it.[26] Another translation was later given by Sophie de Grouchy, the wife of his great friend Condorcet[27] (1798).

In any case, this infatuation with Adam Smith's work could not but bring La Rochefoucauld closer to Colbert, Brienne's protégé who had known and guided the Scot in Languedoc: it was in fact at Brienne's estate, where Seignelay liked to stay, that the Abbé Morellet undertook the translation of *The Wealth of Nations*.[28] Morellet was a pupil of Turgot and Brienne, but also of Champion de Cicé (Colbert's predecessor at the bishopric of Rodez and at the Assembly of Haute-Guyenne) and of Boisgelin de Cucé, archbishop of Aix, who was also vicar general of Rouen (1756–1764) with Brienne under Mgr de La Rochefoucauld, and who was Colbert's and Dillon's companion during their time of exile in London. A friend of Voltaire, Morellet had acquired a serious reputation as an economist, and it is known that Adam Smith "attached a certain importance to his relations with the abbé[29]" [Morellet] whom the Scot had met at Helvetius's, the Duchess d'Enville's and the Marquise de

[25] ADAM SMITH, *Des Sentiments moraux de Adam Smith*, trans. abbé Jean-Louis Blavet, Paris, 1775. See M. BIZIOU, "Traductions et retraductions françaises de la *Théorie des sentiments moraux* d'Adam Smith. L'insoutenable légèreté de (re)traduire", *Noesis* (CRHI), 21, "Traduire la philosophie," pp. 229–263.

[26] A. SMITH, *The Correspondence of Adam Smith*, E. C. Mossner, I. S. Ross, Oxford ed., Clarendon Press, 1977, p. 233 (letter from the Duc de La Rochefoucauld, 3 March 1778).

[27] Th. BOISSEL, *Sophie de Condorcet, femme des Lumières, 1764–1822*, Paris, Presses de la Renaissance, 1988; ADAM SMITH, *Théorie des sentiments moraux*, trans. marquise de Condorcet, 2 vols, Paris, Buisson, 1798.

[28] Abbé Morellet stated that in the autumn of 1776, while staying with Loménie de Brienne, he was busy translating Smith's *Wealth of Nations*, which he had come to know on his trip to France. He adds that when Brienne was at the ministry, he asked him in vain for funding to print the book, which was refused. It is interesting to find Brienne's trail here… for the translation of a work of which an original copy can be found in Colbert's library. See, Morellet, André. 1821. *Mémoires de l'abbé Morellet*, de l'académie française. T. 1. Paris: Ladvocat. pp. 326–327. The catalogue of Colbert's library is here: http://bvmm.irht.cnrs.fr/resultRecherche/resultRecherche.php?COMPOSITION_ID=13944.

[29] *The Correspondence of Adam Smith*, *op. cit.* p. 295.

Boufflers's house,[30] whose very Anglophile salon was for a time hosted by David Hume, Seignelay's "cousin"!

It is interesting to follow Brienne's lead in translating the work of Seignelay's brilliant compatriot, whom the latter had once guided in Languedoc and who later endeavoured to put into practice some of Smith's innovative economic principles as president of the provincial assembly of Haute-Guyenne.[31]

We know that Colbert encouraged the aerostatic experiment of the abbé Carnus, professor at the College of Rodez The *Ville de Rodez* balloon took off publicly on 6 August 1784. The Duke of La Rochefoucauld was president of the Academy of Sciences (whose vice-president in 1788 was Brienne) and he was fascinated by Montgolfier's experiments. He was the first president of the Commission for aerostatic machines (November 1783), and the first two meetings were held at the Hôtel de La Rochefoucauld. It is likely that eight months later, the Bishop of Rodez (Brienne's feal) related in detail his successful experience to his host, who was himself engaged in aerostatic attempts in his land of La Roche-Guyon.

All this should demonstrate that Colbert, both before and after his accession to the see of Rodez, was a familiar figure to the La Rochefoucaulds, and these links were only strengthened under the Constituent Assembly when he became vice-president of the Comité de Mendicité, under the leadership of the Duc de Liancourt, an attentive reader of Adam Smith.[32]

The Comité de mendicité recruited another active member on the probable advice of Brienne and/or Colbert: this was Jean-Baptiste-Auguste de Villoutreix de Faye, who was for a long time at Colbert's

[30] Let us point out a letter n° 91 from a "Gr[and] vic[aire] eccossais" (probably Colbert) written "on 18 February 1766 to "Adam Smith, philosopher of Glasgow, [...] what are you doing, my dear friend, How are you governing the Duchess of Enville and Mad. De Bouflers?" *The Glasgow Edition of the Works and Correspondence of Adam Smith*, VI: *Correspondence*, ALI SMITH, ADAM SMITH, Clarendon Press, 1987; see also A. ALCOUFFE, Ph. MASSOT-BORDENAVE, *op. cit.*

[31] Colbert, bishop of Rodez, remained faithful to Adam Smith's ideas when, in 1784, he pushed the Academy of Montauban to create one of the first agricultural competitions in France. Ph. MASSOT-BORDENAVE, "L'influence des Écossais...", art. cité, pp. 345–360.

[32] J.-B. MASMÉJAN, art. cit.

side as vicar general of Brienne (of whom he was a relative[33]) and chancellor of the University of Toulouse,[34] before being appointed bishop of Oloron in 1783.

It is likely that Colbert's exile in London followed many leads opened by the Duke of Liancourt across the Channel. With Liancourt, there are many such leads and each time they cross paths with the English traveller Arthur Young, after Adam Smith. It is Young who confirms in several places that the bishop of Rodez was a regular guest at the La Rochefoucauld hotel.

As D'Argenson wrote in 1750: "the wind has been blowing from England for several years[35]". The peace of 1763 revived the Anglomania which pervaded the La Rochefoucauld circle as well as many other Parisian salons. Thus Liancourt, during a first trip to England, made a lasting friendship as early as 1769 with Arthur Young, whom he met at his home in Bradfield and again in 1778, even sending his two sons to him for their Grand Tour of budding economists across the Channel[36]: François de La Rochefoucauld spent no less than 14 months at Young's home in Bury St-Edmund until February 1785, including an excursion to Ireland and Scotland (did he meet Adam Smith there?) before returning to spend 3 months at Bury; his brother Alexandre did the same (1786[37]). It was only afterwards that Liancourt received Young not only in the Parisian hotel of his aunt, the Duchess of Enville (1788–1790), but also many times in private at La Roche-Guyon and in his own estate of Liancourt, where he was developing his experimental farm, factories and a Technical School, the embryo of the School of Arts and Crafts (*Arts et Métiers*).

Later, in 1799, Liancourt even gave a French translation of Sir Frederick Morton-Eden's groundbreaking work, *State of the Poor, or History*

[33] Originally from Flavignac in Limousin, he too was related to the La Rochefoucaulds since 1662 See A. JEAN, *Les évêques et les archevêques de France depuis 1682 jusqu'à 1801*, Paris et Mamers, 1891, p. 46.

[34] It was he who, on the advice of Brienne, made the encyclopaedist Gardeil, a friend of d'Holbach, a regent doctor at the Faculty of Medicine in 1773.

[35] MARQUIS D'ARGENSON, *Journal et mémoires du marquis d'Argenson*, E. J. B. Rathery ed., Paris, Renouard, 1859–1867, vol. VI, p. 320.

[36] L. and J. MARCHAND, 'Une amitié internationale au XVIIIe siècle; La Rochefoucauld-Liancourt et ses fils, Maximilien de Lazowski et Arthur Young', *Annuaire-bulletin de la Société de l'histoire de France*, vol. 81, no. 1 (1945), pp. 45–74.

[37] N. SCARFE, *To the Highlands in 1786: The Inquisitive Journey of a Young French Aristocrat*, Woodbridge, Boydell & Brewer, 2001.

of the Working Classes of Society in England... It is a pioneering work of political economy and sociological enquiry, which Malthus and Karl Marx regarded as the masterpiece of the only true disciple of Adam Smith with Arthur Young in the eighteenth century; it had only been published for 2 years (1797) when Liancourt set about translating it into French. The work was to be published without the name of the translator (at his request) but Roederer demanded that he be honoured.[38]

Colbert de Castlehill, also a lover of political economy despite his episcopal status, but also president of a Provincial Assembly and undertaking great works in the line of Turgot, could not have had a better president in the Begging Committee of the Constituent Assembly, just as Liancourt had a vice-president worthy of supporting him....

In any case, when the Duke of Liancourt, after the assassination of his cousin the Duke of La Rochefoucauld at Gisors (1792), was forced to emigrate by the back door via Rouen (where he was lieutenant general) and Le Crotoy, it was quite natural that he crossed the Channel (18 August 1792[39]), not without tribulations, disguised as a sailor, and took refuge for a year in Bury-St-Edmunds at the home of Arthur Young.... No doubt this is a possible exile trajectory of Colbert de Castlehill who, it is true, had no trouble finding hosts by virtue of his ancestry, but his proximity to Liancourt and the Englishman Young during the early days of the Revolution should give pause. In several places Young shows us the two presidents of the Comité de Mendicité, Seignelay, Liancourt and/or his cousin, dining in the hotel of the Duchess of Enville or in Versailles. "The day after our arrival, I was introduced to the Larochefoucauld society with whom we live"; on 22 June 1789, when 149 deputies of the clergy joined the Third Estate following Colbert and four other prelates, Young notes: "Dined with the Duke of Liancourt at the Palace: there were many noblemen and deputies of the communes, among them the Duke of Orleans, the Bishop of Rhodez, the Abbé Siéyès and M. Rabaud-Saint-Étienne"[40] and to add among other guests: "we still have

[38] LAROCHEFOUCAULD-LIANCOURT, *État des pauvres* [...], *Extract from the Work Published in English by Sir Morton-Eden, by* Paris, H. Agasse, year VIII (1800), p. 2.

[39] See V. TREMBLAY, "Notice sur M. le duc de La Rochefoucauld, ancien pair de France...", Beauvais, imp. Achille Desjardins, 1856.

[40] Arthur YOUNG, *Voyages en France, pendant les années 1787, 1788, 1789*, Paris, Guillaumin et Cie, 1860, p. 206 (p. 345 of the Paris, Buisson, 1793 edition).

in our meetings: the duke and the duchess of City [for d' Enville], the duchess is one of the best people that I know".

The Lubersac Network, Chartres-Narbonne-London

It is surprising maybe to see Young quoting side by side at a revolutionary dinner at the Hôtel de La Rochefoucauld or in Versailles the bishop of Rodez and the abbé Siéyès, but this was a time when the Revolution had not yet tipped over into the unacceptable for Colbert and a few other liberal prelates who were still campaigning with him for democratic, economic and societal reforms. Above all, the apparent familiarity with Siéyès links Colbert to a second network, that of Mgr Lubersac, bishop of Chartres. Lubersac was, with the Duke of La Rochefoucauld, one of the twelve members and the only prelate of the Comité des Recherches (de Sûreté ou d'Instruction) of the Assemblée Nationale, dedicated to "the defence of the Revolution.[41] In the two most important committees of the Constituent Assembly, we thus find three long-standing relations of the bishop of Rodez. If the links with the La Rochefoucaulds have been amply commented on, those which link Colbert, directly and indirectly, to the bishop of Chartres Lubersac, need examining. He was a prelate who was initially liberal like himself, and it should be pointed out that the sister-in-law of the Duc de Liancourt was the daughter of the Marquis de Surgères, sovereign grand master of the Order of the Holy Spirit and, like her father and son, governor and grand bailiff of… Chartres (1760–1789).

Jean-Baptiste-Joseph de Lubersac (1740–1822), chaplain to the King (1767), then First Chaplain to Madame Sophie (30 May 1775), the King's aunt, he was first consecrated Bishop of Tréguier where he was assisted by Abbé Siéyès, whom he insisted on taking with him when, in 1780, he was transferred to the see of Chartres: there he appointed his indispensable right-hand man ("Abbé Siéyès is my only book", he used to say) as canon, chancellor and grand vicar. Elected deputy of the clergy to the Estates-General in 1789, Mgr de Lubersac was, as Brissot (one of his diocesans with Pétion and Siéyès) says, one of the four "first of his

[41] Fr. Furet, preface to P. Caillet, *Les Français en 1789, d'après les papiers du Comité de Recherches de l'Assemblée Constituante (1789–1791)*, Paris, Éd. du CNRS, 1991.

order to join the Third Estate[42]", with Colbert, and to accept the abolition of privileges. Brissot, who early on esteemed him highly, said that "he had a philosophical mind and the most enlightened spirit, but he backed down when it was necessary to put theory into practice[43]". Opposed to the Civil Constitution of the Clergy CCC, he emigrated by ways that are poorly understood by biographers who often confuse him with his cousin the abbé of Lubersac, who will be mentioned soon again later. Exiled as far as Münster, where he met up with fifteen or so prelates, including the archbishop of Rouen,[44] La Rochefoucauld, he ended up, unlike Seignelay, by accepting to resign from his see at the time of the Concordat.[45]

The early links between Lubersac and Colbert were so numerous and intimate that the bishop of Chartres can be considered a mentor of Seignelay in the same way as Brienne and Dillon: in fact, it was Lubersac who served as a character witness and guarantor for Colbert[46] during the assessment of information prior to his appointment as bishop of Rodez (1782). He then declared himself to be living in Paris on the rue du Bac (as did Dillon). These links constitute a convergent path with Mgr Dillon and the English exile. In fact, Dillon took as his vicar general in Narbonne the cousin of Mgr Lubersac, and, in exile in London, he remained strongly linked with Colbert, as noted by Abbé Grégoire during his visit to England: "In London, "Dillon periodically has bishops' dinners at his house" and to quote in the first place "Colbert, bishop of Rodez[47]" whom he could not help but continue to esteem despite their divergence after 1792. This respect is surprising for two reasons:

[42] J.-P. Brissot, *Mémoires de Brissot... sur ses contemporains et sur la révolution française, publiées par son fils; notes et éclaircissements historiques par M. F. de Montrol*, Paris, Ladvocat, 1830, t. I, p. 202.

[43] Ibid., vol. 1, p. 201.

[44] NWS Münster, Msc.AV nr. 195 f°3 v°.

[45] See E. Sevrin, *Mgr Clausel de Montals, évêque de Chartres (1769-1857), t. I*, Paris, Vrin, 1955, pp. 47–48; M. de Lamase, "*Jean-Baptiste-Joseph de Lubersac, évêque de Chartres, d'après sa correspondance inédite*", *Annales historiques de la Révolution française, t. XXXIX*, 1967; "*Jean-Baptiste-Joseph de Lubersac*", in A. Robert and G. Cougny, *Dictionnaire des parlementaires français*, E. Bourloton, 1889–1891.

[46] 3 February 1781, Arch. Nationales, MC/ET/LXXXII/581 (File found at the Archives Nationales by Ronan Tallec, kindly transmitted by A. Alcouffe).

[47] H. L. Carnot, *Mémoire de M. Grégoire, ancien évêque de Blois [...] précédé d'une Notice historique sur l'auteur*, Paris, J. Yonet, 1840, t. II, *Mémoires ecclésiastiques, politiques et littéraires de M. Grégoire, ancien évêque de Blois* (rédigé en 1808), vol. 2, pp. 256–257.

firstly, Abbé Grégoire took as vicar general of the Loir-et-Cher in Blois the defrocked Capuchin Chabot, a Convention member who was not very commendable, to say the least, and who was formerly a diocesan of Colbert's in Rodez, who had to ban him from saying mass because of his antics (1788). Chabot then enjoyed a shameless political omnipotence before following his victims to the scaffold for fraud in the liquidation of the East India Company. Apparently, he did not succeed in sullying the reputation of his former bishop with Abbé Grégoire, who therefore retained his esteem for Seignelay. However, and this is the second reason for astonishment, Grégoire, in December 1789,[48] joined the Société des Amis des Noirs founded by Brissot with the support of the protégés of Mgr de Lubersac,[49] Petion and his vicar general Siéyès, together with the Duc de Liancourt, Condorcet, etc., all active supporters of abolition. There was also in this society the Marquis de Valady (1766–1793), from a Rouergat family and soon to be a Girondin deputy to the Convention (Dec. 1792).[50]

No doubt Colbert saw fit to conceal from his progressive friends the slaving activities of his two brothers, Lewis Colbert/Cuthbert, who had long since made his fortune in the West Indian plantations and the slave trade and who travelled back and forth between England and Jamaica, and George, who replaced him at the office of the Provost-Marshall of Jamaica (1785–1788). However, Seignelay did not break with his brother Lewis, despite the source of his wealth, and he hosted him for some time in Toulouse (around 1766) before his departure for Jamaica. Lewis even visited him in Paris during the revolutionary turmoil in 1792, thus shortly before his exile[51] (and, possibly, to help with his exfiltration…). Well before the Revolution, he even recommended some of his protégés to him, so much that surprisingly, this admission is related to Napoleon

[48] M. Dorigny, B. Garnot, *La Société des Amis des Noirs, 1788–1799. Contribution à l'histoire de l'abolition de l'esclavage*, Paris, UNESCO and UNICEF Publishing, 1998; M. Dorigny, "Grégoire et le combat contre l'esclavage pendant la Révolution", *Revue française d'histoire d'outre-mer*, t. 87, n° 328–329, 2e semestre 2000.

[49] *Mémoires de Brissot…*, Brussels, vol. III (1832), p. 88 and p. 133.

[50] Guillotined on 6 December 1793 in Périgueux for not having voted for the death of the king.

[51] Ch. Fraser Mackintosh, 'Letters of Two Centuries, Chiefly Connected with Inverness and the Highlands, from 1616 to 1815', Inverness, A & W Mackenzie, 1890, p. 171.

in the *St Helena Memorial* from the very pen of Las Cases that he [Las Cases] "...saw the opportunity to make a fortune [...] A bishop from Rodez, Colbert, a Scotsman by birth, who liked me very much, proposed that I follow his brother to Jamaica". He was going there [as] the head of the executive power, and was one of the most important planters; he would have entrusted me with the management of his property and made me have that of his friends. The bishop guaranteed me a real fortune in three years. I preferred to continue a miserable life away from the French coast.[52]

This "hard-hearted" brother, according to Lady Nugent,[53] remained in close contact with the refractory bishop, whom he sheltered, whether in Clifton near Bristol, Walcot, Bath, London[54] or even Edinburgh. When Colbert began his British exile (summer or autumn 1792), he admits that he was eager to see the Duke of Buccleuch (a disciple of Adam Smith) in Edinburgh, but one of his letters of apology tells us that he had to postpone his visit in order to meet this brother who was leaving for Jamaica. Shortly before embarking, moreover, Lewis Cuthbert was consulted by *the House of Lords* on the possibility of abolishing slavery and in his reply of sixty pages long, he persisted in advocating the maintenance of the triangular trade, even though he acknowledged that a minority of masters mistreated their slaves... There is no doubt that Seignelay had to cast a modest veil over this unfortunate compromise, even though it was commonplace at the time and he did not have to take responsibility for the sins of his brothers. Nevertheless, he remained on the sidelines in this ethical struggle, where several of his relations, unlike him, did not hesitate

[52] LAS CASES, NAPOLEON, *Memoirs of Saint Helena. Le manuscrit retrouvé*, P. HICKS, Fr. HOUDECEK, Th. LENTZ éd. 2018. The young Las Cases was a pupil at the Collège de Sorèze *long before* Colbert became its commendatory abbot (1789). However, he must have found the prelate in London where he published his *Atlas géographique et historique* (1799), helped by the widow of his fellow student at Sorèze (the Marquis Izarn de Valady, a diocesan of Colbert) who became the Countess Walsh de Serrant. See Chr. VIALELLE, "La comtesse Walsh de Serrant...", *Société d'histoire de Revel Saint-Ferréol, Les cahiers de l'histoire* n° 18 p. 73 [online].

[53] See LADY NUGENT, *Journal of her Residence in Jamaica from 1801–1805*, Ph. WRIGHT ed, University of the West Indies, 2002. She met Lewis Cuthbert in September 1791.

[54] His London residence was 43 Gloucester Place, from where Seignelay signed a letter on 6 October 1800. SLA-GBDB.

to go to the front line. It is likely that Seignelay was caught in the crossfire between two mentors, Lubersac, who was rather sincerely anti-slavery, and Brienne, who was rather evasive and dilatory in this regard, according to Brissot's testimony: thus, when Lafayette tried to obtain the support of the Archbishop of Sens, then a minister, in this abolitionist struggle, "Brienne [......] pretended before him to see with pain the existence of the trade and slavery of the negroes; he wished more than anyone, he said, that a way could be found to abolish them, reconciling this abolition with the interests of the planters [...] All this was real court talk and Lafayette knew it as well as I did...".[55] Colbert had to prudently adopt the same duplicity in this respect as his first mentor...

In any case, Abbé Grégoire adds some interesting details about Colbert's hesitations concerning the oath to the Constitution which he himself took first of all, specifying "an anecdote which is unknown [...]: it is that various bishops such as those of Langres, Besançon, Blois, *Chartres [Lubersac], Rhodez* had already taken measures to organise their dioceses on the plan of the C.C.C. Suddenly they changed direction, when [...] they believed that their combined resistance would make the new law fail [...]". Then Grégoire evoke some anecdotes linking Colbert and the bishop of Chartres: "one day (it was shortly before the time fixed for the taking of this oath); I found him [Lubersac] discussing with Colbert, bishop of Rhodez: the latter claimed that the oath was licit, and nevertheless he refused it. Retired to England, he even showed himself one of the most opposed to the resignations requested by Pius VII. Lubersac gave it and returned to France[56]". AndGrégoire repeats himself further: "Colbert, bishop of Rodez: I heard him maintain to the former bishop of Chartres [Lubersac] that it was necessary to take the oath even though he himself refused to do so[57]".

This may give some credibility to a late account given by Abbé Servières,[58] according to which it was Abbé Malrieu, his colleague in the Assembly,[59] who is said to have distracted him in extremis from taking

[55] *Mémoires de Brissot*..., *op. cit.* t. 2, p. 245 ff.

[56] *Mémoires de Grégoire, ancien évêque de Blois*..., *op. cit*, vol. II, pp. 15–16.

[57] Ibid., vol. II, p. 257.

[58] Abbé Servières, *Histoire de l'Église du Rouergue*, Rodez, 1874, pp. 551–552.

[59] Jean-Pierre Malrieu (1740–1824); see H. Affre, *Biographies aveyronnaises*, Rodez, pp. 243–244.

the oath and urged him to go into exile.[60] The anecdote is weakened by the date error: 4 January 1791 was the deadline for taking the oath, but Colbert emigrated in the spring of 1792. In addition, Abbé Servières did not hear it directly from Abbé Malrieu, but from one Docteur Marion.[61]

It is known that in France there were only "4 bishops who swore out of 135", and among these 4 oath takers, there was Brienne, Colbert's long-time protector, and Jarente, bishop of Orléans who was, like him, Brienne's vicar general in Toulouse, both of whom rallied to the arguments of Abbé Grégoire and Abbé Siéyès, the right-hand man of his other mentor, Lubersac. It is easy to understand why, under these contradictory influences, Seignelay was able to remain indecisive for some time.

It should be noted that several witnesses and historians still link Lubersac and Colbert in the very start of the revolutionary process: the Marquis of Clermont-Gallerande writes: On 22 June, "149 members of the clergy, headed by the bishops of Chartres and Rhodez, and the archbishops of Vienne and Bordeaux, came to meet the Third Estate" to "submit their powers to the common verification[62]" and to specify in a note: "The bishop of Chartres [M. de Lubersac] had been chaplain to the king and had spent his life at Court; M. de Colbert, bishop of Rhodez, was the friend and obliged of the archbishop of Sens [Brienne] and in the same principles". Then, according to him, Champion de Cicé (predecessor of Colbert in Rodez), influenced by Necker and coveting the post of *Garde des sceaux* (Keeper of the Seals), persuaded his three confreres to join the Third Estate: "Seduction and weakness led the bishops of Chartres, Rhodez, and the archbishop of Vienne to follow him". Toulotte and Beaulieu repeat the same narrative, always closely associating Lubersac and Colbert.[63]

[60] Abbé Servières, *op. cit.*, Rodez, 1874, pp. 551–552.

[61] *Revue historique du Rouergue*, "A propos d'une lettre de Mgr de Seignelay de Colbert et de la chapellenie de Saint-Laurent, à Millau", May–June 1942, no. 3, pp. 25–27; *Semaine catholique des diocèses de Rodez et de Mende*, 19 July 1865; *Journal de l'Aveyron*, 15 July 1865: "Notice biographique sur Mgr de Colbert", [by Dr Marion].

[62] M. de Clermont-Gallerande, *Mémoires particuliers pour servir à l'histoire de la Révolution qui s'est opérée en France en 1789*, Paris, J.-G. Dentu, 1826, t. I, pp. 80–82.

[63] E. L. J. Toulotte, *La Cour et la ville, Paris et Coblentz ou l'Ancien régime et le nouveau…*, Paris, A. Costes, 1828, t. I, p. 164; Cl.-Fr. Beaulieu, *Essais historiques sur les causes et les effets de la révolution de France: avec des notes sur quelques événemens et quelques institutions*, Paris, Maradan, 1803, t. I, p. 257 and 279.

There are many other links between the two prelates: we can find them through the intertwining of Mgr Lubersac and Mgr Dillon, two of Colbert's mentors with Brienne and Liancourt. Thus, when Dillon was transferred from the archbishopric of Toulouse (where he was succeeded by Brienne, with Colbert as vicar general) to the archbishopric of Narbonne, he chose as his vicar general two figures of great interest. Firstly, his childhood friend, Abbé Edward Booth, an Englishman born in St-Germain-en-Laye (1711), where he kept a flat in the royal chateau until the 1780s.[64] His father was an officer of the House of James III and Abbé Booth's godfather was Ralph Sheldon, an officer of the King's House,[65] an interesting connection since Arthur Dillon's wife was a Sheldon and the Sheldons attended the wedding of Mr^{gr} Dillon's niece, along with the Jerninghams and Maitlands, relatives of Seignelay ...

Beside this Jacobite who followed him from Toulouse to Narbonne, Mgr Dillon named the abbé Charles-François de Lubersac, cousin of the bishop of Chartres... Now this abbé of Lubersac, abbot of Noirlac and Brive, found himself in London (where he died[66]) among the emigrated French prelates. Residing in 1802 at 24 Queen Ann Street East, he published a precious *Historical and Religious Journal of the Emigration and Deportation of* the *Clergy from France to England*,[67] which is very detailed and in which Dillon and Colbert are mentioned several times,[68] thus confirming their complicity as indicated by Abbé Grégoire. This is hardly surprising given their common British ancestry and Brienne's decisive patronage of Seignelay's career. Brienne and Dillon were both at the same time vicars general of the archbishop of Rouen, before becoming bishops. Didn't Colbert, who became Brienne's vicar general in Toulouse, meet Dillon when he guided Adam Smith and the Duke of Buccleuch to attend the sessions of the Estates of Languedoc presided

[64] Edward Corp, 'The Jacobite Presence in Toulouse During the Eighteenth Century', *Diasporas* 5 (2004), p. 139.

[65] Ch. Edm. Lart, *The Parrochial Registers of Saint Germain-en-Laye, Jacobite Extracts of Births, Marriages and Deaths*, London, The St-Catherine Press, 1919, 2 vols.

[66] Fr.-X. Plasse, *Le clergé français réfugié en Angleterre*, Paris, V. Palmé, vol. 1, 1886, p. 258.

[67] Abbé de Lubersac, *Journal historique et religieux de l'émigration et déportation du clergé de France en Angleterre,... par l'abbé de Lubersac, vicaire général de Narbonne, abbé de Noirlac et prieur royal de St-Martin de Brive, émigré françois*, London, 1802.

[68] Notably ibid. p. 20 and 169.

over by Mgr Dillon (1763)? Colbert was closely associated with Dillon's relatives, Richard de Barnewall (1708–1778), found in Toulouse of a Masonic lodge[69] (1741) and especially his son Nicolas (1726–1813) who returned to Ireland in 17,900 The Nugents and the Barnewalls were related since the sixteenth century. The godmother of Mgr Dillon was a Mary Nugent, grandmother of General Nugent, whose wife was the lady who, in the West Indies, disapproved of the harshness of Colbert's slave-owning brother.... We also know that Nicolas Barnewall was only able to be recognised as his father's sole heir thanks to a transaction concluded on 10 May 1779 "under the auspices of *the Abbé de Colbert* and the Baron de Puymaurin[70]". Colbert was then vicar general of Toulouse, under Brienne, in concert with Félix de Malaret, provost of St-Étienne (1732–1792) whose brother Joseph de Malaret, lord of Fontbeauzard and Blagnac, an active Freemason, welcomed the Lodge of the Barnewals in their *hotel particulier* in Hautpoul.

After the summer of 1792, there were reunions across the Channel between Colbert, Dillon, Barnewall, the Abbé de Lubersac, Count Grant de Vaux, etc. and, on the death of Mgr Dillon in July 1806, Seignelay and Nicolas Barnewall were found conducting the funeral ceremony in St Pancras Church in London.

This network, whose intertwining is ancient and becomes even closer in exile across the Channel can be examined in more detail.

In a letter to the Duke of Buccleuch, dated Cossey near Norwich, 21 October 1792, Colbert tells us that from Edinburgh he came to "the county of Norfolk, where I have come to spend some time [...] in the neighbourhood of the castle of Mr. de Jerningham, with whom I am at this moment[71]". This information is valuable in strengthening the conviction of a network of exiles. Colbert's host is Lord William Jerningham, 6th baronet of the name (1736–1809) who married Frances Dillon (born in 1747), sister of General Arthur Dillon and niece of the archbishop of Narbonne, on 16 June 1767. This link can be enriched thanks to the *Journal d'une femme de cinquante ans*, written by Henriette-Lucie Dillon,

[69] M. Taillefer, *La Franc-maçonnerie toulousaine sous l'Ancien régime et la Révolution, 1741–1799*, Paris, ENBS-CTHS, 1984; G. Lamoine, "Jacobites et francs-maçons à Toulouse: autour de la famille de Barnewall", *Lumières*, (PU Bordeaux), n° 7 (2006).

[70] AD H-G, 3 E 6477 ff. 153–160; M. Taillefer, *op. cit*, p. 20, note 36.

[71] A. Alcouffe, A. Moore, *Smith's encounters...*, *op. cit.*

the future Marquise de La Tour du Pin,[72] who mentions in many places her links with her Jerningham cousins.

From 1780 to 1786, Mgr Dillon took his grand-niece Henriette-Lucie with him every year when he went to Montpellier to preside over the Estates of Languedoc, sometimes (in 1785) going as far as Toulouse, Montauban and even to Bordeaux, where they stayed for seventeen days with the archbishop, M. de Cicé, Colbert's predecessor at Rodez, hoping to find her a good match. When the agreements were made, it was also Dillon who celebrated her marriage to Count Frédéric-Séraphin de La Tour du Pin Gouvernet (1759–1837) in Montfermeil: She writes "On my wedding day [21 May 1787] … the company consisted, on my side, of my grandmother, my great-uncle [the Archbishop of Narbonne], my aunt Lady Jerningham, her husband, daughter and eldest son, now Lord Stafford; Messrs. Sheldon, their elder brother, Mr. Constable, my first witness, and the Knight Jerningham, mother's friend and mine, my second witness. It was all my family. The guests included all the ministers, the Archbishop of Paris, the Archbishop of Toulouse, some of the bishops of Languedoc present in Paris; M. de Lally-Tollendal[73] […]".

We learn from the bride's pen that the wedding was refused several times by a very cantankerous grandmother who gave in wearily to pressure from the family of the intended who, she says, "made us circumvent on all sides[…]". These details reinforce the idea, if not of endogamy, at least of a network which extends or becomes denser. Indeed, among Brienne's vicars general in Toulouse, we find not only Colbert de Castlehill (until 1782), Villoutreix de Faye, future member of the Comité de Mendicité with Liancourt and Colbert, but also the Abbé Alexandre-Henri de Blot de Chauvigny.[74] The latter, who became bishop of Lombez, consecrated by his patron Mgr de Brienne (August 1787), took as his vicar general Jean-Antoine Robert de Razebourg, whose brother was vicar general of Chartres under Mgr de Lubersac, while Mgr Dillon had as his vicars general the Irishman Edward Booth and the abbé of Lubersac, cousin of the bishop of Chartres and moral guarantor of Colbert! A new circle appears.

[72] Born in Paris, rue du Bac, on 25 February 1770.

[73] Marquise de LA TOUR DU PIN, *Journal d'une femme de cinquante ans, 1778–1815*, Paris, Librairie Chapelot, 1920 (2e ed.), pp. 105–107.

[74] Quoted as such in *La France ecclésiastique… 1782*, p. 261.

It can therefore be estimated that, among all this elite gathered with the Jerninghams of Cossey by Mgr Dillon for the marriage of his grand-niece, the marquise of La Tour du Pin, the bishop of Rodez was probably present, between his two mentors Brienne and Dillon: we know indeed that he was then in Paris to attend the Assembly of the Notables which had been held since 22 February and which was coming to an end three days later. The hypothesis can be crowned with a genealogical argument which can be conclusive. It can be found in the genealogical record of the Marquis Charles Grant de Vaux, based in Normandy near Bayeux at Vaux-sur-Seulles, a relative of Colbert de Castlehill who celebrated in London (1793–1794) his remarriage and the wedding of his two daughters.

It is in fact Viscount Grant de Vaux himself who pointed out that his close friend M. de Litteau had for brother-in-law the Marquis de Marguerye de Vierville who had just married Annabella Henriette, the daughter of Count Louis Drummond de Melfort, an excellent match since he was a lieutenant-general and a Grand Cross of Saint-Louis. He was related to Seignelay and the Grants as well as to the Dillons and was the uncle of Colbert's vicar general in Rodez, as his daughter, who became Marquise de Vierville, was his cousin! She "was placed with Madame Elisabeth", sister of the king,[75]insisted Charles Grant who also felt the need to publish in his file a letter in which his friend Litteau told him on 12 December 1783: "I am obliged to go tomorrow to Magny, having just learned that the Baroness de La Tour du Pin is in bed[76] ... It is not far from your home...". Indeed, Vaux-sur-Seulles is 2 km from the château of Magny-en-Bessin, very close to the summer residence of the Bishop of Bayeux in Sommervieu. It should be added that the vicar general of Bayeux was a Rouergat, the Abbé d'Albignac de Castelnau (1742–1814). The latter had built a house adjoining the said château of Magny before being promoted to the bishopric of Angoulême (1784) and then joining Colbert in exile in London. It can be noted that it was with the help of a relative of Abbé d'Albignac de Castelnau, Abbé Gaston de

[75] Ch. Grant, *op. cit.* p. 377 (letter of 13 September 1784).

[76] Ibidem, p. 376.

Sambucy,[77] that Madame Elisabeth was able to secretly receive absolution[78] on the day of her execution (10 May 1794), in the absence of her confessor, Abbé Edgeworth, who was wanted at the time and who took refuge for a time near Bayeux, in the château de Vierville-sur-Mer (as will be mentioned later).... It should also be noted that when Viscount Charles Grant de Vaux was belatedly made a knight of St Louis on 27 July 1790, it was the Minister of War, La Tour du Pin, Comte de Paulin, who countersigned the King's letter.[79] It is likely that Colbert, cousin of the Grant de Vaux and the Drummonds and staying in Paris at the time, did attend the marriage of the future Marquise de la Tour du Pin, née Dillon. The only person *apparently* missing from the wedding was Lubersac, the bishop of Chartres, but this is far from certain.... Above all, the Sheldons are mentioned among the bride's attendants, including, no doubt, the future revolutionary general; yet Abbé Booth, vicar general of Mgr Dillon in Toulouse and Narbonne and colleague of Abbé de Lubersac, was the godson of M. Sheldon, vice-chambellan of James III Stuart. Given all these strong links between Colbert, Dillon, Brienne and Lubersac, and their respective tropisms for England, is it any wonder that most of them ended up in London, Cossey, Bath, Edinburgh, Stafford, the Jerninghams or with Arthur Young during the time of their emigration across the Channel?

It is interesting to note that Mgr Dillon's relative, Catherine Dillon, a nun in the Carmelite convent at Pontoise (where Dillon and then Brienne were Grand Vicars) before being promoted to Prioress of the Carmelites of Saint-Denis (1758), emigrated to Bodney Hall in Norfolk, not far from Cossey, at the beginning of 1793, where lived Lady Jerningham. Colbert stayed not only in Bath and Edinburgh, but especially, at the beginning of his exile, in Cossey at the Jerninghams' house.[80]

Besides, in referring to his marriage, Mgr Dillon's niece, the Marquise de la Tour du Pin, recalls that her "first witness" was Sir Thomas Hugh

[77] The brother of the future bishop of Angoulême, Count Claude-François d'Albignac de Castelnau (1740–1822), married in 1772 Henriette *de Sambucy* de Vandeloves, from a collateral branch.

[78] See J. de Viguerie, *Le sacrifice du soir. Vie et mort de Madame Élisabeth, sœur de Louis XVI,* Paris, Cerf, 2010.

[79] Ch. Grant, *op. cit.* pp. 417–418.

[80] Letter to the Duke of Buccleuch, Cossey 21 October 1792, quoted in A. Alcouffe, A. Moore, *Smith'sencounters*, *op. cit.*

Clifford, later Clifford Constable (1762–1821), 4th Lord Clifford of Chudleigh whose parents had converted to Catholicism. In Bath (where Colbert was for a time to be found with his brother Lewis in Walcot) he took as his confessor Abbé Caron "the good Samaritan of the priests emigrated to England", whom he welcomed with such generosity that in 1813 Louis XVIII showed his gratitude by coming to dine at his house and endorsing his appointment as baronet in May 1815.[81] Lord Clifford Constable had studied at the Collège de Navarre, where he met professors and students linked to Colbert, for the network to which Seignelay was linked in many ways can be further enriched by the covalent links that connected him to the Sorbonne, the Court and Ireland.

From the Sorbonne to Maynooth

As mentioned above, Mgr Dillon had a Jacobite, Edward Booth, born like him in Saint-Germain-en-Laye (1711), as his vicar general in Toulouse; when he was transferred to Narbonne, Dillon took his childhood friend with him and added the Abbé de Lubersac, cousin of the Bishop of Chartres (Colbert's guarantor), who not only had the Irishman Mackarty, from the diocese of Kerry, among the canons of his cathedral (1788), but also chose the Irish Abbé Aherne (1735–1801), also from Kerry, as his vicar general. The latter serves as a link with the Sorbonne since he probably taught Lord Clifford Constable: Aherne was indeed a doctor of the Sorbonne (7 October 1766), a professor of philosophy and a member of the Société de Navarre before becoming vicar general of Lubersac in Chartres. Having refused the oath, Aherne returned to Ireland where he became professor of dogmatics at the recently established Royal Catholic College of St. Patrick, Maynooth[82] (1795), where he found or attracted many colleagues or former Sorbonne students: Delahogue, Peter Flood, the Rouergat Anglade....

Is it by pure coincidence that the Abbé de Lubersac in his *Journal de l'émigration* dwells particularly on a colleague of Aherne, the vicar general of his cousin the bishop of Chartres? He praises "De la Hogue, doctor [May 1764] and professor of Sorbonne before the Revolution,

[81] *Annuaire nécrologique* of 1824, p. 387 and 1821, p. 115.

[82] See for example Fr.-X. Plasse, *Le clergé français réfugié en Angleterre*, Paris, V. Palmé, 1886, vol. 2, p. 336 ff and John Healy, *Maynooth College: Its Centenary History, 1795–1895*, Dublin, Browne & Nolan, 1895...

canon of the chapter of St. Honoré in Paris [...] never for a moment idle since the day of his emigration until the present moment"; he cites "among the great number of books he published in London during his exile [...] an *Exposé des motifs qui ont déterminé le Clergé de France à fuir la Persécution et à se retirer en Pays étranger*" where he "proves that flight was an obligation of conscience"; and concludes: "M. l'abbé de la Hogue, during his exile in England [in London], after having thus made himself useful to his fellow citizens, his great merit for theology being known for a long time in Ireland by the Catholic clergy who are very numerous there, was called in 1798 to profess theology in the magnificent Royal Catholic College of Maynooth, established by the King and the nation, and endowed with their benefactions, for the education of 200 Irish ecclesiastics".[83]

The expression "magnificent college" would tend to prove that the Abbé de Lubersac visited this establishment, which was indeed grandiose, and which constituted the first Catholic "academy" in the British Isles finally authorised by the English. An important element can be added to this reconstruction of a network: Professor Delahogue, when he was contacted to go and teach in Maynooth in the summer of 1798, had been staying for a year with Lord Clifford,[84] a relative of the Dillons and Drummonds of Melfort, who attended the marriage of the Marquise de La Tour du Pin, née Dillon, with her cousins Jerningham and almost certainly Seignelay Colbert de Castlehill and Brienne! The Colbert-La Tour du Pin-Dillon-Clifford-Maynooth link was thus further enriched, and all the more so as a Sorbonne colleague of Aherne and Delahogue soon joined them in Maynooth and played an essential role. This was indeed, and as if by chance, a diocesan of Colbert, François Anglade (1757–1834).[85] He was the son of a carpenter from Rodez and a convert, granddaughter of Camisard chiefs and relative of the man hanged in the famous Calas Affair.[86] In spite of everything, he

[83] Abbé de LUBERSAC, *Journal...*, *op. cit.* pp. 216–218.

[84] Fr.-X. PLASSE, *op. cit.* 2, pp. 348–349.

[85] Patrick FERTÉ, 'L'odyssée irlandaise du père Anglade', *Études aveyronnaises* 2021, pp. 163–184.

[86] His mother, from a family of Camisard chiefs from Camarès, was sister-in-law of the widow Calas and cousin of Siméon Valette-Falgous, Voltaire's 'Poor Devil'. See Patrick FERTÉ, "Du nouveau sur l'Affaire Calas. Un réseau rouergat autour de Voltaire', *Études aveyronnaises*, 2018, pp. 187–216.

had completely broken with his heterodox roots and benefited from an exemplary Catholic education at the Royal College of Rodez under excellent teachers, including Abbé Carnus, already mentioned, and Abbé Malrieu, who was elected deputy to the General Estates at the same time as Colbert. Anglade, who had gone to Paris to take Holy Orders, attended the Sorbonne, particularly the lecture of a fellow countryman, Abbé Dièche, who had been a fellow student of Abbé Carnus at the Sorbonne and at the Seminary of Saint-Nicolas-du-Chardonnet before both were ordained on the same day.[87] After his graduation, Anglade was for a time a reader at the College of Rodez (thus during the episcopate of Seignelay), before being appointed professor of physics at the College of Plessis-Sorbonne on 2 December 1790 where he taught until 1791. Non-juror, he spent six years in England and Wales[88] before being recruited by his former Sorbonne colleagues to fill first a chair of logic, metaphysics and ethics at Maynooth (24 February 1802) and then of moral theology (1810), which he held until his death in 1834. It was the bishop of Rodez Colbert who signed his dimissory letters for his ordinations to the sub-diaconate in Paris on 1er March 1784, to the diaconate in Amiens on the following 21 May,[89] and to the priesthood in Paris on 28 November of the same year.[90]

While the professor of Rodez, the aeronaut Abbé Carnus, was killed by the "Septembriseurs", his bishop and his pupil were luckier: Colbert found an escape route and made it safely to England, as did Abbé Anglade,[91] who later went to Maynooth to meet up with many of his Sorbonian colleagues, Delahogue, Flood and Aherne.

Shortly before their exile, Delahogue, "professor of Scripture at the Sorbonne", and Peter Flood, royal professor of morals at Navarre and

[87] P.-A. Verlaguet, J.-L. Rigal, Martyrologe, Rodez, 1951, t. II, pp. 18–19.

[88] The garden at *St. Patrick's College*, Maynooth, is said to have been created by Anglade who had spent six years as a gardener in Wales. See TURNER, 'The French Connection with Maynooth College, 1795–1855', *Studies: An Irish Quarterly Review 70*, no. 277 (Spring 1981), pp. 77–87; see also P.J. CORRISH, *Maynooth College, 1795–1995*, Dublin, Gill and MacMillan, 1995.

[89] AD Aveyron, G 300 f°71 and f°81.

[90] AD Aveyron, G 300, f° 76.

[91] Fr.-X. PLASSE, *Le clergé français*..., *op. cit.*, vol. 1, p. 258 et vol. 2, p. 343 sq.

future president of *Maynooth College*,[92] had co-signed on 16 November 1791, the *Letter of the professors of theology at the Sorbonne and Navarre to the administrators of the Directory of the Department of Paris*.[93] The co-author was precisely their Rouergat colleague, Abbé Dièche,[94] professor of morals at the Sorbonne since 1774, who had taught Abbé Anglade. Born in Rodez (1748), Abbé Dièche, also a canon of Rodez, was visited as such by his new bishop Colbert, who is likely to have consulted him in the same way as his fellow theologian Asseline at the time of the oath to the C.C.C., when the prelate was, according to several accounts, wavering between refusal and acceptance.

In any case, the *Letter*, signed by Delahogue, Flood and others, in justifying the refusal of the oath to an "obviously heretical" and "manifestly schismatic constitution", condemned all the refractory clergy to martyrdom or exile. It was then that the persecuting countries swapped, and the tropisms reversed; their homeland having become more tolerant, the Irish refugees educated and established in France crossed the Channel again, taking in their wake their French hosts of yesteryear in a just return of things. Away in London for a time and then in Ireland, they invited several of their colleagues to join them at the new Catholic seminary in Maynooth, all the better for having been among the promoters of the foundation of Maynooth, along with Edmund Burke. These Irishmen who had previously taken refuge in France and been educated at the little Irish college in Toulouse and/or at the Sorbonne, whether during the episcopate of Mgr Dillon or that of Brienne, whose vicar general was a certain Colbert de Castlehill (1763–1782)…. So was Francis Moylan, Bishop of Cork, who was linked in one way or another to our network and in particular to Seignelay Colbert, Dillon and Lubersac. In this new skein can be detected converging tropisms and less visible but no less solid links running from the Irish seminary in Toulouse to Maynooth via the Sorbonne.

[92] Master of Arts in Paris on 8 June 1774, being a deacon; licentiate in theology (1780); headmaster for Leinster at the Collège des Lombards (1779) and prefect of studies since 1782; professor at the Collège de Navarre (1783–1789). L. W.B. Brockliss & P. Ferté, *Archivium Hibernicum*, LVIII, 2004, p. 13, no. 10.

[93] Paris, Crapart, 1791.

[94] According to Abbé P. d'Hesmivy d'Auribeau and Cardinal Gerdil, *Mémoires pour servir à l'histoire de la persécution française*, vol. III-IV, Roma, May 1814. t. I, p. 234, note 1.

Mgr Dillon, when he was Archbishop of Toulouse, had hastened to erect the little College of the Irish of Toulouse (Sainte-Anne-la-Royale), created in 1659, into a diocesan seminary on 13 October 1761.[95] When he was transferred to Narbonne, Brienne succeeded him and took the Abbé Colbert as his vicar general, who, as such, had to take care of the "hibernian" college. Many young Irishmen were educated there, perhaps the young Barnewals, certainly Francis Moylan, future Bishop of Cork, Robert MacCarthy, vicar general of the former, and Abbé Henri Edgeworth of Firmont. It should also be noted that the consecration of Colbert de Castlehill as Bishop of Rodez (1781), although he was a Scot by birth, had some impact in Ireland as it was widely reported in the Scottish and Irish press.[96]

Francis Moylan, of Cork (1735–1815), initially a boarder in Paris at the Irish college known as the Collège des Lombards, came to Toulouse to study: a seminarian at the small local Irish college, he did his *quinquennium* at the university, took his doctorate there and was ordained a priest on 7 March 1761 during the episcopate of Mgr Dillon.[97] In Toulouse he formed a lasting friendship with the young Henry Essex Edgeworth[98] known as the Abbé de Firmont, who, after being housed at the seminary in 1752–1753 and educated, it is said, at the local Jesuit college, then went to Paris to study law, where he passed his licence on 17 May 1777, and met up with his friend Moylan, who was at the time vicar general in Paris (at Chatou) while acting as secretary to the Archbishop of Paris. Moylan also formed a lasting friendship with two professors at the Collège des Lombards and/or the Séminaire des Trente-Trois, Peter Flood, who had already been at the Sorbonne (1783–1789) and was later to become a Maynoothian, and Jean-René Asseline, professor of Hebrew and theology at the Sorbonne and vicar general to the above-mentioned Archbishop of Paris: while Moylan returned to Ireland as Bishop of Kerry and then Cork (1786–1815) and campaigned for the foundation of Maynooth College,

[95] This happens to be the tragic day that inaugurates the Calas Affair.

[96] *Dublin Newsletter*, 18–22 May 1781 (p. 2); *Scots Magazine*, Friday 1er June 1781; *Caledonian Mercury*, Monday 14 March 1781.

[97] See L. W. B. Brockliss, P. Ferté, art. cité, n° 596, p. 72.

[98] Cf. P. Ferté, "The Counter-Reformation and Franco-Irish Solidarity: Irish Clerical Refugees at the Universities of Toulouse and Cahors in the Seventeenth and Eighteenth Centuries", in *Irish Communities in Early-Modern Europe*, Th. O'ConnorA. Lyons ed, Dublin, Four Courts Press, 2006, p. 66 and *passim*.

his friend Asseline was appointed Bishop of Boulogne, consecrated on 2 January 1790, while Edgeworth evangelised the lower quarters of Paris, lodged in the Seminary of the Foreign Missions, rue du Bac, before having to confess on the block the deposed King and his sister Mme Élisabeth....

Is it by coincidence that Moylan, once he became bishop of Cork, took as his vicar general Robert MacCarthy, an Irishman from Toulouse, who had become superior of the local Irish seminary (1771–1792), where Moylan and Edgeworth had once stayed[99]? It should be noted that this MacCarthy directed the Toulouse seminary for ten years (1771–1781) precisely during the vicariate general of Colbert, who certainly frequented it. Is it also a coincidence that this MacCarthy later became director of the Institute of the Sisters of the Presentation of the Virgin Mary founded in Maynooth precisely by Father Anglade,[100] a professor at Maynooth College who was ordained a priest and protected by Seignelay?

Was it, finally, by a happy coincidence that Peter Flood, who emigrated after co-signing Abbé Dièche's *Lettre des professeurs de Sorbonne* with his colleagues Delahogue, Aherne, Anglade, Asseline, etc., first took refuge in Edgeworthtown,[101] the birthplace of Louis XVI's last confessor? What a small world! It was only afterwards that, thanks to Burke and his friend Moylan, the Catholic Academy of Maynooth was finally founded,[102] and it was Edgeworth who was first approached to take charge of it, even if, in the end and despite his friend Moylan's insistence that he return to the mother country, he declined the offer and became attached to the exiled French King. However, it was then that a number of Sorbonnians were invited to take up the pulpit at the new St Patrick's College in Maynooth, Flood, Delahogue, Daré, Anglade, Ferris, and also Aherne, vicar general of Mgr Lubersac, Colbert's friend and cousin of the Abbé de Lubersac, admirer of Maynooth and vicar of Dillon in Narbonne.

[99] P. FERTÉ, 'List of Superiors of Irish College, Toulouse (1618–1793)', *Archivium Hibernicum*, p. LXIII 2010, p. 298 and L. W. B. BROCKLISS, P. FERTÉ, art. cité, n° 499.

[100] Fr-X. PLASSE, *op. cit.* v. 2, p. 345.

[101] Flood was, like H. Edgeworth, a native of the diocese of Ardagh, County Longford. L.W.B. BROCKLISS, P. FERTÉ, art. cit., p. 13, no. 10.

[102] Fr-X. PLASSE, *op. cit.* 2, p. 330 ff. See also the importance of these two men in the foundation in J. HEALY, *Maynooth College: Its Centenary History, 1795–1895*, Dublin, Browne & Nolan, 1895.

Rouergat Entryism in the Court

With the Lubersacs, a full circle is achieved with a few last links connecting to the very heart of the Bourbon monarchy through the chaplains and confessors of the royal family and among whom we find a number of characters of great interest for our study, the two Lubersac cousins but also many diocesan or vicars general of Colbert de Castlehill.

Thus, the Bishop of Chartres Lubersac, Colbert's moral guarantor, was first chaplain to the King in 1767 and, in 1773, became first chaplain to Madame Sophie de France [aunt of Louis XVI]. He was then appointed bishop of Tréguier despite the very active intercession of Mesdames Adélaïde and Sophie to obtain for him the see of Blois which he would have preferred. He was nevertheless consecrated in the chapel of Versailles on 6 August 1775, before being transferred, to Chartres (1780). When Mme Sophie died in 1782,[103] he was offered the post of chaplain to Mme Elisabeth, but he declined the offer as he said he was too busy with his double service at Chartres and at Court, as Versailles was part of the diocese of Chartres. Then he clearly withdrew from court life and from then on, the entourage of the royal family and especially of the count and countess of Artois was populated by abbés directly or indirectly linked to Colbert and his diocese. Indeed, wherever he went, a Rouergat was rarely without contacts at that time; under the Ancien Régime, one never ventured out without a godfather or a recommendation: one acted in a network. This writer has elsewhere[104] underlined the effectiveness of Rouergat entryism to monopolise the good places at Court, once one of their number has succeeded in establishing himself there; this will be even more true in exile. Thus, in the eighteenth century, they constituted an active network of court abbés who gravitated towards the royal family and had every facility to favour their compatriots who had gone to Paris and Versailles.

Even before the appointment of Colbert de Castlehill, the Rouergats were therefore very close to the sovereign. Needless to say, they were then at their best with their new bishop, who moreover shared their loyalty to the Bourbon monarch. Other chaplains were so well known

[103] L'Almanach royal 1782, p. 140.

[104] P. Ferté in D. JULIA, J. REVEL, *Histoire sociale des populations étudiantes*, Paris, Éd. de l'EHESS, 1989, t. II, pp. 540–542.

that they obtained an episcopal see and, in return, called their compatriots as vicars general or reserved for them some canonry.[105] One of the keystones of this network of court abbés and highly influential prelates was the Rouergat Jean Armand de Bessuéjouls de Roquelaure (1721–1818), bishop of Senlis since 1754[106] and first chaplain to the King in 1764. An Academician, Commander of the Holy Spirit, protected by Mme Adélaïde and her sisters, he was particularly listened to at the Court and took advantage of this to favour the appointments of his compatriots who had moved to Paris. We can get a glimpse of the density of Rouergats around the monarchy during the coronation of Louis XVI or on religious feasts such as Holy Wednesday 12 April 1775[107]: the bishop of Senlis, as well as his vicar general, Abbé Vezins de Lévézou,[108] also chaplain to the King and abbot of Chateaudun (1778) in the diocese of Mgr de Lubersac, and the abbot of Mostuejouls,[109] first chaplain to "Madame" (1772–1790), as well as the three Gaston de Pollier brothers, Abbé Auguste de Gaston, chaplain to Queen Marie-Antoinette, his brother Abbé Gaston,[110] sub-preceptor of the Children of France, then bishop of Thermes (1779), first chaplain to the Count of Provence (the future Louis XVIII), in charge of the leaflet of the prince's benefits and abbot of Locdieu in Rouergue, and his other brother, Jean-Louis, who is abbot of Notre Dame de la Couronne[111] and, in 1783, district chaplain to the Count of Artois: all Rouergats! And their nephew, Abbé Jean-Claude de Gaston (born 1756 in Rodez) was also appointed chaplain to the Count of Artois while serving as vicar general to Colbert de Castlehill. When Mgr Gaston died (1785), it was another of Colbert de Castlehill's grand vicars who took over his command of Locdieu Abbey, Abbé Drummond

[105] On the court chaplains, see J. Pontet, M. Figeac, M. Boisson, *La noblesse, de la fin du XVIe au début du XXIe; un modèle social* ? I, M. Boisson dir., Atlantica, 2002.

[106] see also *La France ecclésiastique*...1768, and subsequent years until 1790.

[107] *La clef ou Journal historique sur les matières du temps*, pp. 395–396; *Journal historique et politique des principaux événemens des différentes cours d'Europe*, 1775, 20 août 1775, n° 23, Geneva, 1775, p. 406 ff.

[108] *La France ecclésiastique pour l'année 1783*... Paris, 9e ed., 1783, 4e part, p. 248. Jean-Jacques de Vezins de Lévézou.

[109] Claude Charles de Mostuéjouls (born in 1725), sub-preceptor of the Children of France in 1760.

[110] Joseph Albert de Gaston de Pollier (1720–1784).

[111] Jean Louis Gaston de Pollier.

de Melfort.[112] This abbé seems to be Charles Édouard Auguste Drummond de Melfort who propounded a thesis on mathematics at the Collège Mazarin on 25 March 1771[113] directed by Professor Jacques André de Frasnes, a colleague of Abbé Marie,[114] a diocesan of Colbert's—once again—who was we soon to be chaplain to Louis XVIII in exile; Melfort was then reported as a cleric of Uzès and a canon of the cathedral before becoming Colbert's vicar general in Rodez for 20 years. Son of the Duke of Melfort and Count of Lussan, he was born at his mother's castle in Lussan (diocese of Uzès) not far from Avignon, where the deposed King Charles III Stuart resided and who held him in the baptismal font in January 1752 and made him his chaplain.... After the death of his brother (1800), he was exiled to Rome where he died in 1840 as a prelate of the Holy See Through his Franco-Scottish vicar general, a collateral who was godson and chaplain to Prince Charles III Stuart, Seignelay was thus as close to the exiled King of England as he was to the French King and his brother the Count of Artois before and during their wanderings through the Rouergat network of court abbés which deserves further scrutiny.

Thus, the chaplain of Mmes Henriette and Adélaïde, the King's aunts, was, until October 1766, another Rouergat, Abbé René-François d'Adhémard de Panat, doctor of Sorbonne, abbot of Conques (1754), whose brother François-Louis, *maréchal de camp*, was attached to the count of Artois: The latter, deputy of the nobility to the General Estates alongside Colbert, Malrieu and Villaret, died in the Army of the Princes in 1791. Both their mothers were D'Albignac[115]: by this, they were both related to the bishop of Angoulême, chaplain to the King also of Rouergat origin, Mgr d'Albignac.[116] First encountered in Bayeux when he was vicar general and neighbour of Mme de La Tour du Pin in Magny, of Mme Drummond de Melfort, of the Grants in Vaux-sur-Seulles (relatives of

[112] *La France ecclésiastique ou état présent...*, 1787, p. 247; see also P. Clarke de Dromantin, *Les réfugiés jacobites dans la France du XVIIIe siècle: l'exode de toute une noblesse 'pour cause de religion'*, Bordeaux, PU Bordeaux, 2005, p. 280.

[113] *Theses mathematicas propugnabit Josephus Chaurand de Lépinay, Nanetensis. Aperiet Carolus Eduardus Augustis Drummond de Melfort, clericus Uzeticensisnecnon in Sancti Emiliani Ecclesiaecanonicus. (25 March 1771) in Mazarinaeo*, BNF.

[114] B. Noguès, "Répertoire des professeurs et principaux de la faculté des arts de Paris aux XVIIe et XVIIIe siècles", online, rhe.ish-lyon.cnrs.

[115] *Histoire généalogique et héraldique des pairs de France...*, t. 3, p. 37.

[116] Philippe-François d'Albignac de Castelnau (1742–1814).

Seignelay) and of the Jerninghams, and who soon met them again in London. As for Frédéric Joseph, abbot of Panat, he was vicar general of Rouen and grand vicar and official of Pontoise, thus succeeding Brienne and Dillon. This is hardly surprising since the de Panats were also close relatives of the archbishop of Rouen, Mgr de La Rochefoucauld[117] and it was "Monsieur frère du roi" who was lord of Pontoise[118]: this links this other network to the first circle analysed above of the La Rochefoucaulds, with D'Enville, D'Estissac, Liancourt and Colbert, as well as to the one built around the Lubersacs, a protégé of Mme Adélaïde and Henriette, since the governor of Chartres was at that time the Marquis de La Rochefoucauld-Surgères (1735–1789), the father-in-law of the Duke of Liancourt.... Jean Simon de Panat, another canon and archdeacon then vicar general of Rouen, nephew of the archbishop of La Rochefoucauld, exiled near Colbert and Dillon, died in London in October 1811, as did his own nephew the Marquis de Panat (1795), while their relative Jean-Pierre Brunet de Castelpers de Panat was auxiliary bishop of Lavaur under Mgr de Boisgelin de Cucé (1756–1765), who was himself previously vicar general of Rouen (1754–1765) at the same time as his fellow student Loménie de Brienne, and also migrated to London as Abbé de Lubersac points out.[119]

Furthermore, Jean-Antoine Seconds (1734–1792), was the King's preacher in 1788: this other Rouergat, murdered in September 1792 with other compatriots and sorbonian colleagues, including his colleague from Rodez, the abbé Carnus, was a relative of Jean-Chrysostome de Villaret,[120] a former teacher at the College of Rodez, vicar general of Colbert and elected deputy to the General Estates alongside his bishop.

It can be added that the baron de Curières de Castelnau, another Rouergat, had been First Falconer since June 1773 and joined the count of Artois in March 1799 at the time of the exile in Edinburgh and then in London[121] where he died, watched over by the count of Artois

[117] L. DE LA ROQUE, *Armorial de la noblesse*, I, 1860–1863, p. 161.

[118] See E. SERÉ-DEPOINT, "Trois catastrophes à Pontoise en 1788, 1789, la grêle, le grand hiver, la disette", Pontoise, 1880, p. 120.

[119] Abbé de LUBERSAC, *Journal...*, *op. cit*, pp. 47–48.

[120] Future concordat bishop of Amiens and then chancellor of the university.

[121] P. DE GMELINE, J.-B.-G. DE CURIÈRES de CASTELNAU, *De la Cour à l'exil, 50 ans de correspondance d'un gentilhomme du Rouergue*, Nouvelles éds latines, 1981, p. 300.

(November 21, 1800): he is buried in the cemetery of the church of St. Pancras, the traditional parish of the emigrants, where Colbert celebrated the funeral of Mgr Dillon five years later.

During this time, it was another Rouergat who was Louis XVIII's chaplain during his pitiful exile across Europe, the Abbé Marie Joseph François Marie.[122] Born in Rodez, this professor at the Collège du Plessis (1760) and then at the Collège Mazarin (1762–1784), who for a long time hosted the scientific dinners of the Duchess of Enville and the Duc de La Rochefoucauld, had also been sub-preceptor of the sons of the Count of Artois (1782). When he learned that the wandering King had to flee again and leave Blanckenburg to take refuge in Mittau with Tsar Paul Ier, the abbé killed himself, sincerely mourned by the King. He was then replaced by a new chaplain who came to join him, after having served as chaplain to Mme Elisabeth, confessed Louis XVI at the foot of the scaffold and visited the Count of Artois in Edinburgh: This is the Irish abbé Edgeworth already mentioned who serves to connect the various circles that have been linked to Colbert, from Toulouse, Narbonne and Rodez to London, Edinburgh and Maynooth, passing through Chartres, the Sorbonne and the Court.

It has been said that the Abbé de Lubersac, vicar general of Mgr Dillon and cousin of the Bishop of Chartres, whose vicars general were Siéyès and the Irishman Aherne, a Sorbonnian and Maynoothian, was ordinary chaplain to Mme Victoire,[123] the King's aunt. He did not, however, accompany her on her wanderings with her sister to Italy and Trieste, where she died in 1791[124] but, having remained in Paris, this is how he relates that he owes his life to Madame Elisabeth, the sister of Louis XVI. Having written a "detailed account of [...] the appalling day of 20 June 1792", he sent "printed copies to their majesties [...], as well as to Mme Élisabeth de France. This august princess having learned a few days later that in the number which one had assured to be registered on the list of proscription, the abbé of Lubersac was included: she

[122] B. Noguès, "Répertoire des professeurs et principaux de la faculté des arts de Paris aux XVIIe et XVIIIe siècles", November 2008 [online] http://rhe.ish-lyon.cnrs.fr/?q=pfap-record/4418, site du Larhra, UMR 5190.

[123] *Almanach royal 1782*, p. 138 and 412; *idem* in 1783, 1788 and in 1790.

[124] Ed. de Barthélemy, *Mesdames de France, filles de Louis XV*, Paris, Didier et Cie, 1870, p. 411, n. 1; A. de Beauchesne, *La vie de Madame Élisabeth, sœur de Louis XVI*, Paris, Plon, 1869, vol.

had the charity to make it known to him by a person of confidence, the 23 of July of then: without delay, the abbé of Lubersac benefited from this generous opinion and emigrated from Paris and France very few days afterwards by Strasbourg, from where he was joined to the body of the emigration, then to Trier, where their royal highnesses were still on the point of leaving in campaign[125]"; it was only afterwards that he joined the prelates who had taken refuge in England around Dillon and Colbert, while Mme Elisabeth attached herself to the abbé Edgeworth de Firmont whom she recommended to accompany her royal brother as an improvised confessor on his last night and on the scaffold. This Irishman, educated in Toulouse with his friend Francis Moylan, one of the promoters of the College of Maynooth, had resided for 18 years at the Seminary of the Foreign Missions on rue du Bac and had not yet emigrated since his status exempted him from the oath to the CCC imposed on prelates and parish priests.

Thus, after having confessed the King at the foot of the guillotine, he had a secret correspondence with Mme Élisabeth[126] while being obliged to hide near Paris until the execution of the princess (10 May 1794). It has been said above that it was during the transfer from the Temple prison to the scaffold that she received absolution clandestinely from the Abbé de Sambucy, a Rouergat disguised as a locksmith in order to approach the condemned woman: The latter, a diocesan of Colbert, was a relative of the vicar general of Bayeux residing in Magny-en-Bessin, the Rouergat d'Albignac[127] who later became bishop of Angoulême and later anti-concordat with Colbert in London. Moreover, this Abbé de Sambucy was chaplain to the Princess of Lamballe, and Edgeworth was actively sought when it was discovered that "a letter from the Princess of Lamballe had been delivered to the King, before her death, by the Abbé Essex[128]" (*alias* Edgeworth de Firmont). His case was all the more desperate as the Archbishop of Paris, Mgr de Juigné, had seen fit to appoint him his (clandestine) vicar general for the diocese of Paris in his absence, before fleeing like his other vicar general, Peter Flood, who had emigrated with

[125] Abbé de LUBERSAC, *Journal*, *op. cit.* p. 235 ff..

[126] Abbé EDGEWORTH DE FIRMONT, *Mémoires de M. l'abbé Edgeworth de Firmont, dernier confesseur de Louis XVI*, recueillis par C. SNEYD EDGEWORTH et traduits de l'Anglais par le traducteur d'Edmond Burke, Paris, Gide fils, 1815, p. 128.

[127] See notes 98 and 99.

[128] *op. cit.* p. 170.

several of his Sorbonne colleagues to Maynooth. Thus, doubly exposed, Edgeworth, who had indeed promised Mme Elizabeth to pass on her last wishes to her two brothers,[129] soon had to emigrate himself in their footsteps, not without tribulations through Lower Normandy.[130] Is it any wonder that he was found wandering in search of an escape route via Bayeux, where he hid for 18 months,[131] near Magny-en-Bessin, Vaux-sur-Seulles, Vierville-sur-Mer, in short in the vicinity of Mme de La Tour du Pin-Surgères, the Grant de Vaux, the Drummond de Melfort and the Marguerye de Vierville: in search of a passage to England between Vierville,[132] Ver-sur-Mer and Meuvaines, where the Chouan leader Louis de Frotté had established a perilous clandestine "Correspondence" with England,[133] the abbé hid for three months in the area, mainly in the castle of Vierville and/or the adjoining manor of Than and precisely at the home of the sieur de La Marguerye: The latter's son had been guillotined in 1793 after having rescued his wife, Anna Bella Drummond de Melfort, lady-in-waiting of Mme Elisabeth[134] and cousin of Colbert's vicar general, Abbé Charles Édouard Drummond de Melfort[135] ! Once his wife was safely across the Channel, he returned to take care of his two young children left with his father before being arrested in Bayeux and guillotined in Paris (1793). His daughter, who later became Countess

[129] Ibid., p. 140.

[130] A. Pic, o. p. ed. in Abbé Edgeworth de Firmont, *Correspondance, récits, lettre inédites 1771–1806*, Paris, Cerf, 2013; see also *Mémoires de M. l'abbé Edgeworth*..., *op. cit.* pp. 136 and 175–180; https://vierville.cordelle.eu 6432, 'La fuite de l'abbé Edgeworth en 1796'; V.M. Montagu, *The Abbé Edgeworth and his friends* (1923), reprinted Wentworth Press, 2019.

[131] He himself says "18 months"; his nephew says "three years": Ibid., p. 136 and p. 175.

[132] *Mémoires de M. l'abbé Edgeworth*..., *op. cit.* p. 180: a typo twice disfigures the name of the château, which becomes 'Vienville'; but the parish priest of Anière, a neighbouring village of Vierville, is quoted. See also P. Ferté, 'Franco-Irish Ecclesiastical Networks and the Career of François Anglade in the Royal Catholic College of St Patrick at Maynooth, 1757–1834', *Archivium Hibernicum* 2022 (in press).

[133] See L. de La Sicotière, *Louis de Frotté et les insurrections normandes (1793–1832)*, Paris, Plon, 1889; https://vierville.cordelle.eu 6432, online.

[134] See W.-R. Newton, *Almanac of the Court*, 2e ed, 2020, p. 4166.

[135] *La France ecclésiastique* of 1783, p. 237; 1782, p. 18 and 234; *idem* in 1790.

de Hautefeuille, testified to this in her books[136]: It was not him but his own old father who, after having been imprisoned and saved by the fall of Robespierre and having returned to reside partly in his hotel of Marguerye in Bayeux and partly in his castle of Vierville, welcomed and hid Abbé Edgeworth, the confessor of Louis XVI and Mme Elisabeth with the help of Chouans allies from Bessin (the area around Bayeux). Having finally found a boat at Ver-sur-Mer, a parish adjoining the marquisate of Magny, Abbé Edgeworth even reports in his memoirs that the boat was paid for with 400 L by the Royal Correspondence Fund on a mandate from M. de "Marguerye" (i.e. the châtelain de Vierville or Than[137]). He finally embarked, after five attempts, on the evening of 20 August 1796, meeting an English ship which took him to Portsmouth: from there Edgeworth went first to Edinburgh (August 1796) to confer with the Earl of Artois at Holyrood. On his return to London, Edgeworth promised to see his friend Moylan again in Ireland, but circumstances led to him taking counter-revolutionary plans to Louis XVIII, then a refugee in Blanckenburg (Lower Saxony). This simple mission lasted for a long time, since the exiled King wanted to keep him as chaplain (1797), together with Abbé Marie, his Rouergat chaplain, who soon died of despair. Abbé Edgeworth never returned to his homeland and died with Louis XVIII in Mittau (now Jelgava in Latvia).

It was Mgr Asseline, the last bishop of Boulogne, who replaced him with the King, whom he followed to England (November 1808), to Aylesbury near Hartwell, where he died in April 1813, buried in the cemetery of Old St. Pancras, where Colbert had once celebrated the funeral of Mgr Dillon. Appointed shortly before the Revolution as Bishop of Boulogne, Asseline was for a long time a supporter of Colbert's refusal to the Concordat resignation. It is not known whether he attended the funeral of the bishop of Rodez. Finally, there are several last converging clues: it was Edgeworth who wrote to his friend Moylan, co-founder of Maynooth, that "one of your acquaintances, M. Asseline with whom you were at the Thirty-Three had just been appointed bishop

[136] Anne-Marie-Caroline de MARGUERYE, Comtesse de Hautefeuille, *Souffrances*, Paris, Baudouin, 1834, preface.

[137] *Mémoires de M. l'abbé Edgeworth...*, *op. cit*, pp. 136 ff; *vierville-omaha*, 6432, online. This may be the Seigneur de Vierville or his relative, Count Jacques Bertin Louis Henry de Marguerye, a Chouan (1764–1836).

of Boulogne[138]". Sorbonnard and leader of the refractory, Asseline was also with P. Flood, the future president of Maynooth, grand vicar of the archbishop of Paris, an office which fell to Edgeworth in the turmoil, while the bishop of Boulogne emigrated to Hildesheim where he found Mgr de Lubersac, bishop of Chartres and moral guarantor of Colbert. It was only afterwards that Asseline followed the King to London where Colbert was staying. Boulogne was also home to members of Colbert's family, the Drummonds of Melfort and the Maitlands of Melfort,[139] themselves related to the Lauderdales and the Duke of Gordon.[140] Sophie Maitland had married on 30 September 1670 John Drummond, 1st *Earl of Melfort* whose mother was *Lady* Ann Gordon, and an Abbé Gordon was Principal of the Scots College in Paris, where Colbert studied, no doubt through the intercession of his uncle Alexander Colbert, while his other Grant de Vaux relatives (based in Bayeux) were at the same time Principals of the Scots Colleges in Rome and Douai. Another of Seignelay's uncles, Lachlan Cuthbert de Castlehill, also of the Royal Scots, had settled not far from Boulogne, in Calais, where he had married the daughter of the burgomaster of Dunkirk and where he died in 1770, leaving his widow and son Roger. It is also known from Abbé Grégoire that the Bishop of Rodez in exile "was much welcomed, especially by the Duke of Gordon[141]"; he adds that the Jacobin Lord James Maitland Lauderdale "said that this prelate [Colbert de Castlehill] by his virtues honoured humanity[142] of whom the next [Conzié, Bishop of Arras] is a disgrace [as] the driving force behind the conspiracies against France...". When Edgeworth came to report to Monsieur on the last moments of his royal brother and sister, it is quite possible that Colbert was already in Edinburgh: In any case, we know that he was there a few months later, in May 1797, since he himself states that he discussed with Conzié, the Count of Artois' trusted man, about the "Robespierre monster[143]"

[138] Ibid., letter to Moylan, Paris, 28 October 1789, p. 31.

[139] Th. Hindley, *The Royal Scots Regiment During the Scottish Campaign, 1745–1746*, master 2 (2013–2014) [online], p. 166: Louis, William and John Drummond, servicemen of the Royal Scots, all retired to Boulogne.

[140] Ch. Grant, *Memoirs...*, *op. cit.* p. 363, note.

[141] H. Carnot, *Mémoire de Grégoire*, *op. cit.* II, p. 257.

[142] Ibid.

[143] Sir J. Sinclair, *op. cit.* 1831, pp. 252–258.

and that he passed on this information to Sir John Sinclair, a Scottish economist who was a friend and pupil of Adam Smith and whose first wife was a Maitland[144]! Once again, everything comes together and connects us to the Drummonds of Melfort, the Grants of Vaux and the vicar general of Seignelay[145] via Boulogne.

Boulogne is an apt place to finish, residence of Colbert's cousins, the Maitlands of Melfort and bishopric of Asseline, friend of Moylan and Edgeworth. It was via Boulogne that the archbishop of Rouen, Mgr de La Rochefoucauld, embarked for Dover on 20 September 1792. Boulogne was also for a long time the headquarters of Brissot, protected (at the beginning) by Lubersac[146]; it was also in a Boulogne family that Brissot found his wife, Boulogne where he animated a progressive Society of the Friends of the Constitution before founding the Society of the Friends of the Blacks, helped by Lubersac, by the duke of Liancourt and by his friend Jacques Cavillier, an enlightened burgher and a local memoirist at times, at whose house he stayed every time he came back to Boulogne.[147] The last known letter written by Seignelay from France before his exile is dated 8 May 1792. It is addressed to citizen Gillet [de Laumont] of the Conseil des Mines: he recommends to him a certain Augustin Cavillier, a young mining engineer in search of alum deposits in the Aveyron.[148] A positive proof of a family link between the two Cavilliers has not yet been found; perhaps it is just a pure example of homonymity; but perhaps it is also another milestone in a network that is already plethoric in its significant interweaving...

* * *

[144] Sarah Maitland, only daughter of Alexander of Stoke-Newington, married in 1786.

[145] *La France ecclésiastique* of 1783, p. 237; 1782, p. 18 and 234; 1790. The printer often mistakenly calls him *Drummond de Milord*...

[146] The correspondence between Brissot and Mgr de Lubersac (1789–1791) can be consulted at AN, 446AP/7 (Brissot fonds), dossier 2, 87–107.

[147] Sainte-Beuve, a relative of the Cavilliers, was able to verify Mme Roland's eulogistic judgements about Brissot (Sainte-Beuve, *Portraits de femmes*, Garnier, frères, 1845, p. 181).

[148] I owe this information to Alain Alcouffe whom I thank. See the Mines ParisTech digital library Archives Gillet de Laumont, dossier 2 (the record erroneously dates this letter to 5 August).

It was a long time ago that Adam Smith regretted that his guide in Languedoc, the young vicar general of Brienne, in Toulouse "was almost as much of a stranger to the region as we are".[149] Through his personal qualities, his sociability, his open-mindedness, and his dynamism in the management of the administrations entrusted to him, Colbert was able to make a name for himself in the various philanthropic circles where he was received in the wake of his mentors, and succeeded in establishing solid relational networks for the better and, in the long run, for the worse. In exile, he reflected on his candour when he expressed his enthusiasm to Count Barnewall during the preparation of the General Estates and the *cahiers de doléances*: "It is a great revolution that is going to take place. I have no doubt that it will turn out for the better and I desire it more than I can express to you[150]".

In the end, disillusioned and bewildered by the oddities of Providence, he had seen the reversal of all his early hopes: his progressive efforts diverted by extremists; his pacifist convictions and his utopian project of European order annihilated by a bloody continental melee; his philanthropic friends either immolated by the "dagger of the Jacobins and the rabble of Paris", or, for some, passed into the camp of "the monster" and the executioners (Brienne, Grégoire, Jarente, Siéyès, the Marquis de Valady...) and/or adhering to "all the injustices, all the cruelties and all the turpitudes of a regicidal, tiranic and atheistic assembly[151]"; the country that welcomed and educated him became a persecutor at the hands of "cannibals" and the country that forced him into exile became "a land of freedom and safety[152]"; Finally, the head of his Church made a pact with the "usurper" and abolished *sine die* the mission, sacrosanct in his eyes, of his episcopate, with the blessing of many of his companions in exile. He persisted in his refusal to obey the Concordat and to deny himself, even in exile: "Our principles and our souls will remain, if it pleases God, pure and invariable[153]". He had already written from Paris

[149] Quoted in A. ALCOUFFE, Ph. MASSOT-BORDENAVE, *Adam Smith à Toulouse et en Occitanie*, Toulouse, Privat, 2018, p. 117 (letter n° 82, Campbell Mossner).

[150] G. MARTIN, "Les élections aux États généraux dans le Sud-Ouest. Quelques documents inédits", *La Révolution française: revue historique...*, 1928, p. 236.

[151] SLA-GBDB, letter from London, 6 April 1796.

[152] Letter to the Duke of Buccleuch, Cossey 21 October 1792, quoted in A. ALCOUFFE, A. MOORE, *Smith'sencounters*, *op. cit.*

[153] SLA-GBDB, letter from London, 6 April 1796.

on 11 March 1792: "Our resistance must be reduced to refusing iniquity and infidelity. If we are mistreated, if our throats are slit, our only resource is to flee", a conviction that he repeated over and over again, certain that "flight was our only resource and today everything is lost for us except our honour".[154]

[154] Ibid. and letter of 21 October 1792.

CHAPTER 12

The London Exile: Bishop Colbert de Castlehill and the French Bishops in London, 1791–1814

Dominic Aidan Bellenger

Abstract The chapter provides an overview of the life and thought of the French Bishops resident in London following their emigration consequent on the Civil Constitution of the Clergy published in 1790. Their life, in great contrast to their former existence, was dependent on the charity of the British state and limited self-help. It was centred on the French chapels which provided spiritual and material comfort. They had an uneasy relationship with their English fellow Catholics and their leaders, the Vicars Apostolic of the London District and were aware that their identity as Catholics and Frenchmen made them doubly suspicious. Leadership among the bishops themselves was provided by the Bishop of St Pol de Léon in Brittany, a devout and business-like prelate who acted as an intermediary with the British authorities. Others like Dillon of Narbonne and Colbert himself had personal links with their land of exile. Colbert cultivated his British contacts who included Horace Walpole and

D. A. Bellenger (✉)
Von Hugel Institute, University of Cambridge, Cambridge, UK
e-mail: dtjbhome@gmail.com

A. Alcouffe (ed.), *Seignelay Colbert de Castlehill (1735-1811)*,
https://doi.org/10.1007/978-3-031-75273-5_12

busied himself alongside his episcopal colleagues in presenting a united front of opposition to Napoleon's Concordat. Their 'memoir' was a spirited defence of the pre-Revolutionary Gallican Church of which they regarded themselves as the 'faithful remnant'.

Keywords Colbert of Castlehill · Catholicism · Civil Constitution of the Clergy · Concordat · Episcopacy · Exile · Gallicanism · Relief committee · Schism · Ulramontanism

The Civil Constitution of the Clergy in 1790 had huge consequences for the French Church. Its revolutionary restructuring, including the reorganisation of France's historic dioceses, led to a deep schism in which more than half the clergy chose dispossession, and the exile which that implied, rather than signing up to the new Church order. Many thousands of these clergy sought refuge in the British Isles, enemy of the new French Republic, where, despite ingrained anti-Catholicism, the emigration became disproportionately ecclesiastical and the priests were accorded a friendlier reception than in many Catholic countries.[1] In the decades after 1790 the British Isles, and more especially London, hosted a considerable number of bishops, many of them remaining in London until their deaths.[2]

The great majority of the French lesser clergy exiled in the British Isles were *curés* and *vicaires* from Brittany or Normandy, although the bishops came from across the country, including the south. The most senior of the bishops by rank were Boisgelin of Aix[3] and Dillon of Narbonne[4] but leadership was provided by Jean-François de La Marche, bishop of the

[1] See Dominic Aidan Bellenger, *The French Exiled Clergy in the British Isles After 1789* (Bath, 1986).

[2] For the bishops and the Concordat see Dominic Aidan Bellenger, 'The Last Ditch: The French Émigré Clergy in Britain and the Concordat of 1801', in Laure Philip and Juliette Reboul, eds, *French Emigrants in Revolutionised Europe: Connected Histories* (London, 2019), pp. 257–75, and Xavier Maréchaux, 'Reorganiser l'Église après la Revolution: les évêques d'Ancien Régime et Le Concordat de 1801', *Napoleonica: La Revue* 33 (2019), pp.67–98.

[3] See E. Lavaquéry, *Le Cardinal de Boisgelin (1732–1804)*, 2 vols (Paris, 1920).

[4] 'Arthur-Richard Dillon', *Bulletin de la Commission Archaéologique et Litteraire de Narbonne* 51 (2008).

small Breton see of St Pol de Léon, whose austere piety and sound business sense made him a more acceptable figure to the British authorities than his grander and sometimes less edifying colleagues. His collaboration with the great anti-revolutionary Edmund Burke, his early arrival (1791) in the emigration, and his willingness to work hard all contributed to his influence.[5]

The ecclesiastical exiles of the French Revolution received a remarkably positive reception in Britain. They were presented as martyrs for Church and Crown by Pitt's administration and received considerable financial support from well-wishers and later from the State. A voluntary fund, one of several, was established under the chairmanship of John Wilmot, a Member of Parliament who had previously been involved with fund-raising for the welfare of American Loyalists, another group identified by their fidelity to Church and Crown.[6] As the stay of the clergy became prolonged, and voluntary contributions dwindled, the government provided money in the form of a parliamentary grant for 'the relief of the suffering clergy and laity of France'; this 'effectively married the philanthropic compassion of the elite from across the political spectrum with the Tory Pitt's ministry's concerns for national security'.[7] Bishops received ten guineas a month, all lower clergy thirty-five shillings. For a state with an undeveloped tax system, a major war with France on its hands, and a small population, large sums were involved. Distributed by the Treasury, the funding became associated with the nascent Aliens Office and the monitoring of the émigrés. Much of the distribution of funds to individual recipients was administered by Bishop La Marche. He relied on old diocesan networks, especially through the good offices of former vicars general, to ensure that the grants did not get into the wrong hands. The political monitoring of the State was mirrored in La Marche's energetic pursuit of correct clerical behaviour and opinions.

Unlike his Breton and Norman counterparts, Colbert de Castlehill had few of his diocesan clergy with him in exile. Only seven of them appear on the Treasury lists, including a vicar general, Pierre-François d'Esparbes.

[5] See Louis Kerbiriou, *Jean-François de La Marche, évêque-comte de Léon, 1729–1806* (Paris, 1924).

[6] Juliette Reboul, *French Emigration to Great Britain in Response to the French Revolution* (London, 2017), pp. 96–8.

[7] Caroline Shaw, *Britannia's Embrace: Modern Humanitarianism and the Imperial Origins of Refugee Relief* (Oxford, 2015), p. 31.

The others were François Anglade, Charles-Joseph Bevy, Charles-Gabriel Blanchy, Jean Castanes, Simon Chabot and Claude-André de Pierrefitte.[8] Anglade, a theologian, had a productive exile after his early years working as a gardener in Wales. The British authorities had endowed a seminary near Dublin, in Ireland, the Royal College of St Patrick at Maynooth, at least in part to prevent future Irish clergy from studying in continental Europe. Anglade became part of the foundation staff and was an important influence on the Irish clergy of the time, publishing a three-volume manual of philosophy in 1815–1817, ensuring that the scholarly traditions of the French Church were to be continued in Ireland.[9] Charles-Joseph Bevy, a Maurist Benedictine and a historian of French royalty and ritual, was well known enough in London's intellectual circles to be elected a Fellow of the Society of Antiquaries in 1793.[10] Later, after his return to France, he became librarian to the Ministry of War. Among his numerous and very substantial publications was his *Manuel des Revolutions* (1793) which placed the French Revolution in the continuing context of dissent since the Middle Ages. With its plots and conspiracies it reflected the world picture of the émigrés.

In London the French clergy, as part of the wider émigré society, had a well-developed sub-culture, but their lives were complicated not only by their identity as 'aliens', Catholics and Frenchmen, but also by their ecclesiastical status. Although in many ways, and especially as members of what were national, established Churches, the French clergy had more in common with the Church of England, with its endowments, bishops, cathedrals and parochial structures, they were Roman Catholics and that meant in Britain they were part of a small, struggling and barely tolerated community.

The London Catholics had ten or so places of worship, many of them in the 1790s still attached, at least formally, to Catholic embassies: notably the Bavarian, Spanish and Sardinian chapels.[11] The last of these, in Lincoln's Inn, Holborn, was the most substantial of the chapels and

[8] Bellenger, *French Exiled Clergy*, pp. 142–280.

[9] See Patrick Corish, *Maynooth College 1795–1995* (Dublin, 1994).

[10] *A [printed] list of the members of the Society of Antiquaries* (London, 1798).

[11] Bernard Ward, *Catholic London a Century Ago* (London, 1905).

was the setting for many of the principal Catholic functions in London.[12] A few new chapels, reflecting the gradual lifting of anti-Catholic legislation following the First Catholic Relief Act of 1778, were built by prosperous Catholics. Of these the most important was St Patrick's, Soho, which catered for a growing Irish population. It was situated in an area long associated with French-speaking immigrants, mostly but not exclusively Protestant.[13] London Catholicism was on a small scale but was not negligible. The city was home to a Catholic bishop, the vicar apostolic of the London District, one of the four vicars apostolic in England and Wales who, as bishops working in 'missionary' areas, were directly answerable to the office of Propaganda Fide in Rome.[14] From 1790 to 1812 the office was held by John Douglass.[15] Born in Yorkshire, he was educated at the English College at Douai in northern France, the oldest of the English seminaries in Europe, and taught at another English college, that of Valladolid, in Spain, from 1753 to 1773. He had lived in and seen at first hand the Catholic Church as a majority faith. He worked in his native county until his appointment as vicar apostolic. The vicariates supplied various chaplaincies and Mass centres, but not canonical parishes. The number of priests, all educated outside England, was not great; it included not only secular priests but Jesuits—after the suppression of the Society known as ex-Jesuits—Benedictines, Dominicans and Franciscans, all 'missionary' in their work.[16] The spiritual jurisdiction of the London District was perhaps surprisingly large as it not only covered London and the South of England, but the West Indies with the exception of Trinidad, and the Channel Islands of Guernsey and Jersey; before the American War of Independence the vicar's remit had also included the Thirteen British Colonies in North America. As Catholic ordinary in London, the French émigré clergy, including bishops, came under his episcopal aegis; he had the power to grant faculties for the sacraments. This sometimes brought

[12] Rory O'Donnell, 'The Architectural Setting of Challoner's Episcopate', in Eamon Duffy, ed., *Challoner and His Church* (London, 1981), pp. 55–70.

[13] See Dan Cruikshank, *Soho: A Street Guide to Soho's History, Architecture and People* (London, 2019).

[14] See Nicholas Schofield and Gerard Skinner, *The English Vicars Apostolic 1688–1850* (Oxford, 2009).

[15] For Douglass see Geoffrey Scott in *ODNB*, https://doi.org/101093/ref:odnb/7943.

[16] Dominic Aidan Bellenger, *English and Welsh Priests 1558–1800* (Bath, 1984), p. 248.

him into conflict with the French, especially when it came to marriages, a difficult area because of the Anglican monopoly of the solemnisation of matrimony. The difficulties could be exacerbated by the 'class' issue, the plebeian Douglass against the aristocratic 'évêques'. Douglass died at his residence, 4 Castle Street, Holborn, on 8 May 1812, was succeeded by Bishop William Poynter, his coadjutor since 1803, and was buried at St Pancras; his body was later taken to the college of St Edmund in the Hertfordshire countryside north of London, which had been founded to replace the college at Douai closed by the French Revolution. The unpublished manuscript diary he kept provides one of the most vivid archival sources for the period.[17]

The Castle Street residence was a brick-built terraced house of a type widely found in London. It was a relatively humble place, far removed from the bishops' palaces associated with the episcopal residences of Anglican or French bishops. There is a contemporary description of the house and its occupant by Henry Digby Best, an English convert to Catholicism, in an account of the circumstances of his reception into the Church in 1798.[18] The ground floor, the entry level, had a dining room and a waiting room. The bishop's study was on the first floor. The study was darkened by smoke (the writer does not say whether this was owing to coal or tobacco) and had on its walls a crucifix, a portrait of Cardinal Allen, the Elizabethan English cardinal and founder of the Douai College, and a print of Pope Pius VI. The bishop, attired in a black suit, wore a little close white wig and sported a pectoral cross and an amethyst ring. The writer said the bishop welcomed him in French and that there was a French priest in attendance. The bishop had many preoccupations, chief among them the closure of the English colleges in Europe and the working out of a satisfactory arrangement to provide a *modus vivendi* between Catholics and the British State. The French priests, by their sheer numbers, were a pressing problem too, much eased in the short term by the work of Bishop La Marche, whose own home and office, shown in a contemporary print taken from a portrait by Danloux, was not far away from Dr Douglass' residence; La Marche is pictured attired

[17] Archives of the Archbishop of Westminster, London. Bishop Douglass' Diary (henceforth Douglass Diary).

[18] *The London Magazine* 16 (1826), pp. 98–9.

in the same understated way as Douglass.[19] Catholic London and émigré London were close neighbours; many of its Catholic clergy were French educated.

Kirsty Carpenter's work on émigré London has provided a detailed description of the milieu in which the émigrés operated. In 1796 32% of émigrés, clerical and lay, lived in Soho and 29% in Marylebone, a more prosperous district.[20] Bishop La Marche lived in rented accommodation in Little Queen Street, Holborn, not far from Soho or from the Sardinian Chapel. His landlady was Dorothy Silburn, a Catholic widow, who gained the epithet 'mother of the French exiled clergy'. His residence was known as La Providence and provided the central point of émigré life and support.[21] There were numerous social outlets and amenities provided for the French, many of which were listed in Abbé Tardy's invaluable guide for the French in London.[22] In Soho Square there was a French bookshop which provided a useful rendezvous. Enforced leisure led to many publications and the reading of numerous newspapers.[23] Central to the clergy were the chapels. Given the limited number of altars available in the existing chapels, the celebration of Mass by the numerous priests was difficult, and gradually, with Bishop Douglass' consent, as many as eight French chapels had been opened.[24] Later, a number of other chapels were built by French priests, as much for the use of the London Catholics as for émigrés, including one, opened in 1816, in Hampstead, on the northern fringes of London, which is the only one

[19] Henri-Pierre Danloux's portrait of La Marche, now in the Louvre, was painted in 1793 with an engraving, by William Skelton, following in 1797. See Angelica Goodden, 'Danloux in England (1792–1802): an Émigré Artist', in Kirsty Carpenter and Philip Mansel, eds, *The French Émigrés in Europe and the Struggle Against Revolution, 1789–1814* (London, 1999), pp. 165–83.

[20] Kirsty Carpenter, *Refugees of the French Revolution: Émigrés in London, 1789–1802* (London, 1999), p. 197.

[21] Kirsty Carpenter, 'Bulletin de la Commission French Émigrés in London in the 1790s', in Debra Kelly and Martyn Cornick, eds, *A History of the French in London* (London, 2013), pp. 69–90, at pp. 76–7.

[22] Marie-Joachim Tardy, *Manuel du voyageur à Londres* (London, 1800).

[23] Kirsty Carpenter, 'London: Capital of the Emigration', in Carpenter and Mansel, *Émigrés in Europe* (1999), pp. 49–50.

[24] 'Notes on French Catholics in London after 1789', in Kelly and Cornick, *French in London*, pp. 91–8.

to survive, albeit in a much altered state.[25] The chapels in Little King Street, Portman Square, Marylebone and Somers Town became the most celebrated. The Annunciation Chapel in Portman Square is very well documented; adjacent as it was to the residences of many of the most distinguished of the émigrés, including Colbert, as well as members of the Bourbon family, it took on something of the character of a chapel royal.[26] In Somers Town, a new area of speculative housing providing cheap and convenient accommodation, the chapel of St Aloysius was to become the focus of the many philanthropic activities of the Abbé Guy Carron, a Breton priest of marked personal holiness, with a genius for good works and a ready pen. His numerous initiatives included care for the sick and the elderly, as well as a soup kitchen and several schools.[27]

Somers Town was in the Anglican parish of St Pancras, and its Church, one of the oldest in London, still stands near the London Eurostar Terminal. Its churchyard, often extended, was the burial place of numerous French exiles of the Revolution. It had long been the favoured place of rest for London's Catholics: 'The aristocratic and Catholic, Jacobite and émigré tombs set the tone and character of the cemetery – a tone of plaintive intensity, characterised by an aching sense of loss, not merely of the individual dead, but of noble causes and traditional ways of life'.[28] In 2002–2003 major archaeological excavations were made on the site of what is now the extension to St Pancras Station. Among the burials discovered and recorded were those of Arthur O'Leary, the founder of St Patrick's, Soho,[29] and two of the French bishops, Dillon and Godart de Belbeuf, last bishop of Avranches.[30] Colbert was also interred there but his remains were not disturbed.

There were at least twenty French bishops resident in London at any one time in the 1790s and they seem to have met often, not least in the solemn requiem Masses which punctuated the emigration. Colbert

[25] See Dominic Aidan Bellenger, *Fearless Resting Place* (Bath, 2015), pp. 164–8.

[26] UCL blog: The French Chapel in Marylebone by the Survey of London (7 September 2018). Filed under South-West Marylebone.

[27] See Bellenger, *French Exiled Clergy*, pp. 104–9.

[28] Philip A. Emery and Kevin Wooldridge, *St Pancras Burial Ground: Excavations at St Pancras International, the London Terminus of High Speed 1, 2002–3* (London, 2011), p. 92.

[29] Ibid., p. 103.

[30] Ibid., p. 209.

himself appears from time to time in the surviving records. In 1793 he was at the King's House in Winchester. This was a disused royal residence set aside as a temporary home for many hundreds of priests, where life was modelled on a French seminary. There, in its large chapel, Colbert ordained to the priesthood Jean-Baptiste Marest of the diocese of Coutances.[31] In June 1794, when the Scots vicar apostolic of the Lowlands, George Hay, visited London, Colbert facilitated a meeting between Hay and La Marche which attempted to direct some French priests to the Scottish mission.[32] On 16 November 1799 he was among the French bishops present at a requiem Mass for Pope Pius VI at St Patrick's, Soho, where he performed one of the absolutions.[33] On 11 July 1806 he presided at the funeral of Archbishop Dillon in the King Street Chapel, which was 'hung in black'. Colbert was 'in his full pontificals' and assisted by 'all the other French Bishops now in London'. As well as pontificating at the Mass, he also officiated at the graveside at St Pancras.[34] On 8 April 1808, the feast of the Seven Dolours of the Blessed Virgin Mary, he blessed the Abbé Carron's new chapel of St Aloysius in Somers Town and celebrated a Solemn High Mass 'in pontificalibus'. The choir of the Portuguese Chapel sung and 'cards of invitation were sent to many Protestants as well as Catholics for the occasion'.[35] By then, on account of numerous deaths, including that of La Marche, he was probably seen as the most prominent of the remaining French bishops and it may be that as early as 1806 he took it on himself to grant faculties to all the French priests.[36] On the other hand, as we shall see, relations between the London vicar apostolic and the French had become problematic.

Colbert's Scottish family connections gave him a social entrée which many of his fellow bishops lacked; only Dillon was better connected.[37]

[31] See Bellenger, *French Exiled Clergy*, p. 273.

[32] J. F. S. Gordon, *Journal and Appendix to Scotichronicon and Monasticon* (Glasgow, 1867), p. 369. For Colbert's Scottish context see James McGloin, 'Some Refugee French Clerics and Laymen in Scotland, 1789–1814', *Innes Review* 16 (1965), pp. 27–55.

[33] Douglass Diary, 16 November 1799.

[34] *The Gentleman's Magazine* (1806), p. 685.

[35] Douglass Diary, 8 April 1808.

[36] Bernard Ward, *The Eve of Catholic Emancipation* (London, 1911), vol. 2, p. 226.

[37] For Dillon's social context see F. Jerningham, *The Jerningham Letters 1780–1843*, ed. E. Castle (London, 1896) 2 vols, and *Memoirs of Madame de La Tour du Pin*, ed. Felice Harcourt (London, 1970).

This gave him the ability not only to have a non-émigré network in London but also—surprisingly in a time of war—to journey to Scotland, as he did in 1797.[38] Among his London circle was Charles Grant, Viscount de Vaux (1749–*c.* 1818) at whose second marriage Colbert officiated.[39] Grant, born in Mauritius, came to Britain in 1790 and became interested in the scheme for the settlement of French exiles, clergy and laity, in Canada. This utopian plan, aimed at replanting Old France in a Canada, now under British rule, that was no longer New France, failed to materialise, although the despatch of a number of French priests did help to reinvigorate the Canadian Church.[40] The British government had its reservations: William Windham, secretary of state for war, was adamant that the French royalists were 'to be kept apart from other French emigrants there'.[41] Colbert's friendship with Francis Gray, 14th Lord Gray (1765–1842) went deeper; his London address, 43 Gloucester Place, was a Gray property and he died, of inflammation of the bladder, at Gray's residence at Twickenham. A Tory peer and gentleman of letters, Gray was to become president of the Society of Antiquaries of Scotland from 1813 to 1823; Colbert attended a meeting of this learned society during his 1797 visit to Scotland.[42] In July 1796 he visited Horace Walpole, then at the end of his life, at Strawberry Hill[43] and in 1800 he was in conversation with Miss Mary Berry, another author resident in Twickenham, about the biography of Walpole, a close friend of hers, that she was writing.[44] An unexplored line of enquiry might be the Jacobite credentials of Colbert's family and milieu.[45]

[38] John Sinclair, *Correspondence* (London, 1831), vol. 6, p. 252.

[39] Charles Grant, *Mémoires ...de la Maison Grant* (London, 1796).

[40] M. G. Hutt, 'Abbé P.J.L. Desjardins and the Scheme for the Settlement of French Priests in Canada, 1792–1802', *Canadian Historical Review* 39 (1958), pp. 93–124.

[41] British Library Add. Ms 8075 (Puisaye Papers 104) ff. 14–17.

[42] *Account of the Institution and Progress of the Society of the Antiquaries of Scotland*, Part 3 (Edinburgh, 1831).

[43] *The Yale Edition of Horace Walpole's Correspondence* (New Haven, 1944), vol. 12, p. 250.

[44] Ibid., pp. 378–9.

[45] Edward Corp, 'The Jacobite Presence in Toulouse in the Eighteenth Century', *Diasporas* 5 (2004), pp. 124–45, and 'Jacobite Books in Toulouse', *Journal of the Edinburgh Bibliographical Society* 1 (2006), pp. 71–85.

The bishops in London met on a number of occasions to discuss a response to the transformation of society in France and to provide instructions to 'missionaries' in their effort to rechristianise the country. Thirteen bishops met between 1 June and 30 September 1793 in an attempt to evolve an articulated political theology in response to the French Revolution and its secularisation. Throughout the emigration bishops kept in touch both with each other and with their old dioceses and planned for a return to office in the very changed circumstances of France, where the Constitutional Church was struggling to capture the support of the faithful. Any sort of meaningful restoration became less likely after the papal brief of 5 July 1796, which effectively recognised the new French Republic and seemed almost impossible after the Napoleonic Concordat. The papal bull *Qui Christi Domini* of 28 November 1801 suppressed all the dioceses of the historic French Church and called for the resignation of all existing bishops. The French bishops in London had been pre-warned by a papal representative, Charles Erskine, who had been sent to England to break the news and brought letters from Rome to each of the bishops, 'requiring the French bishops in England to resign their Bishoprics into his hands' as 'necessary for the restoration and preservation of the Catholic religion in France'.[46] In response, after a series of meetings on 19, 21 and 23 September held at Dillon's residence in Theyer Street, Marylebone, most of the bishops resident in London, including Colbert, compiled a *Mémoire* eventually published in 1802 which not only made clear that resignation was not an option but that their vision of the Church was the only one they would accept; at its heart was a very exalted concept of the episcopate.[47] They had long anticipated the Concordat: in 1796 and 1797 they met to address the plans for the restructuring of the French Church drawn up for Louis XVIII, which included the redrawing of the French dioceses.[48] The stance taken in 1801 was to remain intact until most of the bishops were dead and was to be a vital part of resistance to the Concordat, which showed itself in France with the birth of the Petite Église despite the public determination of the bishops 'to prevent

[46] Douglass Diary, 15 September 1801.

[47] *Mémoire des évêques français* (London, 1802).

[48] Bernard Plongeron, *Théologie et Politique au Siècle des Lumières (1770–1820)* (Geneva, 1973), pp. 130–1.

a schism'.[49] In England, after 1801, the French bishops, although never excommunicated, were distanced from the vicars apostolic; the local variation of non-compliance with the Concordat, Blanchardism, took hold among the remaining French clergy, while the English vicars apostolic attempted to stamp it by imposing an oath.[50] In the last decade of his life it is not clear how much contact Colbert had with dissident clergy in his former diocese, one of the great centres of the Petite Église, and to what extent he encouraged resistance to the new Church order.

Colbert's period of residence in London was lived among a sizeable French community which, during the period of exile, developed in solidarity and identity. It was, nevertheless, a coda to an ecclesiastical career cut short by the French Revolution and far removed from that day, on 25 June 1789 when, as a member of the Third Estate, he was carried shoulder high through Versailles.

References

Dominic Aidan Bellenger, *English and Welsh Priests 1558–1800*. Bath: Downside Abbey, 1984.

Dominic Aidan Bellenger, *The French Exiled Clergy in the British Isles After 1789*. Bath: Downside Abbey, 1986.

Dominic Aidan Bellenger, *Fearless Resting Place*. Bath: Downside Abbey, 2015.

Dominic Aidan Bellenger, 'The Last Ditch: The French Émigré Clergy in Britain and the Concordat of 1801', in Laure Philip and Juliette Reboul, eds, *French Emigrants in Revolutionised Europe: Connected Histories* Cham, Switzerland: Palgrave Macmillan. 2019, pp. 257–75.

Patrick Corish, *Maynooth College 1795–1995*. Dublin: Gill and Macmillan, 1994.

Arthur-Richard Dillon, *Bulletin de la Commission Archéologique et Littéraire de Narbonne* 51, 2008.

Eugène Lavaquéry, *Le Cardinal de Boisgelin. 1732–1804*, 2 vols. Paris: Plon-Nourrit, 1920.

Louis Kerbiriou, *Jean-François de La Marche, évêque-comte de Léon, 1729–1806*. Quimper: Le Goaziou, 1924.

A [printed] list of the members of the Society of Antiquaries. London, 1798.

[49] Douglass Diary, 31 March 1802.

[50] Ward, *Eve of the Catholic Revival*, vol 1, pp. 83–98 and vol 2, pp. 221–32.

Dan Cruikshank, *Soho: A Street Guide to Soho's History, Architecture and People*. London: Weidenfeld & Nicolson. 2019.
Douglass Cf. Geoffrey Scott in *ODNB*, 101093/ref:odnb/7943.
Archives of the Archbishop of Westminster, London. Bishop Douglass' Diary.
The London Magazine 16, 1826, pp. 98–9.
Kirsty Carpenter, *Refugees of the French Revolution: Émigrés in London, 1789–1802*. London: Macmillan 1999.
Kirsty Carpenter, The Novelty of the French Émigrés in London in the 1790s, in Debra Kelly and Martyn Cornick, eds, 2013, pp. 69–90.
Edward Corp, The Jacobite Presence in Toulouse in the Eighteenth Century, *Diasporas* 5, 2004, pp. 124–45.
Edward Corp, Jacobite Books in Toulouse, *Journal of the Edinburgh Bibliographical Society* 1, 2006, pp. 71–85.
Philip A. Emery and Kevin Wooldridge, *St Pancras Burial Ground: Excavations at St Pancras International, the London Terminus of High Speed 1, 2002–3*. London: Museum of London Archaeology. 2011.
J. F. S. [James Frederick Skinner] Gordon, *Journal and Appendix to Scotichronicon and Monasticon*. Glasgow: J. Tweed, 1867.
James McGloin, Some Refugee French Clerics and Laymen in Scotland, 1789–1814, *Innes Review* 16, 1965, pp. 27–55.
Charles Grant and Vicomte de Vaux, *Mémoires... de la Maison Grant*. London: s.n. 1796.
Maurice G. Hutt, Abbé P.J.L. Desjardins and the Scheme for the Settlement of French Priests in Canada, 1792–1802, *Canadian Historical Review* 39, 1958, pp. 93–124.
The Gentleman's Magazine, 1806, p. 685.
Frances Dillon Jerningham, *The Jerningham Letters 1780–1843*, ed. Egerton Castle. London: R. Bentley and son, 2 vols, 1896.
La Tour du Pin, Henriette Lucie, and Felice Harcourt. 1969. *Memoirs of Madame de la Tour du Pin*. London: Harvill P., 1970.
British Library Add. Ms 8075. Puisaye Papers 104. ff. 14–17.
Mémoire des évêques français, London, 1802.
Debra Kelly and Martyn Cornick, eds, *A History of the French in London*. London: Institute of Historical Research, 2013.
Xavier Maréchaux, Réorganiser l'Église après la Révolution: les évêques d'Ancien Régime et le Concordat de 1801, *Napoleonica: La Revue* 33, 2019, pp. 67–98.
Bernard Plongeron, *Théologie et Politique au Siècle des Lumières. 1770–1820*. Genève, Droz 1973.
Nicholas Schofield and Gerard Skinner, *The English Vicars Apostolic 1688–1850*. Oxford: Family Publications. 2009.

Caroline Shaw, *Britannia's Embrace: Modern Humanitarianism and the Imperial Origins of Refugee Relief*. Oxford: Oxford University Press, 2015.

Marie-Joachim Tardy, *Manuel du voyageur à Londres*. Londres: Chez L. L'Homme, 1800.

Bernard Ward, *Catholic London a Century Ago*. London: Catholic Truth Society, 1905.

Bernard Ward, *The Dawn of the Catholic Revival in England 1781–1803;* en deux tomes. Farnborough, Hants: Gregg, 1909.

Bernard Ward, *The Eve of Catholic Emancipation*. London, 1911.

CHAPTER 13

The Pastoral Correspondence of Mgr Seignelay Colbert (1789–1810)

Marie-Paule Biron

Abstract Marie-Paule Biron examines Colbert's correspondence with his priests in Rouergue, revealing his reactions to the Revolution. Mgr Colbert, a liberal prelate, was elected as a deputy for the clergy to the General Estates and left Rodez in March 1789. Initially enthusiastic about the early reforms, his optimism turned to doubt when the Constituante's religious reforms disrupted the balance between society and the Church. As a Gallican, Colbert had navigated the balance of power between royalty and the Pope but realised a separation of powers was needed to oppose the Civil Constitution of the Clergy.

With the Concordat, Mgr Colbert found himself faced with two protagonists who undermined his principle of the separation of powers. While he sought to fight openly against Bonaparte, who wanted to tame the Church through the Concordat, he wanted, through dialogue and with the support of his Gallican confreres in exile in London, to make the

English revised by Jennifer Morag Henderson.

M.-P. Biron (✉)
Société des Lettres Sciences et Arts de l'Aveyron, Rodez, France

A. Alcouffe (ed.), *Seignelay Colbert de Castlehill (1735-1811)*,
https://doi.org/10.1007/978-3-031-75273-5_13

Pope recognise that, under pressure from temporal power, he had exercised a power not granted to him by the Church to dismiss the bishops. Faced with his failure in the face of Bonaparte and the Pope's refusal to listen to him, Mgr Seignelay fell back on the "Little Church", whose ideals he did not necessarily share.

Keywords Colbert de Castlehill · French Revolution · Gallican Church · Concordat · Bonaparte · Pope Pie VII · Constituante · Petite Eglise · Catholic liberalism · Separation of powers

Colbert's pastoral correspondence with his priests in the period 1789–1810 allows us to identify both the ideas that underpinned his thinking and the principles that guided his conduct throughout this turbulent period.

Mgr Colbert was very active in the Assembly of Haute-Guyenne, of which he was president during the first seven years of his episcopate in Rodez. He was in agreement with the ideas put forward by the philosophers of the Enlightenment and in favour of the reforms advocated by the economists. His natural tendency was to focus less on the spiritual direction of his diocese than on its temporal well-being. Always keen to play a political role, he accepted King Louis XVI's invitation to take part in the two assemblies of notables in 1787 and 1788, which were responsible for bringing reforms to the kingdom in crisis. It was quite natural, in this climate favourable to future reforms that he stood as a candidate for the deputation of the clergy to the General Estates. In his candidacy campaign, he was acknowledged for his positive action as president of the assembly of Haute-Guyenne, while his clergy in Villefranche "reminded him of his obligation of residence, and pointed out to him that the absence of the first pastor obliged young clergymen to delay their ordination or to go and be ordained by the bishop of another diocese".[1] The reality is that he fell more into the category of the "province administrator" prelate than the "sacrament administrator".[2] He was elected to

[1] Gaston ALARY, *L'Église en Rouergue sous le choc de la Révolution 1789–1801*, Éd. Spéciale hors série, l'Église en Rouergue, May 1989, p. 30.

[2] Pierre de la GORCE, *Histoire religieuse de la Révolution Française*, Tome I, Librairie Plon, Paris 1925, p. 158.

the *sénéchaussée* of Rodez by only one vote because of his tendency to be a little too liberal.

Bishop Colbert left Rodez for good in March 1789. From then on, he communicated with his priests only by correspondence. In his first letter of 14 March to his clergy, he expressed his euphoria at the approach of the opening of the General Estates, evoking a great revolution "which", he said, "I have no doubt will turn out well, and I desire it more than I can express to you".[3]

Mgr Colbert actively participated in the first reforms by joining the first seven bishops who favoured the reunion of the orders. It was in this same euphoria that he voted, on the night of 4 August 1789, for the abolition of his own privileges, as confirmed by the letter he sent to his diocese on 25 August,[4] in response to the decree of the Assembly which ordered that a Te Deum be sung in all the parishes of the dioceses, in thanksgiving for the decisions taken on the night of 4 August. When the Assembly decreed the suppression of ecclesiastical tithes on 11 August 1789, Mgr. Colbert did not vote for it, not to oppose this measure which he did not consider anticlerical at the time, but to preserve the Church's property with a view to a separation of powers which he still believed possible. He returned to this measure in a more lucid manner in his mandement, or pastoral letter, concerning the election of M. de Berthier on 20 March 1791, published on 12 May 1791,[5] in which he admitted that he had not seen the Revolution coming.

As a commissioner of the meeting hall of the Assembly, Mgr. Colbert was able to take part in the preparatory work for the Declaration of the Rights of Man. He took part in the 6th bureau responsible for drafting Article 16 on the separation of powers. He showed himself to be a liberal prelate influenced by John Locke, by formulating the proposal reported by Le Moniteur Universel: "The rights of citizens can only be guaranteed

[3] La Révolution Française, Revue Historique, T. 81, Jan.–Dec. 1928, p. 231/6 BNF Gallica.

[4] Mandement de Mgr. Colbert, Évêque et comte de Rodez, le 25 août 1789, à Rodez. Printed by Marin Devic, printer to the King, of Monseigneur l'Évêque et comte de Rodez.

[5] Mandement et Ordonnances de M. l'évêque de Rodez au sujet de l'élection le 20 mars de M. de Berthier, curé de la paroisse de Layole, au diocèse de Rodez, par MM. Les électeurs du département de l'Aveyron, en qualité d'évêque du même département. Seignelay Colbert de Castlehill. At Brille. Libraire à l'Assemblée nationale, rue de Chartres, au coin de celle de Saint-Nicaise, 1791, 46 p. Given in Paris on 12 May 1791.

by a wise distribution of powers"[6] Because of his liberal tendencies, which made him share the principles of the Revolution in progress, he had not considered it necessary to communicate with his clergy on measures which he thought did not concern them. He was far from imagining that, in the discussions in which he took part, a new law was being developed which would upset society and upset religion.

The Constituent Assembly, which wanted religious reform, passed the law of 12 July, sanctioned by Louis XVI, on 24 August 1790, better known as the Civil Constitution of the Clergy. This law was based on the Declaration of the Rights of Man to reorganise the Catholic Church in France, creating a new balance of power, without any prior agreement with the Papacy, solely by virtue of the sovereign powers it believed itself to have.

The oath voted by the Constituent Assembly on 27 November 1790, imposed on all ecclesiastical officials in order to force them to make up their minds about this Constitution, gave a new twist to Bishop Colbert's correspondence with his clerics. In a letter he sent on 8 January 1791, replying to a parish priest and vicar of his diocese, who had asked him what conduct to adopt with regard to the taking of the oath.[7] We note that the initiative did not come from him but from a question from his clergy. His answer "I can only offer you my example and the reasons which dictated my determination". His advice is interesting for us because it allows us to follow his path. Bishop Colbert recognised that the Civil Constitution of the Clergy had caused him to enter a period of doubt and indetermination and admitted that he had not found in the "Exposition des principes",[8] which he said he had signed with eagerness, the arguments necessary to refute this Constitution.

This seemed quite logical if one thinks that the deputy bishops held both to episcopal Gallicanism, which allowed them "to hold the king as the protector of their independence from Rome while preserving their

[6] Moniteur Universel, p. 192.

[7] Copy of the letter written by M. l'évêque de Rodez, to M*** Curé et Vicaire forain de son diocèse. In Paris, 8 January 1791. Bibliothèque universitaire de l'Arsenal (SCD Toulouse I) Res. 34777/2.

[8] Exposition des principes sur la Constitution Civile du Clergé par les évêques députés à l'Assemblée Nationale, 30 October 1790.

spiritual independence from the state".[9] Likewise, the Enlightenment emphasised a separation of powers. In the Exposition of Principles, they had not been able to identify any special links between these two tendencies, leaving Mgr Colbert in a state of uncertainty, which was further accentuated by the oath voted by the Constituent Assembly. It was only at the very end, during the meeting of 4 January 1791, at which he had to take this oath, that he discovered what was really at stake in the Civil Constitution of the Clergy, after having heard a detailed presentation on "the distinction between the two spiritual and temporal authorities, the immutable norms which separated them, the characters and the action which belonged to each of them". He understood how the encroachment of political power on the religious sphere caused the Church to lose its freedom and rights. Finally, he held in the liberal principle of the separation of powers the argument to refuse the oath and to fight the Civil Constitution.

But in seeing a conflict of powers as the only reason for opposing this Constitution, Mgr. Colbert did not suppose that it could affect the very principles of the Church, which he advised his interlocutor to follow as if nothing had changed. On 10 February 1791, Bishop Colbert addressed a more directive letter to "the parish priests and vicars of a district of his diocese"[10] asking them to defend "to the last extremity the doctrine of the Church and Catholic truths... by a constant and invincible refusal to take an oath which is incompatible with their principles". This reminder was undoubtedly heard, since in the spring more than three quarters of his clergy refused the oath.[11] The origin of this refusal should not be sought solely in their bishop's supplication, but in their solid training on the basis of the French school of spirituality, their state of mind and their attachment to their parish, which led them to be sometimes less hesitant to commit themselves to the refusal than their bishop.[12]

[9] Professor Bernard CALLEBAT, The Gallican tradition of the French clergy in the face of the French Revolution. Course handout.

[10] Copy of the letter written by the Bishop of Rodez, to the parish priests and vicars of a district of the diocese. In Paris, 8 January 1791, Bibliothèque universitaire de l'Arsenal (SCD Toulouse 1) Res. 34777/2.

[11] Timothy TACKETT, *La Révolution, l'Église, la France*; Éd. du Cerf, 1986, p. 354.

[12] Bernard CALLEBAT, La tradition gallicane du clergé français à l'épreuve de la Révolution française. Course handout, Institut catholique de Toulouse.

With the establishment of the Constitutional Church, the Archbishop took on the task of reminding his clerics of the canonical rules governing sacred orders and the functions associated with them, a role which he fulfilled with all the more competence as he had received training in Roman and Canon Law at the College of Harcourt. He also made a point of informing his clerics of the attitude they should have towards swearers.

To a parish priest who had consulted him on this subject, the bishop replied: "I will answer you according to my principles". The word "principle" is often used in his writings, for the Bishop had given himself a number of principles which governed his conduct and inspired his advice. In this letter it was a principle of governance, which was not a matter of advice but an obligation for his clerics, which he summarised in these terms: "one must not confuse 'swearers' [those who have sworn the oath] with 'intruders' [those newly appointed to positions in the church] and break entirely with the former, one must wait for the latter until a sentence of excommunication has deposed them from the Church and forbidden them from their ministry". He relied on another principle, that of not making a pact with any temporal power. Bishop Colbert remained faithful to his two principles.

On 27 February 1791, he spoke to his friend Mazars,[13] parish priest of Saint Amans de Rodez, warning him that "intruders" would soon come to take their places, and, concerned about the harm their arrival might do to their pastoral responsibilities, confirmed that "this was not the time to abandon our respective flocks, but to watch over them more than ever".

The election of the first constitutional bishops was the occasion for Pope Pius VI to respond to the signatories of the "Exposition on Principles". His apostolic letter "Quod aliquantum" dated 10 March 1791 was not only a condemnation of the Civil Constitution, but also a refutation of the principles of equality and liberty of the Declaration of the Rights of Man.

The writ pronounced censures declaring the consecrations of the new bishops illicit, illegitimate and sacrilegious.

Mgr Colbert addressed a letter on 12 March 1791,[14] (14) to the prior of the Madeleine, on the occasion of the election of a new bishop for

[13] Letter from Colbert to Abbé Mazars, parish priest of Saint-Amans de Rodez, 27 February 1791, MS SDL7188/9.

[14] Letter of 12 March 1791, to the Prior of the Madeleine.

Rodez, in which his liberal spirit shone through, considering that this forthcoming election infringed the public freedom which was the right of the Church, even before recognising that it was a breach of its discipline.

On 20 March, M. de Berthier was elected bishop of Rodez.

In his apostolic letter "Caritas" of 14 April 1791, Pius VI showed that the constitutional bishops had, by their election alone, no legitimacy or power that only his investiture could confer on them. He appealed to the resistance of pastors and gave priests and bishops exceptional powers to come to the rescue of religious life in these troubled times.

In his turn, Mgr. Colbert announced, in a letter of 17 April, to M. Mazars for MM. Les Ecclésiastiques de Rodez[15] the unceasing sending of a uniform plan of conduct in order to avoid as far as possible the dangers and inconveniences of the present situation, but also a mandate concerning the "intruder". Mgr. Colbert took advantage of the opportunity offered by Pope Pius VI, who granted exceptional powers, to issue, on Holy Thursday 21 April 1791, his "Agenda for the Time of Schism"[16] (16) in which he developed, in the first eight articles, the warning with regard to the intruder bishop because of the suppression of his see or the reunion of dioceses. He then granted a delegation which strengthened and extended the powers of his vicars-general and parish priests to ensure, in difficult circumstances, the good government of the diocese which was about to go underground. As for the mandement, which he had promised concerning the election of M. de Berthier,[17] he did not address it until 12 May 1791, after having waited, he said, for more learned people than himself to take up the pen. He was referring to the Declaration of the legitimate bishops, deputies to the Constituent Assembly of 4 May 1791, which was their reply to the two papal briefs of 10 March and 14 April.

Certain traits of his personality, as well as his state of mind in the face of the revolutionary measures, emerged from Bishop Colbert's letter. His vocabulary betrayed his impregnation with the spirit of the Enlightenment when he evoked a state of mind of "tolerance", "peaceful" sentiments, a "beneficent" religion and clerics "apostles of peace". However, his ideas on the Civil Constitution of the Clergy, which he shared with his fellow

[15] Letter of 17 April 1791, to M. Mazars, MS SDL 7194/5/6.

[16] Agenda for the time of the schism. Paris, 'written in our hand'. MS SDL 7333–47 notebook.

[17] Op. cit., note 5, p. 1.

deputies, were opposed to the analysis made by the Pope, who held the philosophy of the Enlightenment and the Rights of Man responsible for the Civil Constitution and affirmed that the first charge against the Constituent Assembly was to have taken upon itself spiritual power with the aim of annihilating the Church. The Bishop did not want to see in the Declaration of Rights and the Constituent Assembly a desire to destroy the Church, but a purely political reason to make it lose its rights and its freedom.[18]

As a liberal prelate, Bishop Colbert had called for sweeping reforms, but he was far from imagining that they would one day revolutionise ecclesial institutions. The time had come for disillusionment. For example, he took a clearer look at the ecclesiastical tithes.[19] He suspected that those who had despoiled them wanted to make the Church lose its freedom and destroy its sacred rights. But as he did not share the Pope's arguments, he preferred to attribute the origin of the evils he denounced to a principle of error and system, which he could not explain.[20]

Mgr. Colbert took advantage of this letter to praise the episcopal Gallicanism professed by the old Sorbonne where he had been trained. When he wrote: "We acknowledge that the temporal power has all authority to govern the things of this world..." this was a way of recognising a separation of powers.

In this Gallican spirit, he mentioned the wish of his fellow deputies who, seeing the refusal of the Constituents to negotiate with the Pope, proposed to convene a national council with authority equal to that of the Pope. The Constituents' wish was doomed to failure.

His Gallicanism was finally revealed in the way he presented the sacred authority due to the pope. He envisaged three levels. The highest corresponded to an absolute primacy, the Civil Constitution presented the lowest level, "since it hardly kept a trace of this sacred authority".

[18] Letter of the Bishops Deputies to the National Assembly. Paris, Guerbart's printing house. 64 p.

[19] Arch. Parlementaires p. de 1787 à 1850 - Première série (1787–1799) Paris. First series (1787–1799); Librairie administrative P. Dupont 1875. Volume VIII, p. 398.

[20] Jean DE VIGUERIE (professor), Les évêques français et les brefs du Pape de mars et avril 1791, Actes de la treizième Rencontre d'Histoire Religieuse tenue à Fontevraud les 6 et 7 octobre 1989 "L'Église catholique et la Déclaration des Droits de l'Homme", Presses de l'Université d'Angers, 1990.

As for the intermediate level, it was represented by that moderate Gallicanism which Mgr. characterised as "a primacy tempered by a reasoned homage, more just, regulated by maxims and certain laws".

The bishop said that he did not want to take this oath because it would mean recognising the destruction of episcopal authority. On the contrary, should we not see a link with the observation that Mgr. had just made about the sacred authority due to the pope? For, after all, the Constituents had only applied to its logical conclusion the principle which the Gallican bishops themselves had used to weaken the sacred authority due to the Sovereign Pontiff, by granting to the parish priests, through the Civil Constitution, a share of the authority which had hitherto belonged to the bishops.

Bishop Colbert felt that he was the victim of a system of which he was, in fact, the instigator. However, he understood that the radical measures taken by the Constituents had upset the balance of power by which tradition had hitherto been exercised in the Gallican Church, and that it was now necessary to fight to restore freedom to this Church.

This was so central that in a letter dated 6 June 1791, Mgr. Colbert called for Gallicanism to be the real issue in his resistance to the Civil Constitution. "May the immortal lessons of Bossuet, the most illustrious defender of her liberties, never fade from the memory of the true children of the Gallican Church".[21]

In an effort to save the Gallican Church at all costs, Mgr Colbert, together with his fellow members of the Assembly, had chosen to remain on the Episcopal Committee, which had no legal power but was nevertheless tolerated, and which was, until the end of the Constituent Assembly in September 1791, the representative body in Paris of the Gallican Church. Contrary to popular belief, this date did not mark his departure for London. In fact, in the papers of Abbé Mazars given to the *Société des Lettres de l'Aveyron*,[22] there is mention of 8 letters which Mgr. Colbert sent him from Paris, as well as 2 letters to Abbé Girard, which are all dated February or March 1792. But his correspondence with Abbé Anselme Viguier de Grun, his former vicar general, would put back to at least 14 months the time beyond which he was supposed to have gone

[21] Letter given in Paris, 6 June 1791, in response to the Holy Father's brief of 13 April last. Arch. Diocesan Archives of Rodez.

[22] See minutes T. XIX, pp. 111–113 and T. XXIII, p. 4.

into exile. Whatever the date, Bishop Colbert was not leaving as a fugitive, but was joining in London some thirty French bishops, all of them royalists and Gallicans, whom he regarded as forming the Gallican Church of France exiled in London, on which he could rely to guide the conduct of his administrators.

The regime of the Terror was to put a stop to the correspondence of Mgr. Colbert with his vicars-general, who were themselves hounded by persecution.

In article IX of his "Agenda for the time of the schism", Mgr Colbert had foreseen exceptional dispensations which would only be granted until January 1, 1793, unless they were renewed if the good of religion so required. This premonitory measure arrived in this crucial period of the Terror, when, especially after the death of the King, Rouergue saw the birth of, an even more radical spirit of resistance within a small group of priests, which was transformed into a true political insubordination. This was not to the displeasure of Mgr Colbert, who saw it as a means of supporting a resistance to the revolutionary government that he now wanted to be more direct.

The application of Bishop Colbert's principles was to be put to the test by the revolutionary laws concerning worship, starting with the Thermidorian law of 3 Ventôse year III (21 February 1795) which allowed a certain freedom of worship in return for submission to the laws of the Republic. The vicar-general, Anselme Viguier de Grun, on his return from exile in Spain, decided with the other administrators, but without the agreement of Mgr. Colbert, which he never obtained, to respond favourably to the new law, which in their eyes guaranteed them a certain freedom. Faced with this group, another group of refractory priests, gathered in an association, said they were "obeying the orders of the former bishop of Rodez, who himself approved of the Pope's non-assent. They swore to remain faithful to the old faith and to die a thousand deaths rather than break Catholic unity".[23] It was only on 6 April 1796 that Mgr. Dujols[24] (24) in which he explained the dilemma which had prevented him from deciding between the vicars-general who had violated his principle of not making a pact with any temporal power, without recognising

[23] R.P. Mouly, *Concordataires, Constitutionnels et Enfarinés en Quercy et Rouergue au lendemain de la Révolution*, Rodez, 1945, p. 94.

[24] Letter of 6 April 1796, London archerd Strait No. 27. SDL MS. 6p SDL 7750/1, 3p 7753/4/5.

them as prevaricators, and the clerics, whose refusal he said he fully shared, while accusing them of having launched anathema against those who had not wanted to imitate them. The bishop had not measured the extent to which this submission had fractured his clergy and his belated letter was far from calming the battle that was beginning to rage between the two clans.

The consular law of 7 Nivôse An VIII, (28 December 1799) promulgated 3 decrees which in principle put an end to religious persecution. The 3rd decree stipulated that the old oaths of fidelity were suppressed and replaced by a simple "promise of fidelity to the Constitution". The consular government, seeing the disturbance of conscience which this promise caused in the clergy, charged the minister of the general police to warn, by the organ of the Moniteur of 1 January 1800, that by the promise of fidelity one did not ask for the adhesion to the Constitution of the Year VIII, nor approval of the existing laws, but only the engagement not to disturb the established political order.

This time the Bishop intervened in a letter he addressed on 13 July 1801 to Messrs Viguier de Grun and Dumas[25] in which he described this promise of fidelity prescribed by the Consuls as "a subtle and more or less hidden venom, the pernicious side of which lay in the fact that it was presented under a false impression of liberty which had found favour with a large number of faithful and enlightened clergymen". This was the reason why he did not want to break off abruptly, recognising that "this promise depended on the power which demanded it, not on those who are subject to it".

Mgr. did not wish to decide until the French government had determined the meaning of the word fidelity. He declared himself entirely in favour of the opinion of the majority of the faithful ministers for whom "a promise of fidelity said much more than a passive obedience, it would be an active promise which would contain an illicit disposition, to approve and serve the unjust and vicious Constitution to which one had promised to be faithful". But above all, the Bishop agreed to suspend his principle of breaking communion with the swearers, because the Church had not yet pronounced on the legitimacy or illegitimacy of this declaration. He called on his faithful ministers to take nothing upon themselves and to await his decision before venturing any solution themselves. He gave

[25] MS SDL 7282–7307 47 pages.

his vicars-general confidence in asking them to turn to him in matters of discipline or doctrine, but specified that "if he could not answer he would consult his illustrious colleagues, whose results might be regarded as the doctrine of an important part of the teaching Church". He even went so far as to propose that they return to his diocese to support their zeal and share their sorrows.

The administrators had refrained from making the promise of fidelity. Only Mr Jouéry had made it, and he addressed a long letter to Mgr. Colbert on 20 August 1800[26] explained the reasons for having taken the oath, including that of having committed himself only to passive obedience to the government. For Mgr. Colbert, who had warned that regarding this promise of fidelity, he would defer to the decisions of the Church, the time had come to send Father Fajole to let the clerics and the faithful of his diocese know that they should adopt his principles, which were also those of the majority of the bishops.[27] His answer to the swearers was now clear: it was either recantation or rupture. The Bishop had switched from a benevolent wait-and-see attitude to the most absolute intransigence in enforcing his principles simply because they had been confirmed by his peers.

The division was such within the clergy as well as among the faithful that Abbé Antoine Dujols appealed to Mgr. Colbert, in a letter dated 10 September 1800,[28] to bring back peace. He ended his letter in these terms: "See, Mgr. in your wisdom, what means you believe you should take to stop and cure the evil which is always increasing".

In his letter of 6 October 1800, Mgr Colbert[29] replied to Messrs Anselme Viguier de Grun and Dumas whom he thanked for having informed him of the state of his diocese, but he did not propose any remedy. In contrast to his words of thanks to de Grun and Dumas, he condemned the other clergy who were opposed to their views, the "swearers" of the oath, about whom he did not have a good word to say, describing them as "these unfaithful guides… These ecclesiastics who soiled themselves by equivocal, immoral or impious oaths lost forever my

[26] Letter from M. Jouéry to Mgr. Colbert, 230 August 1800, giving his reasons for taking the oath. Arch. of the diocese of Rodez.

[27] MS SDL 7219–20 (Copy SDL 7425/6/7/8).

[28] Quoted in Mémoires de la Société des Lettres (1887–1893) T. IV, p. 48.

[29] MS SDL 7212 /3/4/5, 6p.

confidence…" He suffered no less when he wrote: "How painful it is to learn that those who have taken on the care of this sacred deposit have not all lived up to the trust I had placed in them". Was he thinking of Mr Jouery, whom he had appointed vicar-general on 30 October 1794, having given him all the powers, especially those of governing his diocese?[30] Colbert's inflexibility with regard to the "swearers" did not augur well for him to take a wise measure capable of bringing peace to the diocese, as Abbé Dujols had asked him to do a month earlier.

Colbert's fight against the Concordat took on another dimension, not only because it involved his own future with regard to Bonaparte and Pope Pius VII, but also because it involved the future of the Gallican Church whose freedom he continued to defend.

Bonaparte demanded the abolition of all existing bishoprics and the resignation of all bishops, accompanied in case of refusal, by their deposition by the Pope, whom Bonaparte had forced to legislate in this matter by granting him more power than his office conferred. Pius VII published the Encyclical "Ecclesia Christi", which reorganised the episcopate in France.

This was accompanied by three briefs. In the first, "Tam multa", the Pope committed his responsibility to transform the transmission of power in the Church, by asking his own defenders to renounce their seats. In the letter that Mgr. addressed on 29 September 1801, to Abbé Viguier de Grun,[31] he addressed this brief when he wrote: "We have received a brief from the Pope which asks each of us to resign his diocese. The French who are in London have gathered on this subject and have taken the request into consideration. I was one of those who refused it in the most decisive manner". [end quotes?] Bishop Colbert was accustomed, when he had a text to sign, to use qualifiers which reinforced the eagerness of his acceptance, as well as the determination of his refusal.

He addressed an instruction to his diocese on 8 November 1801[32] in which he declared: "To consent provisionally to the exercise of the powers of Mgr. de Grainville delegated by the Pope as Vicar Apostolic and to transmit his powers of jurisdiction directly to his vicars-general to

[30] Letter from Paris 27/02/1791. MS SDL 7188/9.

[31] MS Copy SDL 7221/2/3.

[32] Servières Louis-Bernard (canon), Histoire de l'Église du Rouergue, p. 599.

remedy the insufficiency of the title and this without derogating in any way from our jurisdiction which we retain in full".

On 29 November 1801, Pope Pius VII was forced to issue a new bull "Qui Christi Domini", in which he declared the 85 bishoprics of old France to be abolished and reduced to 60. It was through this same bull that Bishop Colbert learned not only of the loss of his jurisdiction, but also of the extinction of his see at Rodez. Feeling humiliated by this final outrage and considering this abandonment of power as a forfeiture, he refused the Concordat in its entirety and continued to correspond with his vicars-general and secretary of the bishopric.

On 23 December 1801, Bishop Colbert signed the Memorandum of the Gallican French Bishops of London stating that he had not resigned but had no intention of making a schism with Rome, and if he refused the Sovereign Pontiff's requests it was not in an absolute manner but in a dilatory manner.

On 31 August 1802, Mgr Colbert sent Abbé Dujols the letter he had promised him, explaining the reasons for his refusal of the papal brief.[33]

He confirmed that he had received his letter, dated the 12th of this month and addressed to the "former" bishop of Rodez, but he wanted to re-establish the situation by telling him that he was not the "former" bishop of Rodez, but the "present" bishop of this see. He then went on to explain the reasons for his refusal, emphasising "that which is most inviolable on earth", the institution "which came from the divine author of religion and has passed intact from the apostles to us in an unbroken succession. A bishop holding his see is of divine right". He then went on to set out the limits that the Pope cannot exceed in the matter of removal from office on the basis of canon law. Finally, he listed the evils of his transgression as "an attack on the discipline of the universal Church, a manifest infringement of the liberties of the Gallican Church, an attack on the most sacred rights of the Catholic Church and on the stability of the episcopate". This letter brought together all the grievances brought by Mgr. Colbert against Pope Pius VII.

Colbert was able to rely on Mgr Arthur-Richard Dillon, who was in London one of the most ardent opponents of any conciliation with the new consular power, to forcefully manifest the liberal character of his struggle; making Bonaparte responsible for having distorted the Church

[33] Letter from Mgr. Colbert to citizen Dujols, London, Gloucester place, n° 43, August 31, 1802, ADA. L927 (correspondence relating to the police of cults).

in its ministers, rights and principles, but above all in the transmission of powers, considering this prerogative to be the ultimate infringement of the Church in the exercise of its freedom.

He showed his opposition to it by seeking to combat not only his administrators in charge of the application of the Concordat in the diocese, but also the newly promoted people in charge of the new Concordat Church. To carry out his fight he relied on the small group of rebellious priests who were also determined to fight the Concordat Church but for a much more pragmatic reason than their bishop. They were seeking to get out of this Church and the straitjacket of the Organic Articles, which they found difficult to live with on a daily basis, and saw no other way out than to enter into conflict with the consular power, nor any other way out than to return to the faith of the Ancients and to the traditions of the Church, for which they were nostalgic. These reasons seemed far removed from those of Mgr. Colbert.

This battle that they waged together is revealed to us in a letter of 27 Brumaire X, addressed by the prefect of Aveyron, Mr Sainthorent, to the State Councillor Portalis,[34] which states that "Abbé Daunat and his small number of refractory members were circulating a copy of a letter which he claimed to have received from Mgr. The purpose of this letter was to strengthen their opinion in opposition to the Concordat, and if possible to create further divisions in which the people would be called upon to take part". Then he specified "Bishop Colbert would have acted politically taking advantage of the conflict of France with England to continue to sow discord in the diocese from afar. A role he was playing on principle while we were at war with England". He does, however, grant the bishop an extenuating circumstance, that he thought "given the date on which this letter was written, that he must have been unaware that peace had been signed between England and the Republic If he had written his letter later he would have ceased his manoeuvre". The Scottish origins of Bishop Colbert de Castlehill and his exile in England could only lead to further distrust in political circles at the time.

A letter from the State Councillor Portalis, in charge of the department of Religion or Public Worship, to the prefect of Aveyron, dated 15 September 1802,[35] carried the accusation that "The priest Dujols,

[34] ADA L923 927 An X.

[35] Ibid.

former private secretary to the bishop of Rodez, would maintain suspicious correspondence with his former bishop, who had not resigned, of Rodez. Such correspondence must be classed as that which is maintained with the enemies of the State". This correspondence certainly went up to the 1st Consul, because Portalis continues his letter in these terms: "The intention of the 1st Consul is that you mandate the Dujols priest to firmly defend him from maintaining direct or indirect relations with his former bishop and to make him foresee the severe measures to which one would be obliged to have recourse if such relations continued".

Bonaparte could only be suspicious of this dignitary who, according to his information, seemed to defy him by fomenting unrest through his support for the priests who remained loyal to him.

Bishop Colbert, who still did not wish to break with the Pope, had made several attempts at conciliation with his confreres in London. In April 1803, he joined the 38 Gallican bishops who addressed a memorandum to Pius VII entitled "Canonical and Respectful Claims". In it, they defined their position and motivated their refusal of the Concordat by opposing in particular the bull Qui Christi Domini, which suppressed all ecclesiastical jurisdiction in France from a canonical point of view. The Pope replied by placing the question from a theological point of view, thus upsetting the arguments of the bishops who were convinced that he had exceeded his rights and powers. The Supreme Pontiff reminded them that: "Rome has never admitted the maxims of 1682, the fullness of power belongs to the Vicar of Christ". This was the Holy Father's disavowal of the Gallican principle based on a hierarchy of powers that recognised only a limited role for the Pope in favour of the episcopal body. It was on the basis of this disavowal of the Gallican principle that Bishop Colbert broke with the Pope. This break was soon confirmed in a letter dated 16 April 1803, when he replied to a priest who asked him what attitude he should have towards those whom the Pope would send to replace him. His answer was formal: "They would be usurpers, intruders and thieves..."[36] In this spirit of rupture, a small number of priests entered into dissidence after having refused the order of Mgr. de Grainville of 6 September 1803, enjoining the priests to return to the ranks and to submit to the orders of the Grand Vicar of Aveyron, Abbé Fajolle.

[36] Letter of 16 April 1803, from C. to a priest... MS SDL. 7282–7307.

As for his administrators, they preferred to withdraw. The aspirations of Mgr. did not seem to correspond either to the contestation of the priests or to the expectations of his administrators. Faced with this failure, he was forced to fall back on the "Little Church" he had founded in Rouergue, relying on his most radical clerics in order, as Camille Latreille writes in his work on religious opposition to the Concordat, to wage what could be "his last battle against the absolutism of Rome".[37] Father Mouly, who has studied the Salesses Fonds of the Archives of Aveyron on the "Petite Église", points out that the correspondence between Mgr. Colbert and his chief, Abbé Delhom, very often concerned only the settlement of internal quarrels, which allowed the Abbé to frequently recall the sanctity of the cause and its living representation: Colbert, the legitimate bishop.[38] The absence of any real pastoral leadership suggests that Mgr. Colbert was not really trying to support the "Little Church" in Rouergue, or even to rely on it, because the centre of his struggle was now elsewhere. As early as 3 April 1804, he signed an "apostolic correspondence of the legitimate French bishops" in which he made it known that the archbishop of Narbonne had made him the depositary of his authority. This archbishop was none other than Mgr Arthur-Richard Dillon, the leader of the Gallican bishops exiled in London, whose torch Mgr Colbert was in a way carrying on. The death in London in 1805 of the bishop of Lombez, Mgr. Alexandre-Henri de Chauvigny de Blot, was an opportunity for Mgr. Colbert to send a letter, on 4 March 1806,[39] to Lucrès, Vicar General of Lombez, to inform him, after discussion between the bishops of London, that given the difficulty or absolute impossibility of exercising the sacred ministry by themselves, it had become necessary to establish capable and experienced men to take their place in exercising our powers and representing the Gallican Church in France. The Bishop assured him, in the name of the president of the assembly and in his own name, that all the powers, both ordinary and extraordinary, necessary for the guidance of souls, would be given to him.

[37] Camille Latreille, L'opposition religieuse au Concordat de 1792 à 1803, Paris Hachette, 1910, 290 p., p. VIII.

[38] R.P. Mouly. Op. cit., p. 113. Fonds Salesses A.D.A.F. dossier de la Petite Église, 11° paquet, n° 32.

[39] Extract from a letter from Mgr. Colbert, Bishop of Rodez, addressed to M. Lucrès, Vicar General of Lombez, dated London 4 March 1806. Politique Chrétien, Ier quarter 1815, T. Premier. In Paris, at Beaucé, Libraire rue Guénégaud n°18, 1816, pp. 406–407.

In another letter to the same vicar, dated Edinburgh, 30 July 1806,[40] Colbert answered his question about what was meant by extraordinary powers and gave him guidelines for leading souls. The year 1810 marked an important stage in Bishop Colbert's pastoral correspondence, since he announced that he had just been chosen by his peers in the Gallican Church in London to be their spokesman. This would explain the letter of 1 January 1810, entitled "Pastoral letter, from our masters in the faith, the undismissed bishops, composing the true Gallican Church". In the same month he addressed Mr. Lucres, advising him "not to have any spiritual communication with heretics and schismatics, but, as with intruders, to maintain external peace and charity with them, especially if they had the desire to return from their error to Catholic unity". He ended his letter in a somewhat disillusioned manner. "We are", he said, "scattered soldiers still fighting…".[41]

We have a letter from Mgr. Colbert which he addressed this time to the bishop of Pamiers, whom he knew to be in agreement with his ideas, to advise him: "You will have to keep simply to the decision of the bishops resident in London, which you must consider as that of the whole Gallican Church…" This injunction recalled that which he had made to his vicars general during the discussions on the consular law concerning submission to the laws of the Republic. He ended his letter by speaking of the Concordat Church, in these terms: "This so-called Church has Pope Bonaparte as its author…".[42]

If his correspondence showed him to be quite distant from the struggle of the "Little Church", he was no closer to his former diocesan clergy in that he had found in neither of them the desired profile to represent the Gallican Church.

In conclusion: Colbert's correspondence shows that he had set himself the task of fighting the Civil Constitution of the Clergy which had

[40] Extract from a letter from Mgr. Colbert, Bishop of Rodez, addressed to the same vicar-general of Lombez, at the beginning of January 1810, Politique chrétienne gallicane et variétés Ier Trimestre, 1815, Tome I in Paris, Chez Beaucé, Librairie rue Guénégaud n° 18, pp. 406–407.

[41] Letter from C. to Lucrès, early January 1810, Politique chrétienne gallicane et variétés I° trimestre, 1815, Tome I in Paris, chez Beaucé, Librairie rue Guénégaud n°18, pp. 408–409.

[42] Letter from C. to the Bishop of Pamiers 1810, GABENT "Les Illuminés", (Gallica) 1904, p. 144.

destroyed the Gallican Church of the Ancien Régime, based on a traditional balance of power.

He saw in the separation of powers the possibility of restoring the Church's rights and freedom. This was why his letters to his diocesan administrators were essentially about refusing any oath, submission, or promise of fidelity. With the Concordat his correspondence was to take a new turn, for from now on he was not only affected in his own function, but he felt the need to reinforce his fight to have the Gallican Church recognised as having rights and freedom by Bonaparte but also as having principle by the Pope. His last pastoral letters sought, with the support of his fellow Gallicans in London, to find the frameworks for reviving the Gallican Church in France. His struggle was perhaps not as futile as appearances might suggest. In a paper on "French Bishops and the Papal Briefs of March and April 1791", Professor Jean de Viguerie pointed out that in the nineteenth century a school of thought emerged which advocated the harmony of the Revolution and Christianity. This school was Catholic liberalism, whose motto was "A free Church in a free State". One wonders whether its origins could not be found in the legitimate episcopate of 1791, of which Mgr. Colbert was a perfect example.

PART IV

Some Contemporaries of Colbert

CHAPTER 14

Colbert de Castlehill, Raynal and the Provincial Assembly of Haute-Guyenne: The Bishop and the Abbé, from Reform Ideas to the Clash of Ideas

Gilles Bancarel

Abstract Bishop Colbert de Castlehill came to Rouergue following his appointment to Rodez on 28 January 1781, for a period characterized by great instability due to revolutionary events. He played an active role in the development of his diocese, presiding over the work of the Provincial Assembly of Upper Guyenne initiated by his predecessor Champion de Cicé. This innovative institution of the Ancien Régime, initiated by Louis XVI and his ministers, which put into practice the ideas of decentralization

English revised by Andrew Moore

G. Bancarel (✉)
Société d'Étude Guillaume-Thomas Raynal, Millau, France

A. Alcouffe (ed.), *Seignelay Colbert de Castlehill (1735-1811)*,
https://doi.org/10.1007/978-3-031-75273-5_14

on the eve of 1789, disappeared with its instigators with the arrival of the new regime.

Mgr Colbert de Castlehill was confronted with the implementation of the Civil Constitution of the Clergy. From his exile, he had to fight against the enemies of the clergy and respond to the expectations of his faithful in need of guidance.

Abbé Raynal, both the first benefactor of the provincial assembly and propagator of the ideas that were to lead to its downfall with the advent of the French Revolution, was one of Mgr Colbert's correspondents when he presided over the institution.

This article will examine the evolution and future of this institution in the light of the initiatives taken in its favour by Mgr Colbert and Abbé Raynal.

Keywords Colbert de Castlehill · Provincial Assembly of Upper Guyenne · Decentralization · Reforms · Administration · Agriculture · Raynal Guillaume-Thomas · Philanthropy

Following his appointment as head of the diocese of Rodez on 28 January 1781, Bishop Colbert de Castlehill became president of the Provincial Assembly of Haute-Guyenne. In this capacity, he participated in the development of his diocese with the support of the Abbé Raynal.

What is the origin of this institution? What are its works? What was the joint action of Colbert and Raynal in favour of the Rouergue? What were the consequences? These are the questions we intend to answer.

The Provincial Assembly of Haute-Guyenne

The Provincial Assembly of Haute-Guyenne,[1] created in 1779—one year after the Provincial Assembly of Berry[2]—occupied the territory of the generality of Montauban and included the former provinces of Rouergue

[1] Gérard Boscary, *The Provincial Assembly of Haute-Guyenne (1779–1790)*. Thesis for the doctorate in law, 1932.

[2] Claude Michaud, "L'Assemblée provinciale du Berry (1778–1789)" in: *Les Assemblées d'États dans la France méridionale à l'époque moderne*, Montpellier, 1995, pp. 215–238.

and Quercy (today's departments of Lot and Aveyron with part of Tarn-et-Garonne).[3] It was born of the will of Minister Necker, according to the plans he had outlined in his *Memorandum given to the King in 1778*:

> If your Majesty could institute an Administration which, by smoothing the path of his justice, would be a possible obstacle to abuses of power, this would perhaps be a point of perfection in his eyes, since after having made his people happy during his reign, he would still be their benefactor in the most remote times; I am looking for new reflections to answer this.[4]

> Experience and theory also indicate that it is not with superior men, but with the great number of those whom one knows and has known, that it is right to compare a Provincial Administration, and then all preference will remain with the latter; For, in a permanent commission composed of the principal proprietors of a Province, the combination of knowledge, the succession of ideas, gives consistency to even mediocrity, the concurrence of general interest increases the sum of enlightenment, the publicity of deliberations forces honesty; and if the good comes slowly, it comes at least; and once obtained, it is safe from caprice and is maintained: instead of a Steward full of zeal and knowledge, being soon followed by another who disturbs or abandons the projects of his predecessor.[5]

The reform projects aimed at greater social justice, reducing inequalities and simplifying the public finance system. They were opposed by some of the nobility and the bourgeoisie, who saw this as a disruption of the established social order, as well as by the provincial administrations: intendants and parliaments, whose power was contested and called into question.[6]

The 20 years of the Assembly's existence were marked by the presidency of two bishops of Rodez who promoted the institution with as much zeal as energy: Bishop Jérôme Marie Champion de Cicé[7] from July

[3] Léonce de Lavergne, *Les Assemblées provinciales sous Louis XVI*, Paris, 1863, chap. V, 'La généralité de Montauban', pp. 67–99.

[4] Jacques Necker, *Mémoire donné au Roi en 1778* [1781], p. 18.

[5] Jacques Necker, *Memoir* (op. cit.), p. 21.

[6] Gérard Boscary, *L'Assemblée provinciale de Haute-Guyenne*, op. cit., p. 169 (Cour des aides de Montauban, 1780, 1781, 1782).

[7] Jérôme Marie Champion de Cicé (1735–1810), bishop of Rodez in 1770, archbishop of Bordeaux in 1781, deputy of the Bordeaux clergy to the General Estates, Keeper of the Seals on 4 August 1789, resigned on 20 November 1790, refused to take the oath to

1779 to January 1781, followed by Bishop Seignelay Colbert de Castel Hill[8] from January 1781 to December 1789.

Bishop Champion de Cicé, who was the first president, at the request of Necker, had been the general agent of the clergy from 1765 to 1770[9] before being appointed to Rodez on 24 June 1770. Installed on 8 August 1771, he devoted his first works to a fairer distribution of taxes and the improvement of communication routes. Thus, as soon as he arrived, he launched a major survey of the state of the diocese of Rodez in 1771,[10] then from 1780[11] a vast undertaking consisting of the complete reassessment of the province's land register, entrusted to J.F. Henry de Richeprey.[12] The latter noted in his preliminary work[13] the enthusiasm of the bishop and the population for his undertaking:

> Mgr Colbert, the new president, satisfied with the project and the work begun, defended it. He obtained favourable decisions from the Court and conciliated all the spirits in the province. It was a spectacle worthy of the admiration of good citizens, to see the enthusiasm with which the Bishop

the Civil Constitution of the Clergy, emigrated in 1792. Appointed Archbishop of Aix in 1802. F. Cadilhon, *L'honneur perdu de Monseigneur Champion de Cicé*, Bordeaux, 1996.

[8] Seignelay Colbert de Castel Hill (1735–1811). In 1789 he was elected deputy to the Assembly of the Estates-General by the clergy of Rodez. He remained in office until 1791 when he was replaced by the constitutional bishop Debertier appointed on 22 March 1791. After this date he took refuge in England.

[9] Gilles Bancarel, "Quand le Rouergue expérimentait la décentralisation et les inventions techniques sous l'impulsion de l'abbé Raynal", *Études Aveyronnaises*, 2005, pp. 71–84.

[10] The answers will be recorded in the *State of the diocese of Rodez in 1771* according to the answers made by Mrs. the priests to the questions which were sent to them on October 15, 1771 by the bishop. The work was published by the archivist Louis Lempereur in 1906.

[11] As early as 11 April 1780, Mgr Champion de Cicé announced that he had just found 'in the offices of M. Necker a subject who agrees to take care in the province of the operation of the cadastres'. cf. Henri Guilhamon, *Journal des voyages en Haute-Guyenne de J.F. Henry de Richeprey*, Rodez, Commission des archives historiques du Rouergue, 1952, p. xxxvii.

[12] Henri de Richeprey (1751–1787). Put at the disposal of the Provincial Assembly by the minister Necker, after having spent five years at the Contrôle Général des Finances from 1775 to 1778.

[13] *Rapport sur les règles à employer pour le renouvellement des cadastres communaux et la meilleure répartition de la taille, lu à l'assemblée de l'administration provinciale de Haute-Guienne*, par M. Henry de Richeprey, [Rodez], Impr. de M. Devic, [1784], 112 p. in 4° (p. 6).

of Rodez and your intermediate Commission devoted themselves to the public good and how each of you gentlemen and your correspondents supported them.

In 1785, Richeprey published the *Description des sols de la Haute-Guyenne*,[14] a work intended to serve as a manual and guide to surveyors for the evaluation of income from land and he left a valuable travel journal.[15]

The Work of the Provincial Assembly

At its first assembly, held in Villefranche de Rouergue on 14 September 1779, five offices were set up[16]:

- the *Office for the taille and the vingtièmes* which dealt with the allivrement i.e. the fixing of the base of taxation estimated according to nature, surface and quality for any property. This led, on the one hand, to an identification and description of the nature of the land and, on the other hand, to its distribution by owner.
- the *Office for Capitation*, which dealt with the household tax.
- the *Bureau of Rules*, which dealt with the internal organization of the Assembly and the composition of the bureaux.
- the *Bureau des grands chemins*, which was responsible for the construction and maintenance of main roads.
- the *Office of Foreign Affairs and Public Welfare*, which dealt with education, agronomy, agriculture, health, living conditions, charity and navigation.

[14] J.F. Henry de Richeprey, *Description des diverses qualités de sols de la Haute-Guyenne ou plus simplement Description des sols de la Haute-Guyenne* en 1785, 1 vol. in 4°.

[15] Published in 1952, Henri Guilhamon, *Journal des voyages en Haute-Guyenne*, *op. cit.* To the credit of Richeprey's work must be added the lesser-known work he carried out at the instigation of Condorcet. Motivated by feelings in favour of the abolition of slavery—inspired by the work of Abbé Raynal in particular—he took over the management of La Fayette's plantation in Cayenne in 1784 in order to try to emancipate the black slaves (Guilhamon, op. cit., p. xxviii).

[16] *Procès-verbaux des séances de l'Assemblée Provinciale de Haute-Guyenne*, September–October 1779, pp. 27–30.

Its members, spread across the clergy, the nobility and the Third Estate, most of whom were in favour of the new ideas, distinguished themselves by their commitment to the public good, as is the case for Jean d'Espradel d'Allaret, an agronomist and physiocrat who introduced the cultivation of sainfoin and clover into the Millavois region and developed knowledge of the potato in the region.[17] He was also the literary inspiration for Claude Peyrot's *La Primo Rouergasso, en formo de Géourgiquos*, as the latter will admit[18]:

> Dins lou cap, Desprodels, més lo pensado
> De descrioure en Potois los sosous de l'onnado…
> S'ogissio pas de mens qué de fa lo pinturo
> De tout ce qué dins l'an nous ouffris lo noturo.

In 1781, under the title *Les Quatre saisons, ou les Géorgiques patoises (The Four Seasons, or the Patois Georgics)*, his definitive work was published with a dedication "to Monseigneur Jérôme-Marie Champion de Cicé, Évêque et Comte de Rodez, Président des États de la Haute-Guienne", to whom he revealed his concern to "retrace the innocent customs and useful labours of the Farmers of our mountains, that precious portion of your Herd, which, although hidden in the bosom of the Rocks, is neither less known nor less dear to you".[19]

The *Minutes of the sessions of the Provincial Assembly of Upper Guyenne* published by the printer Védeilhié in Villefranche,[20] were praised by

[17] On Despradel-d'Allaret and his work see: Jean-Marie Tisseyre, "d'Espradel d'Allaret", *Revue du Rouergue*, CXIX (1976), pp. 239–247; Louis Lempereur, "Introduction de la pomme de terre en Rouergue", *Annales du Rouergue et du Quercy*, XI (1888), pp. 163–164; XII (1888), pp. 184–185; XII (1889), pp. 245–247.

[18] [Claude Peyrot], *Poésies diverses, patoises et françoises* par M. P** A.P.D.P. En Rouergue Villefranche-de-Rouergue, [s.n.], 1774, p. 6 'O Moussu Desprodels omic de l'Ogriculturo'.

[19] Monseigneur Jérôme-Marie Champion de Cicé, bishop and count of Rodez, President of the provincial assembly of Haute-Guyenne (1735–1810), initiated a vast survey of the diocese of Rodez published by Louis Lempereur, *État du diocèse de Rodez en 1771*, Rodez, 1906.

[20] For the first session of 1779 published in 1780; for that of 1780 in 1780, both under the presidency of Mgr Cicé (signed JMEC of Rodez) who initiated this publication (Boscary, op. cit., p. 42–43); for that of 1782 in 1783, for that of 1784 in 1785 and that of 1786 in 1787. These last three under the presidency of Mgr Colbert (signed S. évêque

the physiocrat Dupont de Nemours who noted in his *Journal de l'agriculture*[21]:

> If he could have any doubts about the usefulness of the new Provincial Administrations, nothing would be more likely to dispel them than the reading of these Minutes. We will extract from it some articles which will certainly give our Readers a high idea of the wisdom, the lights, and especially of the spirit of Patriotism of the Citizens to whom our beneficent Monarch has entrusted the care of enlightening him on the true interests of that portion of his Subjects which inhabits Rouergue and Quercy.

Bishop Colbert de Castlehill

In 1781, Jérôme Marie Champion de Cicé left the bishopric of Rodez to take over the archbishopric of Bordeaux leaving his place to Monseigneur Seignelay Colbert de Castel Hill. Appointed on 28 January 1781, the new bishop became president of the Provincial Assembly of Haute-Guyenne. The Assembly then had to face resistance from the project's enemies. This resistance was accentuated after 19 May 1781, the date of the dismissal of Necker who had initiated the project. Confronted with the decision of the Intendant of the province[22] who was opposed to the printing of *Procès-verbaux*, Colbert replied to the Minister to defend his institution:

> The printing of our minutes is useful, it excites zeal for the public good, it has given the inhabitants of the Province an energy which they did not have before. This impression cannot compromise the government in any way, because our deliberations are not its work, but ours.[23]

During his term of office, the major projects undertaken by the Assembly were pursued with great energy. The bishop went regularly to Paris to

de Rodez). These volumes will be brought together in a *Collection des Procès-verbaux des Séances de l'Assemblée Provinciale de Haute-Guienne*, in two volumes.

[21] *Journal de l'agriculture, du commerce et des finances* (A Paris), May 1780, p. 157.

[22] Marie-Pierre-Charles Meulan d'Ablois (1739–1814) Maître des requête, Intendant de la Généralité de Montauban (Boscary, op. cit., p. 43).

[23] Letter from Mgr Colbert of 9 April 1783 to Henri Lefèvre d'Ormesson (1751–1808) Contrôleur général des finances from 29 March to 1er November 1783 (Boscary, op. cit., p. 44).

defend the interests of his province and nevertheless remained in close contact with his parishioners who showed him their gratitude, as on that day in October 1781 when, on his arrival in Millau, "he was given a brilliant reception. It surpassed that which had been given in 1771 to his predecessor, Monseigneur de Cicé, and for the costs of which the town had spent a considerable sum of money".[24] A patron of the arts and letters, he sponsored the aeronaut Carnus,[25] the poet Claude Peyrot[26] and the historian Bosc.[27] This made the latter say:

> His frank, loyal, popular and affectionate character made him generally regretted by all his diocesans. I owe a public homage to the care he took to procure the materials which served for the memoirs I am writing on the History of Rouergue. He was like all the Colbert friends of the sciences, and his knowledge in literature had made him associated with the Academy of Montauban. In the administration of the province of Haute-Guyenne, of which he was president, he showed great zeal for the public good.

Under his presidency, the Provincial Assembly took a particular interest in agricultural matters. In October 1782[28]:

> The Bureau of the Public Good, justly persuaded that among the various means which the Peoples of this Province can make use of, to alleviate the overwhelming weight of public burdens, and to acquire some ease, the first, the most useful to all, is the improvement and the perfection of agriculture; it has occupied itself with all the attention that this interesting object deserved, of the precautions to be taken, so that the most precious of all the arts arrives at the highest degree of possible prosperity...

[24] J. Joseph Rouquette, *Histoire du Prieuré et de la Paroisse Notre-Dame de l'Espinasse de Millau*, Villefranche, imp. Veuve Cestan, 1866, pp. 314–315.

[25] Abbé Charles Carnus (1749–1792), professor of philosophy at the Royal College of Rodez, made an ascent in a hot-air balloon on 6 August 1784. An engraving representing this event made by N.T. Candieu professor, will be dedicated to Monseigneur Colbert de Castel Hill (Blanchon sculpt.).

[26] See Gilles Bancarel, "Le succès à travers l'édition ses œuvres" in Gilles Bancarel, "Le succès de Claude Peyrot à travers l'édition de ses œuvres" in: *Claude Peyrot poète occitan (1709–1795)* (colloque Millau, 1995), Millau, éd. du Beffroi, 1996, p. 99–116.

[27] Louis Servières, *Histoire de l'église du Rouergue*, Rodez, 1874, pp. 545–546.

[28] *Procès-verbaux des séances de l'Assemblée Provinciale de Haute-Guyenne*, op. cit. Session of 3 October 1782, pp. 90–94.

> The majority of the citizens of all states inhabit the countryside; the principal inhabitants of the cities go there to stay during the most beautiful season of the year; some attracted by the desire to enjoy a rest which can only be tasted with difficulty in the midst of the tumult of the cities; others, called by the necessity of their business. Agriculture is therefore for all men, either an object of pleasure or an object of utility; it alone unites the interests of all the different classes of citizens, and should be, by this consideration, the most ordinary subject of their research and their reflections; we would even dare to say, the most agreeable subject of their conversations.
> ...but farmers are neither sufficiently educated nor free from the prejudices of previous centuries to be able to choose from among so many different processes those that are most useful and most fruitful.
> ...those who are more particularly concerned with agriculture can be "classified" into two classes; one is that of speculators and writers; the other is that of labourers; it is the latter who are active, and whom it is especially important to train, enlighten and help. Its main fault is that it is given over to a blind routine; it almost never does what was done before. If some local accident disturbs its ordinary course, it does not invent anything to bring itself back into line; it slavishly imitates usage; it stubbornly clings to its habits; anything new revolts and frightens it; and it is only to repeated trials that it surrenders, when one wants to make it adopt a better system of cultivation...
> We therefore propose to deliberate that various agricultural associations be established in the province, under the King's pleasure. Bringing together in each district, a certain number of enlightened men and skilled farmers, to confer together on the present state of culture, on the causes which make it languish, and on the means of putting it into force.

This report seems to be largely inspired by the pages of one of the most widely read books of its time: the *Histoire des deux Indes* by Abbé Raynal[29] in which the author stated as early as 1774 that "Agriculture was the first and true wealth of a state...". He developed his assertion[30]:

> It is the march of the human mind to return to the right path only when it has exhausted itself in wrong ways. It always goes forward; and as it

[29] On Raynal's biography we refer to our book, *Raynal ou le devoir de vérité*, Paris, Champion, 2004.

[30] G.T. Raynal, *Tableau de l'Europe*, 1774, L. 19 ch. VII. The passage will be repeated until the 1780 edition.

> started from agriculture to follow the career of commerce and luxury, it quickly goes round the circle, and finally finds itself in the cradle of all the arts.
> Everything, in fact, depends on and results from the cultivation of the land. It makes the inner strength of states; it attracts to them the riches of the outside world. Any power that comes from elsewhere than from the land is artificial and precarious, either in the physical or in the moral sense. Industry and commerce which are not exercised primarily on the agriculture of a country, are in the power of foreign nations... But a well-cleared, well-cultivated state produces men by the fruits of the earth, and wealth by men...
> The government therefore owes its protection to the countryside rather than to the cities... Wherever the nation is attached to its homeland by ownership, by the security of its funds, of its income, the land will flourish and prosper. Wherever the privileges are not for the cities and the drudgery for the countryside, we shall see each owner in love with the heritage of his fathers, increase and embellish it by assiduous cultivation, multiply his children in proportion to his goods, and his goods in proportion to his children.
> It is therefore in the interest of the government to favour the cultivators above all the idle classes of society. The nobility is only an odious distinction, when it is not based on real services. The clergy is only a profession at least sterile for the land...
> Favouring the arts and neglecting agriculture is like removing the stones from the foundations of a pyramid in order to raise the top...
> If the countryman does not enjoy in peace what he possesses and collects; if he cannot cultivate the virtues of his state, because they are taken away from him; if the militia, the corvée and the taxes, come to take away his son, his oxen, his grains... He will abandon his field and his country. A wise government cannot, therefore, without cutting its wrists, refuse its first attentions to agriculture.
> Indefinite freedom in the trade of commodities makes a people agricultural and commercial at the same time. The circulation of commodities truly brings about the golden age, when rivers of milk and honey flow through the countryside.

As early as 1784, the results obtained by the provincial assemblies were noticed by Necker, who paid tribute to its craftsmen in his work *De l'administration des finances de la France*[31]:

[31] Jacques Necker, *De l'administration des finances de la France*, Paris, 1785, II, p. 274.

> It is rare to combine so much love of the good, so much vigilance in doing it, and so many judicious views with that practical spirit, without which one only increases the list of those vain theories, which have never set in motion one of the smallest wheels of administration: wise institutions need only ordinary men, to become the source of the most interesting advantages in the public order...

Adding, with particular regard to the experimentation carried out in Rouergue:

> On the provincial administration established under my ministry in Haute-Guyenne... This generality, known under the name of Haute-Guyenne, since the time of the provincial administration which was established there in 1779, comprises Rouergue and Quercy. Its extent is 583 3/4 square leagues. Its population is 530,200 souls. That is 903 inhabitants per square league [...] Tribute to the President of this assembly, M. de Cicé, then bishop of Rodez, now archbishop of Bordeaux.

The experience and work of the Provincial Assembly of Haute-Guyenne was set as an example by the *Encyclopédie méthodique*[32] (to which Richeprey contributed),[33] which noted:

> There is hardly anyone else [sic] but them [the provincial assemblies] who can effectively spread enlightenment in the provinces and see to public instruction of all kinds. Their deliberations and the means they adopt to carry them out must therefore be carefully collected. It is moreover an honourable spectacle for the nation, and consoling for humanity, to see the spirit of benevolence no longer remain inactive in the souls of a few citizens; but to move large assemblies and direct their work towards the happiness of the most obscure and most interesting class of society.

The praise received by the Provincial Assembly, complimented from afar, met the ideas of the philosopher Raynal. This communion of ideas, which combined an innovative political and administrative organization with the

[32] *Encyclopédie méthodique. Jurisprudence*, t. 9. In Paris, chez Panckoucke, libraire, hôtel de Thou, rue des Poitevins. 1791 p. 94, note "accouchement".

[33] Richeprey "assiduously frequented the literary circles of Paris, the circles of the *Encyclopédie* and the Economists. One of his cousins introduced him to the bookseller Panckoucke [...] who appreciated him and asked him to collaborate on some of his numerous publications" (Guilhamon, op. cit., p. iii).

philosophical discourse of the *Histoire des deux Indes*, as well as the field of experimentation chosen, the territory of his native Rouergue, which had already benefited from his generosity,[34] were undoubtedly the causes of his commitment. It is not impossible to add to this the close links that the philosopher had with the instigators of the project, first and foremost minister Necker, with whom he always had "regular liaisons".[35]

As for Mgr Colbert, although we do not know, for lack of evidence, whether he had a direct relationship with the Abbé, their age difference—Raynal was 22 years older than him—leads us to believe that they did not frequent the same literary circles in the capital. Nevertheless, we know that the latter, like many ecclesiastics, possessed in his bishopric library the *Histoire philosophique et politique des établissements et du commerce des Européens dans les deux Indes*.[36]

Abbé Raynal's Action in Favour of the Provincial Academy

However, on 1 November 1788, Raynal wrote to Bishop Colbert of Rodez to inform him of his decision to support financially the institution he was presiding over.

> I have had a contract purchased, Monseigneur, for 1200 livres of perpetual annuity on the Hôtel-de-Ville of Paris. This aid, which rich farmers and large landowners would count for nothing, may be of some use when it is intended solely for farmers who themselves cultivate the inheritance which they received from their fathers, or which active industry has enabled them to acquire.
> My plan would be to divide the 1200 livres into twelve equal portions, and to give two, three, but never more, to the country people who have made themselves known by some praiseworthy action, by an extraordinary assiduity in work, by the beauty of their cattle, or by the perfection of their crops.

[34] "3 000 l. to the parish of Lapanouse which must be placed to give annually broths to the sick of the parish. The priest and two inhabitants chosen by the commune will preside over this distribution" (Copy of the will of G.T. Raynal 1791 private funds).

[35] Letter from Raynal to Angélique de Charrière de Sévery, 10 June 1784.

[36] G.T. Raynal, *Histoire philosophique et politique des établissements et du commerce des européens dans les deux Indes*, Geneva, Jean-Léonard Pellet, 1780, 10 vols. in 8°.

> These small encouragements, which would become honourable, could be accompanied by a medal: it would be possible that such an expedient would raise the spirits of those who are too downcast by misery.
> I beg you, Monseigneur, to offer on my behalf the property of the contract to the provincial Assembly of Haute-Guyenne. If it does me the grace of accepting this weak testimony of my zeal; it will be willing to reform in my ideas what will not be reconciled with its lights.
> All of Europe has applauded the sound and profound ideas which form a complete course of political economy in the minutes of the enlightened body over which you so happily preside. I am happy to have been born in a province which all the others have taken or will take as a model.
> I have the honour to be [ ] Raynal.

Raynal's letter was published in the *Journal de Paris*, 8 June 1789,[37] preceded by an announcement:

> Last year, M. l'abbé Raynal instituted three annual and perpetual prizes of 1200 livres each, one at the Académie Française, and the other two at the Académie des Sciences and the Académie des Inscriptions et Belles-Lettres. This year, he has made another kind of establishment; we will see what it consists of.[38]

In 1788, the Provincial Assembly of Haute-Guyenne accepted the said donation. The Intermediate Commission noted the decision in its reports[39] and referred the matter to the Royal Agricultural Society on 5 March 1789[40] in order to implement this foundation. The announcement was made by Mr Dailly, its correspondent:

[37] *Journal de Paris*, 8 June 1789, p. 718: 'Letter from M. l'abbé Raynal to M. l'évêque de Rodez, 1er November 1788.

[38] On the other prizes founded by Raynal, see our articles: [Henri Tachoire and Gilles Bancarel], "L'œuvre de Raynal une machine au service du progrès" in: *L'esprit en progrès*, Institut de France, Conférence Nationale des Académies, Paris, Akademos, 2013, p. 145–155.

[39] Observations of the Intermediate Commissioner of Haute-Guyenne, pages 41 and 42, read by the Secretary of the Society in the session of 5 March 1789: 'the famous Raynal cedes to the provincial administration of Haute-Guienne a contract for twenty-four thousand livres on the Hôtel de Ville de Paris, the interest of which was to be used annually to give incentives or rewards to the farmers who had distinguished themselves the most by works or processes relating to the improvement of agriculture'.

[40] *Mémoires d'agriculture, d'économie rurale et domestique*, Winter 1789, pp. VIII–XIII.

> One could count among the benefits of the Provincial Administration, the interest which this establishment has already inspired in the good Citizens in favour of all objects of public good; a sentiment of which M. l'Abbé Raynal has just given useful proof, by assigning to the Provincial Administration a contract of 24,000 l. on the Hôtel de ville de Paris[41], the interests of which must be annually employed to give encouragement or rewards to the Cultivators who will have distinguished themselves the most by works or processes relating to the improvement of Agriculture.

On this occasion, the Royal Agricultural Society, grateful for what Abbé Raynal has done to encourage agriculture in the Province of Haute-Guyenne, decided that he would be awarded a gold medal at the next public meeting, considering that:

> When one is capable of such sacrifices for the public good, one can only be sensitive to the impulses of honour and virtue; it is these which put us in the position of asking you to accept the token which the Society distributes in its Sessions to each of its Members. We would be very flattered to see such a distinguished and commendable Citizen in our Assemblies: may you long enjoy the fruit of your virtues, and the satisfaction of having cooperated so effectively in the progress of an Art so useful and so interesting for the good of humanity.[42]

Raynal's nomination as a member of the Royal Academy of Agriculture was transmitted to him by a letter from the Permanent Secretary[43] indicating that:

> The Government seems to be convinced at last that it owes its protection to the countryside rather than to the towns, and that the latter will flourish only through the fertility of the fields[44]. We already have some evidence of its happy dispositions in favour of the inhabitants of the countryside,

[41] This suggests that the amount has doubled in the past year.

[42] Royal Agricultural Society to Raynal of 5 March 1789. *Mémoires d'agriculture, d'économie rurale et domestique*, Winter 1789, pp. VIII–XIII.

[43] Pierre Marie Auguste Broussonet, Permanent Secretary of the Royal Agricultural Society to Raynal of 6 March 1789.

[44] G.T. Raynal, *Tableau de l'Europe*, The Hague, 1774, p. 194. On the comparison of this passage with the work of Claude Peyrot, see our study: "Le succès de Claude Peyrot à travers l'édition de ses œuvres" in: *Claude Peyrot poète occitan (1709–1795)* (colloque du bicentenaire Millau, 1995), Millau, Éditions du Beffroi, 1996, pp. 99–116.

most of whom have lost even the desire for a happier lot, and who will all believe that they have received a lot if what was taken from them is ever returned to them.

The wording of the Royal Society, which took up the very terms of the *History of the Two Indies*, had the value of recognition and symbol. This recognition was to be extended by the appointment of Raynal as an associate member of the Academy. This was accompanied by the award of a gold medal to the generous benefactor:

> The Society had announced that it would distribute, at this meeting, Gold Medals to persons who had distinguished themselves by the use of some new or little-known process which had contributed in an effective manner to the progress of Agriculture and to the welfare of the Farmers. These prizes were awarded as follows
>
> - To M. Vilmorin, Marchand Grenetier in Paris and Correspondent of the Society.
> - To M. l'Abbé Rozier, Correspondent of the Society in Lyon, author of several works on rural economy.
> - To Mr. Etienne Caillaux, Master Baker in Arpajon.
> - To M. l'Abbé Raynal, author of the Histoire philosophique des deux Indes, who has ceded to the provincial administration of Haute-Guyenne, a contract for twenty-four thousand livres, the interest on which is to be used annually to give encouragement to the farmers of the Province, who have distinguished themselves the most, by works or processes relating to the improvement of agriculture.
>
> The Society, sure to be contradicted by no one, awards this Prize to the Doyen of French Philosophers, in the name of all the friends of Agriculture and of humanity....[45]

The honorary prize awarded by the Agricultural Society on 28 December 1789,[46] "in the name of all friends of agriculture and humanity", was intended to further the founder's aims. The Society therefore decided to apply this gift to the distribution of the simplest, easiest-to-handle instruments, as close as possible to ordinary instruments. It proposed to involve

[45] *Mémoires d'agriculture, d'économie rurale et domestique*, Autumn, 1789, pp. IX–XI.

[46] *Mémoires d'agriculture*, 1789, op. cit. *History of the Royal Agricultural Society*, IV, p. xi.

the less well-off day labourers in this distribution and to have the agricultural implements it hoped to improve made in French factories. A vast survey was then opened by her, in the various parts of the Kingdom, to find out which were the most useful agricultural tools. This survey was the origin of a large collection intended to compare these instruments, to modify them and to give the mechanics of the time a new lease of life. In addition to the 1200 livres endowed by Abbé Raynal, the Society added 500 livres from the funds it had earmarked for the encouragement prize.

Announced in 1788, the foundation was only definitively established and published in 1789. The sum[47] was made available to the Société d'agriculture by Ferdinand Grand, Raynal's banker[48] and the Société took charge of implementing the competition, the deadline for which was set for the first of April 1791. The candidates had to produce a brief to answer the question:

> *Does a flourishing Agriculture have more influence on the prosperity of the Manufactures, than the increase of the Manufactures on the prosperity of the Agriculture?*[49]

In the spring of 1791, in the absence of satisfactory responses, the Agricultural Society responsible for awarding the prize stated in its report[50]:

> We therefore conclude that part of the sum of 1,200 livres destined for the distribution of agricultural instruments to the inhabitants of the countryside during the course of this year should be used for 1°. To the

[47] One can follow the evolution of the payments and the interests of the annuity in: *Compte rendu à la Société d'Agriculture de Paris, des travaux faits, commencés et projetés, depuis le 30 mai 1788, jusques et compris le 30 septembre 1793, an 3 de la République Françaises; et de l'emploi des fonds qui ont été mis à sa disposition pendant cet espace de temps*, par J.-L. Lefevre, son agent général, secrétaire par intérim. In Paris, year VII, pp. 22–23, 51–52, 153.

[48] Gilles Bancarel, "Raynal et le banquier Ferdinand Grand, une certaine dimension du réseau" in: *Raynal et ses réseaux*, textes réunis et présentés par Gilles Bancarel, Paris, Champion, 2011, pp. 247–266.

[49] *Mémoires d'agriculture, d'économie rurale et domestique*, Autumn 1789, p. XXI. The Prize was to be awarded in the public session of the same year (1791).

[50] Relevé dans les *Rapports fait à la Société royale d'Agriculture depuis le* 31 mars 1791, p. 86.

> necessary expenses for the plates on which Mr. Touroude's machine[51] and the various parts which compose it will be engraved, as well as to those of the printing of the speech which must contain the explanation. 2°. To the construction of a machine of the same size as the one submitted to our examination, which would be used for the first marsh draining that would be undertaken, and where it would be necessary.[52]

In May 1791, the Agricultural Society reported[53]:

> We would have liked the author to go into greater detail on the state of agriculture, to indicate the crops that could be promoted, as he only mentions artificial meadows which are lacking in these cantons, and we would have liked him to draw up a precise table of the agricultural practices and instruments used by farmers to enable the Society to know which would be most suitable for these departments in order to distribute them in accordance with the wishes of Abbé Raynal.

At the end of the deadline, the pieces sent to the competition having in no way fulfilled the conditions of the Programme, the Society allocated the sum given to it by the Abbé Raynal[54] to another prize. In the session of 13 October 1791, a new subject was proposed

> *To make known, by a very careful chemical analysis, the constituent principles of different soils compared with each other in relation to their products, to classify them according to their degree of goodness & to indicate at the same time the easiest method, the most accessible to Cultivators, to know the composition of different soils.*

[51] Touroude, a mechanic from Toulouse who worked for the Canal Royal du Languedoc, presented a memoir devoted to the invention of an "Archimedean screw, intended to dry out marshes, water meadows and drain foundations", *Mémoires d'agriculture, d'économie rurale et domestique*, Spring 1791, pp. 101–122.

[52] The report states: 'We think that if the Society adopts these conclusions, it will fulfil the purpose of the foundation on the one hand, and that on the other hand, giving new publicity to an action which essentially concerns agriculture, the source of an empire's wealth and the happiness of its inhabitants, will give rise to imitators, as one of the members of this company has observed'. *Reports made to the Royal Agricultural Society*, op. cit., p. 86.

[53] *Reports made to the Royal Agricultural Society*, op. cit., p. 99.

[54] *Mémoires d'agriculture, d'économie rurale et domestique*, 1791, Trimestre d'automne, 'séance du 13 octobre 1791' *Histoire de la Société royale d'Agriculture*, III, p. xxvi.

The Competitors will indicate the state of the land where they have taken the samples they have analysed; they will pay attention to the situation, to the fertilisers that have been spread on it, and to the plants that have been cultivated there previously; they will attach some of these samples to their writings. The Society, in proposing this question, wishes above all to engage the Scientists to make a sure application of Chemistry to one of the principal branches of Agriculture, and to put the Cultivators within reach of guiding their course by very simple procedures.
This prize, consisting of 1,200 livres or a gold medal of similar value, was awarded to the Society in 1789 by M. l'abbé Raynal.[55]

We do not know the outcome of this competition, the memoranda of which were to be received until 1er November 1793, and were disrupted by the course of history. Nevertheless, we can see the literary extension of this initiative in the works of Crèvecœur[56] and Arthur Young,[57] which were to take up this initiative in favour of agriculture. We find a link with the thinking that was to preside, around the same time, over the foundation of the collection of the Conservatoire des Arts et Métiers.[58]

We also find an extension of this on the artistic side in the work of the engraver Augustin Dupré.[59] The latter, chosen by Raynal, produced

[55] *Mémoires d'agriculture*, op. cit. *History of the Royal Agricultural Society*, V, p. xxxii.

[56] M.G.J. Crèvecœur, *Voyage dans la Haute Pennsylvanie et dans l'État de New York, depuis l'année 1785 jusqu'en 1798 par un membre adoptif de la nation Onéida*, translated and published by the author of *Lettres d'un cultivateur américain*, Paris, 1801, p. 247: "I was well aware that without a flourishing agriculture there could be no commerce; but never before had I observed in so obvious a manner how much a free export is necessary to excite and animate agricultural industry, and how much the rapid progress of our new settlements is due in part to the prosperous state of our maritime commerce…".

[57] Arthur Young, *Voyages en France en 1787, 1788 et 1789*, ed. H. Sée, Paris, 1931 III, pp. 986–989. Relevé dans *Sources d'histoire de la France moderne XVIe, XVIIe, XVIIIe siècle*, dir. J.F. Solnon, Paris, 1994, p. 669.

[58] L. Passy, *Histoire de la Société d'Agriculture de France*, Paris, 1912, I, pp. 293–295. The *Catalogue général des collections du conservatoire royal des arts et métiers*, Paris, 1818 does not mention Raynal's initiative. Dominique de Place, *L'incitation au progrès technique et industriel en France de 1783 à 1819 d'après les archives du CNAM*, Paris, EHESS, 1981.

[59] R. Trognan, Ph. Sorel, *Augustin Dupré (1748–1833) Graveur Général des Monnaies de France*, collections du Musée Carnavalet, Paris, 2000, p. 23, 157 n. 33.

in 1789 the medal[60] distributed to valorous farmers. It bears the inscription: "To the hardworking farmer" representing Guyenne personified by a woman (tourellée) holding the shield with the arms of her province (a leopard), placing a crown on the head of a farmer leaning on a plough. In the background, peasants are busy harvesting. On the reverse, in a wreath made up of sheaves of wheat and vine shoots, we read: "Prix d'agriculture fondé par G.T. Raynal, awarded by the Assembly of Haute-Guyenne".[61]

We have no knowledge of Bishop Colbert's reply to Abbé Raynal's letter of 1 November 1788. The year 1789 was to destroy their projects concerning the Provincial Assembly, which was to disappear definitively by a decree of 22 December 1789. Raynal's initiatives prolonged the memory of this ephemeral and emulating Assembly, which saw some of its attributions taken up again, after the birth of the departments, by the creation of the Agricultural Society of the department of Aveyron on 28 May 1798 (9 Prairial, Year VI).

In 1791, at the same time as the first prizes were being awarded from the foundation set up by Raynal, ecclesiastics were confronted with the implementation of the Civil Constitution of the Clergy. Bishop Colbert was dismissed in favour of the former parish priest of Laguiole, Debertier, who became a constitutional bishop.[62] To denounce this appointment, the bishop published an ordinance intended for all his faithful[63] dated 12 May 1791, in which he made himself the witness of the events:

> What havoc is not being wreaked at this time by the dreadful licentiousness we are witnessing? Were morals ever so corrupt as they are today?

[60] Probably because of their proximity during the philosopher's stay in Passy. cf. Gilles Bancarel, "L'abbé Raynal à Chaillot au n° 1 de la rue des Batailles", *Bulletin de la Société historique d'Auteuil et de Passy*, n°160 (2015), p. 4–9.

[61] Michel Hennin, *Histoire numismatique de la Révolution Française ou description raisonnée des médailles*, Paris, 1826, pp. 70–72. *Catalogue général illustré des éditions de la Monnaie de Paris* vol. I De l'Antiquité à Louis XVI, Paris, 1977, p. 315 (H). Note the similarity of this medal to the one produced by the engraver in 1781, dedicated to Daniel Morgan, hero of the Revolutionary War, in which the "American Indian" decorates his liberator with a crown.

[62] A.C. Sabatié, *Debertier, évêque constitutionnel et le clergé de Rodez*, Paris, 1912.

[63] Seignelay Colbert de Castlehill, *Mandement et ordonnance de M. l'Evêque de Rodez, au sujet de l'élection faite le 20 mars… de M… Berthier, parish priest of La Guyole, in the diocese of Rodez, by MM. the electors of the department of Aveyron, as bishop of the same department.* Paris [chez Brille], 1791 (pp. 3–4).

> The principles of justice and reason seem to be entirely forgotten or disregarded: there is neither order, nor reserve, nor respect for the public, nor property of any kind: the greatest dangers threaten religion in all parts of this unfortunate kingdom: look at the multiplied attacks directed against it by the errors, passions, and excesses of a misguided multitude; see how it is exposed and compromised by the very laws of the power that was supposed to protect it.

A few weeks later, on 31 May, the National Assembly read out the letter that Abbé Raynal had just sent to it[64]:

> Ready to leave this immense family whose happiness I have ardently desired, what do I see around me? Religious troubles, civil disputes, the consternation of some, the tyranny and audacity of others, a government enslaved by popular tyranny, the sanctuary of the laws surrounded by unbridled men who alternately want to dictate them or defy them; soldiers without discipline, chiefs without authority, ministers without means; a king, the first friend of his people, plunged into bitterness, outraged, threatened, stripped of all authority; and public power existing only in clubs where ignorant and rude men dare to pronounce on all political questions.

Just a few days after the consecration of the constitutional bishop Debertier[65] Raynal and Colbert had the same view of the course of events which was to engulf their efforts, after having provoked the resignation of the Mayor of Millau, Viscount de Bonald, a few months earlier.[66]

The first, defender of this institution which he had called for, belatedly measured the scope of his writings in the *History of the Two Indies* which was the bible of the Revolutionaries, by choosing to publicly

[64] *Address to the National Assembly*, read on 31 May 1791. Paris, Calixte Volland, 1791, 14 p. in 8°. See: Hans-Jürgen Lüsebrink, *L'Adresse à l'Assemblée Nationale (31 mai 1791) de Guillaume-Thomas Raynal: Positions, polémiques, répercussions*, Paris, Société française d'étude du XVIIIe siècle, 2018.

[65] Debertier was consecrated bishop at Notre Dame de Paris on 1 May 1791.

[66] Louis Gabriel Amboise de Bonald (1754–1840). Mayor of Millau on 6 June 1785, he received a civic crown from the commune on 2 September 1789. Re-elected on 19 February 1790, he became a member of the Departmental Assembly on 29 July 1790 and became its president on 9 August 1790. Hostile to the Civil Constitution of the Clergy he resigned and left France on 18 October 1791. See: Gilles Bancarel, "Une correspondance inédite de l'abbé Raynal au vicomte de Bonald", *Revue du Rouergue*, 63 (2000), pp. 485–490.

denounce the excesses of the new regime. The second, refusing to sign the Concordat and fiercely opposed to the installation of the "intruder" Debertier, swore "we must die rather than betray our principles". The philosopher lost his posterity, the bishop entered into resistance, becoming promoter of the *Little Church* and choosing exile, while Louis-Gabriel Amboise de Bonald was to establish himself as one of the major figures of the counter-revolution.[67]

[67] In 1796 Bonald published *Théorie du pouvoir politique et religieux dans la société civile, démontrée par le raisonnement et par l'histoire.*

CHAPTER 15

Comparison Between the Bishop of Rodez, S. Colbert de Castlehill, a Figure Ignored by Historians, and Abbé Sieyès, Icon of the Revolution

Christine Fauré

Abstract Two ecclesiastics, members of the High Clergy or initiated into its administration, became involved in the Revolution in 1789: Seignelay Colbert de Castlehill, former Grand Vicar of the Archbishop of Toulouse, Loménie de Brienne, then Bishop of Rodez; Abbé Sieyès (1748–1836), Grand Vicar of Lubersac, Bishop of Chartres, author in 1788–1789 of the famous Qu'est-ce que le Tiers État? They took part in the provincial states of their regions, respectively Haute-Guyenne and Orléanais. They met in Versailles on 22 June 1789 shortly before the transformation of the General Estates into the National Assembly. On the same day, Bishop

English revised by Timothy R. Day.

C. Fauré (✉)
Centre National de la Recherche Scientifique, Paris, France
e-mail: faure.christine2@wanadoo.fr

A. Alcouffe (ed.), *Seignelay Colbert de Castlehill (1735-1811)*,
https://doi.org/10.1007/978-3-031-75273-5_15

Colbert of Castlehill joined the Third Estate. Sieyès, although belonging to the Clergy, was elected in extremis deputy of the Tiers of Paris, a rare case for a religious. Both became deputies to the Constituent Assembly and, although their arguments differed, they both defended the tithe, that hated tax paid to the clergy, and with what arguments. They had in common an abstract and geometrical conception of the administrative division of the kingdom: they wanted to rationalise the administration of the country for the sake of better communication between administrators and citizens, without taking into account the singularity of the land and the landscape. This Enlightenment conception was not shared by all the Constituents, far from it. They each developed and adhered to a philosophy of natural law that sometimes intertwined with the idea of the happiness of civil and political societies.

The thirteen years separating Colbert from Sieyès his junior, the fact that Colbert did not prolong his stay in France and his participation in the revolution, explain their difference in the implementation of natural law. Colbert chose religion and Sieyès the art of governing to which he was enjoined by events.

Colbert was a man of the Enlightenment, like Sieyès, whose actions constitute a link between the ideas of emancipation and their revolutionary application.

Keywords Provincial Assembly · Colbert de Castlehill · Abbé Sieyès · Vingtième · General Estates · Tithe · Natural law · Sensualist · Jurie Constitutionnaire

The comparison between Seignelay Colbert de Castlehill, Bishop of Rodez, and Sieyès, the famous revolutionary, is not gratuitous. Colbert was born in Scotland in Inverness in 1735 and Sieyès in Fréjus in 1748. Between the life of a young Scottish nobleman sent to France and that of the revolutionary of modest extraction, there are many similarities. The ecclesiastical condition brought them together: Colbert was tonsured in Paris in 1752, ordained a priest in 1762 and appointed, in 1763, vicar general of the archbishop of Toulouse, Loménie de Brienne. From 1781 to 1790, presided over the Provincial Assembly of Haute-Guyenne.

Sieyès, who showed no trace of religious conviction, was tonsured in 1765 when he entered the *Petit Séminaire de Saint Sulpice* in Paris; he was awarded a Master of Arts degree on 3 August 1770[1] at the Sorbonne. He benefited from the support of several protectors: the abbé Meffray de Césargues, vicar general of the diocese of Fréjus, beneficiary of the liberality of his father Honoré Sieyès, then the support of Jean-Baptiste-Joseph de Lubersac, chaplain to the king, a figure of the high clergy called to the bishopric of Tréguier and who was a liberal spirit. He took Sieyès by his side as secretary. Sieyès stayed in Tréguier for short periods; in 1779, he became chaplain to Madame Sophie, daughter of Louis XV. In 1783, Sieyès became vicar general in Chartres, still in the wake of Lubersac. During his stay, he held two important administrative positions: commissioner appointed by the diocese to the Sovereign Chamber of the Clergy of France (14 August 1786); from 1787 to 1788, he represented his order, the Clergy, at the Provincial Assembly of Orléans.[2] His sinuous career therefore contrasts with that of Abbé Colbert.

The Royal Reform

The provincial assemblies provided an opportunity to meet important men. Sieyès was a member of two Bureaux[3]: the *Bureau du bien public et de l'agriculture* and the *Comité pour les vingtièmes*; he was also a member of intermediate Commissions.

Colbert, in his capacity as bishop of Rodez, after Jérôme Champion de Cicé had been appointed archbishop of Bordeaux in January 1781, presided over the opening sessions of the Provincial Assembly of Haute-Guyenne. This new administrative unit opened on 20 August 1779 in Villefranche, being at an equal distance from Rodez, Cahors and Montauban. Several *Bureaux* were created for the *taille*, for the *vingtièmes*, for the *capitation*, and the charity funds as well as the *Bureaux du règlement*, *des grands chemins* and *des Affaires extraordinaires et du bien public*.[4]

[1] Paul Bastid, *Sieyès et sa pensée*, Paris, 1939—Geneva, Slatkine Reprints, 1978, p. 28.

[2] Ibid., p. 41: At the end of the Ancien Régime, there were eight sovereign ecclesiastical chambers: Paris, Rouen, Lyon, Tours, Toulouse, Bordeaux, Aix and Bourges. That of Paris included 18 dioceses, including Chartres.

[3] Orléans Media Library, Minutes of the sessions of the Orléans Provincial Assembly, held in Orléans on 6 September 1787 (H 38).

[4] Gérard Boscary, *Assemblée provinciale de Haute-Guyenne, 1779–1790*, thesis for the doctorate in law, 1932, p. 40.

Seignelay Colbert de Castlehill put all his talent as a conciliator at the service of this Assembly from 1781 until its disappearance in 1790. In order to carry out the repair of the land register, the Provincial Assembly sent a young geometric engineer from Paris, Henri de Richeprey, who had collaborated in the *Encyclopédie* as editor of the article *Imposition*. In 1785, Richeprey left the province and went to Cayenne to exploit a property owned by Lafayette in order to try out the gradual emancipation of slaves. He died prematurely in 1787 at the age of 36. Colbert, who had already made a name for himself by his calming interventions on behalf of the archbishop of Toulouse during the epizootic[5] (an epidemic that struck animals) of 1775, showed great optimism and undeniable diplomatic qualities in Haute-Guyenne. For example, he lifted the ban on publishing the minutes of the 1782 Assemblies and had them printed because there were many conflicts between the Intendant and the Provincial Assembly (Letter from Colbert to Calonne dated 30 September 1784[6]). Colbert's progressivism was also evident in the project to establish child birthing classes in Haute-Guyenne: "It was decided that 24 doctors would be chosen who, in return for a payment of 100 livres, would undertake to provide free care to women of little means".[7] In his diocese of Toulouse, Loménie de Brienne also instituted a free annual course in 1784 for the training of midwives, mainly from the countryside.[8]

Colbert's project was less a question of tax remission than of a general vivification of the province (Colbert's intervention at the end of 1785 gave rise to numerous discussions between Colbert and Calonne). The numerous letters which Colbert sent are nowadays shared between his different interlocutors. The Archives of Rodez hold part of the correspondence between the bishop and the procurators general. Montauban also holds some of these exchanges of letters, for example on the duties imposed on the *innkeepers*. The minutes of the sessions of the Provincial

[5] Claude DEVIC (dom), Joseph VAISSETTE (dom), *Histoire générale du Languedoc*, tome 13ème, Privat, Toulouse, 1877, p. 1265.

[6] Gérard BOSCARY, op. cit., p. 98.

[7] Gérard BOSCARY, ibid., p. 102.

[8] Pierre DAUGA, *Un Prélat politique à la fin de l'Ancien régime: Loménie de Brienne*, thesis for the doctorate in law under the direction of André Cabanis, defended on 16 May 2020 (Atelier National de Reproduction des Thèses, ANRT).

See also Abbé Gentil CORMARY, *Loménie de Brienne à Toulouse, 1763–1788*, Albi, Ginestet, 1935.

Assembly, held in November and December 1786, mention remarkable reports "on the reserved rights, the great roads, the bridges and roads and navigation, the workshops of charity, the woollen animals, the stud farms, the warehouse of the wines in Bordeaux, the mines, on the public courses on child birthing, on the chair of mathematics at the College of Montauban, on the project of the nobility of the province, the general improvements (interruption of the clearing, access to the mineral fountains), the quality of the horned animals and finally, on the regulation concerning the disputes of competence which arose between the intendant and the intermediate Commission and which related to the execution of the Regulation of 1782; with a Report on the product of the harvests devastated in particular by the "hail and the ravines" and finally with a Report on the accountancy between the overtaxed, the less taxed, on the discharges and moderations of the *capitation* and the *vingtième*".[9] All these reports are signed by the bishop of Rodez and Galtié, the secretary-archivist who belonged to the order of the third state.

The role of the Intermediate Commission was also very important in the functioning of the Provincial Administration between sessions. The bishop of Rodez was also a member. Faced with Charles-Alexandre de Calonne, Controller General of Finances from 1783 to 1787, a friend of the *economists* who appointed Dupont de Nemours as State Councillor and Director of Commerce, Colbert had to fight in 1784 against the royal power which seemed to want to reduce the powers of the Provincial Administration. In 1782, he had to fight to have the minutes of the session printed against the advice of the Intendant Meulan d'Ablois, who was appointed in 1780 and who was creating difficulties in Paris, and also against Daniel de Trimond, the very last Intendant appointed.[10] These reports, informative as they are, give us no idea of the discussion between the members of the Assembly. They are the subject of several redactions from documents which are still in the Departmental Archives of Aveyron

[9] *Procès-verbal des séances de l'Assemblée provinciale de Haute-Guyenne, tenues à Villefranche dans les mois de novembre et décembre*, Paris, Crapart, 1787, pp. 52–113. The vingtième, introduced in 1749, was to be one-twentieth of annual income (5%), collected directly by the government. capitation, major direct tax in France before the Revolution of 1789, first established in 1695 as a wartime measure. Originally, the capitation was to be paid by every subject, the amount varying according to class NdT.

[10] Gérard Boscary, op. cit., pp. 90, 96.

and Lot,[11] but we do not know the position that each one defends. All contradictions and oppositions have been erased from the minutes.

The Provincial Assembly of Orléans, in which Abbé Sieyès and Lubersac participated, seems to be richer in information to us. Sieyès was a member of the *Comité du vingtième*, a tax for which a subscription system was to be established: this was a fixed, lump sum that the province undertook to pay to the Royal Treasury. The abbé de Cézargues and Lubersac, who were the successive protectors of Sieyès, were part of this Committee of the *vingtième* with the count of Rochambeau: "November 19, 1787, the merits of the subscription are bitterly discussed there. Ask the provinces that have subscribed since 1756 and obtained this precious advantage, they will tell you the immense sums they have saved and the rest they have enjoyed".[12] Sieyès was also part of the Intermediate Commission to represent the clergy; the chemist Lavoisier represented the third estate. But it appears that Sieyès' presence was intermittent. According to Lavoisier's correspondence, the latter had entered into discussions with Sieyès: "Several of these reflections are good", wrote Lavoisier on 16 May 1788, "But they could have been presented in a more moderate way. All in all, this work needs to be redone".[13]

The aim of this project, drafted by Sieyès, was to achieve "a fair and proportional distribution between the various owners"[14] by means of subscriptions. In the edition of *Lavoisier's Correspondence*, we learn some scandalous facts from Grimaux: the Duke of Luxembourg paid nothing, the baron of Montboissier was under-taxed in relation to the value of his property. With the Committee of the vingtième, the Duke of Luxembourg, President of the Committee and the baron of Montboissier pronounced themselves against the subscription of the *vingtième*. On the other hand, Sieyès, Lubersac and the count of Rochambeau pronounced themselves for it. Sieyès thus embraced a more just popular cause.

[11] Archives départementales du Lot, Série C; Archives départementales de l'Aveyron, Série C-1546 à 1590, *in* Boscary, op. cit., pp. 411, 413.

[12] Médiathèque d'Orléans, H 38, one of the 25 copies of the special print run ordered by the interim commission of the Provincial Assembly of Orléans, 23 October 1787, 13ème session of Friday 20 November 1787.

[13] Édouard Grimaux, *Lavoisier, 1743–1794, d'après sa correspondance, ses manuscrits et ses papiers de famille*, Paris, Alcan, 1899, p. 174.

[14] Médiathèque d'Orléans, op. cit., n°11-1326, pp. 193–194.

The General Estates

The election of Colbert to the General Estates was certainly easy. No comments were made about his election by the clergy of the *bailliages* of Rodez and Millau.[15]

Abbé Sieyès, on the other hand, suffered some setbacks. He was not elected in Montfort-l'Amaury where two priests had won. He took no part to the redaction of the *cahiers de doléances* of the clergy. Moreover, he seems to have given up being the elected representative of the Clergy and decided to represent the Third Estate in Paris. In extremis, on 19 May 1789—the General Estates had opened on 5 May—he succeeded. He was narrowly elected on the 3rd ballot by 127 votes out of 247. His election was challenged without success. In the whole of France, there were only two other clergymen appointed by the Third Estate.

Bishop Colbert did not sign the *Oath of the Real Tennis Room*. For Paris, Sieyès is cited as a signatory.[16]

Sieyès appeared as a divisive figure from the opening of the General Estates. However, according to the English traveller Arthur Young, Colbert and Sieyès met at the home of the Duc de la Rochefoucauld-Liancourt: "On the 21st of June, dinner with the Duc de Liancourt at the palace; a numerous company of nobles and deputies of the communes and among them, the Duc d'Orléans, the Bishop of Rodez, the Abbé Sieyès and Mr Rabaud Saint-Étienne".[17] Young then notes the physiognomy of Abbé Sieyès, his intense curiosity, the mobility of his face and his great prudence. The insignificance of Rabaud Saint-Étienne, despite his undeniable talents, is obvious to him. He said nothing about Colbert, whose manners must have been in keeping with the customs of the time. The presence of the Duc d'Orléans at this Assembly was hardly surprising; he prided himself on representing the new ideas. Sieyès was part of the duke's entourage, although in his much later notice on himself (1795), he denies any proximity to the Duc d'Orléans.

[15] Armand Brette, *Recueil de documents relatifs à la convocation des états généraux de 1789*, by Armand Brette, tome I, Paris, Imprimerie nationale, 1904, p. 481.

[16] Armand Brette, Facsimile of the text and signatures according to the minutes of the manuscript kept in the Archives Nationales, Paris, 1893.

[17] Arthur Young, *Voyage en France, translation, introduction and note by Henri Sée*, Paris, 1931, Tallandier 2009, p. 299.

On 19 June 1789, the clergy asked themselves the following question: "Will the credentials be verified in common in the general hall or will they be verified separately?" The following decree was adopted: "The plurality of the assembled clergy is of the opinion that the final verification of the powers be made in the General Assembly subject to the distinction of the orders and reserved of right". In the list of the plurality of the members of the clergy[18] appear in particular Champion de Cicé, the bishop of Bordeaux, Lubersac, the bishop of Chartres and Colbert de Seignelay, the bishop of Rodez—*sénéchaussée* of Rodez.[19] In the examination of 19 June 1789 by the communes, Sieyès intervened so that one may take account of the modifications which he had made with the text. He seems to have shown an exceptional vigilance; he took the floor to impose himself.

Did Colbert become known as one of the seven bishops who started the movement to bring the orders together? This initiative would have given Colbert great popularity. It is said that he was carried in triumph through the streets of Versailles on 25 June. But this event is not mentioned in the *Moniteur*, in the *Archives parlementaires* or even in Edna Hindie Lemay's *Dictionnaire des constituants*. It is found in Hoefer's *Nouvelle Biographie générale*[20] and then in the *Dictionnaire des parlementaires français*.[21] But on what sources are these biographical notes based? In Buchez and Roux's *Histoire parlementaire de la révolution* and in Thiers's *Histoire de la révolution française*, both of which Hoefer refers to, the day of 25 June 1789 is devoted to the attack on the Bishop of Paris, and the episode of Colbert's triumph at Versailles is not mentioned.

On the other hand, Claude-François Beaulieu, born Claude-Benoît Pioche, a journalist and supporter of the constitutional monarchy, wrote in his *Nouvelles de Versailles* of Thursday 25 June: "The bishop of

[18] *Archives parlementaires* (MM. MAVIDAL, LAURENT, CLAVEAU, PIONNIER, LATASTE et BARBIER), 1ère series, tome 8, pp. 131–134.

[19] The *sénéchaussée* was the area of jurisdiction of a seneschal, an administrative division of *Ancien Régime* France.

[20] Jean-Chrétien-Ferdinand HOEFER, *Nouvelle Biographie générale*, Tome 11, Paris, Didot frères, 1855.

[21] *Dictionnaire des parlementaires français…: depuis le 1er mai 1789 jusqu'au 1er mai 1889*, sous la dir. de MM. Adolphe ROBERT, Adolphe BOURLOTON et Gaston COUGNY, Paris, Bourloton, 1889–1891.

Rodez, whose pastoral virtues are extolled, on his way to the home of Monseigneur l'archevêque de Paris, was taken away by the people, who showered him with blessings: They never wanted to allow him to enter the hotel; his Grandeur was carried in his arms with the greatest respect and was deposited in the neighbouring shop".[22] This abduction, which at first seemed to protect Colbert from any violence, was not a triumph: Was it part of an apologetic construction to accredit the fine role of the high clergy in the first moments of the revolution?

On the Ecclesiastical Tithe in the Constituent Assembly

Colbert and Sieyès took part in the debate on Article 7 on tithes in the project relating to the abolition of privileges, during the session of 10 August 1789.

Colbert wanted to maintain the tithe: "Because of religion and the decency of worship and as a property of the poor".[23] His speech was not transcribed and published in the *Archives Parlementaires*, perhaps because it did not meet the demands of the time. Nevertheless, Sieyès followed suit and took up Article 7 of the Drafting Committee: "The tithes in kind, ecclesiastical, secular and infeudated, could be converted into pecuniary royalties and redeemed at the will of the taxpayers according to the proportion which will be regulated, either by mutual agreement, or by the law, except for the reinvestment to be made by the decimators if it is necessary".[24]

But the tithe was not a tax like any other; removing it would enrich the landlord and condemned the church staff to starvation. Sieyès thus proposed the following wording: "All tithes will be redeemable in kind or in money, by mutual agreement between the communities and the decimators or according to the method which will be fixed by the National Assembly and the price of the redemption of the ecclesiastical tithes will be converted into assured incomes, to be employed in compliance with the law with their true destination".[25]

[22] Thanks to Alain Alcouffe for finding this reference.

[23] *Parliamentary Archives*, Volume 8, 10 August evening, p. 387.

[24] Ibid., p. 387.

[25] Ibid., p. 389.

The question of the tithe paid to the clergy was important in the eyes of Sieyès. One finds there the ecclesiastical administrator that he was before the Revolution; also Sieyès devoted "to the ecclesiastical goods… summary observations" which enriched what he has just said in his speech with the Assembly.

As at other times in his revolutionary career, Sieyès took paradoxical attitudes. He supported the thesis of the redemption of the tithe, the price of the redemption having to be allocated to the maintenance of the ecclesiastical service, which aroused the opinion of the Constituent Assembly against him. The divergences between the thought of Sieyès and the revolution in the course of the events arrived very early: "The people with prejudices blamed me for attacking the privileges. Today, they blame me for defending property… They serve the reigning prejudice".[26] Sieyès was not a gregarious person; his independence manifested itself in spite of pressure from coteries, as when Thomas Payne,[27] under the influence of Condorcet, enjoined him to defend the republican cause and Sieyès seized the opportunity in July 1791 to side, despite the risks, with a non-hereditary and idealised monarchy.

A Common Culture: The Administrative Division of the Territory

In the first moments of the Constituent Assembly, Sieyès' rhetorical superiority shone through.

Colbert, although a man of the *Enlightenment* who had distinguished himself in the management of the Provincial Assembly of Haute-Guyenne, did not find his feet in the Constituent Assembly. He did not seem to be gifted with an exceptional capacity for eloquence, and was ill at ease in the turmoil of the debates. The simple invocation of tradition was no longer acceptable in this early state of the revolution. To rally to the third party was not enough; it was necessary from now on to a violent, brutal public opinion, resentful. As for Sieyès, he turned the revolution into an obstacle course. His assessment of the situation, his audacity as well as his reserve, allowed him to express himself and to survive the events until the return of the Bourbons, under whose reign he went into

[26] *Summary observations on ecclesiastical property of 10 August 1789*, p. 13.

[27] Thomas Payne, English revolutionary, 1737–1809.

exile in Brussels. He had voted for the death of the King. During the Jacobin takeover, he took refuge and made himself forgotten at Madame Helvétius's home in Auteuil. As for Colbert, of Scottish origin, he chose exile in England.

Of the few appearances that Colbert made at the Constituent Assembly, appearances retained by Lemay's *Dictionnaire des Constituants*, there was one where he expressed a positive opinion on the administrative division of the kingdom.

He supported the establishment of the canton in these terms: "There are few regions of an extent of 4 square leagues where there is not a dwelling suitable to form a chief town and where there are not enough educated people who, enlightened by a direct correspondence with the Assembly of departments, are in a position to fulfil the functions which would be entrusted to them. I consequently regard the establishment of the cantons as very practicable and very useful" (12 November 1789).[28]

This is the expression of Colbert's former experience as an administrator of the Provincial Assembly of Haute-Guyenne, which was in charge of repairing the land register. As a practical man, he wanted to rationalise the administration of the territory in the interests of better communication between administrators and the people. In the Provincial Assembly, he had confronted the "effects of the love of independence and the desire to exercise some empire". In line with the spirit of the Constituent Assembly, he defended the general interest against the wills and interests of individuals admitting no reply. He had a taste for topography, equal to that which Sieyès mentions in his *Discourse on the royal veto* (7 September 1789).[29]

Sieyès defended the need to present to the Assembly "a plan of municipality and province such that one could hope not to see the Kingdom torn into a multitude of small states in republican form".[30] In his reflections on municipal power, he drew inspiration from the treatises on topography that he had read, such as that of Robert de Hesseln, "Censeur Royal" (Paris, 1780). In his very extensive archives, which he never wanted to publish during his lifetime and which are held in the National Archives,

28 Parliamentary Archives, 12 November 1789, p. 6. The square league is approximatively 15 km^2 NdT.

29 On 12 November 1789, Sieyès did not participate in the discussion.

30 *Dires de l'abbé Sieyès sur la question du veto royal, 7 September 1789*, Paris, Baudouin, p. 32.

Sieyès wrote: "I call a canton a territorial area of 4 square leagues, there will be 9 in each commune".[31]

The distribution of populations on the national territory was of great concern to the Constituents. Sieyès returned to the question on several occasions from a perspective that was fairly comparable to that of Colbert. His perception was strictly geographical and on the cantons, he writes: "One must take care that the last subdivisions which the committee calls cantons could not without disadvantage be of more than 4 square leagues".[32] All the Constituents, Barère de Vieuzac and Mirabeau in particular, did not adhere to this abstract and geometric vision of a territorial administration that did not take into account the diversity of the terrain and landscapes.

Natural Law and Perpetual Peace

Despite the thirteen years that separated the two men, the cultural universe from which they drew was the same. In 1770, Colbert tried his hand at a now classic exercise with his work *Les éléments du droit de la nature et de la morale naturelle (The Elements of the Law of Nature and Natural Morals)*[33] after the great works of the *jus naturalis* jurisconsults such as Grotius, Pufendorf and Burlamaqui. Colbert quotes them on page XXXI. The tone he adopts is resolutely optimistic and his confidence in the talents of man is unwavering: "Angels of peace, it is your talents, your virtues, your courage duly employed and joined to the docility and submission of the people, which give constancy to Society, which bind it and ensure its happiness and rest".[34] This introduction marks Colbert's orientation of natural law: the search for happiness. In the Index, he reserves eight entries for the word happiness: natural happiness; individual natural happiness; moral happiness; easy, quick, assured happiness; general

[31] "Delineamens politiques", 4ème, *in Des Manuscrits de Sieyès, 1773–1799*, edited by Christine Fauré, Paris, Champion, 1999, p. 367.

[32] *Emmanuel Sieyès, Écrits politiques, selection and presentation by Roberto* Zapperi, Contemporary Archives edition, Geneva, 1985–1994, pp. 250–251.

[33] *Les Éléments du droit de la nature et de la morale naturelle by Monsieur le Baron de C.*, at Basle, MDCCLXX.

[34] "To the Civilised and Policed Nations of Europe" in ibid., p. XVI.

happiness; present, remote, hidden happiness; future happiness; happiness of civil and political societies.[35]

The equality of men from the point of view of their constitution and their destination resounds loud and clear: "one can say that all (men) are naturally equal".[36] Equality of property, like happiness, is measured "in proportion to the work of each man and to the way in which he will direct and measure this work".[37] The question of tyrannicide and that of resistance to oppression is not addressed by Colbert, who is decidedly more of a rationalist philosopher than a revolutionary.

Colbert wrote and published a second work in 1782 entitled *Projet d'un traité de paix générale et perpétuelle en Europe*[38] with an "Address to Louis XVI". In it, he set out his moral and political views on "the right and interest of the Christian nations of Europe and all their subjects". He wanted to alert the King to the state of crisis which "the essential rights of man, the liberty and peace of Europe, of each state and of each individual" were in. Did Colbert have diplomatic ambitions? Did he want to be an adviser to the King on foreign affairs? He signed his proposal in May 1782. This "Address to the King" is followed by "Preliminary Explanations" consisting of three chapters and forming a total of fifty-two pages.

Along Colbert, "convenience and greed" have been the main driving forces behind the actions of rulers and vassals. The overthrow of Empires and the extinction of the original possessors ignore the laws of humanity. "They instituted a situation of violence and persecution".[39] From this disunity arose "anarchy… in public or common law… dissensions, wars, calamities, ruins, great bloodshed".[40] Colbert thus concludes that nations and the individuals who compose them enjoy the same fate. He always maintains this parallel. Thus, a rule of conduct must be instituted, which he defines as follows: "Mutual tolerance of natural freedom of action",

[35] Ibid., Table, p. 229.

[36] Ibid., Book I, chap. XX, p. 44.

[37] Ibid., Book I, Chapter XVII, p. 39.

[38] *Projet d'un traité de paix générale et perpétuelle entre les différentes puissances chrétiennes de l'Europe, précédé d'explications préliminaires par M le Baron de Colbert de Castlehill,* sne, mai 1782.

[39] Ibid., "Preliminary explanations", pp. 1–5.

[40] Ibid., p. 6.

as already stated in the *Decalogue*. He announces that he will devote a special treatise to the principle of the law of nature.[41] This great work does not seem to have been done, perhaps interrupted by other urgencies linked to his function as bishop caught up in the royal reform or by the Revolution.

He goes on to say, "I considered finally that by taking the war outside against the enemies of the Christian name"[42]... thus he proposes in fact a kind of crusade regulated by a "wise, just and beneficent law".

Chapter II is devoted to the summary principles of the law of nature and people: "To give a slight idea of the effective influence of this law on the happiness of men".[43] It provides lengthy developments on a "portrait of man in the whole of his nature... to satisfy his needs and effect his happiness".[44] The reference to the savages of America,[45] who have never ceased to haunt dissertations on natural law, serves as a counterpoint to civilised man. Hobbes, Machiavelli and their followers "do not admit of natural rules of law and natural law of conduct for sovereigns".[46]

Colbert attempts a difficult synthesis between a *fixist* philosophy of natural law and the conduct it inspires, and a discourse on the accidental circumstances of history which open the way to conquest. The union between nations that he proposes on the basis of their mutual interest is an analogy with that of men in political society.

Chapter III (which is the last) returns to the national dimension and the description of its government. The constitution of a political society composed of a great multitude of individuals puts in place checks, conventions and stable hierarchies; the Christian nations of Europe imitate and perpetuate this organisation.

Colbert followed in the footsteps of the Abbé de Saint-Pierre who, in 1713, at the end of the warlike reign of Louis XIV, wrote a *Treaty of*

[41] Ibid., chapter II, p. 16.
[42] Ibid., chapter I, p. 14.
[43] Ibid., chapter II, p. 15.
[44] Ibid., chapter II, p. 16.
[45] Ibid., chapter II, p. 19.
[46] Ibid., chapter II, p. 22.

Perpetual Peace.[47] Alerted by the great misery of the people and by the excessive violence exercised by the sovereigns through continuous wars, the Abbé de Saint-Pierre did not magnify savage societies without law or stability. He was therefore doing *real politik* and examining the balance of power as it exists.[48]

Colbert, in his *Address to the King*, writes "May 1782". Is this a sign of Rousseau's influence on the bishop? Let us remark that Rousseau's notes on the Abbé de Saint-Pierre were published originally in Geneva in 1782 in the complete works edited by Moultou and du Peyrou.[49] Rousseau with regard to the natural man who aspires to rest and tranquillity does not talk of happiness[50] without limits, as Colbert did in all ingenuity: "The limits..." writes Colbert "... allow me to lay down here the great principles, only of the law of nature; to give a slight idea of the effective influence of this law on the happiness of the men whom it has as its object; to make then, by analogy, the application of it to the nations of Europe in their encounters, disentanglements of interest and negotiations together, to mark in the same way the influence of this law on their happiness and to deduce from it the law of nations or of people".[51]

Colbert seems to have shifted from the search for happiness through natural law, already announced in his previous treatise, to a very fin-de-siècle hedonistic impulse which characterises the revolutionary period. Rousseau was of a completely different perspective.

Sieyès, like Colbert, was also a follower of natural law, although professors of public law in the twentieth century saw him as a precursor of contemporary constitutional law: "This modern meaning of the notion of constitution had already been fully perceived and clearly specified by Sieyès at a time when, however, the conceptions of the school of natural law still prevailed in this respect", wrote the publicist Raymond Carré

[47] Charles-Irénée CASTEL de SAINT-PIERRE (abbé), *Projet pour rendre la paix perpétuelle en Europe*, à Utrecht chez Antoine Schouten marchand-libraire, 1713, Paris, Fayard/Corpus des œuvres de philosophie en langue française, 1986.

[48] Charles-Irénée CASTEL de SAINT-PIERRE (abbé), *Interest de chaque souverain en particulier de signer un traité de police durable et d'arbitrage permanent, «Venise»*, p. 570.

[49] Ibid., "Notes and Variations", p. 1551.

[50] Robert DERATHÉ: "In the state of nature, there can be no competition between men for whom happiness is reduced to a sense of physical well-being", in ibid., p. 1557.

[51] COLBERT de CASTLEHILL, *Preliminary explanations*, op. cit. chapter 2, pp. 15–16.

de Malberg in the 1920s.[52] Paul Bastid, the first biographer of Sieyès, claimed that "Sieyès remains the most authentic promoter of the constitutional principles on which we still live".[53] The important thing at the time seemed to be to extract Sieyès from this current of natural law, guilty of political niaiserie and incapable of founding and guaranteeing rights. However, in the sensualist line opened by Condillac, Sieyès, at a very young age, praised individual enjoyment: "To avoid pain and to enjoy, these are the principles of all man's actions. It would be advantageous for him to know the possible means of doing both, and thus he would achieve the greatest possible happiness".[54]

This search for happiness and the means to achieve it is essential in Sieyès' political thought. It links him to the literature of the 1760s, which he had read extensively in his youth. The works of Jean-Henri Samuel Formey (1711–1797), secretary of the Berlin Academy, are at the top of the list of reference works cited by Sieyès in his carefully compiled "Bibliography", which contains more than 200 handwritten pages.[55] *Le Temple du bonheur ou recueil des plus excellents traités sur le bonheur, extraits des meilleurs auteurs anciens et modernes*, attributed by Barbier to L. Castilhon, who is cited three times in Sieyès's selection, includes, in addition to texts by Formey and Castilhon, extracts from *La Vie heureuse* translated from Seneca by La Mettrie and two speeches by Maximus of Tyre translated by Formey. Sieyès, in his "Bibliographies", shows himself to be a lover of natural sciences; he draws heavily on chapter 3 of Gilbert Burnet's *Défense de la religion tant naturelle que révélée*, Tome IV, The Hague, 1738—this chapter 3 corresponded to the physical theory of William Derham (1657–1735), which had appeared in English in 1713, a work that has been republished twelve times in 50 years and translated

[52] Raymond Carré De Malberg, *Contribution à la théorie générale de l'État*, Paris, Sirey, 1920–1922, Volume 2, p. 573.

[53] Paul Bastid, 1939. Volume 2. p. 626. See Christine Fauré, "Actualité de Sieyès selon Bastid", *in* "Sieyès, Rousseau et la théorie du contrat", *Figures de Sieyès* (ed. Denis, Quiviger, Salem), Paris, Publications de la Sorbonne, 2008, p. 223.

[54] Sieyès, "Le Grand cahier métaphysique", manuscript and notes, archival documents written around 1773 in the wake of his critique of Condillac. In *Des Manuscrits de Sieyès, 1773–1799*, under the direction of Christine Fauré with the collaboration of Jacques Guilhaumou and Jacques Valier, Paris, Champion, 1999, p. 96.

[55] "Les Bibliographies de Sieyès", *in Des Manuscrits de Sieyès, 1770–1815*, Tome 2, edited by Christine Fauré, Paris, Champion, 2007.

into several languages.[56] William Derham was a naturalist philosopher, minister of the Church of England and President of St. John's College, Oxford. In contrast, Sieyès, in his selection of books, quotes very little from *the Encyclopédie*.[57]

Throughout his career, the abbé, in his legislative activity, never lost his confidence in natural law. He treated as heretics of natural law, among others, Hobbes, the author of *Leviathan*, Bayle, the author of the *Critical Dictionary*, Mandeville and his *Fable of the Bees* and finally Montaigne with his *Essays*.[58]

Sieyès's fame, which did not wane until the Empire, was due to his role as a constitution-maker par excellence, in tune with the aspirations of the revolutionary people. Edmund Burke, the English politician (1727–1797), in a letter to a Lord, mocked Sieyès and his fondness for constitutions: "Abbé Sieyès whole nests of pigeon-holes full of constitutions ready-made, ticketed, sorted, and numbered; suited to every season and every fancy; some with the top of the pattern at the bottom, and some with the bottom at the top; some plain, some flowered".[59] From this quasi-manic activity, we will retain only the discussion on the Constitution of Year III. It seems to us the most fertile on the subject and anchored in a certain political urgency. It was a question of the Convention providing itself with a new Constitution and it was on this occasion that he made two major speeches on 2 and 18 Thermidor III. These speeches remained largely misunderstood by his contemporaries, who were disconcerted by his formulas. Thus he said in his first speech "In terms of government and more generally in terms of political constitution, unity alone is despotic, division alone is anarchy: division with unity gives the social guarantee without which all freedom is only precarious".[60] Sieyès drew several pictures to show how he imagined this political movement: "Upward action, downward action", the primary Assemblies of the

[56] Ibid., p. 111, note 177.

[57] Françoise Weil "Présentation des bibliographies de Sieyès", *in Des Manuscrits de Sieyès*, ibid., p. 80.

[58] Ibid., p. 156, footnote 387–389.

[59] Edmund Burke, *Letter to a Noble Lord*, London, 1796, p. 44.

[60] "Opinion de Sieyès sur plusieurs articles des titres IV et V du projet de Constitution prononcé à la Convention le 2 Thermidor de l'An IIIème de la république, imprimé par ordre de la Convention nationale", *in Œuvres de Sieyès*, EDHIS, Paris, 1989, p. 3.

Nation are the starting point, the end point is the people reaping the benefits of the law.[61]

"I know of only two systems of division of powers: the system of balance and that of competition or, in more or less similar terms, the system of counterweights and that of organised unity".[62] Sieyès opts for that of organised unity, he rejects everything that brings to mind the English Constitution and its counterbalances; in the process, he asks for the formation of a *constitutional jury*: "It is a body of representatives that I ask with special mission to judge the complaints against all the attacks which will be brought to the Constitution... Do you want to give a safeguard to the Constitution, a salutary brake which contains each representative action within the limits of its special power of attorney, establish a *jurie constitutionnaire* [constitutional court tNdT]; its necessity is so palpable that I pass at once to my second request".[63] Sieyès based his political-constitutional system on the idea of the division of labour that characterises modernity, hence his attraction to the work of Adam Smith.[64] After the Jacobin experience and its despotic drifts, the existence of this elected body, enigmatically called the *Jurie Constitutionaire*, whose purpose is to control the conformity of laws to the principles of liberty and equality borne by citizens, was necessary. But the *jurie consitutionnaire*, in all of Sieyès' drawings, is surmounted by the rights of man and citizen, which indicates an unchanged hierarchy of values despite constant alterations. The rights of man are always mentioned and Sieyès gave them a constitutive force. He writes in his *Manuscripts*:

1. Declaration of rights (common to all men existing on the territory, common to all domiciled, common to every citizen to ensure all his rights, a complete public establishment is necessary from which
2. the French constitution or organisation of the public establishment, organised establishment.[65]

[61] In *Manuscrits de Sieyès*, Tome 2, ibid., op. cit., p. 531. See Drawing in Annex, p. 331.

[62] *1er Speech, 2 Thermidor l'AN II*, ibid., op. cit., p. 4.

[63] Ibid., p. 11.

[64] Pasquale PASQUINO, *Sieyès et l'invention en France de la Constitution*, Paris, Odile Jacob, 1998.

[65] *Des Manuscrits de Sieyès, 1770–1815*, Tome 2, op. cit. "Discussion sur la Constitution de l'An III", p. 514.

This constitutional moment, which is very important for understanding Sieyès, did not make him forget individual human rights.

His *Jurie Constitutionnaire* comes to us partly from Harrington (1611–1677), the English author of *Oceana* (1656).[66] It was simply in Year III that Sieyès decided to reveal himself; perhaps he had been afraid in 1789 that his *jurie Constitutionnaire* would look too much like a power of notables?

What Does the Comparison Between Colbert and Sieyès Bring Us?

Colbert, who was 13 years older than Sieyès, put all his know-how into the royal reform to smooth out the abuses of the monarchy and its fiscal disorder. The Revolution caught him in the midst of his activities in the Provincial Assembly of Haute-Guyenne, which survived until 1790. He displayed an extraordinary energy and epistolary art; he seemed very attached to his friends and his surroundings. We can consider that he left revolutionary France in May 1792, less for doctrinal reasons related to the civil constitution of the clergy voted in 1790 than for social reasons. Like Loménie de Brienne, his mentor, he was unable to bear the revolutionary violence which henceforth marked the relationships of life in society, from which politeness and respect for titles were banished. For him, nobility implied responsibilities from which he never shirked. To the ecclesiastical administrator, he added the civility he found in the customs of the salons. In 1775 he was still in correspondence with Mme du Deffand, who was one of the great supporters of the young Étienne-Charles de Loménie de Brienne.[67]

Sieyès, on the other hand, was a silent man, with an awkward eloquence. Although he made many speeches, they were always accompanied by a publication published within the framework of the *Assemblées de la Révolution*. His political work, from *Qu'est-ce que le tiers-état?* (1788–1789), a major work at the time, to the Discourses of Year III, did not

[66] Christine Faure, "Harrington, une source méconnue du bon gouvernement selon Sieyès (1748–1836)", *in Philosophical Enquiries, revue des philosophies anglophones*, n°8, June 2017.

[67] Letter from the abbé de Colbert to Mme du Deffand, Toulouse, 7 June 1775—letter communicated by Sue Walker, librarian at Yale University, in charge of the Walpole collection.

further evolve. In the 1770s, he started from a body of knowledge gathered through a large number of readings, of which his "Bibliographies" give us a valuable insight. This does not mean, however, that he had read all the books he cited. Nevertheless, we can consider that his main interests were already there: Spinoza, Harrington, natural law, natural sciences, Greek and Latin philosophers, his taste for English authors. It is known that one could read little during the Revolution, so great was the pressure of events. It was the time of pamphlets and Sieyès excelled in short formats. He would use this sum of knowledge as a reserve that he intended to keep secret. Throughout his life, despite numerous requests, he stubbornly refused to publish his archives, which had been lost and then found at the end of the 1960s. This rediscovery, after two centuries, considerably alters his intellectual portrait. He appears more clearly as a man of the *Enlightenment* and his attempt to feed the political current of the Revolution with a culture that goes beyond it has been little understood by the historians interested in him. His singularity seemed enigmatic, but his ability to use powerful formulas ensured him an unparalleled popularity during the Revolution. His work constitutes a link between the *Enlightenment* and the revolutionary period, usually considered as a radical political fracture—which brings him closer to Colbert.

January 2021

Annex: Sieyès' Drawing. cf. Footnote 65

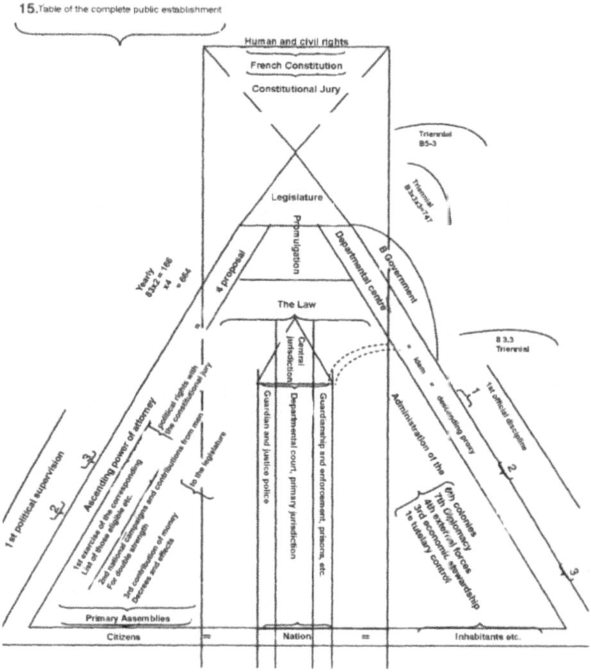

CHAPTER 16

How Patriotism Is a Toulousain Affair…

Maïté Bouyssy

Abstract Maïté Bouyssy is interested in Bertrand Barère. Born in Tarbes in 1755, he became a lawyer at the Parliament in 1775. Her contribution is based on the clues that Bertrand Barère gave in the academic eulogies of his time in Toulouse. Under the aegis of the two great prelates, Loménie de Brienne and Castlehill, Barère tried to place himself in circles that would take him out of the anonymity of the basoche. The set of references and dedicatees of Barère's academic eulogies, discreetly show what he owes them, the course of praising "great men", the then emerging notion of models and the thought of the law concretely forged one of the dimensions of the notion of "national" and "patrie". And one discovers to what extent not only the Philanthropy Committee of the Encyclopaedic Lodge brought together all the youthful forces of the city of Toulouse to set up a local administration, set up a system for defending the innocent who were unable to pay the costs of justice (against the venality of offices). It developed a sense of the authority of the State as guarantor of religious tolerance. Turgotine and Catholic Enlightenment currents of

M. Bouyssy (✉)
Centre de recherches en histoire du XIXe siècle, Université de Paris 1 Panthéon-Sorbonne, Paris, France
e-mail: Bouyssy@orange.fr

A. Alcouffe (ed.), *Seignelay Colbert de Castlehill (1735-1811)*,
https://doi.org/10.1007/978-3-031-75273-5_16

thought were taken up by the Constituante, particularly in the face of the emergency, which immediately led to the creation of the Committee of Subsistence, one of whose first drafters was Bertrand Barère.

Keywords Barère · Loménie de Brienne · Lefranc de Pompignan · Toulouse · "Patrie" · Basoche · Academic eulogies · "Great men" · "Good government" · Religious tolerance · Philanthropy · Indigent relief · Clergy

As a specialist in Barère's writings rather than just in his political career, I can only wonder at the fertile Toulousian soil of the 1780s from which first sprouted the tender shoots of his writing, even though in the shadow of other famous locals: Loménie de Brienne was a major figure in the literary landscape, as was Colbert de Castlehill from the time he was bishop of Rodez and presided over the provincial assembly of Haute-Guyenne. It was here in Toulouse that a vocabulary developed in which the term *patrie* (homeland) came to be used to symbolise the public interest. Neither this term, however, nor yet the divergent positions of these great prelates feature again in 1790 during the debates on the Civil Constitution of the Clergy. Within Barère's observations in his newspaper *Le Point du Jour,* it is not possible to identify the divergent positions of these senior figures, who were reforming administrators, sensitive to misfortune and all too aware of the abuses in the Church of France, just as much as they were of the social problem of begging. Barère (always eager to embrace a good new idea) produced a more viable and articulate strategy than his rather conventional pieces of rhetoric would suggest.

Let us compare him with two other figures. The first is Seignelay Colbert de Castlehill, (1735–1811) who was vicar-general to Loménie de Brienne. He became bishop of Rodez in 1781, and thus president of the provincial assembly of Haute-Guyenne (i.e. Quercy and Rouergue); the second figure is Loménie de Brienne (1727–1794), called to his political destiny as Chief Minister in 1787, had been archbishop of Toulouse since 1763. He was an aristocrat who often chaired major commissions of the national assemblies of the clergy and a member of the Académie française since 1770. The addresses of the speeches under the mask and the civility of the academic eulogies and the choice of emblematic figures to whom crowns are woven in order to affirm a present of shared values are allegiances to Brienne, a figure as powerful as he was enlightened, and also at Montauban, the second place of Barère's philosophical practices, a way of approaching Castlehill according to thought and thinkable possibilities, established or in the making.

The unmasked encomiast flags up his support and the way in which he chooses to show off his talents attracts the attention of Norbert Elias, no less, for the "Mozart case".[1] The glass ceiling that kept the provincial *basoche* (assembly of lawyers) in their place as second-rank Enlightenment figures invites us to wonder about Barère's own journey in search of a role. He found the path that allowed him to become a significant voice; the spokesperson of Committee of Public Safety. No genius, Barère allowed himself a decent period of training in order to be able to remain part of the Revolution, with a real ability to take charge of situations arising from the most difficult of circumstances.

When Barère went to Paris in 1788, he soon found himself taken up by Orleanist circles. This must mean that Barère had behaved in a way not determined by the usual social norms among the clique of the gownsmen lawyers. This would have meant that academic eulogies were used to build networks of chosen relationships, which were also reciprocal within a whole range of possibilities. Axes differed according to different institutional standpoints, and these too spanned a field of choices which were more political than ideological, driven by particular personalities and geographical location. And within that system, Toulouse was a capital city which also had its provinces.

Barère remains a stranger to the worldly games of versification. He does not dream of anacreontic odes or libertine tales, and his muses are not those which often nourished a wealthier pen. His *thirst for eloquence* is a serious style which allows him to develop his thought processes on necessary subjects and which in turn allows him to develop a solid sense of l*a patrie*: a frequently recurring term used when public interest for a place, a territory, a community or a political end is at stake.

As far as distinction is concerned, in both senses of the word (an honour and an acknowledgement of academic prowess) this worthy man of letters can also claim to be a philosopher as the term was understood at the time: a man devoted to the public good. This was the obligatory route

[1] Elias Norbert. 1993. *Mozart: Portrait of a Genius*. Berkeley: University of California Press.

taken by a whole generation of talented lawyers who had their moment of glory during the Revolution, although they hardly ever appeared in provincial academic circles. In Daniel Roche's statistics for the 1780s, these societies offered 618 prizes for a population that was undoubtedly over-served by an abundance of 6000 lawyers (of whom only 2,000 remained at the end of the Empire).[2] In Toulouse, the *basoche* was 250 strong and Barère confessed (in his *Mémoires* and on several occasions in his papers in the departmental archives of the Hautes-Pyrénées, now the ADHP) that this was the only way out of obscurity for anyone who, without being of low birth, was still not sufficiently high-born to get on in professional life. Belonging to a society, as this was called, was less membership of a philosophical society such as the Freemasons, whom Barère never particularly supported after his initiation, but more a *salon* which evolved into a pressure group in a world where favour decided opportunity. Getting to know the discreet cabals that drive (or claim to drive) public opinion did not mean that these cabals then controlled him; it was a necessary evil to allow him the full rights of citizenship.

This article aims to provide a new and provisional overview of Enlightenment figures in Toulouse in the 1780s, drawing on the contributions of Michel Taillefer, *La jeunesse toulousaine de Barère, 1772–1788* and a chapter by Jean-Pierre Thomas in *Barère la voix de la Révolution*, in which Toulouse makes almost no appearance at all.[3] Various specific investigations led me to look at his memoranda and pleadings and his bold undertakings at Betz Park, the estate of the Princess of Monaco, on the same day that Loménie was dismissed, in August 1788.[4] This is the

[2] See Daniel ROCHE, *Le siècle des Lumières en province, Académies et académiciens provinciaux, 1680–1789*, Mouton, Paris-LaHaye, 1978 and Lenard Berlanstein, *The Barristers of Toulouse in the 18th Century, 1740–1793*, Baltimore, 1975.

[3] Michel TAILLEFER, ibid. in Maïté BOUYSSY et alii, *Bertrand Barère (1755–1841)*, ed GuillaumeMauran, pp. 23–34, 2012 and the chapter by Jean-Pierre THOMAS, *Barère la voix de la Révolution,* Desjonquères,1989, "Monsieur de Vieuzac sait son monde", pp. 27–41, where Toulouse appears even less in Barère's first biographer, Robert LAUNAY, *Bertrand Barère, L'Anacréon de la guillotine*, Paris, Taillandier, 1929, reed.,1989.

[4] Maïté BOUYSSY, "Publication of an unpublished text by Bertrand Barère, *Promenades pittoresques dans le parc et jardin de Betz,* rédigées en forme de lettres par Bertrand Barère", *Polia, Revue de l'art des Jardins*, n°6, 2007, pp. 101–139, with a critical presentation: "Un philosophe moral dans le parc de Betz: la promenade de Bertrand Barère en 1788", pp. 89–99.

moment I have dubbed Barère's *political troubadour* period, where hob-nobbing with the aristocratic elite would enable him to forge relationships that would be crucial to fulfilling his destiny. His eulogy of this English park and its owner shows how Barère worked up his texts, and still sees him using a laborious, layered and formulaic approach, purely for effect.

At the same time, what is more, Loménie de Brienne and his cathedral chapter crossed paths with a number of significant figures even before they were seized with revolutionary fervour. They probably differed less in terms of ideology, even if their ideological differences are stressed when presented within the context of the French Revolution as a phenomenon unique in its ideological framework, which the French Revolution is indeed. Those men actually involved however experienced this for real and positioned themselves within a framework nurtured by similar convictions but from contrasting standpoints and viewpoints.

Among the personalities of the aristocratic prelates of the Ancien Régime, some at the pinnacle of power and honours and others nurturing rather more ordinary talents, the chief concern was that of conflict inspired on a religious pretext. No less predominant, if less vocal, however, were their concerns about paupers and begging in the countryside, and these were considered in tandem with abuses of taxation, a vast subject. In the lands of the General Estates and its sub-committees, people tried their hand at philanthropy, and everyone wanted to believe in the benefits of roads and canals. Public utility became a pressingly *patriotic* need, while the sanctity of religion was preserved, if not reserved. The question of justice and fairer taxation linked these subjects, long before the question of the organisation of the Church of France shattered the unified foundations for the shaping of the concept of nationhood—summed up in the phrase *la patrie*.

The Glory of Letters and Knowing Its World, a Game of Clues

Barère's academic eulogies shed light on the local resonance of national themes and their particular ramifications. This autonomy of appropriation through amplification cannot fail to imply possible routes from Toulouse to Paris via Montauban and Bordeaux. His celebrating certain figures and crediting them with an action in a ministerial capacity at the time reveals the extent of Barère's plagiarism in anticipation of his own vocabulary of political power, a vocabulary which was to fuel his career. Indeed, his path leads from eulogy to eulogy; from a dream of limited power with his eulogy of Louis XII, through a personal belief in general laws that would make systemic abuses transparent, to the invention of the supreme word *Patrie*, the title he used as a code with which to anonymise his eulogies of Montesquieu at the Académie de Bordeaux. The facts are clear: Barère had spent the whole decade pondering the unresolved facts and debates from which then emerged the French Revolution.

Michel Taillefer has identified Barère's professional memberships from his writings and actions: the Museum of Toulouse in 1784, the Royal Academy of Sciences, Inscriptions and Belles-Lettres of Toulouse in 1787 and finally the Academy of Floral Games in 1788, which forgot to invite him back when it resumed its work under the Empire, and where, in 1806, as a discreet reminder, he republished his eulogies. He was also a corresponding member of the Académie des Belles-Lettres in Montauban in 1787. All in all, it is a small but honourable contribution. On the other hand, the unusual nature of these contributions can be read not between the lines, but in terms of what happened next, if not at the time: in these we find clues about his search for a place within the field of those anointed for their work. It is therefore necessary to point out the stumbling block that was the national context here, an echo of the possible meaning of his earlier attempts to attract favour, his retreat into the printed word when he could not take part in the official accounts due to his lack of social legitimacy. This ability to speak out in spite of everything will subsequently constitute Barère's greatest strength when he finds himself excluded from the public arena; it will afford him the possibility of continuing to think, to assert his position and to brush up his analyses when excluded from political action. Before any major recognition came his way, he had learned to speak out and believed in doing so, in the debate of ideas, one might say; in his own words: "while the philosophical centuries prove harmful to poetry, they are in turn just as favourable to eloquence".

Barère's first writings coincided with the setting up of the provincial assemblies by Necker, who had just been dismissed. There was one for Haute-Guyenne, which brought together Rouergue and Quercy, as the *generalité* of Montauban previously did. Henceforth, the return to the fundamentals of civil peace, which Rousseau redefined in terms of the Social Contract, dominated the cameral sciences. Montesquieu's success was essential at a time when Calonne and then Brienne were no longer able to resolve the financial crisis, a crisis then succeeded by that of the Parliament and Lamoignon's Courts of Justice. An analysis of the speeches' content reveals that alliances were dismissed or forged which were sometimes not born simply of the silence of an age adept at reading between cryptic lines. Barère attributed two-thirds of his bold audacities in his speeches to the way Montesquieu structured his writings.

With his eulogy of Louis XII (1462–1515), Barère is in search of the good prince, a weak sovereign, a real *loser*, yet the paragon of everything one could want from a more amiable and enlightened despot.[5] This singular monarch knew nothing but personal setbacks and military failures, but his claim to fame was because of something else: he was sensitive, he wept at the misfortunes of his people, and we all know that the gift of tears is a royal virtue. In addition, he convened the General Estates in Blois in 1506 and was described as the Father of the People.

It was 1781–1782 that Necker was dismissed and a plea would doubtless have been made in favour of the sovereign, Louis XVI. The question of the treasury and economies came up again and again, and this Louis XII was seen as miserly, so even if he was drawn into costly wars, it was in spite of himself—and Turgot refused to commit the French treasury in supporting the Americans anyway.

Let us not speak of the sentimental setbacks of Louis XII, who was married for 22 years to a sterile Claude de France; he respected her and only divorced her for reasons of state and in order to marry Anne of Brittany, to whom he permitted just as much autonomy. If we have any feeling for these two ladies, it is very much in terms of the "Queen's party" with which Loménie de Brienne is associated, and without doubt, the prelate of Toulouse can be praised too. The Académie Française then asked for praise for the same monarch but all the same, Louis XII re-emerged from the disarray which provoked the libels which accompanied the successive dismissals of the ministers Vergennes, Calonne and Brienne.

The old institutions of Toulouse, the *Parlement* and the *Capitoulat*, which exist in close complicity, preserve the local autonomy of the city. Thus, when Barère honoured a great jurist of national stature, Furgole (1690–1761), who had been Chief Minister of the *Capitoulat*, he also delivered his eulogy from an autonomous standpoint at the closing session of the Conférence de Charité on 6 September 1783, a creation to which

[5] In *Gaston de Foix, 1512–2012*, ed. J. Barreto, C. Nativel, G. Quaranta, Publications de la Sorbonne, 2015, Maïté Bouyssy, "Gaston de Foix ou le couronnement du roi loser", pp. 97–114.

he had greatly contributed. At the opening on 9 March, Gez (1700–1792) defined its purpose as "A charitable institution formed at the Parliament of Toulouse". Charged with writing reports, consultations and the public defence of indigent or unfortunate litigants in either civil or criminal cases".

The *basoche* was able to make its mark under the enlightened complicity of Parliament but, as a footnote, a line almost hidden within the *Conciliateur*, a text more or less attributed to Turgot, but which we will come back to later and which was in reality written by Loménie indicates and alludes to a respect for religious convictions, a guarantee of civil peace, a certainty which led to Protestants being given civil status as early as 1787 but which had divided much earlier debates.

If praise of Cardinal Georges d'Amboise (1460–1510), a faithful friend of his king, can also be a kind of confirmation that the prince's true friend, a cardinal, would be some kind of Loménie, someone who was not yet a cardinal, but concerned above all with appeasing society. The logic is possible and even probable, as with praise for Chancellor Séguier, another faithful and energetic servant within the context of the Fronde, the year before, under Vergennes, in the face of the *forcenés*—maniacs—of the Parlement. Once again, a liaison between Michel de l'Hôpital and d'Aguesseau is alleged in order to repair what a foreigner, Mazarin—or Necker? had done through a *ténébreuse*—shadowy—administration with devastating consequences.

After a time of seeking tolerance and praising mediators, as Leo Gershoy, the first academic to have worked on Barère, put it, the time came to think as a philosopher, and so to start to look again at Rousseau and Montesquieu, with sensitivity and the cameral sciences (economy, policy-making and finance) becoming everyone's concern. Eulogy followed eulogy, and the rewards, while not major, meant that this kind of recognition became expected of Barère.

This path, which began with an apology from a prince as the father of his people, conforms precisely to what was hoped for in a Louis XVI remodelled by pre-romantic sensibility. This shifted the focus from concern for the common good of administrators and politicians to the affirmation of a community which questioned the public interest. In this context, Brienne's shadow did indeed exist in terms of a political pole in opposition to the parliamentary world of Toulouse. There again Castlehill's less detectable shadow functioned just as clearly, before both men disappeared from Barère's horizon, as positions became entrenched.

Opinion campaigns in which light-hearted words concealed darker meanings became experiments in the tilting-yard of power. From then on, convictions operated according to precise legal protocols, and Barère's good fortune was to benefit from a *happy ending* that had to do with the ladies and the Orléans, the milieu he discovered and into which he introduced himself by leaving for Betz on the very day of Brienne's downfall on 25 August 1788. From then on, Rousseauism, freedom and the rejection of feudal memories created a troubadour style, with a touch of Toulouse about it, to this last political gasp of the Ancien Régime, that of the *Promenades au parc de Betz*.[6]

Beyond Toulouse: A Bigourdan in Search of a Position

It was the thought of the law, but in a Catholic monarchy, and with the desire to preserve civil peace that became the focus of the appearances of a man who had come from his (county of) Bigorre without any prior registration or useful contacts in the Toulouse *milieu*. Barère always welcomed the legal reorganisation necessary to modernise the mechanism of the state, and on three occasions he referred to the general ordinance of 1498, the first model for simplifying jurisprudence in order to increase transparency, combat abuse and unify the law. On the other hand, making justice accessible to all is a slow-burn affair, and working at this is to be commended. There is, however, a second very sensitive issue, that of abolishing the venality of offices.

Choosing Furgole (1690–1761) to remind the Capitouls of the high price of justice, since the aim of the Conference of Charity was to help just causes that could not be heard due to a lack of financial resources, also meant using a modest and competent man as a model, because of his indifference to "corrupting wealth". Barère attacked hard:

> *Merit has no need of ancestors [...] what are these vain distinctions between one man and another when it comes to knowledge and virtue; I leave it to*

[6] Maïté Bouyssy, "Publication... op. cit., pp. 89–99. These letters, minutes and finished form a bundle of 50 sheets ADHP, F116 (210 × 170). The stylistic formatting is based on formulas for effect. They make it possible to observe Barère's working methods and his writing before 1789, cf in *Annales du Midi*, April 1993, t. 105, n° 202, Maïté Bouyssy, "Stratégie d'écriture et pré romantisme, Bertrand Barère en 1788", pp. 247–261.

these slaves of vanity, all occupied with their genealogy, to tell you about the origins of Furgole.

This expert advocate who wrote supplements and authorised responses to d'Aguesseau was poor, stayed poor and if he became Capitoul, it was at the suggestion of the nation. In a final note, Barère mentions, *in cauda venenum*, that he was not born in Toulouse, but in Armagnac, in Castelferrus, and that many other famous Toulouse names were not born *intra muros* either. A citizen is one who lives and contributes his talents to the city, so *la patrie* is there, hovering in the background and claiming its right to exist!

Furgole wrote a *Treatise on Wills and Donations* (1745–1748), which was printed three times, and then worked on the so-called primitive curates:

"He wanted to uncover the odious and singular origin of this kind of regular ministers of the 8th century, who abandoned their monasteries to take up pastoral duties, and who, since then, replaced within the Rule, have given the church the dangerous example of riches without work, parish priests without functions, and perpetual vicars who are more necessary and less fortunate" [...] "altering curial and episcopal jurisdiction".

This indictment led to the exploration of what remained beyond the reach of feudal practices induced by his *Traité de la Seigneurie Féodale Universelle et du Franc-Alleu Naturel*[7] in 1767. Barère was not the least bit worried by the recomposition of facts that proceeded from discursive logic and, another bold move, it was only in a footnote that he ventured to point out that Helvétius had questioned the benefits of wills. Furgole, who was highly respected, like Charles Dumoulin (1500–1566), was more famous after his death than during his lifetime, no doubt because of his modesty. Dumoulin theorised about Gallicanism and ended up declaring himself a Lutheran, a strange evolution.

Little is known about the work of Furgole, a profound scholar with a "fair and broad mind" who was "somehow seduced by Roman law" (sic) after learning French law. Due to a feeble constitution, weakly constituted, this lawyer gave up pleading such cases as "Target, Elie

[7] https://gallica.bnf.fr/ark:/12148/bpt6k9681140n# (Treatise on the universal feudal lordship and the natural fee allod).

de Beaumont, Jamme, Gari"—an allusion that everyone understood, as they had just contributed to the success of Damade, the bourgeois from Castillon (Castillon-la-Bataille, near Libourne), who had been molested and provoked in the street by former officers and an infantry captain in the Marmande regiment. This defamation case was heard in Bordeaux and Toulouse, and had a huge knock-on effect, as the merchant was compensated to the tune of £80,000, and the opposing party, who was as high-born as he was quarrelsome, was ordered to pay the costs.

This portrait of the expert advocate conjures up a pantheon of the Bar and the judiciary which leaves the glories of Toulouse in the shade, for what must be noted is the explicit positioning that Barère's choices represent. No pretext makes him quote the generally famous local pantheon for the first XVIIe century. Nor is there any trace of the last compilers of the eighteenth century, Vedel, Aguier, or de Soulatges who, in 1784, republished Olive's *Questions notables* with simple updates of the great ordinances of Colbert and Aguesseau. Toulousan jurisprudence is certainly conformist, but among its practitioners, Jean de Lapomarède de Laviguerie (1737–1829), called in 1774 to the Maupeou Parliament, could have been included. This magistracy is undoubtedly routine and its faculty of law decrepit compared with the competition of the Parisian bookstore and its dictionaries of law, but especially the choice Barère makes is deliberately, national and political.[8]

On the other hand, Barère cites Pothier or Jean-Baptiste-Jacques Elie de Beaumont, who was a lawyer from a Norman Protestant family, author of a *Mémoire pour les enfants de Calas*, a corresponding member of the Académie de Bordeaux and Treasurer to the Comte d'Artois. Gerbier of the Paris Bar (1725–1788) also appears; he rallied to Maupeou's parliament, an action the meaning of which is fading and becoming less divisive; but above all, he was prosecuted by Linguet, without acquitting himself with the same firmness as Target, who was also cited, and who was dubbed by Beaumarchais "the Virgin of the palace".[9] Armand

[8] See for the general framework, Th. GOURAT, *Les mémoires judiciaires des avocats au Parlement de Toulouse, (1770–1790)*, Toulouse Le Mirail, 1999 besides Michel TAILLEFER «Les avocats dans les sociétés savantes et les loges de l'époque des Lumières», pp. 181–196, in *L'histoire des avocats et du barreau de Toulouse*, éd. J.-L. Gazzaniga, Toulouse, 1992.

[9] The ambassador in London attacked Gerbier for affairs set up by the irascible Linguet, so much so that he left the palace in 1775 and took up a post as Intendant des finances

Gaston Camus (1740–1804) appears at this time, whose widely used and really successful *Lettres sur la profession d'avocat,* enriched with "livres utiles à un avocet"—works useful for a lawyer—was published in 1772 and 1774 by Méquignon in Paris He also wrote on the subject of the matrimonial code, on harmonious inheritance, and on vicars and their rights (Desaint, 1776). Camus also worked for the General Chapter of the Congregation of Saint-Maur, as did Alexandre Auguste Jammes (1736–1818), who studied at the Collège de l'Esquille with the Doctrinaires and who also practised in Tarbes. Jammes excelled very early in his career at praising his teachers in Latin and French. A regular at the Floral Games, this verbally dextrous, literary jurist, advocate to *Monsieur* later defended the city of Toulouse and its Parliament against Lamoignon, and was proclaimed a "chevalier ès lois" along with Gary, for their *Lettre des avocats du Parlement de Toulouse à monsieur le garde des sceaux pour le maintien des droits et privilèges de la ville et de la province.* They returned triumphant from a delegation sent to Paris led by Du Bourg. They were honoured with a medal bearing the inscription *orator patriae.* This Pierre Alexandre Gary (1736–1819), referred to by Barère, came from Cahors, where his father was a member of the Haut-Quercy Presidial Council. He became Capitoul and then, in 1771, Head of the Consistory (the municipal administration of Toulouse). A good orator, a man of integrity and a skilled advocate, he returned to private life in 1789. These middle-class characters, whose average wealth was £20,000, according to Berlanstein, really got stuck into jurisprudence and Barère anointed them as his own. As was his wont, and as what happened next would show, he was able to watch the dynamics at play, and he knew how to position himself among his compatriots from the provinces, the outskirts of Languedoc and the minor ranks of the legal world, but who would, even so, be named *oratores patriae* first for their homeland before they get their hour of national glory.

de Monsieur. Voltaire saw in his *Memoirs*, published at the time, a man who "runs only after the truth". He became President of the Bar in 1787, but the Académie Française admitted no other lawyer than Target (and later Cardinal Maury).

Justice, but Without the Venality of Office

The only bold claims made by this first incarnation of Barère concern the venality of office and although the line he takes in each of his elogies is strong and forceful, he goes so far as to associate it, with some artifice and even if only in a footnote, it is true, with an indication of Montesquieu's support for his position.[10] This is not true, but in 1788 it must have felt necessary in anti-parliamentary polemics. In each of his speeches from the *Praise of Louis XII* to that of Amboise, via those of Furgole and Séguier, the line recurs, without question. For the beginning of Louis XII's reign, he notes:

"The courts were few in number or closed for part of the year. Finally, justice was rife with abuses and dangers, but the venality of offices had not yet added its weight to these offences" (p. 15), although he must concede that he accepted: "an innovation that would have been fatal to justice and to posterity. The same year that offered the rare spectacle of a declaration of war and a tax reduction also offered the example of the venality of offices" (p. 30) and the note specifies:

> He sold royal offices. After him, François 1er sold twenty offices of councillor in the Parliament of Paris; the following year, he sold thirty in the Parliaments of the provinces and soon, they were all allocated according to finance.

Two years later, the *Éloge d'Amboise* reasserts

> You yourself wanted to erase the traces of this odious venality.

And note 12, the place devolved into radicalism. Barère argues that "*the great Hospital*" was "*far removed from the belief that this venality was advantageous or indifferent; he regarded it as a period of opprobrium or reversal*" and makes him say clearly that the magistracy of his era saw itself as diminished by venality before specifying in the *Esprit des lois* what would eventually become *Montesquieu's Éloge*:

[10] In a note, LOISEAU, *Traité des offices*, "it was Montesquieu who said that *the magistracy should be perpetual, not the magistrate*. He thus refuted what Loiseau had said in favour of venality".

> Since then, Montesquieu has written in his immortal "Esprit des lois", that the venality of offices was good for monarchies because it makes people take up as a family trade what they would not want to do for virtue. Voltaire, in t. 8 of his "Quest. sur l'Encyclopédie" refutes Montesquieu's paradox.

As for Séguier, it is said that he was exonerated because he was yielding to the royal will, and loyalty is the duty of a good servant, even if the formula remains that "*one of the greatest plagues of our land as regards the venality of offices*" [...] is the "*venality of the king*".

The Public Good from Séguier to Castlehill via the Provincial Assembly

When Barère thinks of a responsible administrator, he invokes Séguier. An energetic peacemaker even in the face of the most fanatical members of *la Fronde*:

> What is a more important function than that of making laws! A devastating hero and turbulent politics are only passing scourges. The legislator of a great nation creates stability, good and evil, of any empire. When a hero becomes destructive the misfortune which necessarily follows his exploits dies with him and is forgotten with him and is forgotten; only his triumphs are remembered. A bad legislator perpetuates the misfortune of even the most remote posterity... By contrast a legislator embraces the continuation of time; he looks to the future; he spreads benefits over his century, even if unrecognised or slandered at the time; benefits which will make for the prosperity and glory of another age. Ah *l'Hôpital*, ah *d'Aguesseau*! – such immortal legislators!

Not only did the name Séguier relegate his contemporary Advocate General Séguier to his caprices, but also competing in Montauban meant being closer to a new seat of power, as the Provincial Assembly of Haute-Guïenne became a reality after and despite Necker's dismissal. It was held in Villefranche-de-Rouergue, under the authority of Colbert de Castle-hill, and published the minutes of all its reports. Concern for all and the matrix of Barère's practical thinking about good governanceobviously came from there more than from the theoretical writings of Colbert, who nevertheless in his *Projet de paix générale et perpétuelle* book 5, Chapters 7 and 8 consider the "*Causes of the dissolution of a political society*" *and "patriotism"*[11] but Barère prided himself on keeping his distance from the argy-bargy of metaphysics.[12] It was the great administrator who made it possible to raise the practical problems of travel by road and the choices which had to be made and managed locally; the other major economic concern was the creation of canals and the navigability of the rivers, subjects dealt with just after rural begging.

As regards the matter of begging, the Report of the Bureau du Bien Publique [sic] on 5 December pronounced begging to be:

> *...one of the most regrettable scourges afflicting the kingdom; it is responsible for the degradation of the human race, it debases the soul and weakens courage; in short, it is an abyss which swallows up the virtues, the population and all the hopes of a State.* (p. 104)

After this mention is made of the measures taken by the senior administration, including charity workshops for the "able-bodied poor" (p. 104), as a distinction must be made between the "true poor" and beggars—in short, the shameful poor, who have nothing to do with vagrants:

> *"nothing is more distressing for good citizens than the habitual spectacle of this immense multitude of poor people and beggars who infest the towns, roam the countryside, pester the inhabitants, besiege the gates of their houses and are at once the objects of either entirely rightful contempt or ofwell deserved commiseration"* (p. 220)... it is therefore necessary to *"come to the aid of the destitute and outlaw begging"* (p. 221), *"come to the aid of beggars and pursue them to the depths of their dark asylums"* (p. 226), wipe out begging and provide relief for the destitute. (p. 228)

The idea was to set up charity offices in towns and cities, then in rural communities and parishes.[13] We know what political support Barère gave

[11] *Projet de paix générale et perpétuelle* book 5, chapters 7 and 8, nb on the question of the attribution of offices and positions of judges and administrations, p. 208.

[12] As a grumpy agnostic, Barère opened up about this at the beginning of his *Senilia*, his old-age thoughts written day by day in notebooks: "When you want to lose yourself in the murky depths of metaphysics, you have to condemn yourself to reading Aristotle, Mallebranche, Leibnitz, Barclay, Priestley and other authors of this kind who are so unsatisfactory for reason and sterile for society" (F34.1, 1817).

[13] On begging, see: *Procès-Verbal des séances de l'Assemblée provinciale tenue à Villefranche-de-Rouergue* en *1786*, Paris, Chapart, place Saint-Michel, 1787, in ADHER,

to what was still only the communicative action of an autonomous political power, but this was his entry point into one of the major committees of the Constituent Assembly.

The assembly then moved on to laws to protect the future: excessive deforestation would lead to high timber prices, flooding and erosion. As for the personal taxation, which was too heavy, its basis would have to be revised; otherwise, unable to pay it, people would flee their villages, the land would be covered with abandoned and ruined houses; and the countryside would become depopulated. The taxation issue, which was however considered arbitrary, was specifically attributed to the haste with which, following the insurrections of 1666, the taxation structure was too quickly put in place by Intendant Basville's department.

A complete rethink of taxation was therefore the order of the day.

Publications fuelled general political discussion. Different cabals took control of those who wrote libellous newsheets, whether they were paid to do so or not, while the encomiastes kept to their academic reserve. After a first success with the Académie des Belles-Lettres in Montauban for his chancellor Séguier, Barère presented it with one Georges d'Amboise the following year, either because he had no prospects in Toulouse, or because the centre of the action had moved to Villefranche-de-Rouergue. He appeared there again with his eulogy to the Montalbanais Lefranc de Pompignan in 1787. This great lord, President of the *Cour des Aides*, embodied the Catholic Enlightenment, which allowed Barère to speak and feed into the debates of the day of the many trends discussed at this crossroads.

The Shadow of Brienne: Never Persuade by Force

In this half-seen world, religion is always preserved, and if justice is the first need of men, it is only ever within the scope of religion (in *Louis XII*, p. 30); for all that, this religion must preserve individual conscience, whether Protestant, Albigensian or Vaudois or presented as their successors. Right up to the end, Barère's very politicised religion was linked to public order, and therefore to the efforts at conciliation which had

Recueil de documents sur l'assistance publique, les moyens de remédierà la mendicité dans la ville et le diocèse de Toulouse and the commission created by Turgot in 1775.

led Brienne to grant the Protestants civil status.[14] Barère drew from this prelate the intellectual matrix which had also been upheld by the liberal bishops of the Estates-General, with the shadowy power of the *Tiers Partis* (liberal conservatives) running through all his elogies: Louis XII, d'Amboise, Séguier and, more furtively, Furgole. Montauban undoubtedly helped to confirm this liberalism, as yet still unevenly enthused by the idea of reintroducing Protestants as citizens in their own right.

Furgole supported the freedom of the church against the feudal usurpation of rights in religious matters, which is the hallmark of a good magistrate, but at the margins an unexpected theological audacity intervenes: he is accused of having dabbled in a text, published as the *Conciliateur*, a work on grace "*that he undoubtedly had composed and that was found in his papers, begun in 1741, continued in 1759*", only the dates appear to put him in the clear him but the evidence is strong.[15]

The title is that of the 1754 work, diplomatically anonymous but attributed to Turgot either in conjunction with Loménie de Brienne or to Loménie de Brienne alone. This was at least the fruit of their joint reflections according to Abbé Morellet, who knew them when they were young priests with a promising future. This 1754 text defended respect for religion and the position of the bishops on spiritual matters, i.e. in the administration of the sacraments, at a time when there was a parliamentary crisis and the magistrates wanted to impose on them the obligation to administer communion and burial to the Jansenists. It was even thought that in exchange the king would resume the fight against the Protestants, whose persecution had already resumed in Languedoc. However, the argument of M. de Fénelon, archbishop of Cambrai, proclaimed:

> No human power can break through the impenetrable barrier of freedom of the heart. Force can never persuade men; it only makes hypocrites. When kings meddle with religion, instead of protecting it, they place it in servitude. Tolerance should therefore be granted to all in society, not by approving everything with indifference, but by enduring with patience all that God endures, and by trying to bring men back into the fold through gentle persuasion.

[14] See Maïté Bouyssy, "La très politique religion de Bertrand Barère", *Revue d'histoire de l'Église de France*, t. 101, 2015, n° 246, pp. 67–93.

[15] Bertrand Barère, *Éloges Académiques*, Paris: Renouard, p. 130.

The difficulty for the sovereign, as the *Letter* explained, was how to satisfy in one fell swoop the Protestants, the Jansenists, the Parliaments and the bishops. So "justice alone must decide". Showing favour would only reinforce the complaints, with everyone arguing that they had not obtained enough. Only fair and balanced solutions would make it possible to separate civil law from religious law. A second, more theological letter takes up arguments from Tertulian and Athanasius, as well as from Hilary and Augustine, to advocate respect for religious dissidents. A very long final note explores the question of burials, which would be included within civil law. This was a theme dear to Barère's heart, to the point of inclusion in his *Salon imaginaire*, where he returns to the theme when mentioning the impressive painting in the Musée d'Angoulême by the little-known painter Vaflard. A monumental figure, the famous poet Young, haggard-faced, carries his (step-)daughter Narcissa to her burial by night. This dark dereliction earned it a starring role in the exhibition *Faces of Fear, Violence and Fantasy from David to Delacroix*.[16] The painting had been presented at the Salon of 1804, the year in which Barère published a bilingual edition of *Les Beautés poétiques de Edward Young*, his favourite poet. He could not but admire this work so in harmony with his own, especially as the painter was in fact in the service of Louis-Philippe d'Orléans and this represented Barère's last reasons for sticking with the Consulate.

Toulouse in 1770 was less interested in Brienne's election to the Académie française in Paris than in the debates within its Floral Games. In 1771, the eulogy of the Count of Toulouse Raymond VII caused a stir, the content and extent of which we do not know because it was not published; but when it was decided to put Pierre Bayle's eulogy up for the competition, the Councillor at the Portes Parliament opted to read his biography on 31 July 1772 and a complaint was then lodged with Maupeou. Maupeou exonerated Brienne of having manipulated this trial's rhetoric, but as a precaution, they fell back on to a less controversial subject, the eulogy of Saint-Exupère, bishop of Toulouse.

[16] In Jérôme FARIGOULE, Hélène JAGOT, MUSÉE de la VIE ROMANTIQUE, *Visages De L'effroi: Violence et Fantastique De David À Delacroix*. ed. LienArt, 2016, p. 147; the article by Gilles SOUBIGOU, "Les couleurs obscures de l'anglomanie" (The dark colours of Anglomania) presents a later edition of Young's *Nights* translated by Le Tourneur, whereas the current issue was Barère's simultaneous bilingual edition.

These questions animated Toulouse when Barère arrived there as a young student, and they remained part of his intellectual and political baggage. He always clung to advocating persuasion as the only method of conducting disputes and civil conciliations: "The Waldensians were accused of heresy and dragged to their doom by lords more eager to acquire their victims' property than to assure their conversion. Louis arrived in Lyon. The Vaudois fell to the ground to kiss his knees and demand justice": respectable and enlightened prelates were then dispatched (*Éloge de Louis XII*, p. 32). A note goes on to declare: "These were the inhabitants of the valleys of la Vaupute and la Fraisiniere in Dauphiné, unfortunate descendants of the Albigensians, whom fanaticism had persecuted even in the depths of the Alps". This is a personal reflection not taken from Garnier's *Histoire de Louis XII*, which he usually follows, nor can it be attributed to the other historians cited, Danthon, Saint-Gelais or Seissel.

Barere back-tracks on his views of monastic reform in his elogy to Amboise:

> And so, fanaticism denounces to the legate and the monarch the last unfortunate traces of these Albigensians, forced to take refuge in the Alps through persecution. Unfortunate runts of a proscribed litter, d'Amboise's principles should reassure you. The legate is tolerant because of the principles of an enlightened religion just as much as because of a sense of humanity.

And when he talks about Claude de France's marriage to Charles V, which d'Amboise would have prevented, he comments: "which would have divided the monarchy" meaning that without saying so in so many words, *la patrie* figures within his thinking.

The Charity of Religion, the Public Good of Administrations

Jean-Jacques Lefranc de Pompignan (1709–1784), a grand seigneur, President of the Montauban Court of Aids as well as a cabinet minister and member of the Académie française and the Jeux floraux, was a representative of the Catholic Enlightenment and an easy target for Voltaire, but Barère objected:

> *O Pompignan! what a day to remember you by! All unite in sorrow at your loss; magistrates and people of letters, rich and poor, literary senates and charitable institutions, religion and philosophy, foreigners, your fellow citizens, your patrie, all as of one sorrowful voice. They all combine in one sentiment and one voice with which to praise you… tell the philosophers that they can achieve fame by devoting their talent and their vigils to religion. Let them all know that there is nothing greater on earth than genius guided by virtue, and that there is no reputation more lasting than that acquired through morality and good deeds.* (Éloges académiques, op. cit., p. 172)

This note represents Pompignan's final confession of faith, a metonymic tribute to the religious and political figure of Haute-Guyenne, Colbert de Castlehill:

> *In his own eyes, he found happiness in work and in religion. Raising his eyes to the Divine, he no longer found in profane antiquity the nourishment his soul sought, and devoted himself to reading the Holy Books. He explored the ancient structures of religion in a century in which a proud philosophy was rising out of the debris of the beliefs of our forefathers, in which poetry seemed to be attacking our faith, in which the Ode saw its majesty prostituted in the praise of crimes committed by heroes and pagan […] He armed himself against those of impious belief….* (p. 161)

For all concerned, charitable practices and the organisation of the city remained a stumbling block, whether it was the fate of elderly and needy congregational priests or the training of midwives and the education of poor girls in the countryside.

Beyond conformist praise, the impasse represented by philanthropy without means prompted Barère to join the Encyclopédique lodge, which was close to the Neufs Sœurs lodge in Paris. It dealt with everything, but above all philanthropy, agriculture, civic support (whether for foundlings and beggars or for the safety of wet nurses), fine art, philosophy and even masonry in its various committees, each of which had its own colour and a fixed meeting day; very paradoxically, Barère was president of the "sciences" section, a likely sign that his curiosity, if not his strategies, had changed. Under the watchful eye of Delherm, President of the Parliament, a dynamic figure who was able to attract the interest of more than 100 masons and personalities who would later come to the fore such as Mailhe and Larrey, the desire to take in hand the city's problems began to take shape. These members were capable of investigating, forecasting and providing bread for the poor in times of famine. In this way, they truly became champions of the public good, which the return to "eloquence", that which deals with the foundations of society, attempts to explain through sensible reasoning from Rousseau, or practical mechanisms from Montesquieu.

Rousseau and Montesquieu or the Reasons for the Social State

If until then the sublime had been reserved for the Hebrews, endowed with the double prestige of the antiquity of a primitive people and of religion, Rousseau became the authority on the sublime par excellence:

> Before Rousseau, no one had painted with as much energy the appalling picture of the evils created by the social state. Who better than Rousseau to show us the origins of societies, the successive development of goods and evils?

Rousseau was roused at the sight of the subject as did Achilles at the sight of weapons, and Rousseau rose to the challenge where Voltaire would lower himself through satire (p. 243). The essay on spectacles, this sublime letter from Rousseau to d'Alembert is excused for its weaknesses because it is:

> so interesting for morality, although created without order, without connection, without method, full of digression and sophism but where reigns everywhere an original style, and constantly so remarkable by the energetic expression of its love of virtue and its zeal for *la patrie*?

The author can however be forgiven because he was quick to applaud Gluck's *Iphigénie*. Of *Émile*'s "tender and passionate" loves, Barère recalls Julie's walk with Saint-Preux, and then speaks of the "sublime praise of the Holy Scriptures":

> "Who better than he [Rousseau] has proved the existence of God, the freedom of man and the immortality of the soul? What eloquence? Have Bossuet and Fénelon said anything more beautiful and touching? Have they paid more pure and solemn homage to religion? [such as Julie, wife and mother] and then in "the horrors of death": "this sublime scene, where silence, religion and death reign supreme".

The whole eulogy makes this Rousseau compatible with religion. In Part II the eulogy which deals with the educational significance of the work borders on the panegyric, "the benefits of genius for humanity". Rousseau's main aim was to shape mankind, and it is for this that he deserves the recognition of posterity.

Montesquieu's praise is perfect rhetoric, but highlights his successes abroad, in Prussia and England, and for "the sublime idea of the three powers", which, Barère regularly repeats, was no less revolutionary in the cameral sciences than Newton was in his field and must be worth glory in his *patrie*, a word which emerges because it is the code word chosen by Barère to anonymise his manuscript:

> *France, what respects have you paid to the ashes of this great man, whom England and Prussia have celebrated before you? It is to such benefactors that a solemn tribute from the nation should be due: here are the statues that should honour public spaces.[...] But why speak of public honours? He who perfected the theory of social art, who laid the foundations of our laws, and of all the institutions that can influence our destinies, needs neither statues nor inscriptions: his eulogy is in everyone's heart.* (p. 325)

And for the first among citizens and the sublime philosopher:

> There will therefore exist in our Annals a tradition that will teach our ultimate descendants that Montesquieu's influence produced a happy revolution in the legislation, politics and morals of the State. *The Esprit des lois* is the temple where the sacred fire of love of *la patrie*, public good and humanity will always be rekindled.

These thoughts, captured at the time, may be of interest, but they carry little weight when it comes to positions based on the various *habitus* of some and of others. Circumstances shatter glass ceilings but only assign roles according to the grammar of the time. A black-clad *tabellion* (officer of justice) was of little consequence when he arrived at Versailles, and here again, Barère was able to draw on a capital superior to his practice as a *robin* (lawyer), and it was for a particular reason that he entered the circle of the Orléans and that, as a député, he was lodged in the Château by the almoner of the Artois hunts. For all that, he did not give up his quest for academic recognition; Bordeaux submitted Montesquieu to his competition and Barère sent him a third copy from Paris in August 1789, when he was elected to the Estates-General, which had become the National Constituent Assembly, and, because of his newspaper, he was already a recognised protagonist.

But from the Queen's Party to the Orléans, the Future Lies with the Ladies

Louis XII opened up the field of reflection on the monarchy and the good prince as Father of his people, themes opposed to Necker and then Vergennes, and even more surely the theme became topical again in the face of the brittle manners of Calonne and Brienne, when the Académie française took up the subject. The Austrian was no longer an unacceptable Claude de France, but she remained a target, and respect for the ladies argued in favour of the Queen. These texts, some of which were published at the time [note 21], increased the number of advocates, ranging from the most rigorous to the most liberal. A common game would endow numbers with a symbolic value in the hope that a (Louis) XII+ (Henri) IV would make a (Louis) XVI.

It was against this backdrop that Barère set off for the Parc de Betz on the very day that Brienne was dismissed. The Princess of Monaco was welcoming all comers there and had opened the park to the public.

Barère, dazzled, wanted to be an acolyte of this world, a world in which he was not the social equal; unlike Cerutti, who wrote poetry fit for a château. Barère discovered codes of an aristocracy that could perhaps be seen as an alternative to the political embarrassments of the day, and as all hope was lost for Brienne, Barère, an untapped talent and always available, went to see Jean-Pierre Picqué, a doctor from Lourdes and intimate secretary to the Princess of Monaco. Half-introduced to society as he was, Barère stood at the door of the *salon* and looked at this world. He wanted to be the acolyte of these ladies, in addition to the princess, the Duchess of Bourbon, Bathilde d'Orléans, who often stayed there while works were being carried out on the Elysée Palace. We do not know precisely how it happened, but the moment was decisive, as from then on Barère found himself endorsed within the Orléans circle.

It is also possible that one of the half-brothers, a bastard of Orléans and brother of the Duchess of Bourbon (1750–1822), was vicar-general to Loménie de Brienne and brother to another member of a religious order, both children of Madame de Villemonble (1737–1806). Bathilde referred fondly to one as the dark-haired brother and the other as the blond-haired brother. Saint Phar (Louis-Etienne de Saint-Farre, born in

1759) obtained the abbey of Livry, Louis-Philippe, his younger brother, the Count-Abbot of Saint-Albin, was the "dark-haired brother". There may also have been occasional links between these wealthy, worldly abbots via Toulouse or Loménie, one of whom seems to have been vicar-general. Links may also have been created by Jean-Pierre Barère, who found himself very well off in 1789. At Bertrand's wedding in May 1785, this brother priest was able to give him £7,000 from his small and large income: his parish of Ariébat brought him £3,768 in tithes, £1,900 in *casuel*, £100 in *novales*, in addition to the prebends of Lazaur, £397, Saint-Médard, £322, Agos, £161, and Bénébergot, £104, making a total of £6,752 before any gifts in kind.[17] He continued his career by becoming vicar-general, all evidence of a very good introduction into the decision-making circles of the bishops of Tarbes en Bigorre, which came under Condom, but it was Toulouse which shaped Jean-Pierre Barère.

A Few Leads

Such a reexamination of what is said in that most conventional of public official discourse, academic reports and eulogies, allows us to sketch out configurations that give an idea of the choice of possibility. Barère never ceased to want to reflect on what a statesman is; and he remained in the wake of Loménie de Brienne, undoubtedly lucrative, at least for his brother. If we look at the future of the major prelates in the region, their positions had as much to do with attitude as conviction. Brienne could not think outside the categories of a renewing power, Castlehill had already given shape to the practicalities of day-to-day administration, and a young untapped talent such as Barère could only soak up knowledge and take on what was a social stumbling block for everyone, the question of the poor and of begging, and subsequently of high prices and food supplies. In this way, the civil constitution of the clergy secularised the administration of misfortune without in any way reducing its scale.

Trained within the framework of the Ancien Régime, Barère subsumed the weight of religion into a theology of compassion, after a period in politics that saw him report on subsistence and begging: "To which beings did Christ attach himself: the little ones, the poor, the weak, the

[17] See Jean-Pierre THOMAS, *Bertrand Barère*, op. cit., p. 41.

humble, the destitute, the stranger, the widow, the orphan, the persecuted, the proscribed. These were the people he loved best".[18] These forms of words recur, and when he envisages an interiorised religion, it is by declining the figures of Vincent de Paul and the Madeleine, but his theology belongs to his chosen saint, Theresa of Avila, whose definition of the damned he likes to cite as "unhappy people who will never know love"[19].

We could end by saying that Barère's political itinerary is less cryptic than we might have thought and that what followed was simply the application of that which had been written in anticipation. And why not? What is interesting to see, however, is that by shifting too much towards ideology and theology, regulation and the conflicts of religious society, by placing it in competition (or not) with the government, the king and the parliaments which are its judicial administration, we risk forgetting that position still prevails over conviction. This is not primary sociology; the religious question in 1790 was not so much the subject of canonical debates as of alliances whose configuration shifted, which is why it was important for Barère to produce the daily *Point du jour* for his constituents.

[18] ADHP, F 108 f°1333.

[19] Ibid. f°1333, around 1825.

CHAPTER 17

Epilogue: A Farewell to Colbert de Castlehill

Andrew Moore

Abstract With the publication of this book, Andrew Moore has fulfilled a wish that has been close to his heart for almost 40 years. It is dedicated entirely to Bishop Colbert. In what sounds like a farewell letter, he celebrates the man's extraordinary career, and in particular emphasises the dualities that he believes lie at the heart of his entire life and have shaped its course: Scottish and French, Protestant and Catholic, Cuthbert and Colbert, commoner and nobleman. These dualities allowed him freedoms and flexibility not available to the rest of the French episcopate. Without a vocation, but well informed about the currents of his time, he progressed in the French church thanks to his intelligence, talent, charm and capacity for work. He was also able to return to Britain safely and become a thorn in the side of his adopted creed. There is much more to be said and discovered about this remarkable man, and he richly deserves a full biography.

A. Moore (✉)
Independent Researcher, L'Etang Bertrand, France
e-mail: anvmoore@gmail.com

A. Alcouffe (ed.), *Seignelay Colbert de Castlehill (1735-1811)*,
https://doi.org/10.1007/978-3-031-75273-5_17

Keywords Cuthbert/Colbert de Castlehill · Scotland · Rodez · Rouergue · Toulouse. Inverness · General Estates · Bilingual · Lord Gray · Walpole

I am writing this from a very personal view, not as a full-time historian (which I am not), but as the person who probably still to this day knows Bishop Colbert best. It would be presumptuous to say that I 'discovered' him, but I think that I can claim that I wrote the first researched and documented piece on his career. Much of course has been discovered since, thanks to the advent of the internet and Professor Alcouffe's diligent and meticulous work, and that early essay has been superseded.

Alain Alcouffe has nonetheless, and very kindly, asked me to write something for this book, as much of what is known about Colbert and been made accessible to all is the fruit of our collaboration. The very extensive timeline which must be the basis of all further work on Colbert is our creation.

This piece is thus intended as a very personal overview and valedictory salute to an extraordinary man by someone whose acquaintance with Colbert dates back some thirty-five years. There will be no references, as these can all be found on the website, (colbertdecastlehill.com) and many of my assertions might be open to question. No matter. Controversy is an excellent thing, and the spur to discovery and progress.

For background, I will say something of my own past, and of the strange circumstances under which knowledge of the existence of Bishop Colbert was presented to me. This will help explain perhaps why I feel a particular understanding of Colbert the man and why I feel such a strong sense of kinship with him.

I was born in 1950 in Paris in an English family which had settled in France, on my mother's side, in the 1850s. Roughly, when at home in Neuilly I was English, when I stepped out of the door I became French. I am bilingual and bicultural and was educated in France to the baccalauréat, which I took in the extraordinary circumstances of summer 1968. I moved to England in 1970 to work, for a while, in the wine trade. In 1985, I decided to take a 'life-break', and study for a degree in history at Bristol University, in the West of England.

History had long been a fascination, and Bristol was the city I had settled in.

One of the courses I had the good fortune to choose in the second year was 'The French Revolution', taught be Professor William Doyle, Head of the history faculty, writer of many books and eminent historian of the Eighteenth Century, for me the most interesting of periods in the West, during which so many certainties were undermined and so many hopeful avenues explored.

During the early summer of 1987 I started to investigate possible subjects for a dissertation, an option to replace one of the third-year courses, while on holiday at my parents' house in Najac, a spectacular medieval village in the Aveyron département, within the old province of the Rouergue in Southwest France. They had bought the property in 1966 and I knew the area very well. In an attempt to refine my thoughts, I called in at the Société des Lettres in Villefranche de Rouergue, then a sleepy and charming bastide, sous-préfecture and our local market town. I remember a large, well-lit if dusty room on the first floor of an old building near the town centre, lined with glass-fronted bookcases and filled with desks and tables. A smattering of people sat quietly in the heat, intent on books and folders of documents. An elderly man in shorts presided behind a broad oak table placed diagonally in a corner. I began to outline my purpose: I was interested then in exploring the role of the police in an area like the Rouergue, when faced with the exceptional challenges of the revolutionary years.

At this point I heard someone speak up behind me: it was an elderly nun, peering up from a pile of documents. 'You should look into the Bishop of Rodez during the revolution' she said. 'Strangely, he was a Scot, a very interesting man, but little is known about him, and very little has been published as many of the documents that concern him at the archives in Rodez are in English. What is needed is a historian who is also bilingual and knows the region well'. A quite extraordinary moment of serendipity!

The next day I drove to Rodez, spoke to archivists, and arranged to rent a studio for a month. I have rarely been happier than for those few weeks. I spent every possible hour in the old monastery that then housed the Departmental Archives. I poured through the documents held by the Rodez 'Société des Lettres' and those at the Bishop's Palace, where Colbert's portrait still hung. Back in England, Professor Doyle agreed to oversee my work, which was finally handed in the next year with, I recall, four minutes to spare'; I am sure it played some part in my being awarded a first-class degree.

I would have liked to continue my research on Colbert, as there was clearly still so much to discover, so many avenues to explore. Professor Doyle did his very best to encourage and assist, but the grant he obtained for me from the British Academy was just too small and I had no means of my own. After a period working, among many other projects in France and the UK, for the Conseil Général of the Aveyron, I became a teacher of French in Dorset and am now retired, living, appropriately, in a pair of late eighteenth-century cottages in Normandy.

When I first visited Rodez all those years ago and started digging through the Archives Départementales, I was amazed that someone whose journey through life had been so extraordinary was so little known. William Doyle, my supervisor at Bristol, agreed, but life intervened and it is only when Alain Alcouffe, who had discovered Colbert through working on Adam Smith's peregrinations in the South of France, approached me completely out of the blue that I realized that I was no longer Colbert's only fan. Maybe at long last, he would find his rightful place in the history of both France and Scotland! His 'parcours' are absolutely unique. I am certain that no other Scot influenced the history of France at one of its principal turning points the way he did.

When just 14 years old, he crossed the channel, he was not French, not a Catholic, not a Colbert, not wealthy, and not particularly well connected. Some forty years later, a senior member of the episcopate, he walked across Versailles on the 22nd of June 1789 with four colleagues and a host of other deputies of the clergy to join the new National Assembly gathered at the church of Saint Louis. How did he feel on that momentous day? The stalemate was fully broken, momentum increased and he was ready to play his part as events unfolded. He could not fully realise what a momentous decision he had made or what lay ahead for him or for France, but what a journey for the lad from Castle-Hill! It is his 'roman' that fascinates me most. My dream, long shelved, has always been that there should be a biography of Colbert on the bookshelves of scholars and in universities, and that it should henceforth be impossible for him to be ignored.

Here I will try to take a step back, attempt to see him in the round, as a man steeped in two cultures who could access, as I can, two mindsets, two separate 'mentalités'. In my opinion, this affected important aspects of his journey as it has of mine. There are similarities between us I feel, which have added to my fascination with him, a strange sense of kinship.

The principal point is that we were always—in our adulthood—outsiders. Others did not however always perceive us as such, since our 'foreignness' was revealed not in our conversation but by our names or by other people. I have no accent in either language and I am sure as gifted a linguist as Colbert had none either. Our duality, though, affected our perception of the world around us. He was too Scottish (English in my case) to be French, and too French to be British. He like me understood the French and their ways of being very profoundly but could never assume that identity fully. It is not just a question of language or expression (what language did Colbert dream in?) but family roots and ties, of remaining associated simultaneously in two places with current affairs, social and cultural changes. Our nominal 'nationality' is incidental, not fundamental.

It is not that Colbert was not fully committed to his career in France—he clearly was, as his success demonstrates—but that it was not the totality of his life. He had other engagements, duties, cares, as do most people of course, but within a very different context, that of his family in Scotland and elsewhere, and his contacts and peer group there who made use of his integration into French society for their own ends. It remained throughout his life an option unavailable to others. His involvement in the Douglas affair, his friendships with eminent Scottish intellectuals, Adam Smith and David Hume for example, or émigrés like the Barnwalls in Toulouse and other links hinted at in his correspondence show throughout his career his continued involvement with Scottish preoccupations. He proclaimed this in his name, although the 'de' Castle-Hill added a useful implication of nobility which 'of' does not carry in English, where it is purely geographic. He was also close to the other members of the Cuthbert diaspora who had settled in France, not least Uncle Alexander, who flew to his rescue when he badly mishandled business regarding his 'in commendam' abbey of Valricher. Indeed, later the Abbé Alexander died on the return journey after visiting him in Rodez shortly after his inauguration as bishop. Similarly, many members of my family with whom I am in contact have remained in France, some of them hybrids like me.

Colbert alone among the episcopate could leave his Frenchness behind. Even Dillon was born in France. His statement 'If I cannot be a French Bishop, I will be a Scottish farmer' is very striking. In due course, this parallel life would offer him both comfort and a refuge. He alone could slough off his adopted nationality, and even his obedience to his adopted church.

I am convinced he saw his work in France as a job, a set of opportunities, a range of interesting options in which he could engage his energy, intelligence and ambition, his capacity for hard work and his considerable talent as a communicator. In any case, once as a boy he had crossed the channel to enter the Scots College it was, to a great extent, sink or swim. The Colbert connection that sustained his uncles does not seem to have done much for him, and efforts to forward his career via the Jacobites in Saint Germain-en-Laye failed. He had to do it all for himself. That he succeeded to such an extraordinary degree speaks volumes for his talents and his willpower. These must have been noticed by Loménie de Brienne, who would find a beneficial use for such an able assistant, unencumbered by previous loyalties of caste or clan. For Colbert, being offered associate membership of the Brienne clan proved most beneficial, just as no doubt having a Colbert, however fake, as an aide was no doubt useful to the Briennes. As a Vicar General, Bishop, President of a Provincial Assembly, participant in Assemblies of the Clergy or of Notables, member of committees of the Assemblée Constituante, Colbert proved hard-working and as effective as circumstances allowed. He was clearly an avid learner across many fields, languages, law, lay or canon, various sciences and more, but also, importantly, he knew how to make himself liked by those he met, a necessity if he was to progress as he did. We have glimpses of this through his correspondence, from Smith, Barré, Hume, and various reports from his time in Toulouse, Rodez, Paris and elsewhere. He made connections, sought opportunities, accepted challenges and proved his worth. He had nothing to fall back on, and it seems he was not willing to accept the comfortable anonymity of his uncle if he could avoid it.

Later, however, when the opportunities narrowed, when it became clear that the path ahead would lead no further, in Paris or Rodez, he could go elsewhere and pursue another life in an environment in which he felt completely comfortable. He, alone of all the French bishops, did not go into exile. He went home. Not, I am sure without regret and a great deal of bitterness against many in the French clergy, against the Pope, indeed against those French people who had chosen the path of excess, as he saw it, rather than the path of reform and moderation. Enlightened as he was and desirous of change, of which he acknowledged the absolute necessity, he thought complete upheaval was not the way forward. Understandably, as a close and knowledgeable observer, he foresaw this would bring about disaster for the France he was so fond of and understood so well. He perceived better than most, and believed superior, the British way of achieving change through sufficient negotiation. In contrast, as a callow 18-year-old, I must say I expected far more of the events of May 1968, my personal brush with revolution! My disappointment certainly played a part in my own emigration.

I am sure Colbert felt genuinely sorry and concerned for his old parishioners in the Rouergue, exposed to constant waves of change and turmoil, often unwanted, and imposed by faraway institutions as remote from their daily lives as the King and his ministers had been. Beyond words of comfort, he could do little for them though.

I am convinced that once back in Britain he became a Cuthbert again, surrounded by his family and many friends and able to make use of a large network of sympathetic contacts, often but not exclusively within the Catholic community. He could move in to his brother Lewis' London house in Gloucester Place, where he felt safe and free to assume unorthodox positions with regard to the French clergy's hierarchy and indeed the Catholic church at large, joining with other critics in refusing direct instructions from Rome. He had little to lose. He had seen enough before leaving to realise he was unlikely to return. There was nothing there left for him. The clock was not going to turn back. He was not a good enough Catholic to feel he had to toe the line. The French church hierarchy in exile, uncomfortable in a country where they were merely tolerated, had little control over him and he did not really need them. He could do as he pleased and make the best of his new freedom. France had become a foreign country again.

I am convinced also his Catholicism was expedient rather than derived from conviction. I see no evidence in his life of a vocation. Being a priest was the straw he had drawn, within his generation of Cuthberts, and he made the very best of it. He was certainly no dévot. To further his career, he had to demonstrate he knew the métier perfectly, but if nothing else the contents of his library indicate how far the range of his 'technocratic', 'enlightened' leanings are well evidenced, rather than any enthusiasm for devotion. He was not alone in this among the French clergy, and it did not hinder his progress. Throughout his career he behaved independently, advocating tolerance, willingly mixing with all others who shared his interests, often breaching distinctions of class. Occasional instances surface: his attendance at a concert in Rodez, frowned on by bigots, amusing his female companions, his discussions with tenant farmers in the kitchens of the Bishop's Palace, or his delighted conversation in Erse with Scottish drovers. He was not popular with many in the Rouergue during his episcopacy and I clearly remember the suspicion I encountered when asking about him at the Bishop's Palace two centuries later. He was not at the time 'en odeur de sainteté'. He was certainly never ascetic, as his portrait clearly demonstrates. I think of him as a sensual man, a bon viveur, a jolly companion for the Duke of Buccleugh, a witty habitué of the Paris salons, and I can picture him in my mind, a genial guest at the Versailles dinner party that followed the cathartic events of the 22nd June 1789, thick in discussion with Arthur Young, Siéyiès, Rabaud de Saint Etienne and Philippe Egalité. What company to keep at such a key time and in such a place! What a long way to have travelled for the boy from Castle-Hill!

Unlike other Cuthberts, he could put down no roots in France and he acquired no property. The strictures of his profession forbade a family, all descendance. Once he had been forced to flee, there was nothing for him to go back to, no further role for him to play. He could not do what I have been able to manage so far, despite the horrors of Brexit, and spend time on both sides of the channel, thus maintaining my duality. For him, even communicating with the faithful in the Rouergue was fraught and potentially dangerous for his correspondents. Looking backwards was fruitless. He would become a Scot once again, and look for potential new projects, in England where his status was useful to a minority, in Canada, Scotland, maybe Jamaica. He could call on his old friend the Duke of Buccleugh, assist his brother in attempting to recover the family estate at Castle-Hill. He could work with the writer Mary Berry on the correspondence between Mme Du Deffand and Horace Walpole, as he knew them both well. I imagine him ageing gracefully, visiting friends, his numerous family, (he died at the home of his nephew Lord Gray in Twickenham) no doubt a congenial guest in many country houses, bringing a welcome host of diverting anecdotes, carrying with him a strange aura of mystery and foreignness: 'Tell us, Bishop, what was Robespierre really like?' To a much less romantic extent, I know how it feels.

This is a valedictory text, and now I say goodbye to someone I feel I know well and would love to know better. Had we met, I am sure we could have been friends, shared laughs and many anecdotes, and compared stories about both the countries we know so well. All the many documents I collected have gone to their proper place, and are in the hands of Jennifer Henderson in Scotland, a talented writer and a much younger and more recent convert who may choose to pick up the torch. I hope their final destination will be the Highland Archives where others, as I did, may stumble upon them one day and fall under the charm of this very remarkable man.

Index

A. Alcouffe (ed.), *Seignelay Colbert de Castlehill (1735-1811)*, https://doi.org/10.1007/978-3-031-75273-5

E

N

O

The manufacturer's authorised representative in the EU is Springer Nature Customer Service Centre GmbH, Europaplatz 3, 69115 Heidelberg, Germany. If you have any concerns regarding our products, please contact ProductSafety@springernature.com

Printed and bound by CPI Group (UK) Ltd, Croydon, CR0 4YY
01/10/2026
02225953-0014